The Sounds of the World's Languages

The Sounds of the World's Languages

Peter Ladefoged and Ian Maddieson

First published 1996

Blackwell Publishers Ltd
108 Cowley Road
Oxford OX4 1JF
UK

Blackwell Publishers Inc.
238 Main Street
Cambridge, Massachusetts 02142
USA

British Library Cataloguing in Publication Data
A CIP catalogue record for this book is available from the British Library.

Library of Congress Cataloging-in-Publication Data
Ladefoged, Peter.
     The sounds of the world's languages / Peter Ladefoged and Ian Maddieson.
          p.   cm. — (Phonological theory)
     Includes bibliographical references and index.
     ISBN 0-631-19814-8. — ISBN 0-631-19815-6 (pbk.)
     1. Phonetics. I. Maddieson, Ian. II. Title. III. Series.
     P221.L24   1995
     414—dc20   94-49209
                                                                             CIP

Typeset in 10 on 12 point Palatino and Laser IPA (Linguist's Software)
by Light Technology (Electronic Books) Ltd, Fife, Scotland

Printed in Great Britain by T J Press Ltd, Padstow, Cornwall

This book is printed on acid-free paper

Contents

Figures

Tables

Acknowledgments

This book would not have been written without the direct and indirect assistance of a great many people and organizations. We recognize four great debts in particular. Our greatest indebtedness in terms of material support is to the National Science Foundation who have supported much of the first-hand research which is reported in these pages in the form of grants extending over many years. Our second debt is to all our colleagues in the UCLA Phonetics Laboratory who have contributed to the creation of a warm and supportive working environment which has made the writing of this book possible. The third debt is to all our predecessors and teachers in the field of phonetics. We have built on their ideas and data, and sometimes extended their input in ways that they might not approve of. The fourth debt is to the innumerable language consultants in many different parts of the world, who gave us so much of their time, knowledge, and friendship.

We also recognize a large number of more specific ways in which many of our colleagues in the field have contributed to the present book. A precursor to the chapter on stops was written in collaboration with Caroline Henton while she was a visiting scholar at UCLA, and the chapter on clicks owes an immense amount to joint work with Tony Traill. Much of the work on Indian languages was conducted in collaboration with P. Bhaskararao. Our understanding of several aspects of the phonetics of Caucasian languages owes a great deal to Ian Catford, who spent a quarter working in the UCLA Phonetics Lab, and to Sandro Kodzasov. Both generously allowed us to share their data and provided guidance on its interpretation. We have sometimes differed from them in our analyses, but we would have learned much less without their generosity. Ailbhe ní Chasaide, Didier Demolin, Andy Butcher, and Caroline Smith also kindly made available as-yet-unpublished experimental data. More generally, Keith Johnson, a colleague at UCLA for three years, shaped much of our thinking about perceptual matters, especially in relation to vowels. Mona Lindau, another former colleague, contributed greatly from her own fieldwork experience. Pat Keating, the present director of the UCLA Phonetics Lab, provided a congenial environment and gave us continual encouragement.

We were fortunate enough to have had many talented students working with us in this project, among them Victoria Anderson, Barbara Blankenship, John Choi, Edward Flemming, Sean Fulop, Matt Gordon, Rob Hagiwara, Gary Holmes, Michael Inouye, Bonny Sands, Dan Silverman, Siniša Spajić, JulieAnna Thaxter, and Richard Wright. They often contributed valuable ideas as well as providing assistance with data analysis, preparation of figures and other chores.

A very large class of people who have made an essential contribution are all the speakers who shared with us their knowledge of their languages. Over the last 40 years there have been several hundred individuals whose speech has formed the basis for some report in this book; every one of these individuals has made an essential contribution to its completion. We cannot mention all of them by name, but would like to thank especially a few who provided particularly valuable data. These include Gudo Mahiya (Hadza), Dorothy Babuda (Yeletnye), Guhmsa and Boloǁxao (!Xóõ), Herman Batibo (KeSukuma), Harriet Whitworth, Felicité McDonald and Dorothy Felsman (Montana Salish), Froylan Moreño (Mazatec), Helen George and Martha Garrison (Navajo), Nichümeno Chase (Angami), Vasamalli Pothili and Tesh Kwiḍi (Toda), Basanti Devi (Assamese), and Philip Mulley (Badaga).

Technical assistance with a variety of the research methodologies represented in these pages was provided by Henry Tehrani, the technical director of the UCLA phonetics laboratory, Charles Sandrock of Witwatersrand University, and Joseph Perkell, Melanie Matthies, and Mario Svirsky of the Massachusetts Institute of Technology. Programming assistance was provided by Kristin Precoda and Cheng-Cheng Tan.

We are indebted to the following for providing us with the opportunity for doing field work in various countries: Tony Traill in Botswana; Jan Snyman in Namibia; Stephen Schooling in New Caledonia; Calvin Rensch and John Clifton in Papua New Guinea; Herman Batibo in Tanzania; Paul Geraghty in Fiji; Kirk Huffman in Vanuatu; P. Bhaskararao in India; Paul Kirk in Mexico; Sarah Thomason in Montana; Zhongji Wu in China; Jimmy Harris in Thailand; Chiu-yu Tseng in Taiwan; and Kay Williamson in Nigeria. We have been assisted by the Summer Institute of Linguistics and its affiliated organizations in a variety of countries; and we would like to thank government agencies in Botswana, Tanzania, Kenya, India, China and Taiwan for granting permission to conduct fieldwork.

We are also most grateful to all the people who provided comments, criticism or advice on the text at various stages of its preparation. Helpful comments were made by, among others, Abby Cohn, Rosalie Finlayson, Suzi Fosnot, Cécile Fougeron, John Goldsmith, Bill Ham, Sandro Kodzasov, Pat

Keating, Bruce Hayes, Björn Lindblom, J. A. Louw, Joyce McDonough, Hirosi Nakagawa, Geoff Pullum, Dan Silverman, Caroline Smith, Jan Snyman, Donca Steriade, Rainer Vossen, John Westbury, and Kay Williamson.

Caroline Henton read the entire manuscript in near-final form and saved us from many errors and inconsistencies.

This book has been many years in the writing, and we are sure to have overlooked several people who helped us in many ways. Our apologies for these oversights.

We would also like to thank Catherine Macdonald, who got us started again. As always, we are much indebted to Jenny Ladefoged, who was present from the beginning and pushed us through to the end.

1

The Sounds of the World's Languages

The title of this book, *The Sounds of the World's Languages*, implies two very significant claims. One is that it makes sense to talk about entities that can be labeled 'sounds'. The other is that we know enough about the languages of the world to be able to write a book that covers them all. We would like to explain our thinking in selecting this title.

Most of the phonetic literature of the last two centuries assumes that a meaningful analysis can be made by dividing speech into small chunks that can be called speech sounds. These may be described in formalized terms as phonemes, root nodes, or some other theoretical entity, or discussed in more general terms as 'segments'. The tradition of segmental description has proven its utility in many ways. Nonetheless, linguists' views on what segments are have varied greatly. At one extreme are those who regard them as descriptive fictions, invented solely by the linguistic analyst. At an opposite extreme are those who hypothesize that the organization of speech production, and the structure of words in memory are based directly on segments. We do not feel it necessary in this book to take a stand on either side of this issue, but choose to employ segmental descriptions of languages as the most suitable way of communicating the results of phonetic analyses to a wide range of readers.

The second part of the title, the world's languages, also deserves some comment. We believe that enough is now known to attempt a description of the sounds in all the languages of the world. Professional linguists have some knowledge of the great majority of the languages now spoken. This is a state of affairs which has never existed at any time prior to the latter part of this century. The 'global village' effect means that few societies remain outside the scope of scholarly scrutiny. In all probability there will be a sharp decrease in the rate at which previously unknown sounds are drawn to the attention of phoneticians. We are, of course, aware that there are phonetic phenomena in every language that have yet to be described. Speech varies in response to many different circumstances, and we do not have a complete knowledge of the phonetic structure of any language. In addition, languages are always evolving. Thus there can never be a final description of the sounds of any one language. The next generation of speakers will always speak a little differently from their predecessors, and may even create sounds that have never been used in a human language before. We think it probable, however, that any new sounds will be similar to those that now have a linguistic function and will be formed by re-arrangements of properties of sounds that have been previously observed in linguistic usage. In other words, we feel that a basis exists for discriminating between linguistic and non-linguistic sounds.

Using this basis and our intuitions we have sometimes posited the existence of sounds that have not yet been reported in the linguistic literature. These are sounds which we feel reflect accidental gaps in the currently available data, or are absent only by chance from any currently spoken language. Other possibilities are not mentioned at all since we believe they will never have a role in linguistic structure. There are, of course, many sounds that can be made with the vocal organs that are not known to be used in any language. People can whistle, click their teeth, wag their tongues from side to side, and perform a variety of other maneuvers to produce sounds that have never been reported to have a linguistic function. But linguistic phonetics does not have to account for all the sounds that humans are capable of making, or even all of those which can be made just in the vocal tract.

The primary data we will try to describe are all the segments that are known to distinguish lexical items within a language. We have in this way determined the level of description at which we will operate. We are concerned with the lexical segments that account for minimal pairs. (We must admit that in a number of cases we have insufficient knowledge of the phonology of the language being described to be absolutely sure of the nature of all apparent contrasts; but in general, information at the level of minimal pairs is relatively accessible to both the native speaker and the linguist.) The segments we have chosen to describe may not be the same as the underlying phonological segments. Thus standard varieties of English have minimal sets such as *rum, run, rung,* and hence a contrastive inventory that includes three nasal segments, **m, n, ŋ**. The third of these, the velar nasal **ŋ**, has a different distributional pattern from the other two. It never appears initially in a morpheme and it alternates with **ŋg** before the comparative adjectival suffix *-er* in words like *long, longer.* Words like *dim, dimmer; thin, thinner* do not show a parallel alternation between nasal and nasal plus stop. For several reasons of this sort the segment **ŋ** can be said to be absent from the underlying inventory of English, although it serves to establish minimal contrasts. The different status of ŋ is not of concern to phonetics. We want to account for all the contrasts that occur between distinct segments, and in English that includes ŋ.

There are, of course, other situations which are harder to resolve in this way. In particular it is often difficult to decide how to divide a particular phonetic string into segments. There are well-known cases such as the affricates tʃ and dʒ in English, which some linguists regard as one segment and others as a sequence of two segments. From our point of view it does not really matter which of these solutions is chosen. The phonetic facts to be described remain the same in either case. English also provides a useful illustration of another form of this problem in words such as *mew* and *beauty*. Obviously these words differ from *moo* and *booty*, but the difference could be interpreted as a contrast between the presence and absence of the semivowel **j**, or as a contrast between the different vowel nuclei **i͡u** and **u** (where **i͡u** represents a diphthong with a rising amplitude contour). However, again the phonetic facts would not differ according to which view is taken. Our approach in similar situations is to adopt the phonetic description which yields the simplest segment types. Thus, in this case, we would prefer the interpretation with the simpler segment **j** to the complex one **i͡u**.

Although our primary data are the contrasts within languages, we also take note of differences between languages. We hope that the phonetic events observed will be sufficient to form the basis for an overall phonetic theory. This needs to be rich enough to describe those segmental events which distinguish one language or accent from another and which are also sufficiently distinct to serve as potential conveyers of lexical contrasts for speakers of other languages. We will, however, mainly restrict the discussion to those segments that distinguish words in some language.

As we will be discussing only segments, prosodic features such as tone, stress and accent fall outside the scope of the book, even though they distinguish words. So also do most of the variations in segments that result from differences in their prosodic context. Furthermore, variations due to stylistic choices and changes in speech tempo are disregarded. We are implicitly restricting our attention to a careful speech style, and many of our examples are drawn from citation forms, or words spoken in carrier phrases. For the task we have in mind this choice is appropriate as these forms are likely to be the most differentiated at the segmental level.

Our idea of what a phonetic description of these events should be like involves the establishment of parameters along which variation can be measured and a set of categorial values along these parameters. The categorial labels provide a vocabulary that can be used to classify distinctions within a language and to describe cases where sounds in different languages are sufficiently similar to be equated with one another. The parameters and categories that we use are mostly quite familiar ones from the phonetic literature, but we have in each case tried to rethink, through our examination of contrasts in languages, the basis on which any given one is justified. We also discuss the relationship that exists between the phonetic categories we establish and the classificatory features employed in phonological theory. In these discussions we take as our usual point of reference the features that have been used in recent models of feature geometry (see the review by McCarthy 1988), although we also pay some attention to some older proposals and certain newer suggestions. We do not attempt to present our own competing phonological feature system, as we are not examining phonological processes and constraints, but only contrasts (and even these from a largely phonetic point of view). We do, however, point to some areas where we believe that some elaboration or clarification of the usual feature scheme might be advisable. In the Coda at the end of the book we summarize the major findings on segmental contrasts which a phonological theory must address.

We also maintain that a distinction can be drawn between those phonetic parameters that are likely to serve as a basis for the organization of linguistic behavior, and others that can be used to provide a physical characterization of sounds, but which do not relate well to the sound patterns of languages. We could, for example, consider place of articulation to be defined in terms of a single continuous parameter such as the distance of the stricture from the glottis. However, this description would overlook, among other things, the functional and anatomical separation that exists between the lips and the tongue. A more insightful description is therefore one that partitions place of articulation into a number of major zones, within each of which certain categories can be distinguished.

As is detailed in our discussion of place of articulation in chapter 2, this does not mean that boundaries between each category can be easily determined. For example, the tongue has no clearly defined regions, and neither does the roof of the mouth; and there are, of course, similar problems in dividing the continua which underlie other phonetic parameters. Nonetheless, it is very striking that languages often seem to cut the continua in similar ways so that it is possible to equate a sound in one language with a similar sound in another. Our procedure in trying to build up a description of the sounds of the world's languages is to proceed primarily by a series of such equivalences.

Thus, we might encounter two languages A and B, each of which has a set of three sounds that differ only by differences along a single parameter. In each language it will be possible to rank the three sounds according to their values on the parameter in question, A1, A2, A3 and B1, B2, B3. Now, if A1 is judged to be equivalent to B2, and A2 equivalent to B3, there must be (at least) four values of the parameter in question which suffice to distinguish contrastive sounds. The equivalences can be displayed as follows:

1			B1
2	A1	=	B2
3	A2	=	B3
4	A3		

The likely total of contrastive categories along a given parameter is established by considering a set of such equivalences. Of course, judging which two sounds in different languages are equivalent rests on both the evaluation of data and experience.

A particular speech sound is not characterized by a value on only one parameter, but by the set of specified values on all the relevant parameters. We organize our discussion primarily on the basis of integral sounds, not according to single parameters or groups of related parameters. For example, there are chapters devoted to stops, nasals, fricatives, and vowels, rather than chapters which discuss topics such as degrees of stricture, types of phonation, and lip position. There is one significant exception to this general practice: In chapter 2 we survey the places of articulation needed to characterize the sounds of the world's languages, focussing on place contrasts found in stops and nasals. This chapter provides a framework for description of place contrasts among other classes of segments.

The next chapter, chapter 3, describes the remaining aspects of the various types of stops that occur (apart from clicks, to which a separate chapter is devoted). This chapter contains the principal discussion of distinctions in laryngeal activity between segments. The four succeeding chapters discuss other major types of consonants – nasals, fricatives, laterals and rhotics – in terms of the distinctions in place and laryngeal activity previously established, as well as any additional parameters that relate to the specific class of consonants covered by the chapter. Chapter 8 is devoted to clicks. Although sounds of this type occur in relatively few of the world's languages, there is great variety among clicks due to the fact that a large number of ways of modifying them are employed in the languages that use them. The survey then continues with a chapter on the vowels and semivowels observed in the world's languages. A final chapter, on multiple articulations, discusses single segments produced by combining several articulations each of which on its own could have formed a segment. This chapter includes discussion of what are traditionally called secondary articulations.

In these chapters we treat as separate categories only those differences between sounds that occur within the same language and those differences between sounds in different languages that we believe are great enough to be potentially distinctive. However, a descriptive system of phonetic parameters should also be able to characterize many differences at the phonetic level that are unrelated to phonological contrast. Differences in regional or social accents can be maintained by, for example, subtle shifts in vowel quality that are noticeable over a long stretch of speech, but which are not sufficient for distinguishing the meanings of words or phrases. That is, a phonetic theory should be able to make a distinction between those properties of sounds that can or could convey linguistic information (the difference between one form and another within a possible language) and those that convey only sociolinguistic information (the difference between one language or dialect and another). We believe that it is possible to set up a system of phonetic parameters each of which contains categories that taken as a whole, will distinguish all the potential contrasts within human languages. The system also allows for differences between one language and another to be described by different values along the parameters.

In addition to the categories and parameters of our descriptions we sometimes refer to targets or gestures in our accounts of segments. We would like to make clear that we are using these terms without implying any specific theoretical framework. A target can be thought of as either a specific location towards which an articulator is moving or as a more general notion including several properties such as the rate of the movement or its acoustic results. In either case, a target is an abstract goal at which one aims but which one does not necessarily hit. A gesture in our usage is a movement of a single articulator, which may by itself form the basis of a segment, or may require coordination with other articulatory movements for the formation of the sound. This is not the same concept as used in Articulatory Phonology (Browman and Goldstein 1992) but is based on similar insights. We adopt this usage to provide a framework within which to discuss dynamic aspects of speech. Speech is not a static process, but an active one, and it is clear that many properties cannot be understood unless we examine their dynamic aspects.

Although the discussion in this introductory chapter and the general layout of this book are in terms of articulatory properties of sounds, throughout the book we have also taken note of acoustic properties. It is perfectly possible to describe all the systematic phonetic contrasts that occur among languages in terms of the sound-producing mechanism. But this is often not the appropriate way of characterizing contrasts; some phonological statements depend more on the acoustic properties of sounds. In any feature theory that is eventually developed, some features will classify sounds in terms of their acoustic properties, which are presumed to be in a simple relation with the auditory parameters that the perceptual mechanism uses. There is also growing evidence that the mental targets of some sounds (notably vowels) are best described in terms of an auditory theory of speech production (Johnson, Ladefoged and Lindau 1993).

There are many other points that should be taken into account in a theory of linguistic phonetics. We should note that some places of articulation (or some areas within the continuum) are used more often than others. Similarly certain manners of articulation (such as stops) are common, but others (such as trills) occur less often; and within the vowel continuum, some vowels are found in a far wider range of languages than others. We do not at the moment have a complete theory that will account for these facts. There is no doubt that some articulations are easier to make than others. Thus although it is perfectly possible for anybody to make a closure between the blade of the tongue and the upper lip, this gesture is not used in many languages, perhaps because it is harder to integrate into the stream of speech than, say, a bilabial stop. There is also no doubt that some auditory distinctions are easier to maintain than others; the set of vowels **i**, **e**, **a**, **o**, **u** are more distinct than the set **y**, **ø**, **a**, **ɤ**, **ɯ**. Furthermore, as Stevens (1989) has pointed out, some articulatory gestures can vary over a fairly wide range without producing much acoustic change, resulting in what he calls quantal articulations. But while pursuing these topics is undoubtedly of great importance for an adequate theory of phonetics, our aim in this book is more limited, and we will comment on them only in passing.

We have attempted to provide a great deal of documentation of the contrasts we discuss. As a result, we believe that a part of the value of the book lies in its exemplification of a wide variety of types of phonetic data collected by a range of techniques. The data includes still and cine x-ray photography, palatography, spectrograms, waveforms, aerodynamic data, and articulatory movement data obtained by a number of different methods. We have not attempted to explain how to use these methods, as this book is not a handbook of phonetics, but we hope that we have provided sufficient pointers so that readers will understand the significant aspects of the documentation provided. Readers are presumed to be familiar with basic phonetic concepts as expounded in standard textbooks. We are, however, aware that we refer to so many languages that readers are unlikely to be familiar with all of them. With this in mind, we provide an appendix identifying the location and classification of all languages mentioned. In the text itself languages will usually be cited without further identification.

As with any jointly authored work, this book represents the results of some compromises between the authors. Had only one of us been writing the book, some data would have been interpreted differently, and certain arguments would undoubtedly have been stated more forcefully than they appear here, while others would have been omitted altogether. But we both believe that the combination of our efforts has produced a more complete survey than either of us could have produced alone. When we started this project we knew that we were being ambitious. But we did not realize the extraordinary amount of physiological and acoustic data that is available on the little known languages of the world. Our library research has led us to hundreds of books and papers that contain wonderful instrumental data that has never been summarized or otherwise made available to the general phonetician who is not concerned with the particular languages being described in the original work. We also found that our own files and the UCLA phonetic archives accumulated over many years contained a great deal of previously unpublished material. We were often pleased to find that illustrative recordings and analyses of particular sounds cited could be obtained from our own resources. The great wealth of material available to us led to some problems in trying to decide which of many pieces of data we should include. We wanted to write a book that would advance linguistic and phonetic theory. Accordingly we have limited ourselves to discussing just the data required for this purpose. We have not included a number of things that are well known and readily available, such as acoustic data illustrating the contrasting stop consonants in English, or extended discussions of voice onset time.

As our research went on, we also uncovered some notable gaps in the available published data and our own resources. This led to an interesting problem in research management. To what extent should we try to fill these gaps by extending our own investigations? Our solution to this problem was to set a date for the completion of this book, and do what we could within this time limit. As a result we are woefully aware that much more could have been done. We have been able to provide a large number of new analyses of our own previously unpublished data, and to summarize much of the literature. But we can still foresee a lifetime of work ahead of us.

This is the present state of our knowledge about the linguistic phonetic events that occur in the languages of the world.

2

Places of Articulation

In this chapter we will describe the range of different locations within the oral cavity at which the major articulatory events involved in consonant production may occur. This is, in traditional terms, the place of articulation. We will be concerned mainly with stops and nasals, in that we will usually be considering complete closures of the vocal tract. This is in part because it is more straightforward to characterize the location of a closure than to describe the location of a stricture of lesser degree. However, some additional locations are used for fricatives, and where necessary we will supplement our account by describing these sounds. We will also note in Chapter 5, in which we discuss fricatives in more detail, that there are some interrelationships between place of articulation and manner of constriction. In the present chapter we will describe the primary components of each movement, neglecting any secondary articulations. We will also neglect aspects of the vocal tract that are associated with the phonatory activity of the glottis or with the velic opening. All these additional components of sounds will be discussed in subsequent chapters.

The place of an articulation is one necessary parameter in describing the pattern of controlled movements required to generate a sound. The specification of articulatory movements requires three different kinds of statement. We must say what moves, in which direction it moves, and how fast is it moving. This means that we must first characterize the parts of the vocal apparatus that can move; we must then state the possible directions of movement (where the articulators are moving from, and where they are going to); and thirdly we should specify the timing of the movements in these directions.

We should also note that not every aspect of a movement is of equal significance. Although the change of position of each point in the vocal tract in the course of some particular articulation could, in principle, be given by an equation describing its motion, this would not be very insightful. What is of prime importance in the phonetic patterning of languages is the *outcome* of a set of movements. For example, closing the lips always involves some movement of the lower lip. However, the extent to which the lower lip is moved independently or is moved by raising the jaw may vary, and the amount that the upper lip is lowered to meet the lower lip may vary as well. Although understanding how the trade-off between these different possibilities is managed is very important for building a model of how speech activity is actually controlled, such detail is not of any linguistic significance. What matters is the fact that the lips close – the important variable might be labeled lip aperture.

A set of possible linguistically relevant variables of this kind has been proposed by Browman and Goldstein (1986, 1992) in their Articulatory Phonology model. The most significant part of the Articulatory Phonology research program is the central role that is assigned to the dynamics of the articulation. Movements are described in terms of abstract gestural prototypes. These have an inherent time-course and are coordinated with other gestures so that different degrees of temporal overlap can be specified. Our view of speech activity is colored by Browman and Goldstein's work, although we believe that the number of variables needs to be larger in order to deal with the full range of distinct sound types used in the languages of the world, and our use of the term 'gesture' is not exactly the same as theirs. We do not assign any formal theoretical status to gestures, but use the term gesture to refer to a generalized pattern of movement for a family of linguistically equivalent articulations. In what follows we will concentrate on describing the articulators used and the directions of the movements in each gesture understood in this sense.

We will describe articulations in terms of the five major parts of the vocal tract that move. These are shown in figure 2.1 in a sagittal section of the vocal tract. These moveable parts can be called the active articulators. The first set of articulators consists of both the upper and lower lip. There is no doubt that movements of the upper lip play a prominent role in some articulatory gestures, but the larger movements are those of the lower lip, which is often raised and lowered with the assistance of movements of the jaw. Because the two lips usually act together as articulators, we have joined the points indicating what we take to be the approximate centers of their masses by dashed lines. Gestures involving the lips are said to be Labial.

The next set of articulators is the tip and the blade of the tongue. These are the highly mobile parts of the tongue that are forward of the frenulum (the attachment of the tongue to the floor of the mouth). These two parts of the tongue have somewhat different ranges of motion and therefore their movements need to be separately described, but because they are so closely connected only one or the other can be the primary articulator in any given speech sound. The tip of the tongue at rest is just the part that has a mainly vertical aspect (i.e. is largely parallel to the surfaces of the incisors) plus a small area about 2 mm wide on the upper surface. Sounds made with the tip of the tongue are said to be apical. The underside of the tip of the tongue is used in some articulations; sounds made in this way are said to be sub-apical. Behind the tip is the blade, which is the defining part of the tongue for sounds that are said to be laminal. It is difficult to say how far back the blade extends. Probably the most useful definition of the blade of the tongue from a linguistic phonetic point of view is in terms of its relation to the roof of the mouth. It is the part of the tongue below the center of the alveolar ridge when the tongue is at rest. This, of course, requires us to define the alveolar ridge – an equally difficult task. The center of the ridge is the point of maximum slope in the curvature of that part of the midline sagittal section of the vocal tract which is behind the upper teeth. In practice this is often difficult to determine but it is probably the most useful point that can be approximated in a wide selection of individuals. Laminal sounds are made with the part of the tongue that has its center, when the tongue is at rest, immediately below the center of the alveolar ridge. The laminal area extends forward to about 2 mm behind the tip of the tongue, and backward to a point about 2 mm behind the point on the tongue below the center of the alveolar ridge. The tip and blade of the tongue form Coronal articulations.

The body of the tongue is the mass of the tongue behind the blade which can be taken to have its effective center in the neighborhood of the point labeled 'body' on figure 2.1. From an articulatory point of view, it is the surface of this mass that has to be considered. Articulations made with this surface are said to be Dorsal articulations. It is sometimes useful to distinguish between the front and back regions of this surface, the front being that part which is at rest below the hard palate and the back that part which is at rest below the velum. These regions cannot be moved separately from each other.

The root of the tongue and the epiglottis can be moved independently of the body of the tongue, although, as with other articulations involving the tongue, when they are moved the rest of the tongue will be moved with them. The relation between the root of the tongue and the epiglottis is similar to that between the tip and blade of the tongue. They can be moved separately, but because of their proximity only one or the other can be the principal articulator in any given sound. Gestures made by either of them are considered to be Radical articulations.

Lastly, as we will see later, the glottis has to be recognized as an articulator in some circumstances, forming Glottal articulations.

The starting point of the movement for a consonant depends on the position of the vocal tract in the previous sound. The most convenient approach in this chapter is to consider the movement of an active articulator from its position in a neutral state of the vocal tract towards some articulatory target on the upper or rear surface of the vocal tract in the midline. These surfaces are called the passive articulators. The actual target position may be envisaged as being close to or even, in the case of a stop, just above the passive articulator. The painful thought involved in this latter possibility is achieved without

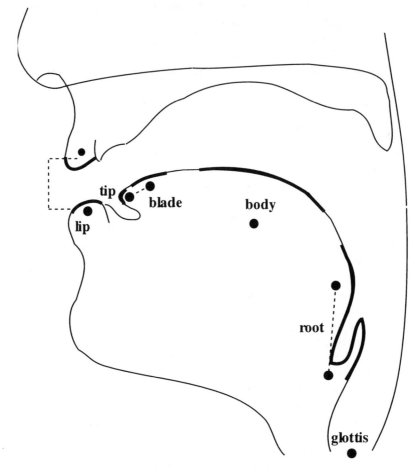

Figure 2.1 The five groups of moveable structures forming the active articulators in the vocal tract.

bloodshed because we never actually achieve these targets. But it is neverthe-less often useful to think of the forceful contact of the tongue or lips in a stop consonant as being programmed in the brain (or in a computer) as an attempt to throw one part of the vocal tract through another. In many other types of consonants, such as fricatives, trills and laterals, the articulators have to be positioned more precisely and this is not the appropriate way to envisage the action.

Although the position of moveable structures away from the midline can be important in differentiating between sounds, the most significant articulatory characteristics can be determined if the midline position is known. Theories of phonetics have virtually always included some notion of place of articulation which is very comparable to the notion of an articulatory target as we have

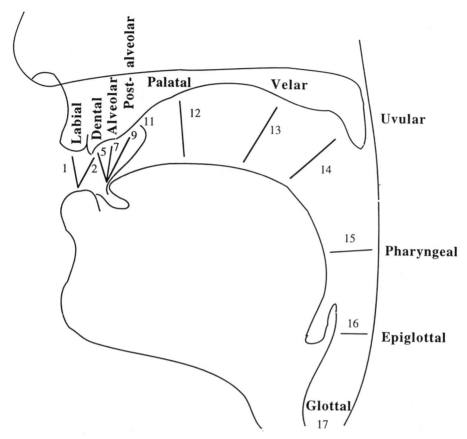

Figure 2.2 The nine regions of the vocal tract that can be considered as target areas for the moveable articulators. The numbered lines show some of the 17 named articulatory gestures, including those in the glottal region. Some additional gestures are shown in the more detailed diagrams of the anterior part of the vocal tract in Figure 2.3.

outlined it above. But the traditional terms are more powerful in that they can be taken to describe both the principal moving articulator and the principal direction of movement. They also, by default, refer specifically to the most highly constricted articulation involved in the production of a sound. We will describe articulations that are produced with more than one constriction in chapter 10.

The traditional terms that specify the target and what moves towards it are shown in figures 2.2 and 2.3, which provide an overview of most of the terms that we will use in the remainder of this chapter. There are nine target regions on the upper or back surface of the vocal tract, which we will term labial, dental, alveolar, post-alveolar; palatal, velar, uvular, pharyngeal and epiglottal. In addition, sounds produced by the vocal folds acting as articulators will be con-

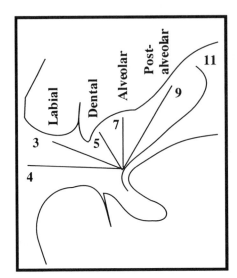
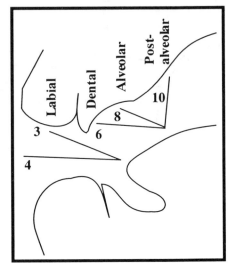

Figure 2.3 More detailed diagrams of the anterior part of the vocal tract in figure 2.2, showing articulations involving the tongue tip and blade.

sidered to have glottal targets. Note that we use the term alveolar to denote only the front part of the alveolar ridge. This seems to be the practice of most phoneticians, although it is somewhat confusing in that it means that the point of maximum curvature in the alveolar ridge forms the boundary between what we call the alveolar as opposed to the post-alveolar region.

Most of the traditional place terms specify both the moving articulator and the articulatory target on the upper or back surface of the vocal tract. It is these pairings between active articulator and articulatory target that are indicated by the numbers on figures 2.2 and 2.3, and not specific positions. Thus 'velar' implies an action involving the body of the tongue and the velar region, and 'epiglottal' implies an action involving part of the root of the tongue (specifically the epiglottis) and the back wall of the pharynx.

In some cases the traditional term does not make a complete specification of the pairing. The term alveolar by itself can refer to sounds that involve the alveolar ridge and either the tip or blade of the tongue, and thus can describe either an apical or a laminal articulation. For some of the sounds in the alveolar region there is a traditional term that incorporates both the apical/laminal distinction and a more precise description of the target region. Thus denti-alveolar is often used to refer to sounds that are articulated in the dental region and involve the blade of the tongue. The name is appropriate in that it seems that laminal dental sounds always involve contact in the front part of the alveolar region as well as on the teeth. Apical post-alveolar sounds are often called (apical) retroflexes; and laminal post-alveolar sounds are called palato-

Table 2.1. Terminology summarizing the place of articulatory gestures

"Place of articulation"	Articulatory target region	Moving articulator	Symbol examples
1. Bilabial	Labial	Lower lip	p b m
2. Labiodental	Dental	Lower lip	ɸ Ꟁ ɱ
3. Linguo-labial	Labial	Tongue blade	t̼ d̼ n̼
4. Interdental	Dental	Tongue blade	t̪ d̪ n̪
5. Apical dental	Dental	Tongue tip	t̺ d̺ n̺
6. (Laminal) denti-alveolar	Dental and alveolar	Tongue blade	t̻ d̻ n̻
7. Apical alveolar	Alveolar	Tongue tip	t d n
8. Laminal alveolar	Alveolar	Tongue blade	t̻ d̻ n̻
9. Apical retroflex	Post-alveolar	Tongue tip	ʈ ɖ ɳ
10. (Laminal) palato-alveolar	Post-alveolar	Tongue blade	t̠ d̠ n̠
11. Sub-apical (retroflex)	Palatal	Tongue underblade	ʈ ɖ ɳ
12. Palatal	Palatal	Front of tongue	c ɟ ɲ
13. Velar	Velar	Back of tongue	k ɡ ŋ
14. Uvular	Uvular	Back of tongue	q ɢ ɴ
15. Pharyngeal	Pharyngeal	Root of tongue	ħ ʕ
16. Epiglottal	Epiglottal	Epiglottis	ʡ ʜ ʢ
17. Glottal	Glottal	Vocal folds	ʔ

alveolars. Sounds in an area behind the alveolar ridge can also be made with the underside of the tip of the tongue, in which case they are called sub-apical retroflex sounds. Articulatory pairings involving the tongue tip and blade are shown in figure 2.3. Table 2.1 presents some of the terminology that is used for labeling articulatory gestures, together with examples of the symbols used for their representation.

The 17 possibilities listed in table 2.1 indicate the major movements of part of the vocal tract from a neutral position towards the center of each target. In the next section of this chapter we will show that each of these possibilities represents one of the different articulatory movements that are used in consonant gestures (all of them, with the exception of the pharyngeal articulation, being used for stop consonants). The final section will consider whether there is a discrete set of places of articulation, which is one possible interpretation of the listing in table 2.1, or whether the 17 possibilities we have been discussing should be considered as terms describing exemplars with which other articulations may be compared.

2.1 Places of Articulation by Target Region

From the linguistic point of view the places of articulation in table 2.1 can usefully be classified into a smaller number of groups based on the articulators they share and on the patterns of linguistic behavior they exhibit. If consonants

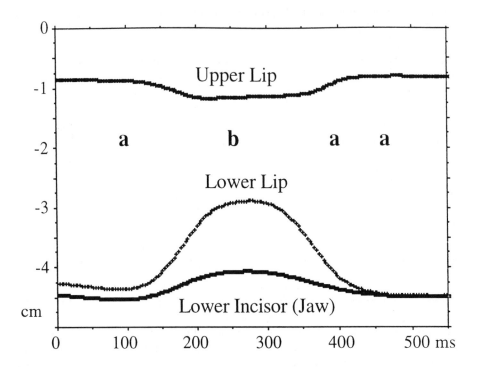

Figure 2.4 Mean vertical movement trajectories over time of the upper and lower lips and the jaw during ten repetitions of the Ewe word **abaa** 'mat' (from Maddieson 1993). Electromagnetic receivers were placed on the outside surface of the lips, hence a gap remains between them even during closure.

in which either the upper or lower lip is involved as an articulator are classified as Labials then there are three place classes among Labial sounds: the lower lip can articulate with the upper lip (bilabial), or the upper teeth (labiodental); and, as we will see, the upper lip can also be the target for the tongue (linguo-labial). If the location of the target on the upper vocal tract surface is taken to define an articulatory group, then only bilabial and linguo-labial places would be included in the Labial group. And if only the lower articulator is used to define a group, then the Labial group would include only bilabial and labiodental places. We will return to consideration of which of these three possible groupings seems most natural in the final section of this chapter.

As we noted earlier, bilabial stops differ from stops at the majority of other places of articulation in that they involve an active movement of the articulator on the upper surface of the vocal tract. The upper lip moves down to meet the upward-moving lower lip to form the closure and moves back up at the release. A typical movement pattern for the lips in producing a bilabial stop is shown in figure 2.4. This figure tracks the vertical position of the lips over time. Partly because both articulators are in motion, and therefore the increase in the cross-sectional area of the oral escape channel occurs more rapidly, the release phase of a bilabial stop is typically shorter than that of stops at other places of articulation. On many occasions (but not noticeably so in the stop shown in figure 2.4), aerodynamic forces may also cause the lips to separate more rapidly than they close (Fujimura 1961). The fact that both articulators are soft tissue may explain why bilabial stops are more likely to be produced with incomplete closure than stops in which the active articulator contacts a less flexible surface. This results in patterns such as that in Japanese, where in native and Sino-Japanese vocabulary /**p**/ is pronounced word-initially as ɸ or **h** (depending on the following vowel), and as **p** in a cluster with another consonant, whereas **t, k** do not alternate with fricatives (McCawley 1968, Shibatani 1990: 166–7).

The use of the labiodental place of articulation is largely restricted to fricatives, so we will defer most of the discussion of that place until chapter 5. There is, however, no doubt that at least for fricatives there is a contrast between bilabial and labiodental articulations. We do not know whether true labiodental stops occur in any language, although they have been reported among languages of Southern Africa, where the symbols **[ɸ]** and **[ɓ]** have been used for their transcription since at least Doke's 1926 study of Zulu. Guthrie reports that "there is a labiodental plosive which is distinct from the bilabial plosive, e.g. -**ɓar**- 'shine', -**bar**- 'give birth to'" in a language in the Nyanja-Tumbuka group that he called Tonga (Guthrie 1948: 61). We have not heard this language, and are unsure how it relates to languages with similar names in the region. In the nearby Tsonga dialects of South Africa, Baumbach (1974, 1987) reports labiodental affricates. Significantly, when an assimilated nasal occurs before these affricates Baumbach affirms that it shares the labiodental place, just as a nasal before the labiodental fricatives **v, f** does. Therefore, these sounds are not sequences of a bilabial plosive followed by a labiodental fricative. If they are indeed true affricates with a complete stop closure, then the stop portion of the affricate must be labiodental in place. Words illustrating these sounds, together with some other contrasting labials, are given in table 2.2.

We have heard labiodental stops made by a Shubi speaker whose teeth were sufficiently close together to allow him to make an airtight labiodental closure. For this speaker this sound was clearly in contrast with a bilabial stop; but we suspect that the majority of Shubi speakers make the contrast one of bilabial stop versus labial-labiodental affricate (i.e. bilabial stop closure followed by a labiodental fricative), rather than bilabial versus labiodental stop. Sounds described as labiodental affricates also occur, for example in German, in which the stop closure is bilabial, although the fricative release is labiodental.

Table 2.2 Words illustrating some of the labial consonants of the XiNkuna dialect of Tsonga (from Baumbach 1974, 1987)

	BILABIAL PLOSIVE	BILABIAL FRICATIVE	LABIODENTAL AFFRICATE	LABIODENTAL
VOICELESS UNASPIRATED	**papa** 'cloud'	**ɸu** 'finished'	**tiɱɡpfuβu** 'hippos'	**ɱfutsu** 'tortoise'
VOICELESS ASPIRATED	**pʰapʰaṭani** 'butterfly'		**ɱɡpfʰuka** 'distance'	
VOICED	**kuba** 'to hit'	**kuβaβa** 'to be painful'	**ʃileʤvu** 'chin'	**kuvumba** 'to guess'
BREATHY VOICED	**jimbɦo** 'ostrich'		**ɱʤvɦuβu** 'tree (sp.)'	**kuvɦeṭa** 'to scratch'

Labiodental nasals occur in many languages. As in Tsonga they are usually the result of coarticulation with a following labiodental fricative. The Yoruba word ɱfé 'want, like (imperfective)' is formed by preposing an imperfective marker consisting of a syllabic nasal with no inherent place to the verb stem fé. Labiodental nasals have, however, been reported as segments contrasting with both bilabial nasals and labiodental fricatives in the Kukuya dialect of Teke. Paulian (1975) describes these sounds as "réalisé comme une occlusive nasale, labiodentale, toujours sonore; l'occlusion se produit entre les dents du haut et l'intérieur de la lèvre inférieure; elle est accompagné d'une forte avance des deux lèvres." We do not know if a true occlusive could be made with this gesture, when we take into account the gaps that often occur between the incisors.

The third known possibility for an articulation concerning the Labial region involves moving the tongue forward to contact the upper lip. A series of linguo-labial segments has developed in a group of languages from the islands of Espiritu Santo and Malekula in Vanuatu (Maddieson 1989a). These languages have stops and nasals with a linguo-labial gesture, contrasting with bilabial and alveolar gestures, as illustrated by the Tangoa words in table 2.3. Some of the earlier literature on these languages (e.g. Tryon 1976, Fox 1979) describes these sounds as 'apico-labials' but, as they are often not apical, we have adopted the term linguo-labial suggested by Lounsbury (personal communication) for a similar articulation reported in Umotina. The IPA transcription for sounds of this type is the diacritic [̼] placed under a symbol for a coronal sound of the appropriate manner class. In recommending this transcription, the IPA implicitly classifies this place of articulation among the Coronals, and not in the Labial group.

The production of these sounds involves a movement of the tongue blade forwards so that it contacts the lower edge of the upper lip, which is drawn back somewhat to meet the advancing tongue. The time-course of this movement can be seen in the three frames in figure 2.5, taken from a videotape of a

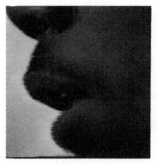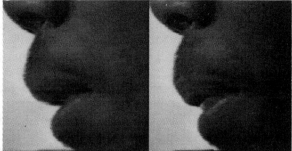

Figure 2.5 Three frames from a videotape showing the tongue and lip contact in the production of the word **naṇḍak** 'bow' by a speaker of Vao.

Table 2.3 Words illustrating bilabial, linguo-labial and alveolar places of articulation in Tangoa (from Maddieson 1989, Camden 1979)

	BILABIAL		LINGUO-LABIAL		ALVEOLAR	
PLOSIVE	**peta**	'taro'	**teṭe**	'butterfly'	**taṇa**	'father'
NASAL	**mata**	'snake'	**ṇata**	'eye'	**nunua**	'messenger spirit'
FRICATIVE	**βiliu**	'dog'	**ŏatu**	'stone'	**sasati**	'bad'

speaker of Vao. The first frame shows the starting position of the upper lip, as the tongue begins its forward movement. The second frame, 60 ms later, shows a downward and backward motion of the upper lip toward the advancing tongue. The third frame, another 60 ms later, illustrates the culminating phase of the articulation, with a complete occlusion formed between upper lip and tongue blade.

An even more unusual sound occurs in Pirahã, a Mura language spoken by approximately 100 people in Brazil. According to Everett (1982) this language has "a voiced, lateralized apical-alveolar/sublaminal-labial double flap with egressive lung air. In the formation of this sound the tongue tip first touches the alveolar ridge and then comes out of the mouth, almost touching the upper chin as the underblade of the tongue touches the lower lip." We have seen a videotape of this sound, which confirms the general description provided by Everett. However, this sound is only used in certain special types of speech performance and it is not clear to us that it should be included in the present enumeration of articulations.

The second group of places of articulation contains those made with a contact against the upper teeth or that part of the roof of the mouth relatively near the teeth. As a group, these articulations are known as Coronal. The group includes most articulations made in the dental, alveolar and post-alveolar regions shown in figure 2.1, but the group is often most usefully limited to those articulations in which the tongue tip or blade makes the constriction. If the group is defined by the use of the tongue tip or blade as the active articulator, then linguo-labials and at least some articulations in the palatal region will be included. Again, we will discuss the linguistic merits of different groupings in the final section of this chapter.

Apart from labiodentals, articulations in the dental region can be made only with the tongue tip or blade as the active articulator. The tongue more commonly contacts the back of the teeth, but the tip may also project between the teeth so that the blade makes contact with the underside of the upper teeth. The special term for this articulation is interdental. We have included a distinction between dental and interdental places of articulation in table 2.1 and figure 2.2, but we do not know of any use of this distinction to form phonemic contrasts. It seems that some languages may consistently use one or the other possibility while others permit the use of either of them. As we will discuss in chapter 5, speakers of American English from California typically use an interdental fricative in words such as 'think', but nearly all speakers of British English use a dental fricative in such words. A similar variation between dental and interdentals is apparent when we examine Australian languages. Dixon (1980) notes that Australian languages often have interdental stops in which the "teeth are slightly apart, and the blade of the tongue projects between and touches both sets of teeth," whereas Butcher (in progress) notes that both postdental and interdental articulations occur among speakers of the same language. In postdental stops the tip of the tongue may be turned down so that it touches the back of the lower teeth, while a closure is formed by the tongue blade contacting the upper teeth.

A difference between apical dental and interdental gestures with different manners of articulation occurs in Malayalam. Some of the speakers we investigated used an interdental nasal n̪ in words such as **pun̪n̪i** 'pig', but they made **t̪** as a dental stop without tongue protrusion in words such as **kut̪t̪i** 'stabbed'. This may be related to the fact that Malayalam has a contrast between dentals and alveolars for both stops and nasals. Acoustically, both dental and interdental stops are quite distinct from the contrasting alveolar stops in their bursts as well as their formant transitions. The nasals have virtually no bursts, and are distinguished almost entirely by their formant transitions (the differences in the nasal murmur itself are not at all salient). Those speakers of Malayalam who have interdental nasals might thus increase the difference by producing more distinct formant transitions as a result of the interdental articulation.

Many languages contrast dental and alveolar stops. This difference is almost always accompanied by a difference in laminality. All four of the possibilities, apical dental, laminal dental, apical alveolar and laminal alveolar occur, but languages rarely have contrasts in which one sound is apical and the other laminal with the contact being made at the same place on the roof of the mouth. In the languages we have investigated, dental stops are usually laminal

Table 2.4 Words illustrating dental, alveolar and sub-apical retroflex stops in syllable final position in Toda

	VOICELESS		VOICED	
DENTAL	**poṭ**	'ten'	**moḏ**	'churning stick'
ALVEOLAR	**paːt**	'cockroach'	**mod**	'village with dairy'
RETROFLEX	**ṭaṭ**	'churning vessel'	**maḍ**	'head'

rather than apical, with contact on both the teeth and the front part of the alveolar ridge, whereas the alveolar stops are often apical, with contact usually on the center of the alveolar ridge. This is the pattern in widely dispersed languages such as Malayalam, Tiwi, Ewe, and Dahalo. In many languages (including all those just mentioned) the dental stops typically have a long contact region in the sagittal plane, and might better be regarded as laminal denti-alveolars rather than pure dentals. Similarly, in these languages in which there is a contrasting coronal articulation, it is always apical with a smaller contact area. It is sometimes in the region in front of the center of the alveolar ridge, making it what we have defined as an alveolar articulation, but it may be on the center of the alveolar ridge, making it what we have called post-alveolar.

Some Dravidian languages have a three way contrast between places involving the tongue tip or blade, distinguishing dental, alveolar and what for the time being we will label retroflex stops. Toda examples are given in table 2.4. We investigated the articulatory characteristics of the Toda stops using palatographic analysis techniques which are fully described elsewhere (Ladefoged, in press). The basic procedure was to paint the tip, blade and front of the tongue with a mixture of edible oil and finely powdered charcoal. The speaker then said the word to be investigated, which was always carefully chosen so that it had only one coronal consonant. The pronunciation was recorded using a video camera, which was also used to photograph a mirror placed in the mouth so as to show the area of the upper part of the vocal tract that had been contacted. The procedure was then reversed, painting the upper part of the vocal tract, and observing which part of the tongue had made the contact. In palatograms and linguograms made in this fashion the area of contact is indicated by a darkened area where the medium is transferred. This is the opposite of what is seen in some of the other palatograms reproduced in this book in which the area of contact is indicated by an area that is wiped clean. Dental impressions were made of each speaker's upper teeth and palate, so that an accurate scale could be applied to the photographs, and sagittal sections of part of the upper surface of the vocal tract could be drawn. We have records of five speakers of Toda (three men and two women) made in this way.

All five speakers made the dental stops with the tip and blade of the tongue making contact with the upper front teeth and the alveolar ridge, as exemplified in the upper pair of photographs in figure 2.6. Often, as in the case of the

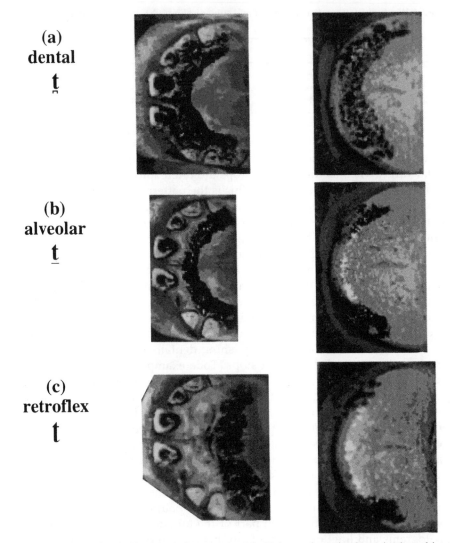

**(a)
dental
t̪**

**(b)
alveolar
t̲**

**(c)
retroflex
ʈ**

Figure 2.6 Palatographic and linguographic records of the Toda words **poṯ** 'ten', **paːṯ** 'cockroach', **ṭɑṭ** 'churning vessel'. The photographs have been retouched so as to remove reflective highlights. The dark areas on the backs of the subject's front teeth are stains and not the result of tongue contact during the articulation.

speaker illustrated, a considerable part of the alveolar ridge was involved. We noted above that dental stops are often formed in this way, making them laminal denti-alveolar stops. The middle pair of photographs in the figure illustrate the alveolar stops. Note that the dark areas on the backs of the subject's front teeth in the left-hand photograph are stains and not the result of tongue contacts. These stops were always made with the tip of the tongue contacting the middle of the alveolar ridge, making them clearly apical alveolars. The retroflex stops, exemplified in the lower pair of photographs, show very little contact on the tip of the tongue, as, instead of the tip itself, it was the underside of the tip that was involved, making these sounds sub-apical. The contact was between the curled back tip of the tongue and the roof of the mouth well behind the alveolar ridge, in the region of the hard palate. We will compare this retroflex articulation with others that have been labeled retroflex in a later section.

In general, if a language has only a dental or an alveolar stop, then that stop will be laminal if it is dental and apical if it is alveolar. But generalizations such as these should be treated with reserve. Most textbooks describe French **t, d, n, l** as laminal dental and English **t, d, n, l** as apical alveolar. But Dart (1991) has shown that 20–30% of her sample of 20 speakers of French used alveolar gestures for some of these sounds (the percentage differing for different members of the set), and similar percentages of Californian English speakers used dental articulations.

There are comparatively few languages in which a dental stop is required to be apical. This is, however, the case in Temne, a West Atlantic language spoken in Sierra Leone, which breaks the generalization that languages that contrast dental and alveolar stops have laminal dentals and apical alveolars. In Temne the stop made on the teeth is articulated with the tip of the tongue, and the one made on the alveolar ridge, which is slightly affricated, involves the blade of the tongue.

Similarly there are not many clear cases in which a laminal articulation is required for alveolar gestures for stops or nasals; but, from the x-ray tracings in Stojkov (1942, 1961), it seems as if the major part of the difference between plain **t, d, n** and what are traditionally called palatalized **t, d, n** in Bulgarian is that the former are produced with an apical alveolar gesture, and the latter with a laminal alveolar gesture, i.e. as **t̪, d̪, n̪**. As Scatton (1984: 60) remarks "the extent to which the mid-body of the tongue is raised is not very much greater than that of their non-palatalized counterparts." The difference between **n** and **n̪** may be seen in figure 2.7. Whereas in **n** the contact is formed just behind the teeth and has a relatively small area, in **n̪** the contact area is larger, extending a little further forward and also further back towards the palatal region. Stojkov's tracings show even less difference in the tongue profile behind the closure for the stops than appears in these nasals.

Another generalization is that if a language has both an apical and a laminal stop consonant, then the laminal consonant is likely to be more affricated. This can be demonstrated by reference to Isoko, which contrasts laminal dental and apical alveolar stops. Spectrograms of words illustrating this difference are shown in figure 2.8. The affrication which occurs with the laminal articulation is quite evident. There are also clear differences in the formant transitions which are due to using the blade of the tongue in the dental (denti-alveolar) as

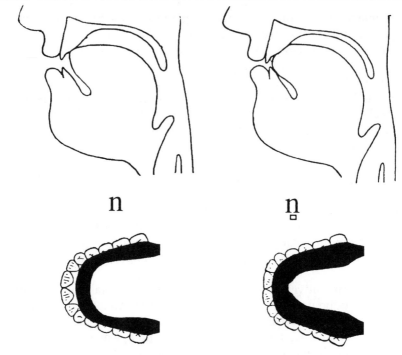

Figure 2.7 Tracings from x-ray photographs and palatograms of apical and laminal alveolar nasals in Bulgarian (after Stojkov 1961).

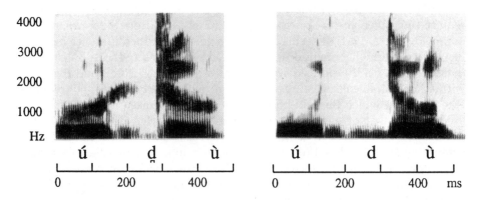

Figure 2.8 Spectograms illustrating the difference between a laminal dental ḏ and an apical alveolar **d** in Isoko in the words úḏù 'farm' and údù 'chest'.

opposed to the tip of the tongue in the alveolar articulations. The locus of the second formant is lower for the laminal dental stop. The closely similar frequencies of the third and fourth formants at the stop release, and the unusual second formant which can be seen in the first part of the laminal dental closure,

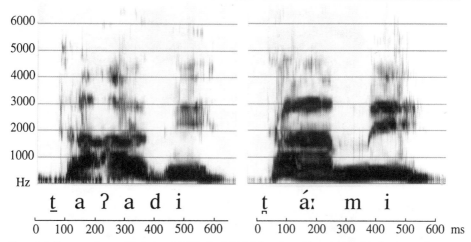

Figure 2.9 Spectrograms of Dahalo t̪aʔadi 'fruit of *shitinke*' and t̪aːmi 'grass, thatch', illustrating longer and noisier release for alveolar than for dental plosives.

occurred in a number of utterances of this word by this speaker. Dart (1991, 1993) also found a significantly higher F2 prior to closure and lower F3 and F4 at both closure and release of apical alveolar stops in 'O'odham, in comparison with the laminal dentals.

An exception to the generalization that laminal consonants are likely to be more affricated is provided by Dahalo. The contrast between the laminal dental stops and the apical alveolar stops in this language is illustrated by the spectrograms in figure 2.9. The noisy part of the release of the alveolars is roughly three times as long as that of the dentals. In having greater affrication in the alveolar stops, Dahalo is unlike most of those languages of India, Australia and the Americas in which dental/alveolar contrasts are found.

The next question that we should consider is the nature of retroflex articulations. We illustrated a retroflex articulation in Toda in figure 2.6, but there is considerably more to be said about such articulations. The term 'retroflex' has been used for a variety of different articulations, which are linked as much by the shape of the tongue involved as the region on the upper surface of the mouth. A retroflex articulation is one in which the tip of the tongue is curled up to some extent. In addition to the sub-apical palatal articulations that occur in Toda, there are also retroflex gestures in which the tip of the tongue is curled only slightly upwards, forming an articulation in the alveolar or, more usually, post-alveolar region. We will symbolize articulations of this kind by a subscript dot beneath the symbol for the alveolar sound. This usage has been explicitly disavowed by the International Phonetic Association (1989), but we have retained it so that we can differentiate between two degrees of retroflexion, using ʈ, ɖ, ɳ for articulations of the Toda type, but t̠, d̠, n̠ for those with a less retroflexed tongue shape.

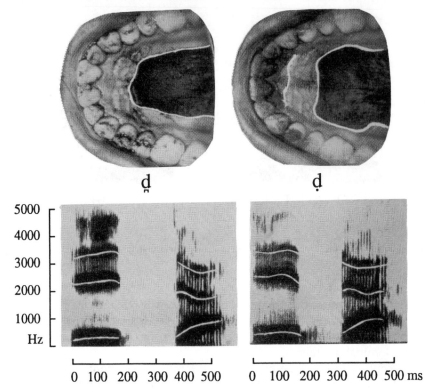

Figure 2.10 Spectrograms and palatograms illustrating the difference between laminal denti-alveolar ḓ and apical retroflex ḍ in Ewe in the phrases é ḓà 'he throws' and é ḍà 'he cooks', based on Ladefoged (1968).

We examined the contrast between ḓ and ḍ in two dialects of Ewe (Kpando and Peki) and in some of the neighboring Central Togo languages. Instrumental records were obtained from a total of six speakers using this contrast. The principal articulatory difference between these two sounds is in the part of the tongue that is used. The denti-alveolar ḓ is articulated with the blade of the tongue against the teeth and alveolar ridge, much as in the majority of other dental sounds we have been considering. The sound represented here as ḍ is articulated with the tip of the tongue against the alveolar ridge (usually but not always, the posterior part), making it similar to the alveolar stop in Toda, but with a slightly more retracted articulation. Figure 2.10 shows palatograms of a speaker of the Kpando dialect of Ewe saying the phrases é ḓà 'he throws' and é ḍà 'he cooks'. The other five speakers investigated all produced very similar sounds. The palatograms show that the area of contact between the tongue and the roof of the mouth is smaller in the second phrase than in the first. Examination of the speaker's tongue after the pronunciation of each phrase also made it clear that in the case of é ḍà only a small part of the tip about 5 mm

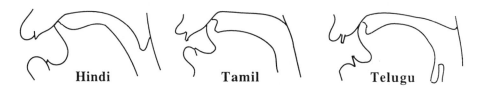

Figure 2.11 X-ray tracings of the apical retroflex ɖ in Hindi and the sub-apical retroflex ɖ in Tamil and Telugu (after Ladefoged and Bhaskararao 1983.)

long in the sagittal plane had touched the roof of the mouth. As the area of contact on the roof of the mouth is longer than 5 mm the tip of the tongue must have moved as it made contact, an action that we find typical of retroflex sounds. Spectrograms for these words are shown on the left side of the figure. The acoustic difference produced by these slightly different articulations is very small, consisting mainly of a greater lowering of F2 and F3 before the closure in é ɖà.

Ladefoged (1968) suggested that the Ewe retroflex ɖ might not be the same as the similarly symbolized sound in Hindi, a suggestion that still seems likely to us. Ewe ɖ does not sound as retroflex as Hindi ɖ. We do not have comparable data on the two languages, so we have no way of deciding this issue. But Ladefoged and Bhaskararao (1983) have shown that languages can differ in the kind of retroflexion that they employ. Figure 2.11 shows typical tongue positions for the retroflex consonants in Tamil and Telugu, two Dravidian languages, and Hindi, an Indo-Aryan language. The Dravidian languages typically have sub-apical consonants in which the underside of the tongue contacts the anterior part of the hard palate, whereas Hindi speakers do not usually have the tongue tip curled so far back and therefore the contact is on the apical edge of the tongue. We use the approved IPA retroflex symbols such as ɖ for sub-apical palatal (retroflex) sounds, and dotted symbols such as ɖ for apical post-alveolar (retroflex) sounds. We do not know of any language with two contrasting retroflex stops, apical and sub-apical. The Dravidian languages are the best known languages that have sub-apical retroflex stops, but Butcher's work (in progress) shows that sub-apical palatal articulations also occur in Australian languages, and Khanty may also have a sound of this kind (Gulya 1966). In several of the Native American languages of the southwestern USA what is important in the contrast between dental and alveolar sounds is that the shape of the tongue should be what we might call slightly retroflex, with the part of the tongue behind the tip hollowed to some extent (Langdon, personal communication).

The acoustic results of retroflexion have been studied by a number of authors. The general concensus seems to be that retroflexion affects mainly the higher formants. Fant (1968) notes that a retroflex modification of alveolar

sounds lowers F4 so that it comes close to F3; but a retroflex modification of
palatal sounds modifies F3 so that it comes close to F2. Stevens and Blumstein
(1975) remark that "the overall acoustic pattern is characterized by a clustering
of F2, F3 and F4 in a relatively narrow frequency region." The latter point is
confirmed by Dave (1977), who also notes that in both his data and that of
Stevens and Blumstein (1975) there are much greater formant transitions going
from a vowel into a retroflex consonant than going from a retroflex consonant
into a following vowel. This effect, which is also evident in our data, indicates
that the tongue tip first bends back into the retroflex position, and then, during
the closure phase, straightens out somewhat, so that by the time of the release
of the closure it is in a less extreme position.

We have now considered all the articulatory gestures required for stops
made in the dental and alveolar regions, and those made with the tip and the
underside of the tongue in the post-alveolar region (the apical and sub-apical
retroflex sounds). Laminal sounds made with the upper side of the tongue in
the post-alveolar region are usually called palato-alveolar.

Australian languages are particularly well known for the large number of
contrasting coronal articulations they use. Many Australian languages contrast
laminal dental, apical alveolar, apical post-alveolar (retroflex), and laminal
post-alveolar (palato-alveolar) stops. In the Australianist literature, sounds
made with this last articulation are usually referred to as 'palatal', but as we
will show, the articulation is further forward than the sounds traditionally
called palatal. Words illustrating the four coronal places for stops and nasals in
Eastern Arrernte are given in table 2.5.

Palatograms of the words in the first row of table 2.5, made available to us
by Andrew Butcher, are shown in figure 2.12. Above each palatogram is a
sketch of the articulatory position in the sagittal plane inferred by Butcher
from a combination of palatographic and linguographic evidence. Gridlines on
the palatograms and sagittal sections correspond. The laminal dental involves
a contact over the entire denti-alveolar region. The apical alveolar articulation
is made directly on the alveolar ridge. The articulation here designated apical
post-alveolar, conventionally called 'retroflex', involves a sub-apical contact
well behind the alveolar ridge; in fact this particular example is so far back that
the location of the contact could be described as on the palate. The midline
contact for the fourth category, the laminal post-alveolar, is considerably further forward, and extends over the alveolar and post-alveolar regions. The

Table 2.5 Words illustrating the plain coronal stops and nasals of Arrernte

	Laminal DENTAL	Apical ALVEOLAR		Apical post- ALVEOLAR		Laminal POST-ALVEOLAR	
Plosives	aṯəmə 'grind'	atəmə	'burst'	kwəʈə	'smoke'	aṯəməjə	'mother's father'
Nasals	aṉəɟə 'sitting'	anəmə	'sitting'	aɳə	'tree'	aləṉə	'tongue'

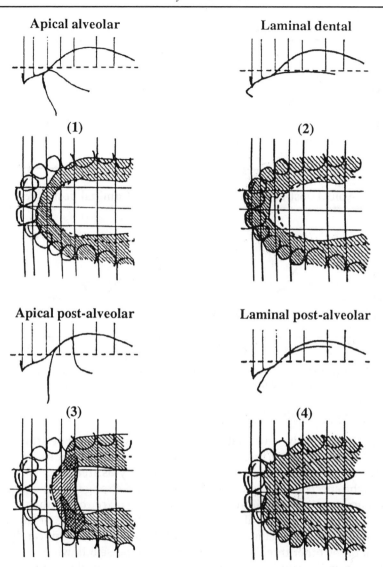

Figure 2.12 Palatograms and inferred articulatory positions for intervocalic coronal stops in Eastern Arrernte (Courtesy of Andrew Butcher). The words illustrated are (1) atəmə 'burst', (2) a̪t̪əmə 'grind', (3) kwəʈə 'smoke', (4) aʈəməjə 'mother's father'.

large amount of contact along the sides seen in the palatogram of this sound indicates that the tongue body is high, as shown in the sagittal section.

Mean spectra of the bursts of ten repetitions of the four coronal stops in Arrernte are shown in figure 2.13. These data are from our own measurements on a different speaker. A natural grouping of these four spectra into two sets

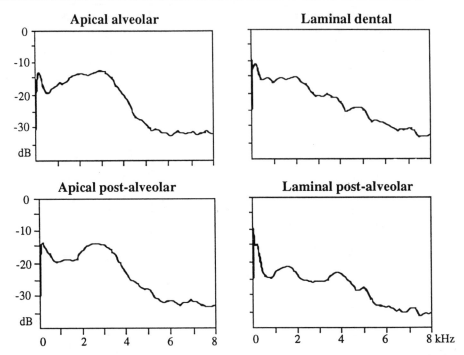

Figure 2.13 Mean spectra of the release bursts of the four Coronal stops of Eastern Arrernte. Each panel of the figure is calculated from ten tokens of words containing the stop in question in varied contexts.

according to the active articulator shape, rather than place of articulation, is apparent in these data. The spectra of the two laminal stops show a general tendency for amplitude to decrease monotonically as frequency increases. In contrast, the spectra of the two apical stops show a strong mid-frequency peak. This is narrower in bandwidth for the post-alveolar (retroflex) than for the alveolar. Further differences also appear when the time-course of the articulations is considered. The closure duration of the alveolar is significantly shorter than that of the other three, whereas the frication noise following the release of closure is significantly longer for the laminal post-alveolar. The voice onset time is shortest for the retroflex. A combination of duration and spectral cues thus serves to separate all four of these segments acoustically.

There is considerable variation in the articulation of laminal post-alveolar stops. This can be exemplified by reference to Ghanaian languages for which we have data from a number of speakers. In the sounds written as 'ky', 'gy' in the local orthography, some speakers made the stop closure with the blade of the tongue, and others with the front of the tongue. In all cases the tip of the tongue was down behind the lower front teeth, and the center of the tongue was raised towards the hard palate. There was usually considerable affrication. These sounds are therefore laminal post-alveolar affricates tɕ, dʑ or palatal stops c, ɟ or palatal affricates cç, dⱼ. In most of the West African languages in which these sounds occur there is a contrast between non-labialized and labialized counterparts (written 'dw' and 'tw' as in the name of the Akan dialect 'Twi'). But the labialized and non-labialized sounds do not necessarily have the same tongue gesture. Thus our main speaker of the Fante dialect of Akan had the same mid-point of articulation in the voiced labialized consonant in ɔ́dʷè 'he calms' as in the voiceless non-labialized consonant in ɔ́tɕè 'he catches'; but the extent of the contact was greater during the labialized consonant. Our main speaker of the Akwapem Twi dialect of Akan had very little affrication in the corresponding sounds, and had the same center point of articulation in ɔcʷà 'he cuts' and càcà 'mattress'; but in this case the contact was greater in the non-labialized consonant. In Nzima we found the articulations to be affricated palatal stops in both ɔcçè 'he divides' and ocçʷɛ 'he pulls'.

Some of the variations noted above may not be differences among dialects of Akan, as we have been implying, but simply differences among individual speakers. The problem is further complicated by the fact that there are large individual anatomical differences in the coronal region, making it hard to make precise remarks about articulation. Keating and Lahiri (1993), who have summarized articulatory descriptions based on x-rays of speech sounds in the palatal and velar regions, note that different sources provide quite different articulatory pictures of what are claimed to be the same sound.

As we have noted in the case of the West African languages the actual area of contact in sounds of this type may vary over a wide range, so that it is often hard to decide whether a given sound should be classified as a palato-alveolar or a palatal. Languages seldom distinguish between sounds simply by one being a palatal and the other a palato-alveolar, preferring instead either to have affricates in the one position and stops in the other, or in some other way to supplement the contrasts in place of articulation with additional variations in the manner of articulation. For example Ngwo has palatal stops and laminal post-alveolar affricates in a stop system which includes d, dz, dʒ, ɟ, g. The middle three terms in this series are illustrated in Figure 2.14, which shows that there are three distinct places of articulation, which we would now classify as being laminal dental (denti-alveolar), laminal post-alveolar (palato-alveolar), and palatal. (Other palatograms show that g is also distinctly different, but the contact area for d is the same as that for dz.)

When places of articulation are grouped according to the active articulator used, palatal articulations, which use the body of the tongue rather than the blade, fall outside the Coronal class of articulations. Rather, they are connected to the velar and uvular places. We use the term Dorsal for this group. A good example of a palatal articulation of this kind from Hungarian is illustrated by the linguogram and x-ray tracing in figure 2.15, which is based on data that Bolla (1980) provides as an illustration of ɟ. As these records indicate, there is no contact at all on the blade of the tongue. The linguogram shows a rather

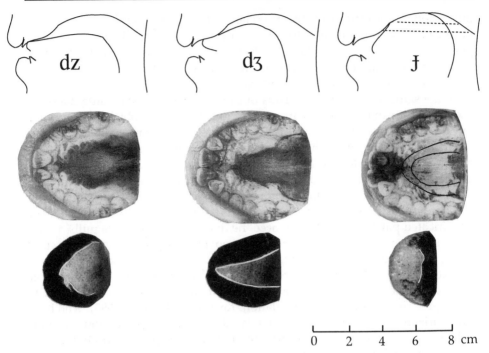

Figure 2.14 Palatograms, linguagrams, and inferred articulatory positions of laminal denti-alveolar, laminal palato-alveolar, and palatal stops in the Ngwo words **èdzé** 'dance', **dʒé** (a species of fruit), **éɟé** 'postpone' (based on Ladefoged, 1968). The contact area on the roof of the mouth is the area from which the marking medium has been wiped away. The dotted lines on the palatal sagittal section correspond to the (solid) contour lines superimposed on the palatogram.

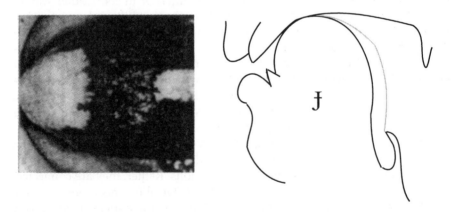

Figure 2.15 Linguogram and x-ray tracing of Hungarian voiced palatal stop (after Bolla 1980). The black tongue outline is the midline; the grey line shows the edge of the tongue.

wide contact area on the tongue front. In the tracing based on cineradiography, the contact on the upper surface is on the sloping area of the palate. Comparing this figure with the laminal post-alveolar from Arrernte illustrated in figure 2.12 above, both the active and passive surfaces involved are distinct in the two cases. Thus, among articulations that have loosely been called 'palatal' there are two quite distinct types involved, as well as a number of intermediate cases, such as some of the Akan types and perhaps the palatals of Czech (see the discussion in Keating and Lahiri 1993).

Lahiri and Blumstein (1984) have argued that phonological theories need not recognize the distinction between palato-alveolars and palatals, because the differences are always, as in Ngwo, supplemented by differences in manner of articulation. However, there are counterexamples. According to both Bubrikh (1949) and Lytkin (1966), Komi has both post-alveolar and palatal affricates (as well as palatal stops). So in this case differences in place of articulation are not supplemented by differences in manner. In addition, some dialects of Malayalam contrast laminal post-alveolar, palatal, and velar nasals. Although the more well-known dialects of this language contrast only six places of articulation, Mohanan and Mohanan (1984) note that there is a dialect that distinguishes seven places on the surface by having both ṇ and ɲ.

It is customary to distinguish three places within the Dorsal region, as indicated in figure 2.2. We have already illustrated the palatal place, and will discuss the contrast between velar and uvular sounds below. The central member of the Dorsal class is the velar place. Virtually every language has velar stops. By definition, these involve a contact on the velum, or soft palate. However, since the active articulator involved is the body of the tongue and this is also involved in the production of front/back contrasts in vowels, the effect of vowel environment on velar stops is different from that seen with other places. Rather than primarily modifying the shape of the tongue behind or in front of the constriction, the location of the constriction itself is affected. In view of this it is possible to distinguish front, central and back velars. Fronted velars may actually make contact on the hard palate. Figure 2.16 illustrates the different location of the constriction in the Ewe words **aká** 'sand' and **eké** 'charcoal'. This figure shows the movement of a point on the tongue dorsum during the whole of these words. Compared with the movement seen in the central vowel environment in **aká**, the entire tongue body is displaced about 8 mm further forward for the execution of **eké**. This figure also shows a forward looping motion of the tongue as the consonant closure is formed and then released. This seems to be characteristic of velars. Similar results to those in figure 2.16 have been shown for English by Houde (1967), Kent and Moll (1972) and others, and for German by Mooshammer (1992).

In most languages the variation between front and back velars is dependent on the vowel, but evidence that this distinction can be contrastive comes from Australian languages that have sounds that are definitely further back than the common laminal post-alveolars, but nevertheless further forward than

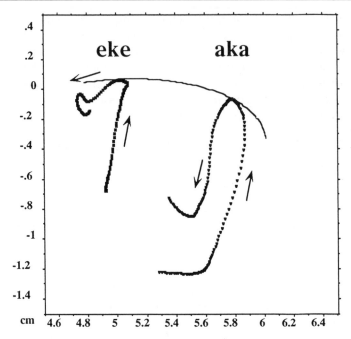

Figure 2.16 Movement trajectories for a point on the tongue rear (mean of 10 repetitions) during the Ewe words **aká** 'sand' and **eké** 'charcoal' (based on Maddieson 1993). Scales are in cm from arbitrary origins. Samples taken approximately 3 ms apart. A curve indicating the estimated location of part of the roof of the mouth has been drawn on the figure.

contrasting sounds that are more nearly in the velar region. These stops are apparently also further back than Hungarian palatals and have been described as palatovelar in Djingili (Chadwick 1975) and Garawa (Furby 1974). Chadwick (personal communication) and Kirton and Charlie (1978) suggest that they may have arisen from a simplification of consonant clusters such as **dg** and **nŋ**, which occur in many of the neighboring languages. In at least one of these languages, Yanyuwa, the palatal stops are in contrast with both laminal post-alveolar and velar stops, so that there are seven places of articulation, as exemplified in table 2.6. (Data from our own field observations with Jean Kirton, supplemented by that in Kirton and Charlie 1978.)

The terms in table 2.6 differ from those used by Kirton and Charlie (1978), notably by the use of laminal dental (denti-alveolar) in place of their apical dental. Their term notes the contact between the tip of the tongue and the upper front teeth, whereas we want to note not only this contact, but also the contact between the blade of the tongue and the front part of the alveolar ridge. There is no doubt that this sound is like that in many other Australian languages, involving what is in our terminology a laminal articulation. We have also used the term palatal (and the regular palatal symbols **ɟ** and **ɲ**) in place of

Table 2.6 Words illustrating contrasts between intervocalic stops and nasals in Yanyuwa

BILABIAL	LAMINAL DENTAL (DENTI-ALVEOLAR)	APICAL ALVEOLAR	APICAL POST-ALVEOLAR (RETROFLEX)	LAMINAL POST-ALVEOLAR (PALATO-ALVEOLAR)	PALATAL	VELAR
wubuwiŋgu 'for a small one (female)'	**wuḍurumaja** 'laugh!'	**wuduru** 'full of food'	**wuḍuḷu** 'in the stomach'	**wuḍuḷu** 'into the grass'	**guɟuḷu** 'sacred'	**wugugu** 'grand-parent'
wumuwaḍala 'in the canoe'	**wuṇuṇu** 'cooked'	**wunala** 'kangaroo'	**waṇura** 'white egret'	**ṇaṇalu** 'tea'	**ḷuwaɲu** 'strip of turtle fat	**waŋulu** 'adolescent boy'

their term palatovelar, although we agree that these sounds are made further back than the sounds that are usually called palatal. In addition the velar stops in Yanyuwa appear to us to be made slightly further back than those in other languages; but they are in no way equivalent to stops classified as uvular in other languages.

A similar distinction to that in Yanyuwa may appear in some languages in the northwest of North America. Both Nuxalk (Nater 1984) and Kwakw'ala (Grubb 1977) are described as distinguishing 'palatovelars' from 'back velars'. Nater compares the 'palatovelar' stop of Nuxalk to the initial sound of the English word 'cube'.

While discussing sounds in the central oral region, we must note another problem in deciding precisely what is meant by a palatal articulation. In several languages our palatograms (and those of others, e.g. Doke 1931b) show that palatal sounds may have two contacts, a tongue tip (or blade) and alveolar ridge contact, and, probably simultaneously, a contact between the tongue front and rear of the hard palate. These contacts are best considered to be due to accidents of the shapes involved, and perhaps in the case of some of the older records made with an artificial palate, due to a less than perfect fit to the subject's mouth. The center of the target articulation can be considered to be in the palatal region, but the target is not reached, and there is only alveolar and postpalatal contact instead.

We have not ourselves heard any language that contrasts palatal stops with both velars and uvulars. Usually, when there are three stops in this area the most forward of the three is a laminal post-alveolar (palato-alveolar) affricate rather than a palatal stop, as is the case in the Quechua words in table 2.7 (note that this is contra Ladefoged 1971 and 1982). There are, however, a few reports in the literature of languages that contrast palatal, velar and uvular stops without making the first of these an affricate. The most convincing case of this kind is that of Jaqaru, a language fairly closely related to Quechua. Hardman (1966)

Table 2.7 Words illustrating contrasts involving palato-alveolar (laminal post-alveolar) affricates, and velar and uvular stops in Quechua

	LAMINAL POST-ALVEOLAR (PALATO-ALVEOLAR)	VELAR	UVULAR
UNASPIRATED	tʃaka 'bridge'	karu 'far'	qaʎu 'tongue'
ASPIRATED	tʃʰaka 'bridge'	kʰujuj 'to whistle'	qʰaʎu 'shawl'
EJECTIVE	tʃʼaka 'hoarse'	kʼujuj 'to twist'	qʼaʎu 'tomato and locoto sauce'

Table 2.8 Words illustrating contrasting velar and uvular plosives and ejectives in K'ekchi

VELAR PLOSIVE	VELAR EJECTIVE	UVULAR PLOSIVE	UVULAR EJECTIVE
ka 'grindstone'	kʼa 'bitter'	qa 'our'	qʼa 'bridge'

describes this language as contrasting not only **c, k, q** but also **ts, tʃ, ts̩**, making it plain that the palatal stop is not an affricate, but actually contrasts with a series of affricates, as well as with velar and uvular stops.

There is very little published data on the difference between velar and uvular stops. Al-Ani (1970) has provided data for a single speaker of Arabic. He notes that the uvular stop lowers F2 for a following **i** or **a**. He also suggests that F2 is slightly raised in **u** following a uvular stop, but this is not so apparent in his spectrogams. What is evident, which he also notes, is that the major energy in the burst of the stop consonant is lower for **q** than for **k**.

We analyzed recordings of 12 speakers of K'ekchi that had been made for us by Ava Berinstein. Each of these speakers said (among many other words) the four words shown in table 2.8 each within a frame sentence. Spectrograms of the four words as pronounced by one speaker are shown in figure 2.17. The bursts that occur on the release of the stop closure are particularly clear for the ejective stops. We found that for all 12 speakers the major energy in the burst was lower for the uvular stops than for the velars. However, F2 was lower at the onset of the vowel for only 9 of the 12 speakers. For these 9 speakers there was also a noticeable lowering of F2 throughout most of the vowel (as may be seen in the case of the speaker in figure 2.17). We found no significant difference with respect to Voice Onset Time for the plosives; the mean VOT for the velars was 52 ms (s.d. 16) and for the uvulars 56 ms (s.d. 21). Nor was there any significant difference in the length of the glottal closure after the release of

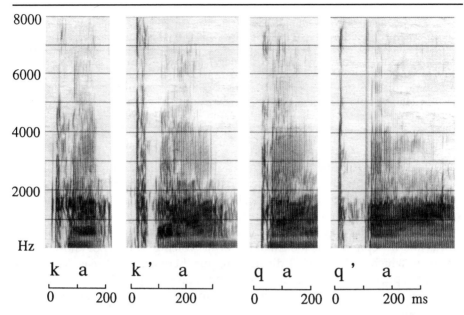

Figure 2.17. Spectrograms of contrasting velar and uvular plosives and ejectives in the K'ekchi words in Table 2.8.

the ejectives, which was 97 ms (s.d. 38) for the velars and 92 ms (s.d. 38) for the uvulars.

Pharyngeal and epiglottal sounds are made in the Radical region, below the uvula. No language makes stops consistently in the upper part of the pharynx, and it is logically impossible to make pharyngeal nasals (as we define nasals), since air cannot come out through the nose while the articulators make a complete closure in the pharyngeal region. Pharyngeal fricatives do occur, but they are not as common as might be supposed from the literature, as most of the sounds to which this label is attached (e.g. in Arabic and Hebrew) are actually what we would call epiglottal fricatives. We will consider this point further in chapter 5, when we discuss fricatives. Meanwhile we will note that there is justification for distinguishing between pharyngeal and epiglottal fricatives, as they contrast in the Burkikhan dialect of Agul. Examples are listed in table 2.9.

As is evident from table 2.9, stops also occur in the epiglottal region. Catford (1983) has suggested that the Chechen 'pharyngeal stop' may be produced by "the epiglottis actively folding back and down to produce an epiglotto-arytenoidal constriction, or closure." We will regard this sound as an epiglottal stop, for which the IPA symbol is ʡ. Epiglottal stops have also been observed by Laufer and Condax (1981), who point out that they occur as allophones of so-called pharyngeal fricatives in Semitic languages. We have also observed epiglottal stops in the Cushitic language Dahalo (Maddieson, Spajić, Sands

Table 2.9 Words illustrating contrasting pharyngeal and epiglottal fricatives, and epiglottal plosives, in the Burkikhan dialect of Agul (data from S. Kodzasov, personal communication)

VOICED PHARYNGEAL FRICATIVE	muʕ	'bridge'	muʕar	'bridges'
VOICELESS PHARYNGEAL FRICATIVE	muħ	'barn'	muħar	'barns'
VOICELESS EPIGLOTTAL FRICATIVE	mɛʜ	'whey'	mɛʜɛr	'wheys'
VOICELESS EPIGLOTTAL STOP	jaʡ	'center'	jaʡar	'centers'
	sɛʡ	'measure'	sɛʡɛr	'measures'

and Ladefoged 1993). Spectrograms of single and medial geminate ʡ are shown in Figure 2.18. Note that this segment usually involves less than a complete closure when it is single and intervocalic, but the geminate involves a full closure. The IPA does not provide distinct symbols for voiced and voiceless epiglottal stops, having accepted the argument that the cavity between the glottis and the epiglottal is too small to permit voicing. We do not know of any language which makes such a distinction, but there are good reasons to consider the epiglottal stop in Dahalo to be phonologically voiced, for example, other single voiced stops also tend to undergo lenition when they are intervocalic.

The larynx, among its many other functions can also serve as a place of articulation for stops. Glottal stops occur in many languages. They frequently pattern with other consonants as in the complex clusters of Tsou (Wright and Ladefoged forthcoming), making it clear that glottal gestures must be taken into consideration when discussing places of articulation that are possible for stop consonants. We will exemplify glottal stops and consider their relationships to other sounds in chapter 3.

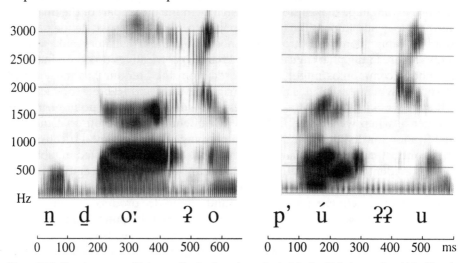

Figure 2.18. Spectrograms of intervocalic single and geminate ʡ in the Dahalo words **ndó:ʡo** 'floor' and **p'úʡʡu** 'pierce'.

Lastly we must mention consonants made with more than one place of articulation, involving two simultaneous articulatory gestures. These gestures will be discussed in chapter 10 which is specifically concerned with multiple gestures.

2.2. Contrasting Places of Articulation

We have now described some (we hope most) of the phonetic events that are significant in characterizing the place of articulation (the moving articulator and the target location for the movement in the articulatory gesture) of consonants. Table 2.10 summarizes the contrasts among the majority of the articulatory gestures mentioned in this chapter that we know to occur within languages. We have heard all these contrasts ourselves, except for those in Jaqaru (Hardman 1966) and Kuvi (Zvelebil 1970), which are accordingly named in italics. In addition, we have heard some, but not all, of the contrasts in Agul; the one italicized contrast is from Magometov (1967). If the 17 gestures specified in table 2.1 are all individually controllable, each of them might be expected to contrast with each of the others. This would make a total of 134 possible contrasts, for which only 80 have an exemplifying language in table 2.10. Our next task is to consider the status of the missing items.

Six of the missing slots on the chart are in the labiodental row and have been marked ssssss. In this row the contrasts all involve fricatives. It would be comparatively easy to name languages in which sibilant fricatives of different kinds contrast with **f** or **v**, and so fill in these gaps. But, as we will see in chapter 7, it is not always clear how the articulations in sibilants should be characterized, so we thought it better to leave these sounds out of consideration at this stage of the discussion. However, we do not consider the gaps marked ssssss to be truly missing contrasts.

Of the remaining 48 contrasts that have not been noted, 11 are associated with missing linguo-labials (marked with ######), and one with a missing epiglottal contrast (marked *****). It seems likely that all 12 of the missing contrasts associated with these gestures are accidental gaps due to the very small number of languages that contain examples of any of these possibilities. If it had so chanced that, for example, V'enen Taut had developed a glottal stop, or one of the languages with an epiglottal fricative had also had a palatal fricative, the gaps would have had a different distribution.

Similar considerations apply to the gaps associated with pharyngeal fricatives, marked ppppp. Agul is the only language we know of that definitely has contrastive pharyngeal fricatives. As we noted, Arabic and other similar languages are regarded as having epiglottal fricatives. Even if the radical fricatives in these languages are considerd to be pharyngeal, they are not in contrast with epiglottal fricatives, as they are in Agul, and therefore would not

Table 2.10 A matrix giving examples of contrasting places of articulation. (Data from our own observations

	(2) LABIODENTAL	(3) LINGUO-LABIAL	(4) INTERDENTAL	(5) APICAL DENTAL	(6) LAMINAL DENTAL	(7) APICAL ALVEOLAR	(8) LAMINAL ALVEOLAR	(9) APICAL POST ALVEOLAR
(1) BILABIAL	ɸ f Ewe	p t̪ V'enen Taut	m n̪ Malayalam	p t̪ Temne	p t̪ Toda	p t Toda	p t̪ Temne	b ḍ Hindi
(2) LABIODENTAL		f z̦ V'enen Taut	f θ English (American)	f θ English (British)	ssssss	ssssss	ssssss	ssssss
(3) LINGUO-LABIAL			#####	#####	#####	t̪ t V'enen Taut	#####	######
(4) INTERDENTAL					------	n̪ n Malayalam	------	------
(5) APICAL DENTAL					ǀ ! !xóõ	------	t̪ t̪ Temne	------
(6) LAMINAL DENTAL						t̪ t Toda	------	t̪ t̪ Hindi
(7) APICAL ALVEOLAR							------	t t̪ Yanyuwa
(8) LAMINAL ALVEOLAR								------
(9) APICAL POST-ALVEOLAR								
(10) LAMINAL POST-ALVEOLAR								
(11) SUB-APICAL PALATAL								
(12) PALATAL								
(13) VELAR								
(14) UVULAR								
(15) PHARYNGEAL								
(16) EPIGLOTTAL								

except in the case of italicized language names, for which the references are in the text.)

(10) LAMINAL POST ALVEOLAR	(11) SUB-APICAL PALATAL	(12) PALATAL	(13) VELAR	(14) UVULAR	(15) PHARYNGEAL	(16) EPIGLOTTAL	(17) GLOTTAL
p t̪ Yanyuwa	p ʈ Toda	p c Yanyuwa	p k English	p q Quechua	pppppp	p ʔ Agul	p ʔ Tsou
sssss	sssss	f ç German	f x Gaelic	f χ German	f ħ Agul	vvvvvv	f h English
#####	#####	#####	t̪ k V'enen Taut	#####	#####	#####	#####
n̪ n̲ Malayalam	ṇ ɳ Malayalam	n̪ ɲ Malayalam	n̪ ŋ Malayalam	------	ppppp	------	θ h English (*American*)
------	------	------	t̪ k Temne	------	ppppp	θ ʜ Arabic	θ h English (*British*)
t̪ t̲ Yanyuwa	ṭ ʈ Malayalam	t̪ c Malayalam	t̪ k Malayalam	t̪ q Urdu	ppppp	t̪ ʔ Dahalo	t̪ ʔ Dahalo
t t̲ Malayalam	t ʈ Malayalam	t c Ngwo	t k English	t q Quechua	ppppp	t ʔ Dahalo	t ʔ Tsou
------	------	------	t̪ k Temne	------	ppppp	------	------
t̪ t̲ Yanyuwa	r r r r	t̪ c Logba	t̪ k Hindi	t̪ q Urdu	ppppp	t̪ ʔ Dahalo	t̪ ʔ Dahalo
	ṇ ɳ Malayalam (*some dialects*)	dʒ ɟ Ngwo	t̪ k Yanyuwa	tʃ q Quechua	ppppp	tʃ ʔ Dahalo	t̪ ʔ Dahalo
		ɳ ɲ Malayalam	ɳ ŋ Malayalam	r r r r	ppppp	r r r r	t̪ ʔ Kuvi
			c k Jaqaru	c q Jaqaru	ppppp	****	c ʔ Margi
			k q Quechua	x ħ Agul		k ʔ Dahalo	k ʔ Dahalo
					ppppp	q ʔ Agul	q ʔ Ubykh
						ħ ʜ Agul	ħ h *Agul*
							ʔ ʔ Agul

serve to diminish the number of gaps in the table. There are 11 missing pharyngeals (marked ppppp), but at least two could be filled in, as Agul has two sibilants which we are not considering at this point. Similarly in the epiglottal column, we could have filled in the contrast in the laminal alveolar row, if we had considered the Arabic sibilant **s** to be laminal alveolar, as it is when pharyngealized (see discussion in chapter 10).

There are three cases, marked r r r r, involving retroflex sounds, with either apical post-alveolar or sub-apical gestures. Ladefoged and Bhaskararao (1983) showed that some languages use one of these possibilities and others the other, making this a reliable phonetic contrast. We conclude that the missing contrasts involving retroflex stops of either kind are also accidental gaps, due to the fact that only a comparatively small number of languages have these sounds. Further evidence to this effect is provided by the case of Kuvi. The best known languages with sub-apical retroflex stops belong to the Dravidian family. Contrastive glottal stops do not occur in most of these languages, so there might well have been a gap in the chart for the ʈ vs ʔ contrast. But phonemic glottal stops do occur in Kuvi (Zvelebil 1970, Reddy, Upadhyaya and Reddy 1974), a little known Central Dravidian language, allowing this gap to be filled in.

It is not clear whether the remaining gaps are accidental or not. These gaps, which are marked with dashed lines, are associated with the laminal interdental, apical dental and laminal alveolar gestures. Contrasts among these gestures are very rare. In our own data, laminal interdental stops do not contrast with either apical dental or laminal alveolars; and these latter two gestures contrast only in Temne and Limba. There is only limited evidence for within language contrasts among apical dental, apical alveolar and laminal dental sounds. We do not know of any within language contrasts of this kind among plosives or nasals, although Albanian seems to contrast apical dental and apical alveolar laterals (Bothorel 1969–70). The clearest evidence for the necessity of distinguishing between apical dental and apical alveolar sounds comes from the specification of the place of articulation in clicks. In many Khoisan languages such as !Xóõ there are two clicks, symbolized |, !. We will discuss these (and other) clicks more extensively in chapter 8, but here we should note that, at the moment just before the release of the anterior closure, some speakers have an apical dental contact for |, and an apical alveolar contact for !. There is thus some evidence for a contrast between apical dental and apical alveolar sounds.

We must now consider the question we asked earlier, namely, are the 17 places of articulation we have been discussing discrete categories such that all consonants fall into one or another of them, or do they simply stand as a set of prototypes against which other articulations can be compared? Putting this another way we can ask whether there is a fixed set of language independent phonetic categories for places of articulation, or whether there is only a phonetic space, definable in terms of general phonetic parameters? The answer is somewhere between these two extremes. The moveable articulators shown in figure 2.1 are the basis for setting up a classificatory system in which there are five active articulator classes: Labial, Coronal, Dorsal, Radical and Laryngeal. Broader classes of this sort predict quite well the types of articulations that can be combined in complex segments, as Halle (1983) pointed out. We also note that, in the normal flow of speech, when segments drawn from two different articulator classes adjoin each other they will often overlap in their production whereas adjoining segments from the same class tend to produce a blended articulation. We have extended Halle's original set of three active articulator classes so as to allow a distinction between Dorsal and Radical articulations, as it is quite possible for epiglottal articulations to occur simultaneously with velar articulations. We have also added Laryngeal because of the similarity between glottal stops and stops made at other places of articulation, and because glottal stops can co-occur with all the other possibilities. We will discuss the various combinations between these classes in chapter 10, but there is another important prediction that the broad classification makes. In a very high proportion of the world's languages, segments with the same manner must be drawn from different active articulator classes. Thus a typical stop inventory is far more likely to contain **p, t, k** rather than **ṭ, t, ṯ** or **c, k, q**.

The five distinct types of articulatory gestures based on independence of articulators can be regarded as establishing a set of major place features. Each of the larger number of individual places we have been discussing can be grouped under one of these major place features, as shown in table 2.11. We have placed the linguo-labial place under the Coronal group, as the active articulator in this case is the tongue blade. As this place cannot be simultaneously combined with another Coronal articulation, the classification is appropriate. However, linguo-labial place cannot be combined with another Labial articulation either. There would thus be good reason to place it under the Labial class as well. This case illustrates the fact that the boundaries between classes are not rigid. Likewise, the numbered elements in figure 2.2 and tables 2.10 and 2.11 are more like the modal possibilities within sets of articulations. They are simply labels for commonly found articulatory possibilities within each continuum. Within the Labial range, articulations are typically bilabial or labiodental. In the case of stops, simple mechanical, physiological, reasons make a bilabial gesture a better target as no population is likely to consist of only people with perfect dentition. But for fricatives, in which the physiology of the vocal tract allows either a bilabial or labiodental gesture, the usual articulation is often somewhere between the two with the lower lip positioned in front of the upper teeth (rather than below them) so that air is directed upwards. In languages such as Ewe, in which there is a phonological contrast between these two possibilities, bilabial and labiodental fricatives may be more clearly distinguished.

Within the Coronal articulations, there is a range of both laminal and apical articulations. Linguo-labial articulations can be made with varying degrees of

Places of Articulation

Table 2.11 The relationship between the major place features and individual places of articulation

LABIAL		1.	Bilabial
		2.	Labiodental
CORONAL	1. Laminal	3.	Linguo-labial
		4.	Interdental
		5.	Laminal dental
		6.	Laminal alveolar
		7.	Laminal post-alveolar (palato-alveolar)
	2. Apical	8.	Apical dental
		9.	Apical alveolar
		10.	Apical post-alveolar
	3. Sub-apical	11.	Sub-apical palatal (retroflex)
DORSAL		12.	Palatal
		13.	Velar
		14.	Uvular
RADICAL		15.	Pharyngeal
		16.	Epiglottal
LARYNGEAL		17.	Glottal

tongue protrusion, involving an articulation between the upper surface of the tip or blade of the tongue and the upper lip. In these sounds there is usually active retraction of the upper lip to meet the protruded tongue, but some native speakers of languages contrasting these sounds use very little upper lip movement. In this case the gestures are very similar to some of the interdental gestures that we have observed in Malayalam, in which the interdental nasal involves not only tongue protrusion between the teeth but also incidental tongue contact with the upper lip. There is thus some shading between linguo-labial and interdental articulations. Similarly the terms interdental, dental, alveolar, and post-alveolar all refer to points within a continuum rather than discrete locations. As has been clearly shown by Dart (1991), when examining the results of a palatographic investigation, it rapidly becomes obvious that the dental region is not clearly separated from the alveolar region; the upper edges of the front teeth are curved, and blend into the alveolar surface. The location of the alveolar ridge itself is also hard to define; many people do not have protruberances of the kind seen in textbook illustrations. In the case of Coronal articulations there are two interacting continua, in that not only is there a range of possibilities for the upper articulator, but also the part of the tongue involved may be anywhere from the underside of the blade of the tongue to somewhere fairly far back on the upper surface of the blade. It might seem as if it should be comparatively simple to determine at least an apical point within this range. But investigators (e.g. Bladon and Nolan 1977) who have tried to categorize x-ray data on articulations have reported that the apical-laminal distinction is often by no means self-evident. In searching the literature in order to find x-ray tracings representing these different possibilities we have found similar difficulties.

Within the Dorsal region, articulations all involve gestures in which the body of the tongue is raised. But some languages (e.g. Yanyuwa) may have an articulation that is between what is usually called palatal and what is usually called velar, while velars in some languages are clearly produced further back (e.g. Kwakw'ala) than in others; again there is a continuous range of possible articulations within this category. Even among Radical sounds there are various phonetic possibilities exemplified among different speakers of Arabic. We have observed some so-called pharyngeal fricatives in which the constriction is in the upper part of the pharynx, although in most cases it is closer to the epiglottis.

Stevens (1972, 1989) has proposed that certain points within an articulatory range are favored in the interest of exploiting the best match between distinctive acoustic structure and the possible articulatory gestures. In this theory, which he calls the quantal theory, these favored places would be the modal places of articulation. A related concept is that some gestures are easier to make than others for physiological reasons. The notions of ease of articulation and auditory distintinctiveness as influences on the phonetic structure of languages were suggested by Martinet (1964) and have been given considerable prominence by Lindblom (1990) and Lindblom and Maddieson (1988). Considerations of this kind probably account for the comparative lack of palatal sounds among the world's languages. The quantal theory and some ease of articulation principle together may account for the preference for use of the modal articulations listed in table 2.11, and for the preference for certain of these articulations over others.

Ladefoged (1993) has suggested considerations that may be relevant in the production of some non-modal places of articulation. His notion is that in situations where there is a contrast between two similar articulations, speakers will tend to use more extreme forms of the gestures involved. In this view, the use of dorsal articulations at non-modal places in Yanyuwa may be a response to the linguistic pressures associated with contrasting seven places of articulation. We will describe in the next chapter another example of what Ladefoged (1990) viewed as the use of more extreme gestures due to the presence of a contrast with a similar articulation in connection with the distinction between bilabial and labiodental fricatives. If this view is correct, the situation for articulatory gestures may be analogous to that described by Keating (1984a) for Voice Onset Time. Keating noted that within the continuum of possible VOTs, languages choose among three modal possibilities: voiced, voiceless unaspirated, and aspirated. She also proposed that there is a polarization principle by which languages keep adjacent pairs within these possibilities further apart. She claims that this polarization principle causes the second possibility, voiceless unaspirated stops, to be realized in two different ways. If a language contrasts a voiced stop series with one other stop series, then that second series will probably be slightly aspirated; whereas, if a language contrasts an aspirated stop series with one other stop series, the second series will probably be slightly voiced. We might also hypothesize that the same polarization principle occurs in the realization of some differences in places of articulation.

3

Stops

In this chapter we will consider the stops that occur in the world's languages. Stops are the only kind of consonants that occur in all languages. They may be distinguished from one another by place of articulation, as we discussed in chapter 2, and by variations in the glottal state, the airstream mechanism, and the articulatory activity during onset and offset. They may also vary in length, and possibly in strength. All these variations, which are summarized in table 3.1, will be discussed in this chapter, except for those associated with nasality and laterality (which are discussed in chapters 4 and 6, respectively). This chapter also contains an account of the different types of glottal stops that have been observed in the world's languages. We should also note that taps or flaps, which might be considered to be very short stops, are discussed in chapter 7. There is a separate discussion of clicks (in chapter 8), which are types of stops in which an oral closure plays a part in forming the airstream mechanism.

3.1 Laryngeal Setting

Most languages have phonemic contrasts between classes of stops which differ in the mode of action of the larynx, or in the timing of laryngeal activity in relation to the oral articulation. Differences of this kind may be considered to be variations in the laryngeal setting. Because some of the terms listed in table 3.1 have been used inconsistently by different authors (ourselves among them), it is important that we describe with some care how we intend them to be understood in this book. We provide brief definitions in table 3.2. These will be expanded and clarified in the more detailed discussions that follow.

Stops

Table 3.1 Variations among stop consonants with example languages

LARYNGEAL SETTING		voiced	most languages
		voiceless	most languages
		creaky voiced	Hausa, Mazatec
		stiff	Jingpho, Korean
		(post-)aspirated	Danish, Thai
		(pre-aspirated)	Icelandic, Gaelic
		breathy voiced	Hindi, Marathi
		slack	Javanese, Wu
AIRSTREAM MECHANISM		pulmonic (plosive)	all languages
		(voiceless) ejective	Haida, Uduk
		voiced implosive	Igbo, Sindhi
		voiceless implosive	Igbo, Lendu
ARTICULATION	during onset	pre-nasalized	Fijian, Fula
	during offset	affricated	German, Navajo
		nasally released	Yeletnye, Arrernte
		laterally released	Navajo, Mixtec
LENGTH		long	LuGanda, Pattani Malay
STRENGTH	articulatory force	fortis	Agul
	respiratory force		Korean

Table 3.2 Short definitions of terms used in this book concerning variations in the laryngeal setting

MODAL VOICE	Regular vibrations of the vocal folds at any frequency within the speaker's normal range.
VOICELESS	No vibration of the vocal folds; arytenoid cartilages usually apart (but they may be together, as for ʔ).
ASPIRATED	Having a greater rate of airflow than occurs in modal voice for a period before or after a stricture; arytenoid cartilages may be further apart than for voiceless sounds.
BREATHY VOICE (= MURMUR)	Vocal folds vibrating but without appreciable contact; arytenoid cartilages further apart than in modal voice; higher rate of airflow than in modal voice.
SLACK VOICE	Vocal folds vibrating but more loosely than in modal voice; slightly higher rate of airflow than in modal voice.
CREAKY VOICE (= LARYNGEALIZED)	Vocal folds vibrating anteriorly, but with the arytenoid cartilages pressed together; considerably lower rate of airflow than in modal voice.
STIFF VOICE	Vocal folds vibrating but more stiffly than in modal voice; slightly lower rate of airflow than in modal voice.

The detailed study of vocal fold activity shows that it is a very complex phenomenon about which much still remains to be learned. Most of the time when someone is speaking, the vocal folds are vibrating in one or other of several possible modes. These modes vary according to how closely together the folds are held. It is useful to divide the continuum of shifting modes of vibration into a number of steps which will be discussed below. Any state in which vibration occurs is a form of voicing. Vibration can be prevented by opening the glottis widely enough so that the folds are too far apart to vibrate, or by pressing the folds together, as for a glottal stop. Vibration will also fail to occur if subglottal pressure is too low (e.g. the speaker is out of breath) or supraglottal pressure is too high (e.g. because air is impounded in the oral cavity by an articulatory closure), even if the vocal folds are in a position that would induce vibration under other conditions. In these latter situations vocal fold vibration may be absent from some part of a spoken utterance without any alteration from a laryngeal setting appropriate for voicing having occurred. As a result there is a conflict between an acoustic and an articulatory definition of voicelessness. For some linguists, voicelessness invariably implies an open glottis, whereas for others it means the absence of vibration, whether produced by active laryngeal control or not. Since stops, by definition, are produced with a supraglottal articulatory closure (unless they are glottal stops), it it important to bear this distinction between active and passive devoicing in mind as we describe the phonatory differences that accompany their production.

We will recognize five steps in the continuum of modes of vibration of the glottis, starting from breathy voice – the most open setting of the vocal folds in which vibration will occur, passing through slack voice, modal voice, and stiff voice, and ending with creaky voice – the most constricted setting in which vibration will occur. An open voiceless state, in which the vocal folds are not vibrating because they are too far apart, may be regarded as the extension of this continuum in one direction; and glottal closure, in which the vocal folds are even more tightly together than in creaky voice, may be regarded as an extension in the other. We have chosen to name only these seven major phonetic categories, which, generally speaking, will be sufficient to enable us to describe the surface phonetic contrasts that we have observed; but we would also emphasize that there is a continuum of glottal opening, and a different number of steps might have been named.

A further term that needs to be noted is aspiration; in at least some cases voiceless aspiration involves a wider opening between the vocal folds than occurs for open voicelessness. This position can be considered as yet a further step along the continuum of vocal fold opening. However, aspiration involves matters of relative timing between laryngeal and oral articulations, and the wider opening can be viewed as an aspect of the control of this timing. We will return to this issue in the detailed discussion of aspiration below.

Note that we are not distinguishing between murmur and breathy voice, nor between creaky voice and laryngealization. These pairs of terms have been used somewhat confusingly, and it seems best not to try to attach specific meanings to each term. We may approximately quantify the differences between the phonation types by comparing the rates of airflow through the glottis, assuming no significant supraglottal constriction is present. For a male speaker with a subglottal pressure of about 8 cm H_2O, during an open voiceless sound there may be a flow rate of as high as 1000 ml/s (milliliters per second); breathy voice will have flow rates nearer 500 ml/s; slack voice might be approximately 250 ml/s; modal voice is usually around 120 ml/s; stiff voice around 100 ml/s; and creaky voice even lower. Obviously, when the glottis is closed there is no airflow.

Modal voice

We will discuss each phonation type in turn, beginning with modal voice. The physiological position for modal voice can be regarded as one in which the arytenoid cartilages are in a neutral position for speech, neither pulled apart nor pushed together (Stevens 1988). The vocal folds would be very slightly apart, if there were no air flow. We assume that the same position as occurs in ordinary voiced vowels and in voiced continuant consonants such as nasals is normally maintained in stops that are phonologically voiced. It is well known that in some languages, English being a familar example, the vocal folds may not vibrate throughout the closure for a voiced stop. Even when surrounded by other voiced sounds, such as vowels, the vocal fold vibration often ceases shortly after the closure is made and only resumes shortly after the closure is released. Most English speakers appear to leave the vocal folds in a constant position throughout such a sequence, but passive devoicing occurs as the supralaryngeal pressure builds up behind the oral closure. There are a number of maneuvers that can be made to assist the continuation of vocal fold vibration during an oral stop closure by expanding the size of the cavity behind the location of the closure; these include a relaxation of the cheeks and other soft tissues around the oropharyngeal cavity so that the pressure will passively expand the volume, as well as active gestures, such as moving the articulatory constriction forwards during the closure, moving the root of the tongue forwards, lowering the jaw, or lowering the larynx (Hudgins and Stetson 1935, Bell-Berti 1975, Ohala and Riordan 1979, Keating 1984c). Some English speakers utilize such gestures to a sufficient degree to produce vocal fold vibration during their voiced stop closures (Westbury 1983), but similar gestures are often executed by speakers producing intervocalic phonologically voiced stops without sustained vocal fold vibration (noted by Kent and Moll 1969). Flege (1982) has shown that the variation in the time at which vocal fold vibration starts near the release of utterance-initial voiced stops in English does not depend on how long before the release the vocal folds are adducted. The target

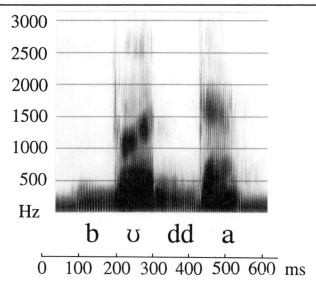

Figure 3.1 Spectrogram of the Ilwana word **budda** 'pelican' showing vocal fold vibration during both utterance-initial **b** and intervocalic geminate **dd**.

for voiced stops in English can therefore be said to include the maintenance of a position of the vocal folds appropriate for voicing, but not to require the employment of other strategies to sustain vocal fold vibration.

In contrast to English and several other Germanic languages, a considerable number of languages have voiced stops which require more energetic efforts to produce sustained vocal fold vibration. Such languages include well-known ones such as French and Thai, as well as more obscure ones such as Ilwana. In languages of this type, the target in the production of voiced stops must be defined as including the presence of actual vocal fold vibration through the articulatory closure period. Figure 3.1 shows the word **budda** 'pelican' from Ilwana. This word contains an initial voiced stop and an intervocalic geminate voiced stop which are both produced with full vocal fold vibration. This occurs despite the fact that these are both positions in which sustaining voicing requires particular additional effort, as has been shown by Westbury and Keating (1986).

In some of the languages in which sustained vocal fold vibration is part of the target for voiced stops, the downward movement of the larynx and the other cavity-enlarging movements used are sufficient to actually rarefy the air in the oropharynx. On the release of the oral closure, some inward airflow occurs. That is, there is a continuum between fully voiced stops and implosives. We will discuss this latter type of stop more fully below; here we merely want to note that implosives and fully voiced stops are not the same thing. For example, they contrast in Ilwana, as a comparison of the intervocalic stops in

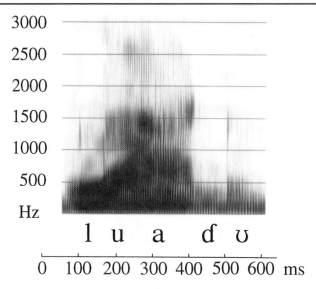

Figure 3.2 Spectrogram of the Ilwana word **luaɗu** 'speed'.

figure 3.1 and figure 3.2 illustrates. We do want to emphasize, however, that voiced stops will have a range of acoustic patterns. But, as far as we know, no language makes use of the difference between stops with the same laryngeal setting for voice but differing solely in the presence or absence of gestures to sustain vocal fold vibration. Thus, although English and Ilwana voiced stops are different, this difference is not one that is available for meaningful contrast within a language.

Of course, a phonologically voiced stop will not necessarily maintain the same laryngeal articulation in all positions. For example, there are phonological processes that result in changing a voiced stop in a particular environment into its voiceless counterpart. Rules of this type are well known in German and Russian. Phonetic studies indicate that such processes often show some gradience. But the acoustically measured variation in the voicing of stops in languages such as English probably does not reflect variation in the actual laryngeal setting.

Voiceless

The great majority of languages of the world have a series of stops in which the vocal folds are not vibrating because they are separated by too wide an aperture. In stops of this kind in intervocalic position, it is quite common to find that the vocal folds continue to vibrate for a short time after the oral closure is formed. This is because the folds have not yet separated widely enough by the time the oral closure is reached. A combination of factors, including the active glottal opening movement and active and passive factors affecting the airflow through the glottis will determine the actual moment at which vibration ceases.

Most languages with only a single series of stops (from the point of view of laryngeal setting) are reported to have voiceless stops (Maddieson 1984a). We suspect, however, that there may be two major types of stops involved. In some languages, such as the Polynesian group (Hawaiian, Maori, Tongan, etc.) actual vocal fold opening seems to be required; in others, such as most of the Australian languages, the stops may be produced with no actual opening required, with vibration ceasing due to lack of efforts to sustain it. Acoustic measurements on intervocalic coronal stops of five speakers of Tiwi (Anderson and Maddieson 1994) showed voicing continuing for approximately 50 ms after the oral closure is formed; this is longer than usually seen, and consistent with models of passive cavity expansion. Comparisons are difficult, but closure durations may be typically longer in Polynesian than in Australian languages, and Australian stops seem to be more prone to having voiced variants.

Creaky voice (laryngealization)

Creaky voice is the term we will use for a mode of vibration of the vocal folds in which the arytenoid cartilages are much closer together than in modal voice. Creaky voice also involves a great deal of tension in the intrinsic laryngeal musculature, so that the vocal folds no longer vibrate as a whole. Sometimes the parts of the vocal folds close to the arytenoid are held too tightly together to be able to vibrate at all; on other occasions the ligamental and arytenoid parts vibrate separately, so that they are out of phase with one another. This can produce pulses with alternating high and low amplitudes. If they are almost exactly 180° out of phase with one another they may produce an apparent increase, often an approximate doubling, of the rate of occurrence of glottal pulses. Languages that exploit some form of creaky voice in the production of stops are areally diverse. They are reported to include Sedang and Pacoh (Austro-Asiatic); Lakkia, Sui and Lungchow (Kam-Tai); Lugbara (Nilo-Saharan); Somali (Cushitic); Hausa, Bura, and Ngizim (Chadic); Karok (Hokan); and Wapishana (Arawakan). We have not heard all these languages ourselves, so we are not sure if each of them uses what we would term creaky voice. The published descriptions suggest that there is some variation: in some of these languages the series of stops in question is described as *pre*glottalized, while in others they are compared to implosives. There does seem to be a range of timing options for the relationship between the laryngeal constriction and the oral articulation. In some languages the laryngeal constriction occurs early in relation to the oral closure, whereas in others it is more delayed. There is also variation in degree of the glottal constriction involved.

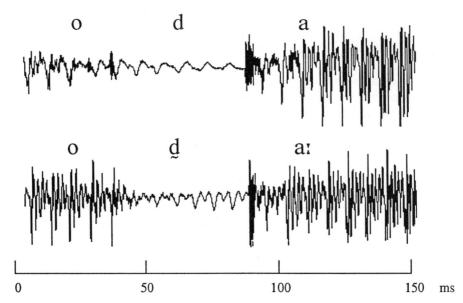

Figure 3.3 Waveforms of consonant closure and portions of adjoining vowels in the Fula utterances
o dari 'he stood' (top) and **o ḍaːnike** 'he slept' (bottom), as spoken by a male speaker from Guinée.

At one end of the range of timing options are the laryngealized stops of
Serer, in which the laryngealization typically consists of a very rapid change
from normal voicing to a glottal stop, followed by a rapid change back to normal voicing again (Ladefoged 1968). The glottal stop usually occurs a few milliseconds before the consonant closure is made. This form of creaky voice is
reminiscent of the glottal catch that occurs in Danish. In this language many
words have a brief superimposed glottal constriction known as a *stød*. This is
clearly not a property of particular stops. It is a suprasegmental or prosodic
feature which applies to words as a whole. A full account of the Danish *stød* is
therefore outside the scope of this book, in which we are limiting the discussion to the segments of the world's languages, but a comprehensive description has been given by Fischer-Jørgensen (1987).

A creaky voice type of vocal fold vibration persisting through the closure of
a stop is often observed in Fula, a language quite closely related to Serer. The
distinction between modally voiced and creaky voiced stops is illustrated by
the waveforms in figure 3.3. Both these closures are of short duration, about 50
ms, and contain approximately five full voicing periods (i.e. they are similar in
fundamental frequency). There are two main differences to note. In the modally voiced stop the amplitude of the vibrations decreases over time, whereas
the creaky voiced stop shows a generally increasing amplitude pattern. The
modal voice pulses are simpler in shape than the creaky voiced pulses, which
show a minor pulse between the major ones. The difference in the amplitude

patterns may indicate more cavity expansion in the creaky voiced stop than in the modally voiced one, perhaps with larynx lowering playing a role. The difference in the pulse shape is an indication that the laryngeal setting itself is different in the two cases.

In other languages the laryngeal constriction occurs closer to the release of the consonant. Voicing may be irregular or absent during the closure, and the first few periods of the vowel following the release also show non-modal voicing. We will illustrate a similar phenomenon when we discuss different types of implosives.

Stops with creaky voice can be considered to be at the intersection of three different continua. One concerns the degree of glottal constriction involved; this varies along a continuum from modified voicing to a simultaneously produced glottal stop. The second concerns the timing of oral and laryngeal movements; this is a continuum from a single segment such as **ḍ** to a sequence such as **dʔ** or **ʔd**. The third concerns oropharyngeal expansion; this is a continuum that links modally voiced stops to implosives. We will return to these perspectives as we discuss co-produced glottal stops and airstream mechanisms below. On the first continuum an intermediate state between modal voice and creaky voice can be labeled stiff voice.

Stiff voice

We are using the term stiff voice to denote a slight degree of laryngealization which may be associated with a contraction of the vocalis muscles. Stevens (1988) has suggested that stiff voice is a distinct state of the glottis. We have found that it is often difficult to say when the degree of muscular activity is sufficiently great for a sound to be considered to have stiff voice as opposed to modal voice. It is also often difficult to distinguish between stiff voice and creaky voice, both of them being simply states of increasing glottal constriction, within a continuum of this kind. There may be quantal states of the glottis as suggested by Stevens, but they are not easy to determine in practice. It is also true that there are no linguistic grounds for postulating a greater number of types of stiff or creaky voice. Languages contrast modal voice with no more than one degree of laryngealized voice. Nevertheless there are occasions when there are clear phonetic differences between stiff voice and the kinds of creaky voice that we have been considering in the previous section. There are a number of languages with stops that have a slight degree of laryngealization. A good example is Thai, which has a three way contrast among stops as shown in table 3.3, in which the pair of segments usually symbolized **b**, **d** are often pronounced with stiff, or even creaky, voice at least during the onset of the closure.

A language using a different variety of stiff voice in consonants is Korean. In word-initial position this language has three different sets of voiceless stops,

Table 3.3 Contrasts involving stops with three different laryngeal settings in Thai. The voiced stops may have a slightly stiff voice, here symbolized with a subscript [ ]

	BILABIAL	DENTAL	AFFRICATED ALVEOLAR	VELAR
VOICED	b̪â: 'crazy'	d̪à: 'to curse'		
VOICELESS UNASPIRATED	pâ: 'aunt'	t̪a: 'eye'	t̪ɕa:n̪ 'dish'	ka: 'crow'
VOICELESS ASPIRATED	pʰâ: 'cloth'	t̪ʰâ: 'landing place'	t̪ɕʰa:m 'bowl'	kʰǎ: 'leg'

Table 3.4 Contrasts between the three sets of stops in Korean. The stiff voiced stops are transcribed p*, t*, k*

	BILABIAL	DENTAL	AFFRICATED POSTALVEOLAR	VELAR
ASPIRATED	pʰul 'grass'	tʰal 'mask'	tʃʰa 'tea'	kʰin 'large'
UNASPIRATED	pul 'fire'	tal 'moon'	tʃa 'ruler'	kin 'measure of weight'
STIFF VOICE	p*ul 'horn'	t*al 'daughter'	tʃ*a 'salty'	k*in 'rope'

as shown in table 3.4. These three series are sometimes described as being aspirated, unaspirated lenis, and unaspirated fortis. The fortis series of stops differs from the other two series in a number of ways, but, as has been shown by Dart (1987) many of the observed differences can be attributed to the laryngeal activity associated with the stiff voice position of the vocal folds. Thus there is a higher F_O at voice onset after fortis stops than after lenis stops. In addition, voice onset after fortis stops is very sharp with relatively undamped harmonics in comparison with the lenis stops (cf. also Han and Weitzman 1970, Hardcastle 1973), which is due in part to the increased tension of the vocal folds.

Kagaya (1974) has also noted that the three Korean stop types have very different laryngeal adjustments. He showed that, for utterance-initial stops, during closure the maximum glottal opening is largest for the aspirated stop, intermediate for the lenis stop, and smallest for the fortis stop, and the timing of the laryngeal gesture relative to articulatory release varies between these stops. For the aspirated stops, release generally occurred near the moment of maximal opening of the glottis. For lenis stops, although the glottis was still quite open at release, there was a more or less continuous decline in glottal area throughout the occlusion. On the other hand, during the fortis occlusion,

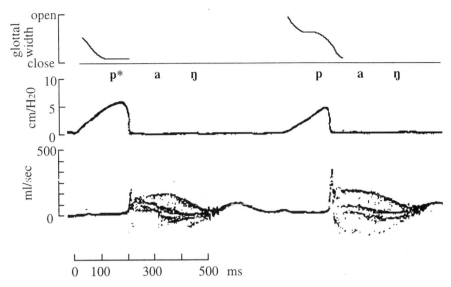

Figure 3.4 Data redrawn from Dart (1987) and Kagaya (1974) illustrating contrasting unaspirated stops in Korean. It should be emphasized that the data combined here were taken from different utterances, and may not truly represent any single speaker.

the vocal folds came together well before release. Fortis closures were also considerably longer than the lenis closures. We should also note that Dart's evidence from modeling indicates tenser vocal tract walls for the fortis stops, and a more rapid increase in respiratory muscle force. Some speakers may exhibit larynx lowering or other supraglottal cavity expansion just before releasing the fortis stop. It is apparent, therefore, that the Korean fortis stops have many distinct phonetic characteristics, a particular laryngeal setting being only one of them. Data from Dart (1987) and Kagaya (1974) illustrating the unaspirated contrasts are given in figure 3.4.

Breathy voice (murmur)

Just as it is convenient to distinguish between stiff voice and creaky voice, so it is also convenient to distinguish between slack voice and breathy voice, using the term breathy voice to describe sounds that have a higher flow rate and a looser form of vibration of the vocal folds than occurs in the sounds with slack voice, which will be described in the next section.

Breathy voice is most readily audible as a distinguishing characteristic of stops only during the release of a closure. The most well-known stops that have breathy voice during their release are those that occur in Indo-Aryan languages such as Hindi and Marathi. However, stops of this kind also occur in

Table 3.5 Words illustrating contrasts between stops with breathy voice and three other laryngeal settings in Hindi

	BILABIAL	DENTAL	RETROFLEX	PALATAL	VELAR
VOICELESS UNASPIRATED	**pal** 'take care of'	**t̪al** 'beat'	**ʈal** 'postpone'	**tʃɛl** 'walk'	**kan** 'ear'
VOICELESS ASPIRATED	**pʰal** 'knife blade'	**t̪ʰal** 'plate'	**ʈʰal** 'wood shop'	**tʃʰɛl** 'deceit'	**kʰan** 'mine'
VOICED	**bal** 'hair'	**d̪al** 'lentil'	**ɖal** 'branch'	**dʒɛl** 'water'	**gan** 'song'
VOICED ASPIRATED	**bɦal** 'forehead'	**d̪ɦar** 'knife'	**ɖɦal** 'shield'	**dʒɦɛl** 'glimmer'	**gɦan** 'bundle'

many other language families in the same general area, including Dravidian languages such as Telugu, Tibeto-Burman languages such as Newari, and Austro-Asiatic languages such as Mundari. Breathy voiced stops also occur in a number of African languages, some of which will be discussed below.

Words illustrating the stop contrasts in Hindi are given in table 3.5. Dixit (1989) has shown that the breathy voiced plosives in Hindi have less activity of the cricothyroid muscle, reflecting a relative slackness of the vocal folds; a moderately open glottis (about 50 percent of that used during aspiration); a high rate of oral airflow; a rapid and brief drop in subglottal air pressure (a feature shared with voiceless aspiration); random distribution of noise in the regions of the upper formants of the following vowel, but with voice also present, and comparatively greater concentration of acoustic energy at the fundamental frequency than at the second harmonic. Very similar results are reported by Kagaya and Hirose (1975) and Benguerel and Bhatia (1980) for Hindi and by Yadav (1984) for Maithili. Their most important findings concern the timing of the glottal opening. As illustrated in figure 3.5, both voiceless and breathy voiced stops are characterized by an abduction of the vocal folds. In the case of the voiceless stops this starts about 80 ms before the release, making it approximately simultaneous with the formation of the closure. For the breathy voiced stop the glottis begins opening at about the mid-point of the duration of the oral closure and reaches its maximum at the time of the release of the stop closure.

A consequence of this timing is that breathy voiced stops in Hindi and many other Indic languages are acoustically distinguished from plain voiced stops by what happens after the release rather than by audible differences during the closure. A breathy voiced stop followed by a vowel shows an acoustically noisy but periodic interval as the glottal gesture overlaps the articulation of the vowel. The spectrograms in figure 3.6 illustrate this contrast in the Hindi words **bal** 'hair' and **bɦal** 'forehead'. During the voiced stop on the left of the

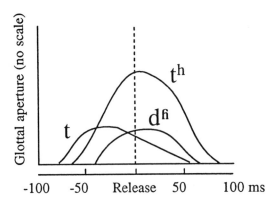

Figure 3.5 Glottal aperture in Hindi stops, based on fiberoptic data in Kagaya and Hirose (1975).

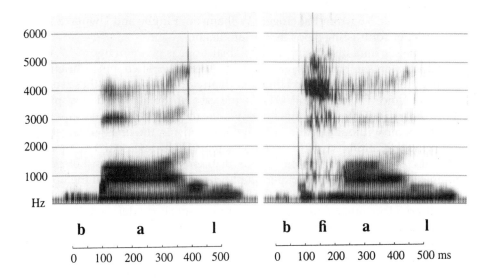

Figure 3.6 Spectrograms illustrating modal and breathy voiced stops in the Hindi words **bal** 'hair' and **bʰal** 'forehead'.

figure there are vocal fold vibrations throughout the stop closure which continue on into the vowel. During the breathy voiced stop on the right of the figure there are also vocal fold vibrations in the first part of the closure, but they become lower in amplitude towards the end as the vocal folds come

Table 3.6 Words illustrating contrasting bilabial and alveolar stops in Owerri Igbo (from Ladefoged, Williamson, Elugbe and Uwulaka 1976)

VOICELESS UNASPIRATED	í̩ pa	'to carry'		
VOICELESS IMPLOSIVE	í̩ ɓa	'to gather'	í̩ ɗa	'to chew'
VOICELESS ASPIRATED	í̩ pʰà	'to squeeze'	í̩ tʰà	'to blame'
VOICED	í̩ ba	'to get rich'	í̩ da	'to cut'
BREATHY VOICED	í̩ bʱa	'to peel'	í̩ dʱa	'to fall'
VOICED IMPLOSIVE	í̩ ɓa	'to dance'		

further apart. For a period of about 100 ms after the closure there are breathy voiced vocal fold vibrations. It has also been shown that vowels before breathy voiced stops tend to be a little longer than before modally voiced stops (Maddieson and Gandour 1977), which may assist in maintaining the perceptual distinction between them.

The breathy voiced stops that occur in languages outside the Indian subcontinent are somewhat different. For example, Owerri Igbo has a four-way stop contrast that is nominally similar to that in Hindi. (Owerri Igbo also has other contrasts involving the glottalic airstream mechanism which we will discuss later.) Table 3.6 (from Ladefoged, Williamson, Elugbe and Uwulaka 1976) shows a set of contrasting stops in this language.

Aerodynamic data illustrating Igbo bilabial stops is given in figure 3.7. Here we will focus on the breathy voice stop, but we will first comment briefly on the other pulmonic stops. As in Hindi and many other languages these sounds contrast in Voice Onset Time (VOT). In the case of the aspirated stop **pʰ**, the airflow record indicates that immediately after the release of the closure there is a burst of air without vibration of the vocal folds; in the unaspirated stop **p** the voicing vibrations start the instant the closure is released. The pressure record also shows that at the onset of both these voiceless stops the speaker continues the voicing for a short period of time after the closure of the lips. As noted earlier, this sort of delay in the voice offset time in voiceless stops has been observed in other languages, including English (Ladefoged 1967). The pressure and larynx microphone records also show that voicing occurs throughout the closure for the voiced stop **b**. The implosives in figure 3.7 will be discussed later in this chapter.

In the case of **bʱ** the pressure record shows that the vocal folds are vibrating throughout the closure, and the airflow record shows a slightly higher than normal flow rate immediately after the release of the closure. In all our records of this language, the difference in flow rate between the voiced and the breathy voiced stops is not very great, but it is sufficient to indicate that during the release of the breathy voiced stops the vocal folds must be slightly further apart (in terms of the distance between the arytenoid cartilages) than they are during normal voiced sounds.

The change from breathy voice to regular voicing often occurs after only a

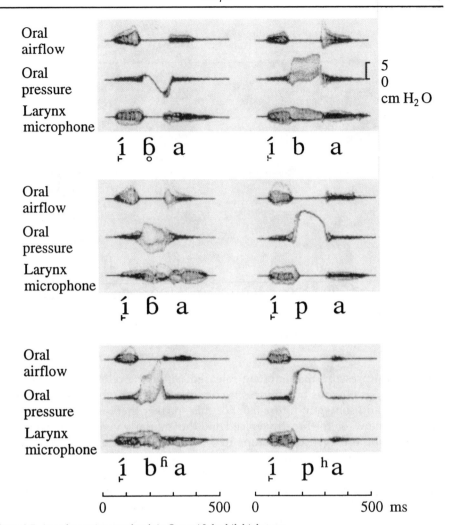

Figure 3.7 Aerodynamic records of six Owerri Igbo bilabial stops.

few vibrations of the vocal folds. It is very difficult to say exactly when the change occurs from data such as the aerodynamic records in figure 3.7. Spectrograms such as those in figure 3.8 are a little more helpful. This figure shows the pronunciation of the voiced velar stop in í **ga** 'to go' on the left, and the breathy voiced velar stop in í **gꟷa** 'to thread' on the right. The voicing throughout the closure is evident for both stops. Spectral components corresponding to periodic vibrations of the vocal folds can be seen in the lower frequencies (near the base line) throughout this interval. As in Hindi, their amplitude decreases during the closure for the breathy voiced stop. The waveform of the breathy voiced stop has greater amplitude in the burst, because of the

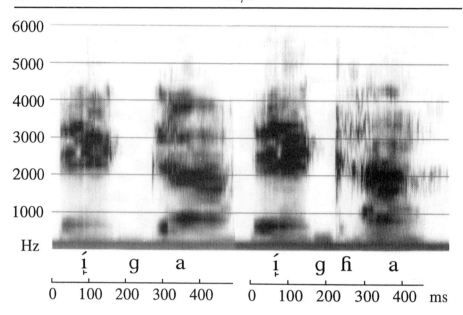

Figure 3.8 Spectrograms illustrating voiced and breathy voiced velar stops as produced by a female speaker of the Owerri dialect of Igbo.

greater oral pressure that is being released. After the release, the interval in which there is obvious breathiness is somewhat shorter (about 30 ms) than in the Hindi stop shown in figure 3.6. For this speaker there is only a very small difference between the breathy voiced and the regularly voiced stop. Generally speaking, the breathy voiced stops in Owerri Igbo appear to have a shorter breathy voiced period, and to have stronger voicing than the corresponding sounds in Hindi and other Indo-Aryan languages. We have no data on the degree of opening of the glottis, but we would expect the glottal area to be less in Owerri Igbo breathy voiced stops than in Hindi breathy voiced stops.

In these Igbo sounds it seems that even during the stop closure the vocal folds are vibrating more loosely than in the regularly voiced sounds. This fact can be deduced from the oral pressure records which show consistent differences between breathy voiced **bʰ** and regularly voiced **b**. In most cases (see Ladefoged et al. 1976), the oral pressure reaches a higher value towards the end of the closure in **bʰ** than in **b**. We must conclude that during the closure (as well as during the release) the vocal folds are vibrating more loosely in the breathy voiced stops, so as to allow more air to flow through the glottis into the mouth in a shorter period of time. The closure duration of the breathy voiced stops is also shorter than that of the voiced stops, which may be an indirect result of the differences in oral pressure.

Yet another kind of sound that might be thought to involve breathy voice occurs in Zhuǀʼhõasi which has contrasts as shown in table 3.7. The initial stops

Table 3.7 Words illustrating some contrasting stops in Zhu|'hõasi

	BILABIAL	ALVEOLAR	VELAR
VOICED	**ba** 'father'	**da** 'skin (blanket)'	**gaba** 'walk pigeon-toed'
VOICELESS UNASPIRATED	**pabu** 'puff adder'	**ta** 'wild orange'	**kabi** 'inspect a trap'
ASPIRATED	**pʰepʰe** 'glutton'	**tʰa** 'bee sting'	**kʰaba** 'to descend'
VOICED-PLUS- ASPIRATED	**bpʰe** 'to spit out'	**dtʰa** 'blanket'	**gkʰaro** 'bed'

in the last row are transcribed **bh, dh, gh** by Snyman (1975) and thus appear to be similar to those in Hindi. In fact, they are something more unusual. As Snyman himself has shown, Zhu|'hõasi has a considerable number of consonant clusters that have the first element voiced and the second voiceless. The initial consonant sequences in the last row of this table are examples of such combinations. We will return to the topic of obstruent clusters with mixed voicing in Zhu|'hõasi in our discussion of ejectives.

Slack voice

As with stiff voice, we should note that slack voice designates a region within the continuum of glottal aperture. In this section we will consider stops with slack voice. These stops have a slightly increased glottal aperture beyond that which occurs in modal voice, and a moderate increase in flow. When there is a considerable glottal aperture and a high rate of flow of air while the vocal folds are vibrating, we will say that the sound is pronounced with breathy voice, as discussed above.

One type of slack voice occurs in Javanese, which has contrasting pairs of what we will call slack and stiff voiced stops at the bilabial, dental, retroflex and velar places of articulation, as shown in table 3.8. Fagan (1988) has noted that these stops have been called light versus heavy, tense versus lax, voiceless unaspirated versus voiceless aspirated, and aspirated versus unaspirated. In initial position neither the stiff nor the slack voice stops have vocal fold vibration during the closure. Hayward (personal communication) investigated these sounds using fiberoptic techniques. She found that the arytenoids remained close together during the closure for the stiff voice stops, much as they do in Korean. The stiff and slack voiced stops differ in that the opening between the vocal folds is noticeably greater for slack voice. The

Table 3.8 Contrasts involving stops with stiff and slack voice in Javanese. In this table slack voiced stops are represented by the regular voiced symbols with an added subscript [̥]

STIFF VOICE	**paku**	**tamu**	**tsariʔ**	**ʈiʈiʔ**	**kali**
	'nail'	'guest'	'piece (of paper)'	'little'	'river'
SLACK VOICE	**b̥aku**	**d̥amu**	**d̥ʒarit**	**ɖ̥isiʔ**	**ɡ̥ali**
	'standard'	'blow'	(type of women's clothing)	'first'	'to dig'

Table 3.9 Contrasts involving stops released with slack voice in the Shanghai dialect of Wu Chinese. In this table slack voiced stops are represented by the regular voiced symbols with an added subscript [̥]

ASPIRATED	**pʰóʔ**	'to strike'	**tʰí**	'heaven'	**kʰʌ́ʔ**	'competence'
UNASPIRATED	**pʌ́ʔ**	'hundred'	**tíʔ**	(particle)	**kóʔ**	'corner'
SLACK VOICE	**b̥ʌ̌ʔ**	'white'	**d̥ǐ**	'earth'	**ɡ̥ə̌ʔ**	(possessive marker)

acoustic difference between these two sounds is manifested at the release. After detailed acoustic analysis, Fagan concludes that the systematic acoustic difference between the pairs of stops lies in the frequency of the first formant, and in the phonation type at the onset of the following vowel (Fagan 1988: 194–5). Our own investigations have also shown that the stops with slack voice exhibit a lowered F1, indicating that larynx lowering occurs. In vowels following these stops, there is a lower F0, and a reduction of energy in the upper frequency range of the spectrum, a notable acoustic property of vowels with slack or breathy voice (see chapter 9). Hayward (personal communication) also noted a slightly longer VOT for the slack voiced stops, reflecting the greater opening between the vocal folds.

Slack voice also occurs in the so-called lenis consonants in Wu dialects of Chinese, such as Shanghai, where the plosives occur at the bilabial, dental and velar places of articulation. As shown in table 3.9, there are three series of stops in this language. One series is plainly aspirated. The difference between the other two series has been the subject of some debate. Some accounts view one series as voiceless unaspirated and the other as voiced during closure and release, but with the release accompanied by weak voiced aspiration; other accounts regard the latter series as voiceless during closure with some voiced breathiness following. We follow Cao and Maddieson (1992), who indicate that the latter account is more appropriate, in that the issue is determined not so much by whether the stops are voiced or voiceless during closure, but rather by a phonation difference at the release of the stops. The so-called voiced stops have slack voice offsets, a quality detectable in the onset of the following vowel, whereas the other voiceless stops are not at all breathy in the comparable portion. Figure 3.9 shows the contrast for the bilabial stops. The spectrograms in the lower part of the figure indicate that neither of these stops

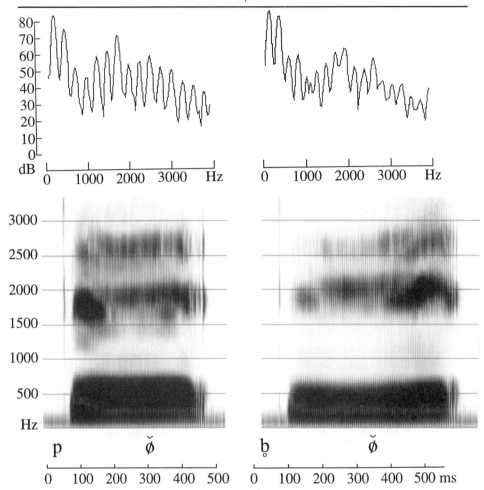

Figure 3.9 Spectrograms and power spectra illustrating the difference between Wu Chinese unaspirated stops. The words are **pø** 'half' and **b̥ø** 'bowl' spoken by a female speaker from Shanghai.

is voiced; in both words vocal fold vibration starts 20–30 ms after the stop release. The power spectra (0–4 kHz) of the first few periods (50 ms) of the vowel in the upper part of the figure show that the difference in amplitude between the second formant and the fundamental is greater for the lenis stop, indicating that it has a more breathy voice. Breathy voice is typically marked by a relative decrease in the amplitude of the harmonics in the middle and upper parts of the spectrum. While the phonological contrast may be thought of as inherent in the consonants, the clearest manifestation is in the following vowel. There is also a greater random noise component in the breathy spectrum.

As is apparent from the preceding discussion, there are many differences in the forms of slack voice that we have been considering. In Javanese there is a form of slack voicing in stops that is phonologically contrastive with some form of stiff voice. In Wu Chinese there is a three-way contrast between stops with slack voice, and both voiceless aspirated and unaspirated stops. The distinguishing aspect of the vocal vibration can be called slack voice in each case, in that in all these segments the vocal folds are vibrating more loosely, but the arytenoid cartilages are not drawn apart as they are in breathy voice.

Aspiration

Voiceless aspirated stops are too well known to need much discussion here; and, indeed, they have already been illustrated in the tables of contrasting stops in Thai, Korean, Hindi and Igbo, and in figures 3.5 and 3.7. In Hindi, as Dixit and others have shown, voiceless aspirated stops are produced with a glottal opening gesture that begins at about the moment that the oral closure is made and reaches its maximum at about the moment that the oral closure is released. This is in contrast to the unaspirated voiceless stops. In these the glottal opening begins at about the same time, but the maximum is reached at about the mid-point of the oral closure duration and the vocal folds return to a voicing position again at about the moment of release. In the aspirated case the maximum width of the glottal opening is also much greater than in the unaspirated voiceless stops. There are two ways of interpreting this greater width; it can be seen as the essential aspect of the production of voiceless aspiration, that is, aspiration is an extra-wide opening of the vocal folds (Kim 1965), or it can be seen as a by-product of the mechanism by which a delay between the offset of the oral and glottal gestures is achieved, that is, aspiration is essentially a matter of the timing between speech movements controlling laryngeal setting and oral articulation (Goldstein and Browman 1986). We will discuss this issue further below. Voiceless aspirated stops are often characterized as having a long VOT, the length of time after the release of a stop closure before the start of modal voicing for the following sound. The extensive work of Lisker and Abramson (1964, 1967) has shown that VOT is a highly effective measure for differentiating stops with different laryngeal actions in a wide variety of languages.

As all the examples above are of stops in initial position, it is worth noting that contrasts between voiced, voiceless unaspirated and aspirated stops also occur in final position. Examples in Eastern Armenian are given in table 3.10. The differences between the minimal pairs in the first two rows of the table is principally a matter of voicing. Waveforms of words with final velar stops of these three types are shown in figure 3.10. The **g** is voiced throughout the closure and vocal fold vibrations continue after the closure is released, whereas **k** has voicing for only a few periods immediately after the beginning of the closure. As is often the case, the voiceless closure is longer. In this particular

Table 3.10 Words illustrating contrasts between voiced, voiceless unaspirated and aspirated stops in final position in Eastern Armenian

	BILABIAL	AFFRICATED ALVEOLAR	AFFRICATED POST-ALVEOLAR	VELAR
VOICED	ab (month name)	bardz 'pillow'	ʃurdʒ 'environs'	bag 'portion'
VOICELESS UNASPIRATED	kap 'bond'	barts 'difficult'	surtʃ 'coffee'	bak 'porch'
			votʃ 'phrase'	tak 'under'
VOICELESS ASPIRATED	kapʰ 'club'	bartsʰ 'high'	votʃʰ 'no'	takʰ 'hot'

pair, there is virtually no difference between the lengths of the vowels before voiced and voiceless stops, although, taking our data as a whole, vowels before voiceless stops are usually a few milliseconds shorter than those before voiced stops.

For this speaker, the difference between the voiceless aspirated and unaspirated stops (the lower pair of words in figure 3.10) is in the strength of the release. The voiceless unaspirated stops are weakly released or (in other data from this speaker) not released at all, whereas the aspirated stop has a shorter closure and a noticeable burst followed by noisy airflow that is sustained for some considerable time. Several of our speakers of Eastern Armenian probably have a glottal closure accompanying final unaspirated stops, and in some cases these sounds are weakly ejective. It should be noted that this three way contrast exists only in Eastern and not in Western Armenian.

It has been suggested that "heightened subglottal pressure is a necessary but not sufficient condition for aspiration" (Chomsky and Halle 1968: 326). This suggestion was somewhat over-energetically decried when it first appeared (e.g. by Ladefoged 1971). At that time there was evidence that heightened subglottal pressure occurred on stressed syllables, but no evidence that it ever characterized a single segment. But Chomsky and Halle were right – for some instances of aspiration. In the case of Owerri Igbo discussed above, the voiceless aspirated stops had a heightened subglottal pressure, despite being shorter than their unaspirated counterparts. One might have expected that the stops with the longer closures (the voiceless unaspirated stops) might have had a higher peak pressure; if the subglottal pressure is produced by a constant decrease in lung cavity size, then the longer the closure the more the pressure would increase. Nevertheless, at least for some speakers, the pressure is significantly higher during the aspirated sounds, and there must be greater respiratory activity to account for it. There is therefore some support for the

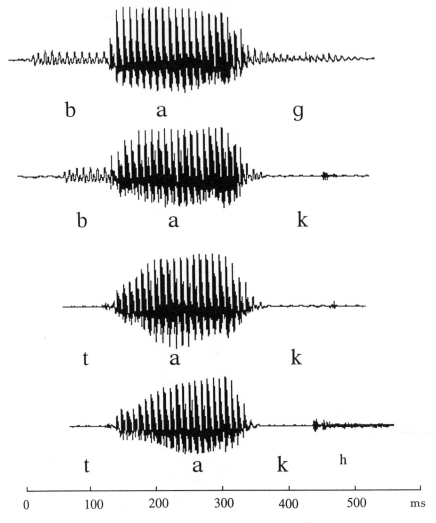

Figure 3.10 Waveforms illustrating contrasts among final velar stops in Eastern Armenian. The words are those in the final column of table 3.10.

suggestion that aspirated sounds are in some languages consistently produced with a heightened subglottal pressure. The pattern of increased oral pressure during the breathy voiced stops of Owerri Igbo might also indicate that these have the same characteristics. However this phonetic attribute is probably never the major distinguishing property in a phonological contrast. It is a secondary mechanism that can be called on to enhance (Stevens and Keyser 1989) the high level of transglottal airflow which a wide open glottal aperture already ensures.

Table 3.11 Aspiration and Burmese causative formation

SIMPLEX FORMS		CAUSATIVE FORMS	
páuʔ	'be pierced'	**pʰáuʔ**	'pierce'
céʔ	'be cooked'	**cʰéʔ**	'cook'
kwà	'peel off'	**kʰwà**	'separate'
mjô	'be floating'	**m̥jô**	'set afloat'
nôu	'be awake'	**n̥ôu**	'waken'
láʔ	'be bare'	**l̥áʔ**	'uncover'

We are now ready to consider further the possible alternative meanings of the term aspiration. We have suggested above that aspiration is one end of a continuum of degrees of opening of the vocal folds during speech. This is similar to the proposal by Kim (1965). Another definition equates aspiration with a period of voicelessness after the release of an articulation, and before the vocal folds start vibrating. The first definition says nothing about the timing; the second nothing about any specific glottal aperture. There are some rather interesting consequences of selecting one or the other of these definitions. The first provides for the occurrence of aspirated segments with no delay of voice onset; all that is required is that the glottal aperture should be wide. Burmese has many pairs of verbs and adjectives that show a morphological alternation between simplex forms with voiceless unaspirated stops and causative forms with voiceless aspirated stops. The parallel alternation in nasals and laterals is usually described as being between voiced and voiceless counterparts. Examples of these alternations are given in table 3.11.

Patterns such as these have suggested to a number of phonologists that aspirated stops and voiceless sonorants share a common feature of aspiration (or [spread glottis]) (Cho 1990, Steriade 1993a). The Burmese voiceless nasals and laterals do not have a voiceless period after their release (see the descriptions in chapters 4 and 6) but what they could have in common with aspirated plosives and affricates is a wider glottal opening. Unfortunately we do not know if this is true as there is no data on glottal aperture in this language. However, we do have some data on airflow in the voiceless nasals and know that it may be well over 500 ml/s (Bhaskararao and Ladefoged 1991). This is very high for airflow through the nose and would be compatible with a relatively wide glottal aperture.

On the other hand, if the definition emphasizes timing, rather than a specific glottal aperture then pairs of sounds such as **pʰ** and **bʱ** in Hindi, Igbo and many other languages can be grouped together as aspirated. At least in Hindi (Maddieson and Gandour 1977, Ohala 1983) and certain other Indic languages such sounds have shared phonological behavior. However, sounds such as **bʱ** do not have a period of voicelessness after the release of the closure, so aspiration cannot be defined in terms of such a period. Instead, if we want to maintain the possibility of quantifying aspiration in terms of VOT, we must redefine it as follows: aspiration is a period after the release of a stricture and before the start of regular voicing (or the start of another segment, or the completion of an utterance) in which the vocal folds are markedly further apart than they are in modally voiced sounds. This definition would allow for voiceless aspirated and breathy voiced aspirated sounds to be grouped together. Note that this does not say that all breathy voiced sounds are characterized as aspirated; only those with this particular articulatory timing pattern.

Pre-aspiration

Before we conclude our discussion of aspiration we should examine pre-aspiration. In pre-aspirated stops there is a period of voicelessness at the end of the vowel, nasal, or liquid preceding the onset of the stop closure. The best-known examples of these sounds occur in Scottish Gaelic, and in Icelandic and Faroese. In Gaelic the pre-aspirated stops occur only in medial and final position, where they are the counterparts of the aspirated stops which occur in initial position. In Icelandic and Faroese, where pre-aspirated stops also occur only in medial and final position, they are realizations of long (geminate) voiceless aspirated stops. All these languages have a contrast between voiceless unaspirated and voiceless aspirated stops in initial position. The unaspirated stops are unchanged in medial position, yielding a surface contrast between pre-aspirated and unaspirated stops. The pattern in Lule Sami (Engstrand 1987) is somewhat similar to that in Icelandic, except that there is no contrast between two series of stops in initial position.

Examples of surface phonetic contrasts involving pre-aspiration in Icelandic are given in table 3.12. Following Thráinsson (1978), we have used **h** rather than ʰ to indicate pre-aspiration because pre-aspiration is longer than the aspiration after a stop release. We have also given the underlying forms according to Thráinsson's analysis. Figure 3.11 shows the patterns of changes over time in the volume of airflow and the width of the glottis which differentiate intervocalic aspirated, unaspirated and pre-aspirated voiceless stops in Icelandic (adapted from ní Chasaide 1985). Thráinsson, surveying the aerodynamic data in Pétursson (1976) and Garnes (1974), notes that "pre-aspiration typically has a normal segment length in Icelandic, whereas postaspiration is much shorter. . . . This suggests that pre-aspiration is not simply the inverse of postaspiration, as its name and some phonetic descriptions might lead us to believe." In all instrumental studies of Icelandic, the duration of the pre-aspiration and stop closure together in **hp, ht**, etc. is about equal to the duration of the stop closure itself in unaspirated geminate stops (Thráinsson's phonemic /bb, dd/, etc.). The glottal opening gesture for a pre-aspirated voiceless stop is wider than for the unaspirated voiceless geminate, but does not take longer. In the pre-aspirated stop, the oral closure occurs when the glottal aperture is near

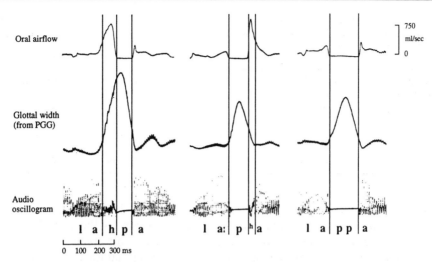

l a h p a   l aː p a   l a pp a

0 100 200 300 ms

Figure 3.11 Intra-oral air pressure and glottal aperture records illustrating pre-aspirated, aspirated, and unaspirated bilabial voiceless stops in Icelandic (from data provided by ní Chasaide). The pre-aspirated and unaspirated stops are phonologically geminate and have a shorter preceding vowel.

Table 3.12 Contrasts illustrating pre-aspirated and unaspirated long voiceless stops in medial and final position in Icelandic. As vowel length plays a part in distinguishing these stops, contrasts between long and short vowels are also illustrated. (Phonological interpretation in accordance with Thráinsson, 1978)

BILABIAL	ALVEOLAR	VELAR
kʰɔhpar /koppar/ 'small pot' [n.pl.]	maɪhtɪr /mættir/ 'may' [2s pt.sub.]	sahka /sakka/ 'sinkstone'
kʰɔppar /kobbar/ 'young seal' [n.pl.]	maɪttɪr /mæddir/ 'distressed' [m.n.pl.]	sakka /sagga/ 'dampness' [ob.sg.]
kʰɔːpar ˋ/kopar/ 'copper'	maɪːtɪr /mætir/ 'meet' [2s pr.sub.]	saːka /saka/ 'to blame'
	maɪhtnɪr /mætnir/ 'meet' [3p pr.ind.]	sahkna /sakna/ 'to regret'
kʰahp ˈ /kapp/ 'zeal'	viht /vítt/ 'wide'	tøhk /dökk/ 'dark' [f.n.sg.]
kapp /gabb/ 'hoax'	vitt /vídd/ 'breadth'	tøkk /dögg/ 'dew'
kaːp /gap/ 'opening'	piːt /bít/ 'bite' [1s pr.]	tʰøːk /tök/ 'grasps' [n.pl.]

Table 3.13 Surface phonetic contrasts between pre-aspirated (upper rows) and voiceless (lower rows) stops in Scottish Gaelic (Lewis dialect), from Ailbhe ní Chasaide (1985 and personal communication)

BILABIAL	DENTAL	POSTALVEOLAR	PALATAL	VELAR
[ʎɛhpəɣ]	[pɔht̪ᵛəlᵛ]	[aɪht̪ʲəvᵛ]	[ɛhcə]	[kr̥ɔ̃hk]
leabthadh	*botal*	*aiteamh*	*aice*	*cnoc*
'bed' [gen.]	'bottle'	'swollen'	'at her'	'hill'
[ʎɛpi]	[pɔt̪ᵛəx]	[aɪt̪ʲə]	[ɛcə]	[kr̥ɔ̃k]
leabaidh	*bodach*	*(ná's) fhaide*	*aige*	*cnog*
'bed' [nom.]	'old fellow'	'farther'	'at him'	'knock'

its maximum, about halfway through the voiceless period, whereas in the unaspirated voiceless geminate the oral closure occurs as the glottal opening gestures starts. Note also that the glottal aperture is no greater for the aspirated than for the unaspirated stop, again suggesting that greater glottal opening is not the defining characteristic of aspiration.

Scottish Gaelic pre-aspirated stops are illustrated in table 3.13. It should be noted that the extent of pre-aspiration varies in different dialects of this language; in Skye Gaelic pre-aspirated stops are comparable in length to those in Icelandic even though there is no reason to analyze them as geminates in Gaelic, whereas in Lewis Gaelic they are as short as other stops (ní Chasaide 1985).

Although pre-aspirated and (post-) aspirated stops are phonologically related in both Gaelic and Icelandic, it is obvious that the glottal gestures in these two categories differ in their timing relationships with the associated oral gestures. Further, at least in Icelandic, the glottal aperture in post-aspirated stops does not seem to be wider than that in voiceless unaspirated stops, although pre-aspirated stops show a wider aperture than either of the others (figure 3.11, also ní Chasaide 1985, Pétursson 1976). Pre- and post-aspiration share the characteristic that a substantial part of the time during which the glottis is open is not aligned with the oral closure.

We also note that pre-aspiration is said to occur in Amerindian languages, such as the Algonquian language Ojibwa (Bloomfield, 1956: 8), and the Arawakan language Guajiro (Holmer 1949). We have not been able to investigate Ojibwa, but it is clear from Bloomfield's account that, much as in Icelandic, the pre-aspiration occurs only before the 'fortis' (long) consonants **pp, tt, cc, kk,** and that these consonants occur only in medial position. We have ourselves analyzed a single recording of Guajiro. In his account of this language, Holmer (1949: 49) states that, at the time of his investigations, many speakers did not use pre-aspiration in medial positions (again, the only position in which it may occur). In a recording of one speaker made approximately 30 years after Holmer's study, we found that the speaker sometimes used a breathy voiced offset to a vowel that was followed by a long stop, but he did not pre-aspirate consistently. In any case pre-aspiration is not used to form phonological contrasts in Guajiro (*pace* Maddieson 1984a: 406).

Pike and Pike (1947) describe the occurrence of **h** preceding a range of voiced and voiceless consonants in Huatla Mazatec (a language of Oaxaca, Mexico). This might be analyzed as pre-aspiration and this is essentially the analysis proposed by Steriade (1993a). However, this case seems different to us, since, when a voiced consonant follows, there is not just one glottal gesture extending over the pre-aspiration and the oral articulation. We would agree with Pike and Pike that these sequences of consonants are clusters. It is interesting to note that in this language **h** forms clusters in a similar manner to **ʔ** in that **h** and **ʔ** may follow as well as precede other consonants in clusters.

Despite its importance in specifying the phonetic characteristics of some languages, we do not know of any language in which it is necessary to regard pre-aspiration as a feature required for distinguishing underlying forms. Stops of this kind always occur intervocalically or finally; there are no occurrences of initial pre-aspirated stops that we are aware of.

Glottal closure

At the opposite end of the continuum of glottal aperture from the kinds of gestures used in voiceless aspirated stops is a full closure of the vocal folds, as in a glottal stop. We will begin by discussing oral stops in which there is an accompanying glottal closure. These can be broadly divided into two types, depending on whether or not the glottal stop serves as the initiator of an airstream. We will discuss the glottalic airstream mechanism below, after we have exemplified stops with simultaneous glottal closure. These are familar as syllable-final variants of phonologically voiceless stops in various, mostly British, dialects of English. Figure 3.12 shows this variation in two utterances of the word *pack*, spoken by Ian Maddieson. In the spectrogram on the left the final velar stop is released and there is no accompanying glottal stop. In the one on the right, the entire velar closure is overlapped by a glottal stop, resulting in the suppression of any audible burst or frication when it is released. In this production it is also possible to see the occurrence of creaky voiced phonation at the end of the vowel. The movement of the second and third formants towards each other typical of a velar closure is very apparent in this token, indicating that the velar gesture is well under way by the time the vocal folds close, but, in comparison with the other token of this word, the transitional movement of the formants is truncated a little by the supervention of the glottal closure.

There are other ways of combining a glottal closure with an oral articulation. In some of the languages described in the literature as having 'glottalized' voiceless stops, a somewhat similar overlapping production of a glottal stop with the oral closure is what occurs. We have heard this phenomenon in

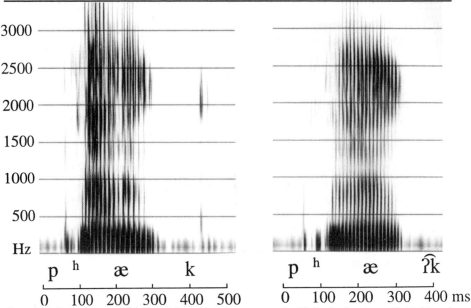

Figure 3.12 Spectrograms of the English word *pack* pronounced with final velar stop with (right) and without (left) accompanying glottal closure.

recordings of Siona, a Tucanoan language spoken on the Colombia-Ecuador border. This language is described by Wheeler and Wheeler (1962) as having a set of glottalized stops which they transcribe **p', t', k', kʷ'**, in contrast with "the simple stop series **p, t, k, kʷ**." They note that "the feature of glottalization is very light, and the glottalized series can best be distinguished by the laryngealization which occurs on the following vowels." Our impression is that there is a simultaneous glottal closure with the 'glottalized' series. Both stop series have a brief delay of voice onset after the release of the oral closure, but whereas this is filled with an acoustically noisy interval in the simple stop series, there is essentially silence between the oral release of a 'glottalized' stop and the beginning of voicing for a following vowel.

Glottal closures can, of course, occur without accompanying oral closure, in which case they form glottal stops. Different types of glottal stops have been observed in the world's languages. In several languages they are part of the regular stop series. This is the case in Hawaiian, in which there are only eight contrasting consonants, as shown in table 3.14. Elsewhere, glottal stops serve to demarcate the boundaries of phrases or other prosodic units. A frequent role of this type (for example, in German) is to indicate the beginning of a word when no other consonant is present. In other languages, however, glottal stops function more as a variation in phonation type. In Huatla Mazatec, as Pike and Pike (1947: 79) note, the glottal stop is sometimes realized as a complete stop, and sometimes as laryngealization of the following vowel. In Jalapa Mazatec

Table 3.14 The eight contrasting consonants of Hawaiian in initial position

pana	'bow'	**kaʔa**	'to roll'	**ʔaʔa**	'dare'
mana	'power'	**nana**	'look'	**haʔa**	'dance'
wana	'sea urchin'	**lana**	'buoyancy'		

the realization is usually entirely as creaky voice on an associated vowel (Kirk, Ladefoged and Ladefoged 1993).

In the great majority of languages we have heard, glottal stops are apt to fall short of complete closure, especially in intervocalic positions. In place of a true stop, a very compressed form of creaky voice or some less extreme form of stiff phonation may be superimposed on the vocalic stream. True stops occur reliably only when it is a matter of gemination. A typical example of these phenomena from a speaker of Lebanese Colloquial Arabic is shown by the waveforms in figure 3.13. In this figure a long silent closure period is

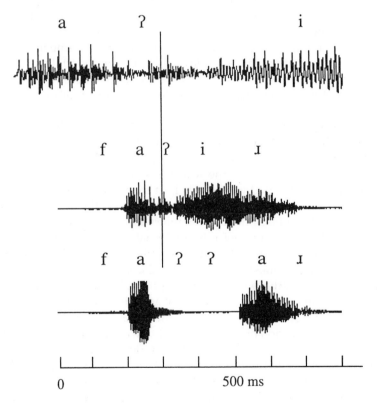

Figure 3.13 Waveforms of Lebanese Arabic geminate and single ʔ in the words **'faʔʔaɹ** 'make poor' (bottom line) and **faʔiɹ** 'poor' (middle line). An expanded waveform of the word on the middle line is shown on the top line. A vertical bar indicates the point at which the expanded portion is aligned with the main waveform.

Table 3.15 Words illustrating intervocalic glottal consonants and directly adjoining vowels in Gimi (suggested by Sam McBride). The segment symbolized by an asterisk is discussed in the text

NO INTERVOCALIC STOP	rahoʔ	'truly'	hao	'hit'
INTERVOCALIC GLOTTAL STOP	haʔo	'shut'	ha*oʔ	'many'

apparent for the geminate glottal stop, but the single consonant above is pronounced with irregular constricted voicing.

A glottal closure obviously precludes any variation in laryngeal aperture, so we would not expect glottal stops to differ in this way. But there are languages that behave as if they had contrasting voiced and voiceless glottal stops, although, quite obviously, this could not literally be the case. One such language is Gimi, a Papuan language of the Eastern Highlands, Papua New Guinea. According to McBride (personal communication), Gimi has a stop system that includes contrasts between voiced and voiceless unaspirated stops at the bilabial and alveolar places of articulation. Where neighboring languages have cognate forms containing **k** and **g**, Gimi has a glottal stop corresponding to **k** and another segment, which we will symbolize using an asterisk, correponding to **g**. From a phonological point of view this segment behaves like a glottal stop, in that it operates in rules which require a glottal stop in the context. For example, there is a rule whereby the nasals **m**, **n** become the corresponding stops **b**, **d** when they occur after a glottal consonant at the end of a preceding morpheme.

Our own recordings of Gimi show that * consists largely of a diminution of energy between otherwise adjacent vowels. Waveforms of the words in table 3.15 are shown in figure 3.14. In each case an expanded version of the intervocalic portion is shown above the waveform of the whole word. A time scale applicable to the expanded waveforms is at the top of the figure; one for the unexpanded words is at the bottom. The waveform for the intervocalic **h** is that of breathy voice **ɦ**, and is similar to the intervocalic **ɦ** in English 'behold'. The waveform for ʔ shows some noise in the initial portion, but is otherwise indicative of a tightly closed glottis. The so-called voiced glottal stop is signaled by slight irregularities in the glottal pulses, and a considerable decrease in the amplitude of the pulses which is probably due to an increase in the glottal stiffness; but there is no indication of anything that would normally be called a stop, glottal or otherwise. There is, however, a clear distinction between * and a simple transition between adjacent vowels as shown in the lower part of the figure. The vowel-to-vowel transition reflects simply the waveform changes that can be associated with the changes in the formant frequencies. In summary, it seems that * in Gimi is voiced, and involves some glottal activity; but it might better be called a creaky voiced glottal approximant rather than a stop.

Thus Gimi uses in a distinctive way what are for most languages simply parts of the range of possible variation in the production of glottal stops.

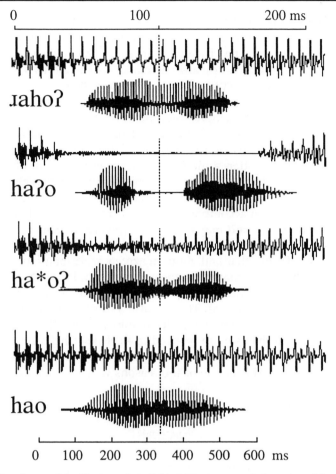

Figure 3.14 Waveforms of the Gimi words in Table 3.15. An expanded version of the intervocalic portion is shown above the waveform of the whole word, time-aligned as indicated by the dashed lines.

Another language which has been reported to have a voiced glottal stop is Jingpho (Maran 1971), but in this case it seems to us preferable to regard the contrasting forms as being distinguished by tonal differences.

3.2 Airstream Mechanisms

Nearly all the sounds of the world's languages are made with the pulmonic airstream mechanism, in which lung air is pushed through the vocal tract by the action of the respiratory system. We have been using the term plosive to distinguish stops made in this way. In the canonical literature on articulatory phonetics two other airstream mechanisms are described, the glottalic and velaric. Some stops (and a few fricatives) are said to be made with an egressive glottalic airstream, in which upward movements of the glottis act like a piston to push air out, forming ejectives. Downward movements of the larynx which lower the pressure of the air in the vocal tract are used to form implosives. We would prefer to lay greater emphasis on the three variables, laryngeal setting, articulatory timing, and changes in oropharyngeal cavity volume, rather than on different categorical labels for airstreams. The presence or absence of a glottalic mechanism is often a matter of degree, with several of the types of stops that we have already discussed in this chapter displaying certain features in common with canonical ejective and implosive stops. For example, stops that occur with an accompanying glottal stop, as in the London English pronunciation of 'rat' as ɹæʔt may have small upward movements of the larynx making them weakly ejective. In addition, fully voiced stops in many diverse languages (e.g. Maidu, Thai and Zulu) are often accompanied by downward movements of the larynx that make them slightly implosive. Nonetheless, the familiar labels ejective and implosive provide a convenient organizational framework for the next sections. There is also a third airstream mechanism, in which movements of the tongue suck air into the mouth. Stops using this velaric airstream mechanism are referred to as clicks. Clicks are quite distinct from other types of stops, whereas plosives differ from implosives and ejective stops by small steps. This is one of the reasons why clicks are discussed in a separate chapter.

Ejectives

Ejectives are not at all unusual sounds, occurring in about 18 percent of the languages of the world (Maddieson 1984a), in language families as diverse as Mayan, Chadic and Caucasian. As we noted, they are produced by the action of the closed glottis, while there is an occlusion in the oral cavity. The larynx is raised rapidly upwards, so that air in the vocal tract above the glottal closure is compressed. The pressure behind the closure in the oral cavity is often increased to about double the normal pulmonic pressure (i.e. from about 8 to about 16 cm H_2O). The oral closure is then released, and, owing to the greater supraglottal pressure, there is a greater amplitude in the stop burst.

Among the places of articulation, velar articulations are the most favored for ejective stops (Haudricourt 1950, Greenberg 1970, Javkin 1977, Maddieson 1984a). Uvular ejectives are also quite common, and are reported in many North American languages such as Haida, Wintu, South-Eastern Pomo and most of the Salishan languages, as well as in Caucasian languages such as Georgian and Kabardian. The ejectives in Montana Salish are illustrated in table 3.16. Palatal ejectives on the other hand are comparatively rare, but not

Table 3.16 Words illustrating the ejectives in Montana Salish and contrasting plosives and affricates (after Flemming, Ladefoged and Thomason 1994)

PLAIN		EJECTIVE	
páʕas	'face is pale, grey'	p'aʕáp	'grass fire'
tám	'it's not'	t'áq'ən	'six'
tsáqʷəlʃ	'western larch'	ts'aɫt	'it's cold'
		tɬ'aq'	'hot'
tʃájɫqən	'cut hair'	tʃ'aáwən	'I prayed'
kapí	'coffee'		
kʷateʔ	'quarter coin'	kʷ'áltʃ'qən	'lid, cover'
qáχeʔ	'mother's sister'	q'áq'ɫuʔ	'vein'
qʷátsqən	'hat'	qʷ'ájəlqs	'priest'

disproportionately so when compared with the palatal plosives. They are reported in Kwakw'ala, Acoma, Bella Coola and Jaqaru. The bilabial place of articulation is relatively disfavored, as it is for plosives. Typically, languages will have ejective stops at the same places at which pulmonic stops occur. This mirroring of behaviors for the two airstreams adds further underpinning to the notion that glottalic and pulmonic systems share more than do pulmonic and velaric.

There are considerable phonetic differences among the ejectives that occur in different languages, some of which have been well documented by Lindau (1984), who compared velar ejectives in Hausa and Navajo, and found significant cross-linguistic variation, as well as some notable inter-speaker differences. Waveforms illustrating some of the differences are shown in figure 3.15. The two languages differ in the relative durations of the different parts of the ejectives: the duration of the glottal closure is longer in the Navajo stop than in the one for Hausa. The Hausa glottal closure is probably released at the point shown on the figure by an arrow, and it is followed by a period of voiceless airflow. The Navajo glottal closure is released into creaky voice which continues for several periods into the beginning of the vowel. Lindau (1984) found that the long glottal closure in Navajo is a highly significant difference between the Navajo and Hausa speakers, and could not be attributed to the overall speech rate, which was similar in both cases. We do not know of any data that addresses the question of the relative timing of the formation of the oral and glottal closures.

This leads us to consider whether it is in any way possible to make ejectives with modal voice during the oral closure, that is, sounds in which although the larynx is being raised and the volume of the supralaryngeal cavity is thereby being reduced, the vocal folds are nonetheless in a position for modal voice and sufficient air is flowing between them to induce vibration. It seems most unlikely that the requisite pressure differential could be produced so as

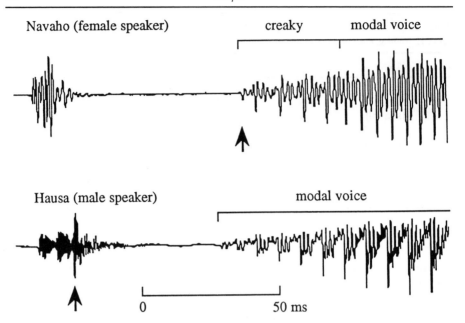

Figure 3.15 Waveforms illustrating differences between Navajo and Hausa ejectives. The arrows indicate the releases of the glottal closures.

to cause sufficient airflow from the lungs to ensure vibration of the upward moving glottis. We do not know of any linguistic use of voiced ejectives.

Sounds that have been described in the literature as voiced ejectives are, in our opinion, misnamed. Voiced ejectives have been reported as contrastive in Zhu‖'hõasi (Snyman 1970, 1975). But as Snyman makes clear, and as Maddieson (1984a: 216) is careful to point out, these 'voiced ejectives' are pre-voiced; the release is voiceless and from a phonetic point of view they are clusters of the form **dt**'. Clusters involving obstruents with mixed voicing in the same syllable are very rare in the world's languages, but they occur in !Xũ languages and in Kelabit (Blust 1974, 1993). We have already noted Zhu‖'hõasi stops with mixed voicing in table 3.7. Further examples illustrating mixed voicing in ejectives and affricates are given in table 3.17. As is evident in the waveforms shown in figure 3.16 (which also illustrates one of the plain stops listed in the earlier table), the initial voiced stops are unexploded. These are not sequences of the form **dᵊt**, but are simply homorganic pairs of stops, with the first member being voiced and unreleased, and the second being voiceless and, on some occasions, also ejective and affricated.

The ejective mechanism can also be used in conjunction with other articulations, including those that do not involve an oral closure. Ejective fricatives are discussed in chapter 5, and ejective accompaniments of clicks in chapter 8. Ejective affricates will be illustrated in a later section of this chapter.

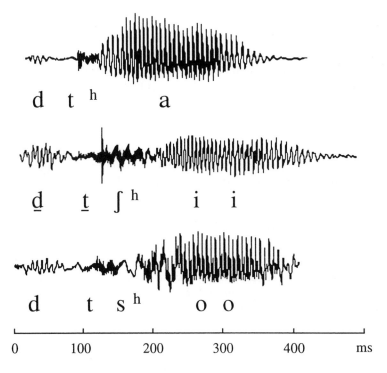

Figure 3.16 Waveforms of clusters with mixed voicing in Zhuǀ'hõasi.

Table 3.17 Words illustrating clusters with mixed voicing in Zhuǀ'hõasi

	ALVEOLAR	POST-ALVEOLAR
VOICELESS UNASPIRATED	tsam 'to stalk'	t∫a 'to fetch'
ASPIRATED	ts^{h}e 'week'	t∫^{h}at̠∫^{h}a 'to sprinkle'
VOICED PLUS ASPIRATED	dts^{h}au 'woman'	d̠t∫^{h}ii 'to carry straddled on shoulder'
VOICELESS EJECTIVE	ts'a 'sleep'	t∫'am 'bird [coracias garrulus]'
VOICED PLUS EJECTIVE	dts^{h}oo 'hartebeest'	d̠t∫'i 'to be wet'

Implosives

Implosives are stops that are produced with a greater than average amount of lowering of the larynx during the time that the oral closure for the stop is maintained. Earlier accounts of this class of sounds generally indicated that they were typically produced with a constricted setting of the vocal folds. It is now recognized that the laryngeal setting can vary, and implosives can be produced with modal voice, with a more tense voice setting, and with a complete glottal closure.

Voiced implosives are stops that are produced by lowering the larynx while the vocal folds are vibrating. If the larynx is lowered rapidly enough, there may be a negative pressure in the oral cavity, so that on the release of the oral closure air flows into the mouth. However, it is often the case that the airflow through the glottis producing the vocal fold vibrations is sufficiently great to prevent the pressure of the air in the oral cavity from becoming negative; consequently there is no ingressive airflow on the release of the stop closure. In fact, there is a gradient between one form of voiced plosive and what may be called a true implosive, rather than two clearly defined classes. Even when there has been a considerable glottal movement, the pressure in the oral cavity is often not very different from the pressure outside the mouth so that the stop burst is less evident.

About 10 percent of the world's languages contain implosives, many of them occurring in West African languages (Maddieson 1984a). Voiced implosives are found at most of the different places of articulation, but there is a tendency for anterior closures to be favored. Bilabial implosives are by far the most common, and voiced uvular implosives are very rare; they are reported to occur in the Ugandan language Ik (Heine 1975). It was once said (Jakobson, Fant and Halle 1952) that languages do not contrast implosives and ejective stops at the same place of articulation, but such contrasts have been reported in a number of languages, including Uduk, a Nilo-Saharan language, as shown in table 3.18.

Sindhi is a good example of a language with an extensive stop system including implosives, as shown in table 3.19. Nihalani (1974, 1991) has provided good aerodynamic data on this language, some of which has been used in figure 3.17. This being a citation form, the utterance begins with an increase in the

Table 3.18 Words illustrating stop contrasts in Uduk, including ejective and implosive stops at the same place of articulation (suggested by Robin Thelwall)

	BILABIAL		ALVEOLAR	
VOICED	baʔ	'to be something'	dèɗ	'to shiver'
VOICELESS	pàl	'to try'	tèr	'to collect'
ASPIRATED	pʰàlal	'centipede'	tʰèr	'to pour off'
EJECTIVE	p'àcʰàɗ	'fermented'	t'èɗ	'to lick'
IMPLOSIVE	ɓàʔ	'back of neck'	ɗek'	'to lift'

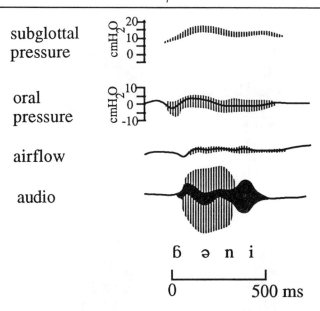

subglottal pressure

oral pressure

airflow

audio

ɓ ə n i

0   500 ms

Figure 3.17 Aerodynamic data (based on Nihalani 1974) for the Sindhi implosive ɓ in the word ɓəni.

Table 3.19 Words illustrating contrasting stops in Sindhi. ɟ and c are affricates, and might be transcribed ʤ and ʧ. The palatal implosive ʄ is often a slightly creaky voiced palatal approximant

	BILABIAL	DENTAL	RETROFLEX	PALATAL	VELAR
VOICED	bənu	d̪əru	ḍoru	ɟətu	gunu
	'forest'	'door'	'you run'	'illiterate'	'quality'
VOICELESS	pənu	t̪əru	ʈənu	cətu	kənu
	'leaf'	'bottom'	'ton'	'to destroy'	'ear'
VOICELESS ASPIRATED	pʰənu	t̪ʰəru	ʈʰəɖu	cʰətu	kʰənu
	'snake hood'	(district name)	'thug'	'crown'	'you lift'
BREATHY VOICED	bʱənənu	d̪ʱəru	ḍʱəɖu	ɟʱətu	gʱəni
	'lamentation'	'trunk of body'	'bull'	'grab'	'excess'
IMPLOSIVE	ɓəni		ɗɪnu	ʄətu	ɠənu
	'field'		'festival'	'illiterate' [var.]	'handle'

subglottal pressure, during which the lips are closed (there is no airflow), and the oral pressure first rises slightly and then decreases while the vocal folds are vibrating. At the moment of the opening of the lips the air can flow into the mouth because of the negative oral pressure. For this speaker, in these citation forms, the implosives at each place of articulation always have a negative oral pressure and a very small ingressive airflow.

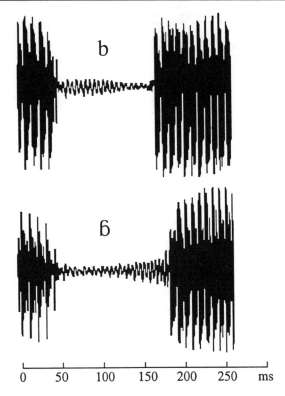

Figure 3.18 Waveforms of Degema showing contrasts between voiced plosive and voiced implosive.

Lindau (1984) studied implosives in Kalabari, Degema and a number of other languages spoken in the southeast of Nigeria. Her examination focused on the bilabial and alveolar voiced plosives compared to the voiced implosives made at the same places of articulation. She did not have any aerodynamic data, but her acoustic records indicate that the implosives in these languages are very similar to those in Sindhi. These acoustic records, exemplified in the lower part of figure 3.18, showed that the amplitude of vibrations typically increased during the time that the oral closure was maintained, indicating that the lowering of the larynx (added to any other cavity-expanding maneuvers during this interval) was more than sufficient to counteract the pressure build-up in the oral cavity. In contrast with the voiced plosives, exemplified in the upper part of figure 3.18, voicing was not only sustained, but grew in ampli-tude. Examination of the shape of the waveforms in detail suggests that the manner of this voicing is generally modal; there are only a few signs of a biphasic pattern and the waveform is not at all heavily damped. Compare these waveforms with those in figure 3.3 where one can see a clear biphasic pattern. There is nothing in these data to indicate that a description of these

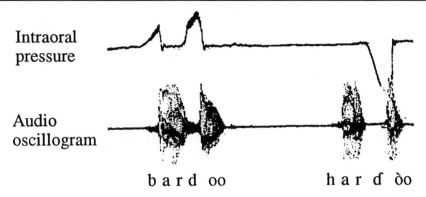

Intraoral
pressure

Audio
oscillogram

b a r d oo   h a r ɗ òo

Figure 3.19 Intra-oral pressure records of the Hausa words **bardoo** 'longtailed dove' and **hardòo** 'Fulani man' (courtesy of R. Schuh).

segments as having a feature [constricted glottis] would match the phonetic facts.

Lindau also studied the implosives produced by a number of speakers of Hausa. All but one of these speakers produced stops in which there was considerable glottal constriction. Lindau notes that "Five out of the 14 speakers produce a voiceless beginning of the closure, presumably from a glottal closure as the larynx descends. One speaker had an implosive just like those in the Niger-Congo languages. The 8 remaining speakers produced an implosive [in which the] closure displays highly aperiodic vibrations" (Lindau 1984: 151).

We have observed sounds of this kind not only in Hausa, but also in other Chadic languages such as Bura, Margi and Ngizim. For many speakers, implosives are produced as in the token illustrated on the right of figure 3.19. In this case substantial negative pressure builds up in the mouth while the oral closure is held, but the vocal folds are too tightly closed for vocal fold vibration to occur during the closure. Voicing does begin shortly before the release, as the oral closure begins to be relaxed. Implosives of this type can be described as creaky voiced implosives, and could be transcribed as ɓ̰, ɗ̰ and so on. In contrast, the voiced plosives from the same speaker, as shown on the left of the figure, have voiced vibrations throughout the stop closure, even though intraoral pressure is positive.

Another view of this Hausa type of implosive is given in figure 3.20 which illustrates the difference between the plosives **b, d** and the implosives **ɓ, ɗ** in utterance-initial position. The data is from a different speaker. All these stops are voiceless during most of the closure in these examples. The differences are primarily in the onset of the vowel. In both **ɓ** and **ɗ** the few periods of voicing during the closure and those at the onset of the vowel are irregular. The Hausa implosives with creaky voice seem to be similar to those in Mixtec as described by Hunter and Pike (1969). It may also be that, as the majority of Hausa speakers have some form of glottal constriction in their implosives, these sounds are

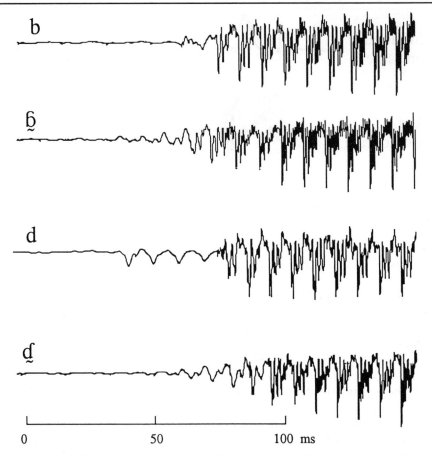

Figure 3.20 The difference between the releases of the modal voice and creaky voiced stops in Hausa.

Table 3.20 Words illustrating the set of so-called glottalized sounds in Hausa, and contrasting non-glottalized sounds

GLOTTALIZED	ɓaːtàː	ɗaːmèː	k'aːràː	kʷ'aːràː	s'aːràː	ʔʲaː
	'spoil'	'tighten (belt)'	'increase'	'shea nut'	'arrange'	'daughter'
PLAIN	baːtàː	daːmèː	kaːràː	kʷaːràː	saːràː	jaː
	'line'	'mix thoroughly'	'put near'	'pour'	'cut'	'he' [comp.]

primarily distinguished from their voiced counterparts by being laryngeal-ized, rather than by having an ingressive airstream. As illustrated in table 3.20, Hausa has ejectives at some places of articulation and implosives at others. This set of sounds, together with ʔ, has been called glottalized by Carnochan (1952), so as to provide a label for a group of sounds that are subject to the same phonotactic constraints.

Table 3.21 Words illustrating voiced laryngealized stops and voiced implosives in Lendu, according to Goyvaerts (1988)

	BILABIAL		ALVEOLAR		VELAR	
VOICELESS	**pà**	'swing' (n.)	**tà**	'become rich'	**kŏ**	'appear'
VOICED	**bà**	'milk, breast'	**dà**	'tongue'	**gŏ**	'heal'
VOICED IMPLOSIVE	**ɓà**	'allow'	**ɗà**	'water'	**ɠŏ**	'follow'
CREAKY VOICED IMPLOSIVE	**ɓ̰à**	'glue' (v.)	**ɗ̰à**	'beauty'	**ɠ̰õ**	'mouse'

Goyvaerts (1988) suggests that Lendu distinguishes between laryngealized implosives and implosives with modal voicing. This would mean that this language contains both implosives such as Hausa **ɓ, ɗ** and Kalabari **ɓ, ɗ**. Examples in accordance with Goyvaerts' interpretation are shown in table 3.21. However, Demolin (in press) has a different interpretation, preferring to interpret the distinction as one between voiced and voiceless implosives, as we will discuss below.

Implosives with glottal closure (voiceless implosives)

For a considerable time implosives were generally regarded as having only one possible laryngeal setting, namely that for voicing. But, as we have just noted, implosives can vary between modal voice and a more constricted phonatory setting. Both Catford (1939) and Pike (1943: 92) mention the possibility of voiceless implosives in the early literature on these sounds. By this, they meant implosives produced with a full glottal closure.

Voiceless implosives occur in Owerri Igbo (Ladefoged et al. 1976). The Owerri dialect of Igbo has a larger number of laryngeal distinctions among oral stops at one-place of articulation than any other known language. We have already discussed the four-way phonation type contrast; in addition there are both voiced and voiceless implosives, making a total of six bilabial stops, as shown previously in table 3.6.

Figure 3.7 illustrated the difference among the Igbo bilabial stops. The implosive **ɓ̥** is clearly a voiceless glottalic ingressive stop. After the lips close, airflow out of the mouth ceases, and the pressure inside the mouth increases very slightly. Then, probably at the time when the small mark on the oral pressure record occurs, the glottis closes. The closed glottis is lowered so that the pressure in the mouth decreases considerably. When it is about -4 cm H_2O the vocal folds start vibrating and the oral pressure starts increasing. Shortly afterwards the lips come apart and air flows out of the mouth.

These implosives are nearly always slightly voiced during the last part of the closure, with voicing beginning about 25 ms before the closure is released. The decrease in oral pressure is about 5 cm H_2O. We may assume that the pressure

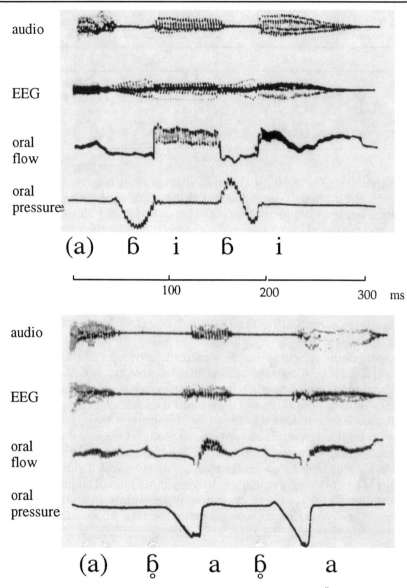

Figure 3.21 Aerodynamic records of Lendu implosives. In the words (a) ɓiɓi̋ 'eaten by insects', and (a) ɓ́aɓ́a 'attached to'. From data supplied by Demolin (personal communication).

below the vocal folds during these implosives is very slightly higher than in other sounds, as the descending closed glottis will cause a slight (less than 1 cm H_2O) increase in the pressure of the air in the lungs. The pressure of the air in the lungs during plosives is typically about 8 cm H_2O for the speaker whose speech is illustrated in the figure. Consequently the pressure drop across the vocal folds at the time when they are set into vibration is approximately 13 cm H_2O, which corresponds to that produced during fairly loud shouting.

The voiced implosive is very different. As we noted in the discussion of voiced implosives in other languages, the flow of air through the vibrating vocal folds may or may not be sufficient to compensate for any decrease in oral pressure due to the downward movement of the glottis. In the voiced implosive illustrated in this figure, there is a slight negative pressure (as, indeed, was typical for this particular speaker). But the distinctive auditory characteristics of these sounds are more probably due to movements of the larynx affecting the formant frequencies at the onset of the vowel rather than to anything that can be more directly associated with the direction of the airflow. Both the voiced and the voiceless bilabial implosives in Owerri Igbo also seem auditorily to be velarized. This is not surprising, as they developed historically from the labial-velars found in other dialects.

Voiceless implosives also occur in the Uzere dialect of Isoko (as well as in several other dialects), in for example oɓa 'rooster' (Donwa 1982). Donwa's thesis contains oral pressure tracings for these voiceless implosives.

According to Demolin (in press), the implosives in Lendu which Goyvaerts describes as laryngealized are voiceless implosives, as Kutch Lojenga (1991) had earlier suggested. The lower part of figure 3.21 illustrates the implosives of this type in the Lendu word meaning 'attached to' which here, following Demolin, is transcribed ɓáɓá. These sounds are in contrast with the voiced implosives, which are illustrated in the upper part of figure 3.21 in the word ɓíɓĩ 'eaten by insects'. In ɓáɓá the lowering of the oral pressure, lack of voicing during most of the closure, and the small ingressive airflow at the release of the closure suggested to Demolin that these are voiceless implosives. Note, however, that voicing starts slightly before the release of the closure, as is particularly evident on the EGG (electroglottograph) recording. This voicing may also be slightly creaky. Demolin notes that the pre-voicing is a consistent feature of these sounds. In view of this property it seems to us that Goyvaerts might be correct, and that these sounds are very similar to those in Hausa. If this is the case, then Lendu would be an example of a language that distinguishes between laryngealized stops and modally voiced implosives.

Pinkerton (1986) has a good discussion of the glottalic airstream mechanism in Kichean (Mayan) languages. In these languages, there is considerable variation across dialects and across speakers in the realization of glottalized stops as implosives, or ejectives or pulmonic stops. Thus, in some towns glottalized uvular sounds are voiceless implosives while in others they are voiceless ejectives. The voiced bilabial stop is produced as an implosive or as a voiced pulmonic stop, or as a voiceless bilabial implosive. The glottalic alveolar stop appears as a voiceless ejective, a voiced implosive and a voiceless implosive. In each case, therefore, some distinct characteristic separates the glottalized consonants from the unaspirated voiceless pulmonic stops with which they contrast. The common feature is a constriction of the glottis, and it is this laryngeal gesture that is the essential target for production, rather than the particular airflow patterns that result from the movements of the larynx

3.3 Affricates

In almost every case, as a stop is released the articulators will pass briefly through a position in which the constriction is narrow enough that it will cause turbulence in the air at the constriction site. This transitory friction is usually considered a part of the release burst of the stop. Affricates are stops in which the release of the constriction is modified in such a way as to produce a more prolonged period of frication after the release. As with many of the types of sounds we have discussed, the class of affricates has no sharp boundaries. Affricates are an intermediate category between simple stops and a sequence of a stop and a fricative. It is not always easy to say how much frication should be regarded as an automatic property of a release; some places of articulation seem to be often accompanied by considerable frication (see chapter 2). At the other extreme, a combination of a stop and fricative that both happen to have the same place of articulation do not necessarily form an affricate. Phonological considerations must play a part in any decision as to whether a stop and a following homorganic fricative is to be regarded as an affricate which is a single unit, or as two segments (or two timing slots), forming a sequence of a stop and a fricative.

Affricate releases may involve only a slight widening of the articulatory constriction of the stop, so that stop and fricative components have identical place of articulation. Some affricates, however, involve a small forward or backward adjustment of the active articulator position. An example is the affricate **pf** in German, usually described as labiodental in place. For many speakers the stop component of this sound has a bilabial closure for which the upper lip is actively lowered to meet the raised lower lip (the position is subtly different from that in simple **p**, in that the lower lip is slightly retracted). The closure is released by raising the upper lip and pulling the lower lip further back into the normal position for **f**. The details of these gestures can be well observed in the photo-strips of lip positions published by Bolla and Valaczkai (1986).

The most common affricates are voiceless and sibilant; the palato-alveolar affricate **tʃ** occurs in approximately 45 percent of the world's languages and dental or alveolar sibilant affricates are also quite common (Maddieson 1984a). Less common affricates occur in Standard Chinese, which has a voiceless aspirated palatal affricate, in addition to the similarly rare voiceless aspirated retroflex sibilant affricate, as illustrated in table 3.22. The fricative components of these sounds will be discussed in chapter 5.

The Athabaskan language Chipewyan has one of the largest and most complex sets of voiceless affricates, as shown in table 3.23. Other unusual affricates

Table 3.22 Words illustrating contrasts between affricates in Standard Chinese

	ALVEOLAR	RETROFLEX	ALVEOLO-PALATAL
VOICELESS UNASPIRATED	**tsa** 'to smack lips'	**ṭṣa** 'to pierce'	**tɕa** 'to add'
ASPIRATED	**tsʰa** 'to wipe'	**ṭṣʰa** 'to stick in'	**tɕʰa** 'to pinch tightly'

Table 3.23 Words illustrating Chipewyan stops and affricates

	UNASPIRATED		ASPIRATED		EJECTIVE	
STOPS	bɛs	'knife'				
	dene	'man'	tʰeli	'pail'	t'óθ	'paddle'
	gah	'rabbit'	kʰe	'moccasin'	k'i	'birch'
AFFRICATES	dðéθ	'hide'	ṭθʰe	'pipe'	ṭθ'áí	'dish'
	dzéke	'rubbers'	tsʰaba	'money'	ts'i	'canoe'
	dʒíɛ	'berries'	tʃʰeθ	'duck'	tʃ'oɣ	'quill'
	dlíe	'squirrel'	tɬʰes	'lard'	tɬ'uli	'rope'

are said to occur in Beembe, which we infer from Jacquot (1981) to have a voiceless aspirated labiodental affricate contrasting with a voiceless unaspirated affricate at the same place in, for example, **pfʰúri** 'cotton' vs. **pfínà** 'duvet'.

Most of the distinctions that can distinguish unaffricated stops also occur with affricates. Slack voiced affricates were illustrated in the discussion of Javanese, and breathy voiced affricates in the discussions of Hindi and Sindhi. Palatal implosives which are usually affricated were noted in the discussion of Sindhi. Other implosive affricates have been described by Hoard (1978) in Gitskan, a dialect of Tsimshian. Affricates with mixed voicing (which we would rather regard as sequences of voiced stops plus affricates) were illustrated in Zhuǀ'hõasi. Lateral affricates and ejective lateral affricates are discussed in chapter 6.

3.4 Length

Stops, like most other sounds, can contrast in length. In fact, long or geminate stops have been referred to earlier in this chapter in examples from Arabic, Ilwana, Icelandic and other languages. The most widely used measure of the length of a stop is the closure duration as measured from acoustic records. In languages with a phonological contrast between long and short consonants, long stops have between one and a half to three times the acoustic closure duration of the short stops in careful speech.

A distinction can be drawn, at least with respect to phonological behavior, between geminates and a sequence of two identical stops, such as may occur across a morpheme boundary in English, as in *hip-pocket*, *book-case*, etc, or in word-initial position in Jeh, as in **bban** 'arm', **ddoh** 'distended' (compare **ban** 'look after', **doh** 'later'). The first parts of these identical stop clusters in Jeh function as the equivalent of 'pre-syllables' (Cohen 1966), which normally have a CV structure. Unlike a sequence, geminates (of any kind, not only stops) may not be separated by an epenthetic vowel or other interruption, neither will one half of them undergo a phonological process by itself (Hayes 1986, Lahiri and Hankamer 1988). They often alternate with short consonants in processes of morphological derivation. Geminate affricates are very clearly different from an affricate sequence, since the sequence has two stop and two frication portions, while a geminate affricate has a long stop closure followed by one fricative portion.

Geminate stops in many languages are limited to word-medial positions where they usually close the preceding syllable, shortening its vowel to some degree, as well as serving as the onset of the following syllable (Maddieson 1985). Japanese exemplifies the rare case where a preceding syllable is essentially unaffected by a long following stop (Homma 1981, Smith 1991). The acoustic record does not reveal whether a long stop is produced with two separate articulatory gestures, the first corresponding to the syllable-closing part and the second corresponding to the syllable-opening part, as was proposed long ago by Sievers (1876). A number of studies have looked at this issue using either electromyography or methods of tracking articulatory movements over time. An electromyographic study by Lehiste, Morton and Tatham (1973) showed that two peaks of activity of the orbicularis oris muscle can occur both for word-medial geminate **pp** in Estonian and for **p#p** across a word boundary in English for one speaker of each of these languages. On the other hand Barry's (1985) dynamic palatographic data on English **k#k** sequences did not show any evidence of two articulatory peaks and Smith's (1992, in press) x-ray microbeam study of word-medial geminates in Italian and Japanese did not show double peaks in the articulatory movement of the lips for geminate bilabial stops in either of these languages, nor was there evidence of any double peaks in the tongue blade movements for alveolar geminate stops in this study. Typical trajectories showing the tongue back movement (for the vowels) and the changes in lip aperture in the production of single and geminate bilabials in Italian are shown in figure 3.22.

It thus seems evident that geminates can be produced with a repeated articulatory movement under some circumstances, but that this is unlikely to be the most common articulatory pattern. Moreover, the presence or absence of a second articulatory peak cannot be taken as diagnostic of whether a long

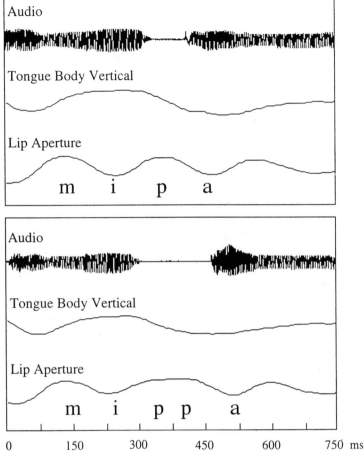

Figure 3.22 Articulatory trajectories for lips and the tongue in the nonsense words **mipa** and **mippa** spoken by one of the Italian speakers in Smith (1991).

closure represents a geminate stop or a sequence of two identical stops.

Most languages with a distinction of consonant length have only two distinctive lengths. Estonian and Sami are among a handful of languages that have been claimed to have three distinctive lengths for consonants. At least in the Lule dialect of Sami (Engstrand 1987) the third consonant length ('Grade III') is actually realized as a consonant sequence containing an epenthetic vowel with predictable quality. In Estonian (Lehiste 1966, Eek 1984–5) the third length is created by further lengthening of long consonants in a stressed syllable.

Word-initial long stops are rare, but they exist, for example, in Pattani Malay (Abramson 1986, 1991), which has a length distinction for initial consonants.

Table 3.24 Words illustrating initial long stops and continuants in Pattani Malay (from Abramson 1986)

	Short			Long	
	bulɛ	'moon'		bːulɛ	'many months'
	katoʔ	'to strike'		kːatoʔ	'frog'
	labɔ	'to make a profit'		lːabɔ	'spider'
	makɛ	'to eat'		mːakɛ	'to be eaten'
	siku	'elbow'		sːiku	'hand tool'

Illustrative contrasts are given in table 3.24. Abramson reports that the mean duration of the closures for the long stops in word-initial and word-medial position measured in a carrier phrase is three times longer than that for the short consonants. Of course, the onset of closure of an *utterance*-initial voiceless stop has no acoustic signature, and hence the durational differences cannot be readily perceived in this position. Nonetheless, Pattani Malay speakers can reliably recognize words contrasting in initial consonant length in isolation. Abramson (1986) suggested that the perceptual cues that compensate for the lack of information about closure duration in initial voiceless unaspirated stops might include intensity of the stop burst, rate of formant transitions, fundamental frequency perturbations, and relatively greater amplitude of the following vowel. In a more recent report (Abramson 1991), he has shown that Pattani Malay listeners are indeed sensitive to amplitude differences in the initial syllable in forming their judgments about the category of utterance-initial stops.

LuGanda also has long and short consonants which contrast in initial and medial position (Ladefoged, Glick and Criper 1968: 40). Initial contrasts are shown in table 3.25. The initial long consonants can be shown to be moraic (they were separate syllables historically, when they were accompanied by a high front vowel). Phonologically speaking these consonants are tone-bearing, although they may be voiceless, as in the examples cited in table 3.25. The audible difference between the words in the two columns in table 3.25 is largely in the pitch of the first vowel. The words in the second column have a lowered high tone because of the influence of the preceding (silent) low tone. The release of the stops in these words is also stronger than in words with simple initial voiceless stops. Long stops in word-medial position in LuGanda are differentiated more straightforwardly by duration but still have an underlying tone.

In addition to the distinctive use of long and short consonant lengths, there are many factors that affect the durations of stops in both their articulatory and acoustic domains. These include speaking rate and style, position in a word and other prosodic structures, the context of surrounding sounds, as well as certain inherent properties in the consonant itself. Since other durational variations are, for the most part, not distinctive we will not discuss them in this

Table 3.25 Words illustrating initial long and short stops in LuGanda (from Ladefoged 1971)

SHORT		LONG	
páálá	'run about madly'	ppááp̀ààlí	'pawpaw'
téékà	'put'	ttéékà	'rule, law'
kúlà	'grow up'	kkúlà	'treasure'

book, except insofar as they relate to the discussion of strength in the next section.

3.5 Strength: Fortis vs Lenis Stops

The terms fortis and lenis have been used with very diverse meanings in the literature. We will discuss two of these uses; in one of these uses the term 'fortis' indicates increased respiratory energy applied in the production of a segment, in the other 'fortis' indicates greater articulatory energy. In both cases, lenis indicates less energy.

The use of increased respiratory energy at a segmental level is a comparatively rare event. The best known example occurs in the Korean stiff voice stops discussed above, in which heightened subglottal pressure accompanies the more constricted glottis and tenser walls of the vocal tract. We have also observed consistent subglottal pressure increases in some (but only in some) contrasts involving aspirated stops, such as those in Igbo, described above.

There is also a heightened subglottal pressure in the formation of some long stops, such as the long initial stops in LuGanda. But these stops may not have an actual increase in respiratory effort. If the volume of air in the lungs is being decreased at a steady rate and a stop closure occurs, then the pressure of the air in the lungs will be increased in proportion to the duration of the closure. This effect in itself may be sufficient to account for the strong release burst of the long stops in LuGanda.

The question of articulatory strength as a parameter of distinctive consonantal contrast has been raised much more often. Many writers prefer to describe the two series of stops in Germanic languages such as English, German and Dutch as 'fortis' and 'lenis' rather than as voiceless and voiced. This is in part because there is often no vocal fold vibration in consonants of the 'voiced' series, so that reference to voicing can be considered misleading, but also because it was felt that the complex of measurable properties which distinguish these series – especially matters of timing such as the longer stop closure and shorter preceding vowel – could all be accounted for on the basis of the strength of the articulation. Alternative terms were used in the nineteenth century, when 'tense' and 'lax' were substituted for voiceless and voiced, a use which persisted much later in Halle, Hughes and Radley's (1957) description of the English stops. Originally the use of these labels was based only on a kinaesthetic sense, but as instrumentation improved a number of researchers began to look for evidence of the hypothesized strength differences. Measures of the force of contact between the articulators or of the peak intra-oral pressure generally failed to show that pairs of stops such as **p** and **b** differed in the expected way (Malécot 1968), and the idea of articulatory strength was widely considered among phoneticians to be discredited (e.g. Catford 1977a). However, rates of articulator movement and muscular activation levels often do differentiate between phonological voicing categories. For example, Smith and McLean-Muse (1987) showed that the peak closing velocity for postvocalic **p** was significantly greater than for **b** in a study of eight speakers of American English, and Slis (1971) had earlier shown EMG activation levels 12 percent higher for the lip-closing activity of the orbicularis orbis muscle in a word-medial **p** than for **b** for a speaker of Dutch. Engstrand (1989) showed a more extended contact area for **t** than for **d** in Swedish in a dynamic palatographic study.

Such differences in the purely oral articulatory movements between consonants that are commonly described by reference to their laryngeal settings are not confined to Germanic. In fact, we believe they are widespread. For example, the Ewe bilabial stops **p** and **b** also differ from each other in their articulatory gestures, as the movement tracks in figure 3.23 illustrate. The closing movements of the upper and lower lips are markedly faster for **p** than they are for **b**, and the peak of the **p** gesture is flatter, indicating more compression of the lips. In the terms of Browman and Goldstein's articulatory phonology, the gesture for **p** has greater stiffness. Older phoneticians might have said it was fortis. Because the lips reach closure earlier, this difference also relates to the longer closure duration of **p** (158 vs 150 ms in these data).

Voiceless stops have a greater mean oral pressure than voiced stops, and also often have a greater peak oral pressure. Accordingly, the greater degree of articulatory activity in the formation of the closure may be an anticipation of this need to make a firmer seal. In principle, the parameters of voicing and gestural stiffness could vary independently. When they co-vary either one might be regarded as primary. As little is known about the articulatory dynamics of most languages, we would caution against making the assumption that phonological voicing differences are associated with articulatory strength differences in any particular case.

Only a relatively small handful of languages have been proposed as possibly having articulatory strength differences that are independent of voicing. Among salient examples are Dagestanian languages such as Tabasaran (Kodzasov and Muravjeva 1982), Archi (Kodzasov 1977) and Agul (Kodzasov 1990: 338–41). Stops, affricates and fricatives in Archi, according to Kodzasov, show a contrast of strength. In the strength groupings that he sets up, weak stops are usually voiced but weak fricatives are voiceless and weak affricates

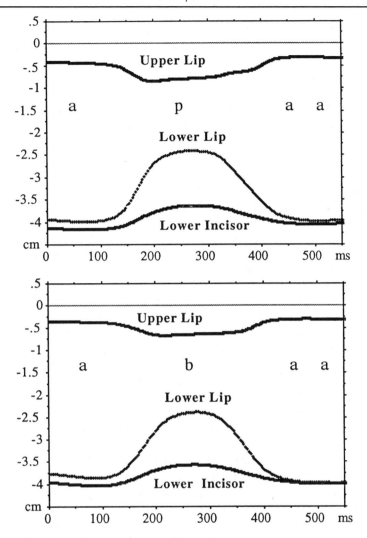

Figure 3.23 Vertical movement trajectories of the lips and jaw in production of **apaa** and **abaa** in Ewe. Mean of ten repetitions by one speaker (from Maddieson 1993).

are ejective, so there is no overall association of the strength and voicing parameters. Although strength is associated with durational differences, Kodzasov argues that the strength is the primary factor involved. In his view "Strong phonemes are characterized by the intensiveness (tension) of the articulation. The intensity of the pronunciation leads to a natural lengthening of the duration of the sound, and that is why strong [consonants] differ from weak ones by greater length" (p. 228). However, "the adjoining of two single weak sounds does not produce a strong one ... Thus, the gemination of a sound does not by itself create its tension." Our own impression from the descriptions available of this language, and from examination of a tape-recording of three speakers made available by Kodzasov, is that length should be given the primary role; strong consonants have approximately twice the duration of weak ones, and they often do result from adjoining two single consonants, at least morphologically speaking. The patterns in other Dagestanian languages are similar, but some Agul dialects have an especially large number of permitted initial long consonants.

The terms fortis/lenis have also been linked to matters of duration in other languages. For example, Bloomfield (1956) equated fortis with long and lenis with short consonants in Ojibwa. Jaeger (1983) also found length to be a significant factor. She summarized the range of phonetic events that have been claimed to produce a fortis/lenis contrast, and concluded that in two quite different languages she was investigating, Zapotec and Djauan, the phonetic factors underlying the contrast were primarily duration, glottal width and possibly closure width. She suggests that in both these languages the prototypical fortis obstruent is long, voiceless, has no variation in stop closure, and has higher amplitude noise; the prototypical lenis obstruent is short, usually voiced but often voiceless, has much variation in closure type, and lower amplitude noise. McKay (1980) concludes that the stops in Rembarrnga, another Australian language spoken in the same region as Djauan, are better described as single vs geminate rather than as fortis/lenis or voiced/voiceless, but measurements from spectrograms show that the closure durations for single stops can be extremely short, especially for coronals. Short stops are often voiced but by no means invariably. McKay comments (p. 346) that the spectrograms show "the geminate stops to be characterized by a more abrupt closure . . . and by a more prominent burst of noise at the point of release, with greater interval before voice onset after the release . . . than the corresponding single stops. These characteristics of the geminate stops may be considered indicators of fortis or tense articulation." There are thus indications that the long and short stops are not produced with articulatory movements that are identical apart from their timing. Neither McKay nor Jaeger provide any aerodynamic or articulatory data, so it is difficult to determine whether the differences they observed were also accompanied by variations in respiratory effort, or in what way the articulatory dynamics might differ, apart from the indication that the articulatory magnitude tends to be less for the lenis stops. We do not know whether any of these sounds should be regarded as fortis by our definition, but again, as when it co-varies with voicing, there does not seem to be independent use of articulatory strength as a contrastive parameter. Rather, it is an aspect of a contrast that also includes length.

The terms fortis/lenis may sometimes provide useful phonological labels for specifying a dichotomy when used language-specifically, as noted by both Jaeger (1983) and Elugbe (1980). But we agree with Catford (1977a: 203) who says "the terms tense/lax, strong/weak, fortis/lenis, and so on, should never

be loosely and carelessly used without precise phonetic specification." We
have tried to provide such a precise specification for some cases.

3.6 Summary

At the end of the previous chapter we summarized the place features needed
to distinguish stops and nasals. It is much more difficult to summarize the
other distinctive attributes of stops. In dealing with places of articulation we
noted that there are no neat boundaries between one place of articulation and
the next. This problem is even more acute in the case of some of the distinctions
among stops. Those due to differences in phonation type cannot be neatly cat-
egorized, as is apparent when we try to draw up a matrix of contrasting states
of the glottis, as shown in table 3.26. Contrasts that we do not know of are
indicated by question marks. Those we think unlikely to exist are marked by
dashed lines. Pre-aspiration has been put at the bottom of the chart because it
probably never forms the basis for contrasts among underlying forms. Glottal
closure is also noted separately, as it is more appropriately considered to be in
opposition to other places of articulation than to different phonation types. The
table then shows languages illustrating the contrasting possibilities of the other
states of the glottis.

There are no problems with the first three rows of the first three columns in
table 3.26. Voiced, voiceless unaspirated and voiceless aspirated stops contrast
with each other in many languages. The fourth column also lists reliable contrasts between creaky voice and the first two possibilities, voiced and voiceless
stops, but it is a little more difficult to list clear cases of contrasts between
creaky voiced and aspirated stops. We feel that this is likely to be an accidental
gap, largely due to our lack of knowledge of phonetic details of languages with
creaky voiced stops. Further problems come with the addition of the terms stiff
voice and slack voice; some of these cases are unlikely to be accidental gaps.
We doubt that creaky voice and stiff voice will contrast, and the same is true of
breathy voice and slack voice. It would also be possible to re-arrange the contrasts that we have shown here, and suggest that Javanese contrasts modal and
slack voice stops (instead of stiff voice and slack voice stops as we have indicated). But this would simply leave a gap at a different place in the table.

Given the evidence of table 3.26, we might be thought to have overspecified
differences among phonation types. There are three comments that can be
made on this observation. Firstly, it may be true – as far as stops are concerned.
When we consider vowels we will be able to illustrate at least one of the contrasts that is noted here as missing or dubious. Secondly, the terms listed describe what Keating (1984a) has called "major phonetic categories." There is a
continuum of phonation types, but phoneticians have no difficulty identifying
archetypal sounds corresponding to each of these terms. Thirdly, although

Table 3.26 A matrix exemplifying languages that contrast stops with different glottal states; thus Hindi is an example of a language that contrasts voiced **b** with voiceless (unaspirated) **p**

	(2) VOICELESS	(3) ASPIRATED	(4) BREATHY VOICED	(5) CREAKY VOICED	(6) STIFF VOICE	(7) SLACK VOICE
(1) VOICED	b p Hindi	b pʰ Hindi	b bɦ Hindi	b b̰ Fula	b b̬ ————	?????
(2) VOICELESS		p pʰ Hindi	p bɦ Hindi	p b̰ Fula	p b̬ Thai	p b̥ Shanghai
(3) ASPIRATED			pʰ bɦ Hindi	pʰ b̬ ?????	pʰ b̬ Thai	pʰ b̥ Shanghai
(4) BREATHY VOICED				?????	?????	————
(5) CREAKY VOICED					————	?????
(6) STIFF VOICE						b̬ b̥ Javanese

(8) PRE-ASPIRATION   (9) GLOTTAL CLOSURE

there are missing or dubious entries, the matrix in table 3.26 illustrates a number of oppositions that would be difficult to describe using a smaller set of terms (but not impossible, with a bit of pushing and shoving). As our main aim in this book is to give good phonetic descriptions of the widest possible set of sounds occurring in the world's languages, we will tentatively suggest that all the phonation types listed here need to be distinguished within whatever feature set is proposed.

Table 3.27 summarizes most of the other contrasts among stops that we have been considering in this chapter. The four possibilities in this set, ejective, voiced implosive, voiceless implosive and affricate contrast with one another, and also contrast with plosives. In addition we have noted that a few languages have stops that contrast in length, and a smaller number still have contrasts in strength, either of the airstream mechanism or of the articulatory gestures.

The phonological representation of stops should take into account all the phonetic parameters listed in tables 3.26 and 3.27, plus the additional possibilities, length and strength. The theory should also make it apparent that stops are subject to continuous variation along a number of parameters, and that within these continua there are no hard boundaries. Thus it should be clear that there is a continuum between voiced stops and voiced implosives, so that it is natural for there to be allophonic variation within this range. There must

Table 3.27 A matrix giving examples of languages that contrast various different types of stops

	(2) VOICED IMPLOSIVE	(3) VOICELESS IMPLOSIVE	(4) AFFRICATED
(1) EJECTIVE	p' ɓ Igbo	p' ɓ̥ Igbo	t' ts Navajo
(2) VOICED IMPLOSIVE		ɓ ɓ̥ Igbo	ɗ dz Avokaya
(3) VOICELESS IMPLOSIVE			ɗ̥ ts Igbo

be other continua linking voiced implosives with both creaky voiced stops and ejectives, and for many more such relations. The stops of the world's languages have to be specified not only in terms of their places of articulation as described in the previous chapter, but also in accordance with other distinctive properties as outlined in this chapter.

4

Nasals and Nasalized Consonants

This chapter describes the types of nasal and nasalized consonants that occur in the languages of the world. It is also concerned with some general questions concerning the timing relationship between oral articulation and velic function. We will divide the discussion into three principal sections; 4.1 on purely nasal consonants, 4.2 on the analysis of consonant elements that are partly nasal (that is, for part of their duration they are nasal and for part of their duration they are oral), and 4.3 on nasalized consonants (where nasal airflow accompanies oral airflow). Nasalized vowels are discussed in chapter 9 and nasalization as an accompaniment to clicks in chapter 8.

4.1 Nasals

A nasal consonant is one in which the velum is lowered and there is a closure in the oral cavity somewhere in front of the velic opening. Hence, air from the lungs is directed out through the nasal passage alone. Note that what we call simply nasals are called nasal stops by some linguists. We avoid this phrase, preferring to reserve the term 'stop' for sounds in which there is a complete interruption of airflow. Ingressive nasals can be produced but they are not known to occur in human languages, although an ingressive nasal accompaniment to clicks occurs in !Xóõ, as described in chapter 8. In principle, nasal segments could also be produced using a glottalic airstream, but we do not know of any language which uses such sounds; so-called glottalic nasals are nasals produced with a laryngeal constriction, but with pulmonic air. As noted in chapter 2, nasals occur at a subset of the places of articulation used for stops. The most retracted possible nasal is a uvular one, since with a closure in the pharynx or larynx it is not possible for air to pass into the nasal cavity. Symbols for nasals at all of the sufficiently forward places of articulation were provided in table 2.1, and examples of many of the contrasts in place of articulation between nasals are included in tables 2.2, 2.5 and 2.6. Since questions of place have already been discussed in that chapter, this topic will not be further reviewed here.

Nasals have an articulatory similarity to stops by virtue of their oral closure, but in other respects they are similar to approximants. This is because there is an uninterrupted outward flow of air that does not pass through a constriction sufficiently narrow to produce local turbulence. There are no fricative nasals. It is quite possible to narrow the velic opening so that friction is produced by the constricted airflow through the velo-pharyngeal port (while maintaining an oral closure). Catford (1977a) mentions a fricative of this type as a potential speech sound, but, as far as we know, languages do not contrast nasal consonants which vary in the degree of velic opening in this way. We believe that distinctions of type of velic stricture are linguistically irrelevant for nasals. Pike (1943) also noted that 'frictionalized nasals' can be produced by making a forward oral closure and narrowing the pharynx sufficiently to create turbulence before the air enters the nasal passage. Again we do not know of any linguistic use of this possibility.

It has, however, been suggested that nasals can differ in degree of velic opening without involving friction in the contrast. In many Austronesian languages, nasals occur alone and in nasal + stop sequences (frequently analyzed as prenasalized units). Commonly, vowels are allophonically nasalized after nasals in these languages, but are oral after the nasal + stop elements. In a number of languages of Indonesia and dialects of Malay a special development has occurred which results in the loss of the stop component in the nasal + stop sequences while preserving the oral character of the following vowels. In at least some cases these newly developed nasals remain phonetically distinguishable from the original plain nasals, as well as having distinct phonological characteristics. Durie (1985) reports that in Acehnese they have a lesser rate of airflow through the nose than the plain nasals. (They also have a longer duration). If a distinction between the width of the velic opening in the new and the original nasals is inherent in these consonants, then open and close approximation of the velo-pharyngeal port distinguishes between types of nasals, i. e. there is a difference of manner of articulation. This is essentially the way that Catford (1977a: 139–40) interprets the Acehnese situation, as a distinction between 'lightly nasal' and 'heavily nasal' nasal consonants with controlled articulatory differences in the velic aperture.

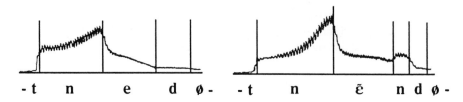

- t   n   e   d   ø -   - t   n   ẽ   n d ø -

Figure 4.1 Difference in nasal airflow in French **ne** *nez* 'nose' and **nẽ** *nain* 'dwarf' spoken in the frame *Dites ___ deux fois*, adapted from Cohn (1990: 110).

There is, however, another possibility and that is that in order to produce the required phonological contrast of oral and nasal vowel *after* a nasal which the new phonological situation requires, a start must be made on the velic closure *during* the nasal to avoid nasalization spreading to the vowel when an oral vowel follows. In this view the measured difference between the newly derived and original nasals is a coarticulatory effect. Articulatory and aerodynamic data from other languages where oral and nasal vowels are in contrast after nasal consonants, such as French, lend plausibility to this idea. In a cineradiographic study of a Parisian French speaker, Rochette (1973) found that the velum typically does not reach such a low position in a nasal preceding an oral vowel as it does in one preceding a nasal vowel. Also before an oral vowel the velum has usually been raised most of the way towards its maximum height before the release of the oral closure for the nasal occurs. Measurements of velo-pharyngeal opening from a fiberscopic study of a Swiss French speaker (Benguerel, Hirose, Sawashima and Ushijima 1977) indicate that there is a considerably smaller maximum opening of the velic aperture for the nasal in the syllable **na** than for the nasal in the syllable **nã**, and that the duration of the opening gesture is also substantially shorter. The data in Cohn (1990) shows that nasal consonants in French have lower airflow before an oral vowel than before a nasalized vowel. Her records of the distinction between **ne** *nez* 'nose' and **nẽ** *nain* 'dwarf' are shown in figure 4.1.

Aerodynamic records of a pair of contrasting words from our own investigations with an Acehnese speaker are shown in figure 4.2. These exemplars are representative of at least five repetitions of these words recorded as part of a set of data including all articulatory places (Long and Maddieson 1993). In **tçama** 'sea-mew' (a species of gull) there is an intervocalic plain bilabial nasal. The duration of the labial closure can be seen from that portion of the audio waveform and the oral flow traces in which the amplitude is low. Nasal flow increases markedly during this interval, and remains elevated for two or three vibrations of the vocal cords (about 30 ms) during the following vowel. Oral pressure is only slightly elevated while the lips are closed. (The oral pressure was recorded by means of a small tube inserted between the lips, and therefore does not show the increased pressure associated with the initial stop.) In the lower panel the contrasting pattern for the other type of nasal is shown. To

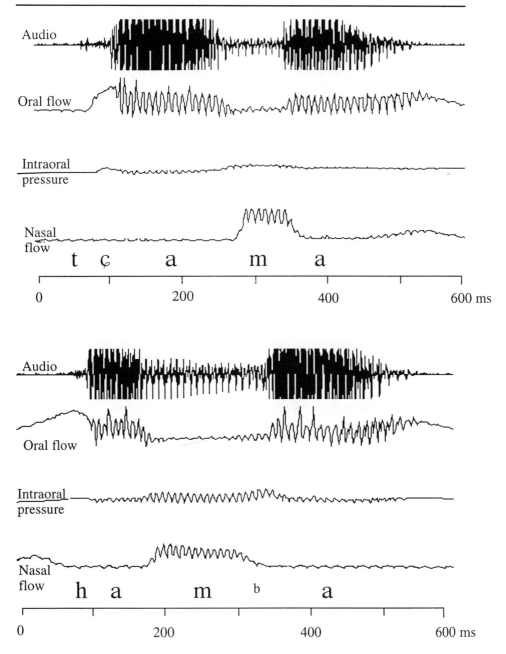

Figure 4.2 Aerodynamic records of Acehnese **tçama** 'sea-mew' and **hamᵇa** 'servant'.

distinguish the nasals this word is transcribed **ham^ba** 'servant'. Several differences are apparent. The nasal in this token is much longer, almost twice the length of the nasal in the upper part of the figure. Somewhat smaller differences in length were observed in other repetitions. In addition the intra-oral pressure has considerably larger amplitude vibrations during the labial closure; and the nasal flow trace is at the base-line by the time the oral release is made. The higher intra-oral pressure variations occur because the velum is not lowered as much. The shape of the intra-oral pressure curve indicates that the aperture to the nasal cavity is particularly small, creating greater resistance to airflow, especially at the offset of the oral closure. Thus velum lowering begins just as oral closure is made and the velum begins to be raised before oral release. The onset of this closing movement can be judged to occur about 40 ms before oral release by noting the time at which nasal flow begins to decline, and the intra-oral pressure increases.

We will call nasals of the second type orally released nasals. From these records, as well as from the experiment briefly reported by Durie (1985), we infer that the mechanism for producing such orally released nasals and preventing the spread of nasality to the following vowel involves lowering the velum to a lesser degree than in the ordinary nasals, as well as timing the whole velum-lowering gesture to coincide quite precisely with the duration of the oral articulation involved. Perhaps to permit time for this precise timing to be executed, the duration of the oral closure is lengthened in comparison with 'ordinary' nasals. The newly derived nasals in Acehnese and other languages mentioned by Durie (1985) may therefore differ from the older nasal segments in these languages simply because they are followed by oral vowels. In other words, the measurable differences in the nasals reflect a coarticulatory phenomenon like that which has been observed in nasals before oral and nasal vowels in French. Acehnese differs from French in the strictness of its requirement that the following vowel be entirely oral, but not in any other way. At this time we continue to believe that no linguistically distinctive use is made of nasals which differ in manner of articulation of the velum.

4.2 Laryngeal activity in nasals

In the great majority of languages all the nasal segments are produced with modal vocal fold vibration. However, a number of languages do employ nasals with different phonatory settings. In addition to modally voiced nasals, nasals occur with breathy voice, creaky (or laryngealized) voice, and with voicelessness due to open vocal folds. As with stops, there are substantial differences between languages in the relative timing of the oral and laryngeal gestures involved. We do not know of a language with four series of nasals differing in phonation type, but several Southeast Asian and North American

Table 4.1 Words illustrating Jalapa Mazatec nasals

	BILABIAL		ALVEOLAR		PALATAL	
VOICED	ma	'be able'	nà	'women'	ɲa	'we'
VOICELESS	m̥a	'black'	n̥ɛ	'falls'	ɲ̥á	'growth, brush'
LARYNGEALIZED	m̰e	'dies, kills'	n̰à	'shiny'		

Table 4.2 Words illustrating Hindi voiced and breathy voiced nasals (from Kelkar 1968)

	BILABIAL		DENTAL	
VOICED	kʊmar	'boy'	sʊnar	'goldsmith'
BREATHY VOICED	kʊm̤ar	'potter'	dʒʊn̤ai	'moonlight'

languages have three. Examples from Jalapa Mazatec exemplifying modally voiced, voiceless and laryngealized nasals are given in table 4.1.

Languages with three series of contrasting nasals are comparatively rare. More commonly, a language has only one series of nasals in addition to the modally voiced ones; this second series being either breathy voiced (e.g. Hindi, Marathi, Newari), or laryngealized (e.g. Montana Salish, Kwakw'ala, Stieng, Nambiquara) or voiceless (Burmese, Hmong, Iaai). Usually every voiced nasal has a corresponding nasal in these other series, although in some languages the voiceless, breathy or laryngealized nasal series has fewer members than the voiced series. For example, the Zhuǀ'hõasi dialect of !Xū (Snyman 1975) has plain voiced, laryngealized and breathy voiced nasals at the bilabial place of articulation, but only voiced nasals at the alveolar and velar places of articulation. Jino (Gai 1981) has voiced and voiceless velar nasals but only voiced bilabial, alveolar and palatal nasals. As shown in table 4.1, Mazatec lacks laryngealized palatal nasals.

Contrasts between modally voiced and breathy nasals in Hindi are illustrated in table 4.2 and figure 4.3. Dixit (1975) has studied this contrast in detail in his own speech. He showed that the breathy voiced nasals (which he calls 'aspirated nasals') have a shorter oral closure duration than their modally voiced counterparts. After the closure is formed, the initial portion of a breathy voiced nasal has modal voicing. The glottal opening gesture for breathy voice starts in the middle of the closure period some 40 ms before oral release. The peak of this glottal opening gesture occurs 30–40 ms after oral release, and 80–90 ms of 'voiced aspiration' is observed at the onset of the vowel. Dixit's photoglottographic data shows that the vocal folds open about as far as they do during an intervocalic **h**. Vocal cord vibration continues throughout the duration of the glottal gesture. Our observations generally agree with the pattern that Dixit reports. In the breathy nasal in figure 4.3 a short period of modal voicing occurs at the beginning of the nasal before breathiness begins, indicated by the greater noisiness in the signal and less well-defined resonance

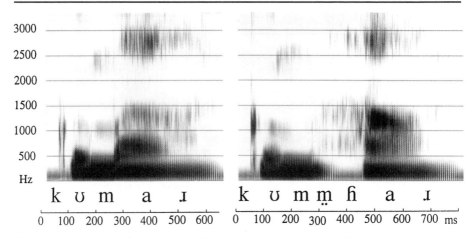

Figure 4.3 Spectrograms illustrating modally and breathy voiced nasals in Hindi in the words **kʊmar** 'boy' and **kʊmar** 'potter' respectively. The transcription below the spectrogram shows additional phonetic detail.

peaks. It is difficult to determine the precise time of the oral release but the duration of breathy voicing is about 100 ms in total and the sequence is voiced throughout. Oral and glottal gestures for intervocalic breathy voiced nasals in Hindi are thus coordinated in a similar way to those for breathy voiced stops, as discussed in chapter 3.

In Tsonga breathy voiced nasals the amount of vocal fold separation is typically much less than in Hindi, but the timing of oral and laryngeal gestures seems similar. In an aerodynamic study of six speakers Traill and Jackson (1988) report that nasal airflow is the same in the early part of both modal and breathy voiced nasals, but the mean peak airflow before the release is 11 ml/s higher in breathy voiced nasals. In their data, 25 ms after a breathy voiced nasal is released the oral airflow in the following vowel is 20 ml/s higher than after a modally voiced nasal, and 75 ms after release it is still 12 ml/s higher. A spectrogram of Tsonga modal and breathy voiced nasals is shown in figure 4.4. We have also observed other differences between languages in voicing and in the degree of breathiness that accompanies breathy nasals. For example, Marathi breathy nasals sound more breathy than those in Newari (Ladefoged 1983), and in Lianchang Yi breathy nasals in initial position have a voiceless onset which extends for about one quarter to one third of their duration. The 'aspirated nasals' of northern varieties of KeSukuma (Maddieson 1991) and of Kwanyama can also be produced with sufficiently open vocal folds so that for part of their duration they are voiceless.

In addition to Mazatec (Table 4.1), we have heard laryngealized nasals in a number of other Native American languages. In Kwakw'ala (exemplified in table 4.3) the laryngeal constriction gesture seems to be centered at the same point in time as the oral closure, so that creaky voice characterizes the middle

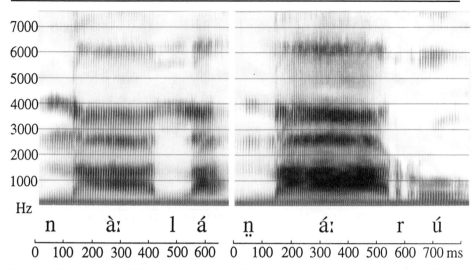

Figure 4.4 Spectrograms of Tsonga modal and breathy voiced nasals in the words nàlá 'enemy' and n̪árú 'three', as spoken by a male speaker.

Table 4.3 Words illustrating voiced and laryngealized nasals in Kwakw'ala

	BILABIAL		ALVEOLAR	
VOICED	**mixa**	'sleeping'	**naka**	'drinking'
LARYNGEALIZED	**m̰um̰uxdi**	'balsam tree'	**n̰ala**	'day'

part of the nasal, but in other languages the laryngeal constriction occurs at the beginning or the end of the nasal. In some cases the glottis may be entirely closed, temporarily preventing airflow through the nose. Figure 4.5 shows an utterance from Columbian Salish that includes two syllabic laryngealized nasals (and also a voiceless nasal). Note that the first of the laryngealized nasals shows strong, almost periodic, low frequency pulses, while the second appears to have quite turbulent airflow. In both cases, the laryngealization of the nasal culminates in a glottal stop. Phonologically speaking, in this language the laryngealization of the nasal could be regarded as an effect of a glottal stop segment, or the phonetic sequence could be labeled a 'postglottalized' nasal. By contrast, the laryngealized nasals in Montana Salish could be regarded as preglottalized nasals, in that they usually have a strong glottal constriction at the beginning of the nasal. Two speakers' productions of sm̰ú 'mare' are shown in figure 4.6. Sometimes the glottalization takes the form of a complete glottal stop followed by a nasal with what appears to be modal voice, as in the case of the speaker on the left of the figure; at other times there is a nasal which is almost entirely creaky voiced, as for the speaker on the right of the figure.

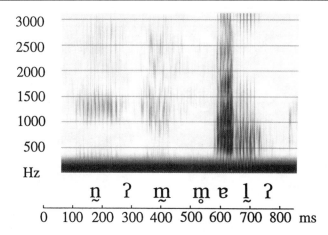

Figure 4.5 Spectrogram of the Columbian Salish word /ṇṃṃaḷ/ 'lukewarm', containing two laryngealized nasals. The transcription below the spectrogram shows additional phonetic detail.

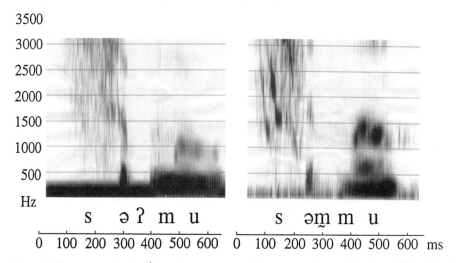

Figure 4.6 Spectrograms of sṃú **'mare'** as pronounced by two speakers of Montana Salish. In both cases there is an epenthetic ə separating the first two consonants in the initial cluster.

When there are sequences of glottal nasals, as in sṇṃṇe 'toilet' the second nasal is better described as having superimposed creaky voice, so that in a narrow transcription this word is usually [səˀnṃˀne]. In final position in Montana Salish the glottal constriction may be followed by a very creaky nasal or even one that is voiceless. Traill (1985) describes glottalized nasals in !Xóõ that "are invariably pronounced with a glottal stop preceding the nasal." He also notes that the duration of the voiced portion of the nasal in this position is shorter than it is in the plain nasals. Kashaya (Buckley 1990, 1993) places the glottal

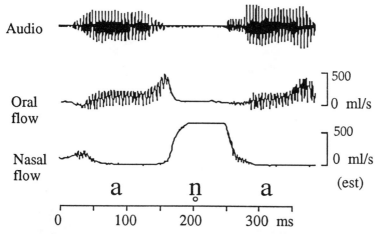

Audio

Oral
flow

Nasal
flow

a   n̥   a   (est)

Figure 4.7 Aerodynamic records of the Burmese word **(a)** n̥a 'nose' that are typical of five of the six Burmese speakers.

Table 4.4 Words contrasting voiced and voiceless nasals in Burmese

	BILABIAL	ALVEOLAR	PALATAL	VELAR	LABIALIZED ALVEOLAR
VOICED	mă	nă	ɲă	ŋâ	nʷă
	'hard'	'pain'	'right'	'fish'	'cow'
VOICELESS	m̥ă	n̥ă	ɲ̥ă	ŋ̥â	n̥ʷă
	'notice'	'nose'	'considerate'	'borrow'	'peel'

constriction at the beginning of the nasal when the consonant is syllable-initial, and at the end when it is syllable-final. There is obviously room for further language-specific variation in the way that these oral and laryngeal gestures are related to each other, but the documentation is not yet very extensive.

Voiceless nasals contrast with voiced nasals in several languages spoken in South-East Asia. Burmese examples are shown in table 4.4. These voiceless nasals usually have an open glottis for most of the articulation, but some voicing for the period just before the articulators come apart. They are also usually longer than voiced nasals, and have a higher F0 at the onset of the vowel (Maddieson 1984b).

We have recordings of the oral and nasal airflow during the pronunciation of sets of Burmese words spoken in the sentence ŋa ___ ko ye ne te 'I write ___'. A typical recording of a word beginning with a voiceless nasal consonant is illustrated in figure 4.7. Six Burmese speakers, three men and three women, all from Yangon, Myanmar, were recorded in this way, each of them saying the

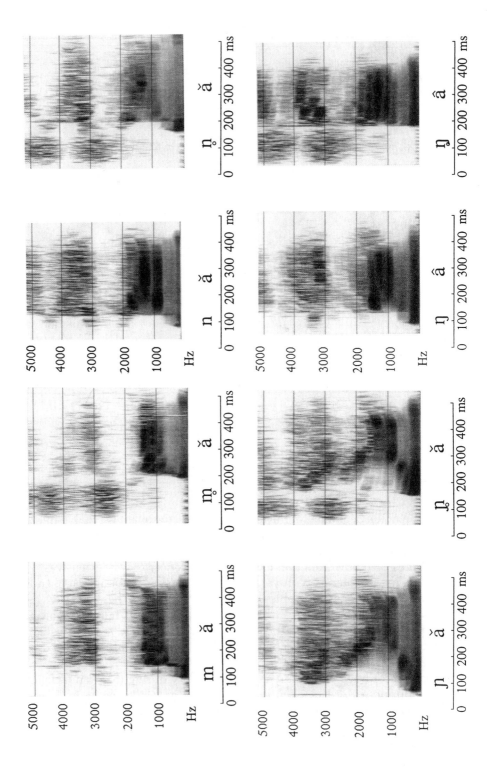

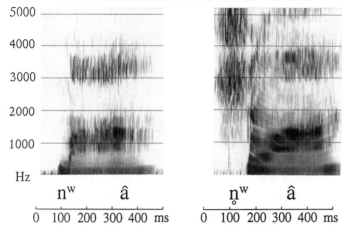

Figure 4.8 Spectrograms illustrating five pairs of Burmese voiced and voiceless nasals. The words are those listed in table 4.4.

four words in the frame sentence once. As discussed in chapter 3, there is a high volume of nasal airflow (often above the limits of the transduction system, as in the figure) suggesting that these nasals are produced with a wide open glottis and might therefore be characterized as aspirated. Measurements indicated that, for all these speakers, in the last part of the oral closure there is substantial voicing, often amounting to almost a quarter of the duration of the segment. We also recorded the speech of three female speakers of the Hmar dialect of Mizo, another language that has voiceless nasals similar to those in Burmese, finding essentially the same situation.

Ladefoged (1971) and Ohala (1975) suggest that an early onset of voicing helps to distinguish one voiceless nasal from another by making the place of articulation more apparent. This is because the voiced offglide from the nasal into the vowel displays formant transitions that are characteristic of each place of articulation. Dantsuji has shown that, in addition, the voiced portions of the voiceless nasals in Burmese "include significant cues which can distinguish points of articulation." (Dantsuji 1986: 1). There are also indications that the spectra of the voiceless portions differ; for example, bilabials may be distinguishable from voiceless nasals made at other places because of greater relative energy in the lower frequency range in the voiceless portion (Maddieson 1983). The spectrograms in figure 4.8 illustrate the contrast of voiced and voiceless nasals in the Burmese words in table 4.4. Here differences in transitional movements during the noise portion of the voiceless nasals distinguish places of articulation quite well. Note also that for these words spoken in isolation there is usually very little voicing before the release of the voiceless nasals.

It might seem that the short voiced portions at the end of Burmese and Mizo voiceless nasals could be regarded as simply part of a transition universally required by voiceless nasals. But this is not the case. Angami, another Tibeto-Burman language, spoken in the state of Nagaland, in northeastern India, has a very different series of voiceless nasals. Examples of the contrasts among Angami voiced and voiceless nasals are given in table 4.5.

Table 4.5 Words illustrating Angami contrasts involving voiced and voiceless nasals (from Blankenship, Ladefoged, Bhaskararao and Chase 1993)

	BILABIAL	ALVEOLAR	PALATAL
VOICED	mẽ	nẽ	ɲiē
	'mouth'	'to push'	'thousand'
VOICELESS	m̥è	n̥è	ɲ̊iè
	'to blow'	'to blow one's nose'	'to paste'

We have recorded a total of 9 speakers of this language. Most of our work was concerned with the Khonoma dialect; six of our speakers used this dialect, and only three were first language speakers of standard Angami. The Khonoma dialect is distinct from standard Angami in many respects, but it uses the same articulatory mechanism for the voiceless nasals. In both forms of Angami there is no voiced portion towards the end of the voiceless nasal consonant. Instead, before the voicing for the vowel begins, the oral occlusion is released while air is still flowing out through the nose.

The structure of these voiceless aspirated nasals may be seen from the aerodynamic records in figure 4.9, which shows examples of each of the three voiceless nasals extracted from a frame sentence. Significant moments in time are marked with arrows in the top example. At time (1) the articulators (in this case, the lips) close, and after a few vibrations of the vocal folds voicing ceases. (In our recordings made for acoustic analysis a longer voiced portion occurred at the onset of these nasals.) The line indicating the oral airflow slopes slightly upwards after the closure, but this is probably not due to any flow but occurs because the lips are being pushed forwards into the mouthpiece. There is a short pause after the oral closure is formed, and then the nasal airflow increases slowly. This is quite different from the sharp rise at closure seen in Burmese (Figure 4.7). At time (2) the articulators open and there is a rapid flow of air from the mouth. At the same time the nasal airflow decreases, but the velum remains down so that there is still a considerable flow of air through the nose. At time (3) voicing starts, probably with somewhat breathy vibrations, as there is a high rate of airflow through the mouth, as well as through the nose. If we take it that the vowel begins at this point, then we must consider at least the first part of it to be nasalized.

A similar sequence of events may be seen in the records for the other two voiceless nasals in this language. The oral airflow on the release of the alveolar closure (at the equivalent of time (2) in the middle set of records) is particularly strong. It even causes some artifacts on the audio record which was made via a microphone held just outside the oral mask. The nasal airflow drops at this moment in time, but it still remains at about 500 ml/s. The voiceless palatal nasal at the bottom of the figure shows a far less sharp release of the oral air. These patterns were consistent across all repetitions for all of the nine speakers

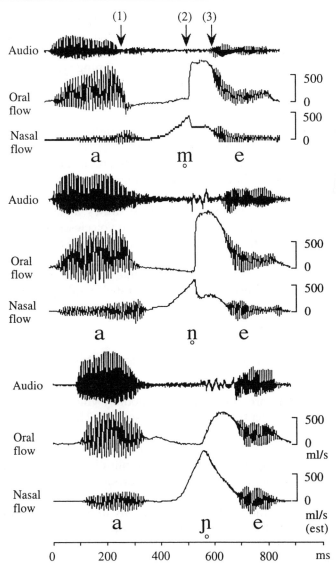

Figure 4.9 Aerodynamic records of Angami voiceless aspirated nasals. See text for explanation.

of Angami that we have recorded. Oral airflow began a little over half way through the voiceless section. Unlike the Burmese and Mizo sounds, in which there is almost always some voicing during the last part of the nasal, in Angami there was never any voicing during this part of the nasal.

Therefore these sounds are not simple voiceless nasals but are more accurately described as voiceless aspirated nasals using aspiration as a description of a timing relationship rather than as a label for a particular glottal width. From the aerodynamic records it can be inferred that the glottal opening gesture begins only after the oral closure is completed, and the peak opening must occur at or after the oral release. This is the same timing relationship between oral and glottal articulations that is seen in aspirated stops (see chapter 3, and especially figure 3.4). In these aspirated nasals the aspiration noise is nasalized for most or all of its duration.

The term 'aspirated nasal' is also sometimes encountered in connection with other voiceless nasals, e.g. in Manley's account of Sre (Manley 1972) which is said to have bilabial, alveolar and palatal aspirated nasals. In this language we suspect that voiceless nasals of the more familiar type were described in this fashion in order to draw attention to a parallel between voiceless nasals and aspirated stops in the phonology. Dai (1985) draws a distinction between voiceless and aspirated nasals; both types having voicelessness during the period of oral closure, but the aspirated type being followed by aspiration at the onset of the vowel. He says that the voiceless nasals of Achang have 'slight aspiration'; as such, they are neither exactly like simple voiceless nasals nor like aspirated nasals. The use of the term 'aspirated nasal' in connection with the breathy voiced nasals of KeSukuma has been mentioned above.

Acoustic structure of voiced nasals

As noted above, nasals are most frequently modally voiced. Voiced nasals are perceptually quite distinct from other speech sounds. The steady state portion of a voiced nasal consonant is characterized acoustically by a low frequency first resonance with greater intensity than the other resonances. The higher resonances have low amplitude. The overall amplitude of voiced nasals is usually less than that of adjacent vowels. During production of a nasal, air flows through the pharyngeal cavity and via the velo-pharyngeal port into the nasal cavity and out through the nostrils. The oral cavity in front of the velo-pharyngeal port forms a side chamber to this pathway. Both theoretical and empirical studies of the spectral properties of nasals indicate that this side chamber contributes a spectral zero or anti-resonance (Fant 1960, Fujimura 1962, Recasens 1983). The frequency of this zero is inversely related to the volume of the cavity, which in turn results from the position of the tongue (and other moveable tissues) in the front of the mouth. A more forward articulation of the tongue or a lower position of the tongue body will produce larger cavity volumes. More retracted articulations or a higher position of the tongue body will produce smaller cavity volumes. The frequency of the first nasal resonance and the oral zero are both higher the nearer the oral articulation is to the uvular region. The increase in the nasal resonance may be due to the decreasing size of the pharyngeal cavity as the tongue is positioned further back, and/or the size of the

Table 4.6 Principal acoustic features of Catalan nasals

	m	n	ɲ	ŋ
FIRST NASAL FORMANT	250	280	290	300
NASAL ZERO	(not given)	1780	2650	3700

Table 4.7 Mean nasal zeros for the four coronal nasals of Arrernte

PLACE	MEAN	s.d.	*n*
DENTAL	1506	188	33
ALVEOLAR	1403	167	44
RETROFLEX	1634	201	41
PALATO-ALVEOLAR	2094	233	22

velo-pharyngeal aperture itself, which is narrower when the back of the tongue is raised. The nasal cavities themselves do not vary appreciably.

There have been relatively few studies of the acoustic distinctions between nasals in natural languages, and many of those that do exist are limited to **m** and **n** (Kurowski and Blumstein 1987, Qi and Fox 1992). However, Recasens (1983) provides some acoustic data on the four contrasting nasals in Catalan. Means of the first nasal resonance from word-final nasals for 13 Catalan speakers are given in table 4.6. His estimates of the nasal zero frequency for one of these speakers are also reported.

We have made our own estimates of the frequencies of the nasal zeros in the four coronal nasals of Arrernte. If the four coronal places involve shifts in only the location of the tongue contact, then the nasal zero will rise as the articulation becomes more retracted. If, in addition, tongue body position differs, then an articulation with a (presumptively) more retracted contact location but lower tongue body position might have a lower nasal zero than one with a more forward contact location.

Estimated values of nasal zeros were obtained for 139 tokens of plain (i.e. non-labialized) nasals in Arrernte from the average power spectrum computed over a 10 ms window located midway through the closure of the nasal. Following a technique analogous to that used by Recasens, the nasal zero was considered to be the largest negative peak located between F1 and F2 in the spectral display. The corresponding wide band spectrogram was simultaneously examined to verify that the chosen value coincided with the center frequency of the appropriate area of attenuated amplitude throughout the nasal. Results of these measurements are reported in table 4.7. A highly significant effect of place was found in a one-way analysis of variance, $F(3,136) = 66.0$, $p > 0.0001$. All place pairings are significantly different at better than the .05 level by Fisher's PLSD test (adapted for unequal cell sizes).

If only contact location was involved in the more forward coronal place contrasts, the alveolar place should have a higher nasal zero than the dental since it is a more retracted place. Instead, the alveolar zero is significantly lower. However, if the dental is pronounced laminally, then the high tongue blade position would reduce the oral cavity volume and raise the frequency of the zero. The combination of higher tongue body (and a raised jaw) in a laminal dental makes for a smaller cross-sectional area between the roof of the mouth and the upper surface of the tongue, hence a smaller oral cavity volume, than for a apical alveolar. If the tongue posture were the same in the dental and alveolar cases we would not see the observed result.

The retroflex and palato-alveolar nasals both have nasal zeros at higher frequencies than the dental or alveolar nasals, as expected. The palato-alveolar has a significantly higher value than the retroflex. While we do not know the specific nature of the Arrernte nasal articulations used by this speaker, the observed values would be consistent with the palatal being laminal and the retroflex apical as we saw for Arrernte plosives in chapter 2, figure 2.12.

Despite these acoustic differences, nasals with different places of articulation are poorly discriminable one from another on the basis of the voiced steady state portion isolated from the transitions which might precede or follow it (Malécot 1956, Nord 1976). Coarticulation with adjacent vowels also may have a strong influence on the perception of place of articulation for nasals (Zee 1981, Kitazawa and Doshita 1984). In particular, these studies suggest that high front vowels present an environment in which bilabial nasals are heard as if produced with a further back articulation. This effect may have contributed to the change of Classical Latin **m** to **n** in Old French in monosyllabic words, such as *rem → rien, meum → mien* (final nasals were lost except in monosyllables, and later changes have resulted in nasalized vowels rather than final nasals), and to the reduction of the number of contrasting final nasals in Chinese (Zee 1985).

4.3 Partially Nasal Consonants

Since the raising or lowering of the velum is independent of the movements of (most of) the oral articulators, an essentially static position of these articulators can be maintained while the position of the velum is changed. In this section we will discuss the existence of sounds which could be described as being partially nasal, that is, the velic position is changed during their production so that for part of their duration they are nasal and for part of their duration they are oral. It is possible to imagine a much larger number of potential categories of partially nasal consonants than those which seem actually to have been observed. If we consider just those consonants produced with the pulmonic airstream, then the observed partially nasal consonants fall into only four classes. These are prenasalized stops (including affricates), prenasalized fricatives,

prestopped nasals, and, perhaps, prenasalized trills. In all but prestopped nasals, the nasal portion of the segment occurs before the non-nasal part. We do
not know of any cases of prenasalized lateral or central approximants; nor do
we know of any types of segments other than prestopped nasals in which the
nasal portion follows the non-nasal portion. Surface 'medionasal' segments –
stops with an oral onset and offset, but a nasal medial portion – are reported in
Kaingang (Wiesemann 1972). These are the variants of prenasalized stops that
occur medially after oral vowels.

Pre- and postnasalization do not seem to occur with glottalic consonants. We
know of no cases of prenasalized implosives. Prenasalized ejectives are at best
marginal. Although voiceless stops preceded by nasals in Zulu may be pronounced as ejectives (e.g. class 9/10 prefix /N/ + stem /-pala/ "antelope" =
[imp'ala]) it is probable that the resulting strings do not have the structure of
prenasalized ejective stops, since the function of the prothetic vowel **i-** found
here seems to be to provide a syllable nucleus for the nasal to attach to. This
would be unexpected before a unitary prenasalized segment, and the nasal
may be taken as simply a coda consonant in this initial syllable. Prenasalization
does occur with clicks, but we will postpone discussion of this type of sound
until chapter 9.

Prenasalized stops

The similarity in the mode of production between plosives and nasals results
in a connection between nasals and stops in the phonology of many languages.
In many cases a sequence of a nasal and a stop must be homorganic; for example, in English, nasal + stop sequences within a morpheme must be homorganic. In such a sequence the nasal portion is terminated and the stop initiated simply by raising the velum. A change in laryngeal setting may also occur
during the sequence. It has often been argued that similar gestural sequences
in some languages should be treated as unitary segments, particularly if they
occur in syllable-initial position. In this case, these segments are known as
prenasalized stops, and are often notated by a superscript nasal symbol preceding the stop symbol, i.e. as **ᵐb, ⁿd, ᵑg** etc., although where no ambiguity
exists it is customary not to use superscripting but to simply write a nasal and
a stop symbol, viz **mb, nd, ŋg**. This raises the question of whether there is a
phonetic distinction between prenasalized stops and nasal + stop sequences.
(Note that we are here concerned only with whether phoneticians should distinguish between prenasalized stops and nasal + stop sequences not with the
question of the phonological representation of such a distinction.) The discussion can also be taken to apply to prenasalized affricates and fricatives, but for
convenience we will confine our examples to stops.

On the face of it, it would seem that we need to make such a distinction,

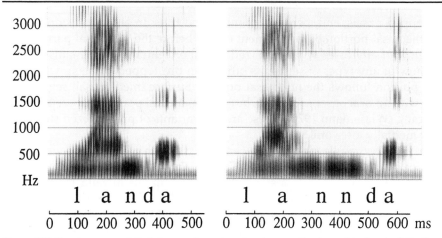

Figure 4.10 Spectrograms of Sinhala words contrasting 'prenasalized stop' in **la.nda** 'blind' and heterosyllabic nasal + stop sequence in **lan.nda** 'thicket'.

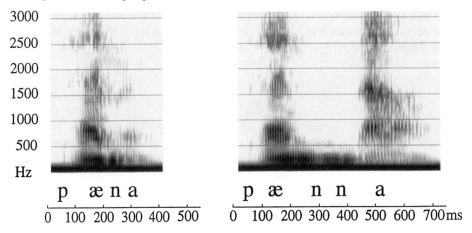

Figure 4.11 Spectrograms illustrating single and geminate nasals in Sinhala in the words **pæna** 'question' and **pænna** 'jumped'.

given that there are reported to be languages which distinguish between prenasalized stops and nasal + stop sequences. One frequently cited example is Sinhala (Jones 1950, Feinstein 1979). The contrast referred to this way is illustrated by pairs of examples such as the words normally cited as **landa** 'thicket' and **la^{n}da** 'blind'. Spectrograms of these words are provided in figure 4.10. We measured the duration of the interval from the onset of the oral closure for the nasal to the burst of the stop in several such pairs in recordings of two Sinhala speakers. For both speakers the mean duration of this interval in the so-called prenasalized stops was close to 100 ms. For one speaker the contrasting sequence was twice as long, and for the second closer to three times as long, 275

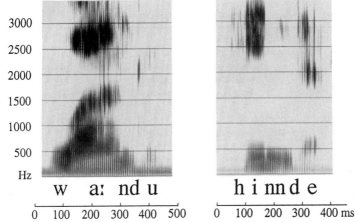

Figure 4.12 Spectrograms illustrating 'prenasalized stop' and geminate nasal + stop in Fula in the words **waandu** 'monkey' and **hinnde** 'steamer'.

ms. The additional duration is added in the nasal portion, resulting in a nasal of comparable duration to a geminate nasal, as may be seen from the Sinhala examples of single and geminate nasals in figure 4.11. Note also that the 'prenasalized stop' in **la^{n}da** is of comparable duration to nasal + stop durations in other languages, such as English, where word-medial nasal + stop clusters have durations in the range 90–80 ms according to Vatikiotis-Bateson (1984) and Lisker (1984). On a phonetic basis at least, this contrast in Sinhala is more appropriately described as a contrast of single versus geminate nasals followed by stops, that is [**mb, nd**] vs [**mmb, nnd**], etc. The phonological difference between these is principally that the geminate nasals are heterosyllabic, but the single nasal + stop sequences form a syllable onset (Cairns and Feinstein 1982).

There is a similar contrast in Fula, but whereas in Sinhala nasal + stop elements only occur word-internally, Fula prenasalized stops may appear word-initially. However, the longer nasal + stop sequence does not occur in initial position. Fula examples are illustrated in figure 4.12. As in Sinhala, we feel that the phonetic difference between these examples is best described as one between single and geminate nasals preceding a homorganic stop. The phonological patterns of Fula certainly support such an analysis: for example, when a suffix beginning with a prenasalized stop is added to a stem with a final consonant, the resulting form has a longer nasal portion (Arnott 1970, McIntosh 1984). Examples of this suffixation process are given in table 4.8.

In our recordings of Fula these 'geminate prenasalized stops' do not have much greater duration than might be expected from concatenation of a single nasal and a stop in some other language. And our measurements on a number of words with non-geminated prenasalized stops from two speakers showed that the total duration of the nasal and stop portions was in the range 45–100 ms, with a mean close to 60 ms.

Table 4.8 Fula single and geminate 'prensalized stops'

No final consonant in stem
    stem **waa** + noun class suffixes **-ndu** / **-ɗi**
                    (initial consonant mutation also relates to noun class)
                    waandu   'monkey'
                    baaɗi   'monkeys'

Final stem consonant
    stem **biC** + noun class suffixes **-ŋga** / **-ko**
                    biŋŋga   'big child'
                    bikko   'big children'

Table 4.9 Mean duration of medial prenasalized consonants and selected other consonants in Fijian

	MEAN	S.D.	N
Prenasalized stops: 11 speakers from three dialect areas			
mb	132	22.2	62
nd	131	23.8	63
nḍ	114	25.5	65
ŋg	114	32.6	65
Other medial consonants: 6 Standard Fijian speakers only			
t	125	19.5	24
k	116	30.1	24
l	117	12.3	21

It might be argued that the shortness of this duration is evidence for a distinction between a prenasalized stop and a nasal + stop sequence. Herbert (1986), in his monograph on prenasalization, suggests that the phonetic characterization of a prenasalized consonant is precisely that it is a sequence of homorganic nasal and non-nasal elements that are approximately equivalent to the duration of 'simple' consonants in the same language. By implication, this means that a nasal + stop sequence would be longer than a simple stop. We feel that this view rests on false assumptions and, furthermore, does not take into account the variability in timing of segments both within and across languages.

As Browman and Goldstein (1986) have shown, the sequences **mp, mb** in English do not necessarily have any longer acoustic or articulatory durations than the single segments **p, b, m**. They also show that the timing of these English bilabials is very similar to that which they find in word-initial **p, m, mb** in the KiVunjo dialect of KiChaka, where **mb** is usually analyzed as a prenasalized stop. Similarly, in Fijian, the acoustic duration of prenasalized stops (Maddieson 1990a, Maddieson and Ladefoged 1993) is very comparable to that of other consonants in medial position as the data in table 4.9 shows. But in measurements from a KeSukuma speaker intervocalic voiced bilabial and velar prenasalized stops had a mean duration of 144 ms, whereas intervocalic voiced bilabial and velar stops had a mean duration of 43 ms after long vowels and 30 ms after short vowels, and intervocalic bilabial nasals a mean duration of 94 ms after long vowels and 73 ms after short vowels.

Variations in the duration of homorganic nasal + stop sequences can be seen as due to variable implementation of a process of gestural economy. Two adjacent segments which require homologous articulatory gestures may be produced with a single combined gesture. In the present case the two oral closure gestures for the nasal and the stop may be pictured as overlapping, with both the release of the first and the closure formation of the second suppressed in the interests of economy. The degree to which potential gestural economy is exploited varies from language to language, and within languages varies according to linguistic environment and speech style. In many Bantu languages, this kind of gestural economy produces a lengthening of a preceding vowel, which extends into the time period 'vacated' by the compression of the nasal + stop. The process operates to different degrees in different Bantu languages; more in LuGanda and CiYao, less in KeSukuma and Runyambo (Maddieson and Ladefoged 1993, Hubbard in press). In Austronesian and Australian languages with prenasalized stops such vowel lengthening has not been observed.

Voicing control in nasal + stop sequences

Another reason, apart from the durational considerations discussed above, for not treating 'prenasalized' segments as distinct elements from the phonetic point of view is the independent control of voicing within the sequence. In most languages that have been said to have prenasalized stops only voiced sequences occur. However, in those languages where the stop component may be either voiced or voiceless the nasal component of the sequence is generally voiced regardless of the voicing state of the stop (Herbert 1986). Thus, in many Bantu languages such as KeSukuma (Batibo 1976) there are both 'voiced' and 'voiceless' prenasalized stops. In KeSukuma the voiceless prenasalized stops are quite strongly aspirated, as illustrated in the aerodynamic records in figure 4.13 (see Maddieson 1991 for further discussion), and this is true for most of the related languages. In phonetic terms the voicing difference between such pairs lies not in the nasal but solely in the stop. In other words, the voicing state is actively changed in the middle of sequences such as **mp, nt, ŋk**. Although nasal segments themselves are usually voiced, a change of voicing within a unitary segment is quite exceptional.

It should not be thought that aspiration necessarily accompanies voiceless prenasalized stops. The distinction between the two series of prenasalized stops in the Hmong dialects of Thailand has sometimes been reported as a

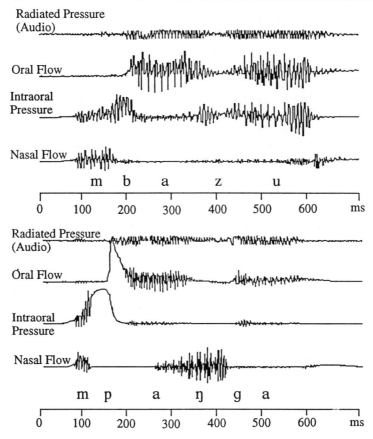

Figure 4.13 Aerodynamic records illustrating voiced and voiceless prenasalized stops in KeSukuma in the words **mbazu** 'goat' and **mpaŋga** 'alive (person)'.

voicing contrast (Lyman 1979). Smalley (1976) transcribes the contrast phonemically in the labial case as between /**mp**/ and /**mph**/ but gives the phonetic realization of /**mp**/ as [**mb**], and so on for other places of articulation, implying that these segments are similar to those in KeSukuma. In fact, the distinction is between voiceless aspirated and unaspirated, with the nasal portion voiced and the non-nasal portion voiceless in both cases. Spectrograms of selected tokens from a word list recorded by a speaker of the Hmong Daw (White Hmong) dialect are given in figure 4.14 to illustrate this point. An additional detail noted in this language is that the duration of the stop portion is strongly related to the place of articulation, increasing the further back the articulation is. The figure shows bilabial and uvular cases in order to indicate the range of variation observed with this speaker. With bilabials the stop closure can be extremely short, as in the examples shown, but

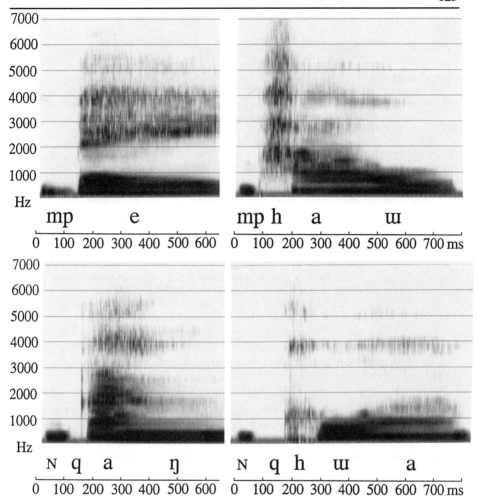

Figure 4.14 Spectrograms illustrating voiceless unaspirated and voiceless aspirated bilabial and uvular prenasalized stops as pronounced by a female speaker of Hmong Daw. The words are **mpe** 'name', **mphaɯ** 'turbulent', **ɴqaŋ** 'thatch' and **ɴghɯa** 'dried up'.

uvular stop closures demonstrate maximum duration. Strong and noisy aspiration follows the release of the aspirated cases. This portion remains relatively similar in duration across differences in place.

On the other hand, voicing assimilation is not unusual in clusters; and some languages do have voicing assimilation in nasal + stop sequences under some conditions. Thus, in Bura, utterance-initial nasals preceding stops share the voicing category of the stop that follows them. This occurs in both homorganic and heterorganic nasal + stop sequences. Spectrograms exemplifying the three-way phonetic contrast of **nd, n̥t, m̥t,** are shown in figure 4.15. When these

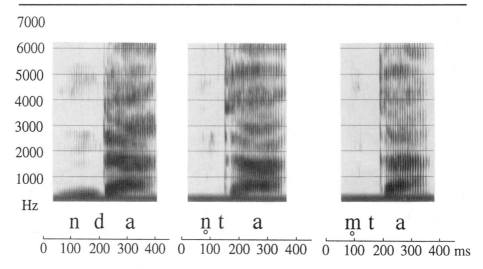

Figure 4.15 Spectrograms illustrating voicing assimilation in homorganic and heterorganic nasal +
stop sequences in Bura in the words /**nda**/ 'cook', /**nta**/ 'tear (vb.)', /**mta**/ 'death'.

devoiced nasals are preceded by a voiced segment in context they are voiced,
and there is no reason to assume that Bura has underlying voiceless nasals
(Maddieson 1983).

Devoicing of nasals before voiceless stops also occurs in a number of Bantu
languages in southwestern and northeastern parts of Africa, such as Ndongo
and Kwambi (Baucom 1974) and Pokomo, Pare, Shambaa and Bondei
(Hinnebusch 1975). We have heard examples from Bondei and note that the
phenomenon is different from that in Bura. Bura has a completely open glottis
and a high volume of airflow in its voiceless preconsonantal nasals so that they
sound similar to the voiceless nasals in Burmese. In Bondei there seems to be a
less forceful airflow and the vocal cords, though apart, are vibrating weakly.
The result is that a very low amplitude periodic component can be observed
for all or part of the duration of the nasal. This phenomenon can be shown
more clearly in a waveform display, as in figure 4.16, than in a spectrogram. In
this token the nasal is acoustically noisy throughout, but at its beginning and
end a weak periodic wave can be observed, indicating vocal cord vibration.
The differences between Bura and Bondei suggest that the manner of the voicing assimilation cannot be quite the same in these two languages. In Bondei,
unlike in Bura, the stop releases are aspirated. This fact is perhaps related to
the differences in the devoicing process, in that the peak of the glottal opening
gesture is presumably later in relation to formation of the oral closure in
Bondei than in Bura.

The Bondei pattern is related to the breathy voiced nasals of Kwanyama and
KeSukuma discussed earlier. In these languages, the oral stop portion of a

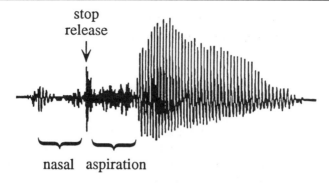

stop
release

nasal   aspiration

Figure 4.16 Waveform illustrating weak vocal cord vibration in devoiced nasal preceding aspirated stop in the Bondei word **ntaa** 'tilapia fish'.

voiceless prenasalized stop has been lost and what remains is a nasal on which a glottal opening gesture is overlaid.

Whatever the facts concerning articulatory timing and voicing may be in a given case, the motivation for talking of prenasalized stops, rather than of a nasal + stop sequence, is often phonological rather than phonetic (in languages which do not have a within-language contrast of the type found in Sinhala and Fula). A unitary analysis may be preferred because the language has no other consonant sequences in any position, as in Fijian (Milner 1956), or has no other consonant sequences in initial position, as in Gbeya (Samarin 1966). We note that the unitary analysis also avoids recognizing a syllable onset with the structure nasal + stop. Syllable onsets with this structure violate the expectation that more sonorous elements (in this case nasals) appear closer to the syllable nucleus than less sonorous ones (stops), in conformity with well-established ideas of the sonority hierarchy (cf. Jespersen 1897–9, Hooper 1976, Steriade 1982). In fact, violations of this particular kind seem to be rather prevalent.

A further question on prenasalization concerns whether any distinction is implied by the use of both transcriptions like [^{m}b, ^{n}d] and like [m^b, n^d], which have sometimes been distinguished as 'prenasalized stops' versus 'poststopped nasals'. The latter were noted by Y. R. Chao in Zhongshan (Chao 1948) and Taishan (Chao 1951), two Yue dialects of Chinese. More recently, Chan (1980) explicitly distinguishes between the two possibilities in her account of Zhongshan phonology. The basis for the proposed distinction lies in the perception that sometimes the nasal and sometimes the stop portion is more prominent. We do not know if this reflects a difference in relative durations of the components, or a difference in the amplitude of the burst for the stop in one case as opposed to the other. Historically, the Chinese poststopped nasals derive from simple nasals, in whose production, as Chao comments "the nasal cavity closed too early and the oral cavity opened too late" in the transition from the nasal to the following vowel. Given this historical origin, it seems quite likely that the poststopped nasals would have a relatively weak burst, but no comparative study has yet been carried out.

Prestopped nasals

Similar questions to those raised in the discussion of prenasalized stops arise in connection with the possibility of a phonetic distinction between a sequence of a nasal preceded by a stop and a unitary segment which might be called a prestopped nasal or a nasally released stop. We do not know of a language in which it has been proposed that these two types of elements contrast, but the phonological patterns suggest that different analyses are appropriate in different cases. In some languages a syllable-initial homorganic sequence of a stop and a nasal is quite uncontroversially treated as a sequence of two separate segments. Russian is one such language. In Russian, many different syllable-initial consonant sequences occur, and stop + nasal sequences are just one of the possible types. Moreover, many of the words with initial stop + nasal sequences appear in paradigms which also include forms that have a vowel separating the stop from the nasal. Some examples are given in table 4.10. From these considerations, the separate status of the nasal and stop elements is clear.

Elsewhere, particularly in Australia, languages have been described as having 'prestopped nasal' segments. In the case of the Australian languages there is often a close connection between a simple nasal and a stop + nasal sequence. In Diyari (Austin 1981), intervocalic apical alveolar and laminal dental nasals following primary stress may optionally alternate with a stop + nasal sequence, provided that the initial consonant is not a nasal. In other positions simple nasals occur. In Arabana and Wangganuru (Hercus 1973) there is a similar, but apparently not optional, rule that also applies to bilabial nasals. Finally in Olgolo (Dixon 1970, 1980), because the initial consonants which controlled the distribution have been dropped, simple nasal and stop + nasal are in contrast in intervocalic position. A similar process has occurred in Arrernte (Dixon 1980). In this language initial vowels have also been dropped, so that

Table 4.10 Partial paradigms of Russian nouns with stop + nasal sequences ('palatalized' stops and nasals are represented as laminal post-alveolars, transcribed as ḏ, ṉ)

	'bottom'	'day'
NOM. SG.	dno	ḏeṉ
GEN. SG.	dna	ḏṉa
NOM. PL.	'doṉja	ḏṉi
GEN. PL.	'doṉjev	ḏṉej

Table 4.11 Arrernte words illustrating plain nasals, and pre- and postnasalized stops (from Maddieson and Ladefoged 1993)

PLAIN NASAL		PRENASALIZED STOP		PRESTOPPED NASAL	
anəmə	'sitting'	ampəɟə	'knee'	apməɟə	'camp'
mwarə	'good'	mpwaɟə	'make'	pmwaɟə	'coolamon'
aɲə	'tree'	aɲʈəmə	'aching'	kəʈnə	'top'
aməŋə	'fly'	aŋkəmə	'speaks'	akŋə	'carry'

the prestopped nasals may occur in word-initial position. None of the unambiguous consonant sequences of the language are permitted in this position. Examples of Arrernte words with pre- and post-nasalized stops are given in table 4.11. Nothing in the descriptions of these languages suggests to us that there is anything phonetically remarkable about the 'prestopped nasals' in these languages, or that they are different in kind from the sequences that occur in Russian. The phonetic problem is again one of stating the timing relationship between oral and velic articulations, and relating the phonetic facts to appropriate phonological structures.

Both phonetically prestopped nasals and post-nasalized stops occur in Eastern Arrernte. The prestopped nasals are variants of plain nasals and are voiced throughout; they are illustrated in chapter 7 in figure 7.23. The post-nasalized stops, exemplified in table 4.11, have a voiceless stop release.

Another instance in which nasal release occurs is in some of the languages which are usually described as having unreleased final stops. A good example is Vietnamese. In this language word-final stops are usually released, but the release is by lowering the velum while the oral closure is maintained, so that a short voiceless nasal is produced.

Prenasalization and trills

Some other sounds combine prenasalization and trilling. Trills are primarily discussed in chapter 7, but we will briefly consider here the occurrence of prenasalized stops with a trilled release. The known types are of two sorts, bilabial and apical (alveolar or post-alveolar in place). Both occur in certain languages spoken in the Admiralty Islands north of the New Guinea mainland (Ladefoged, Cochran and Disner 1977). Kele examples are given in table 4.12. Words containing prenasalized bilabial and alveolar stops with trilled release are illustrated in the spectrograms in figure 4.17.

There are some salient differences in the roles that these two sorts of trills usually play in the phonology of the languages concerned. Whereas apical trills in general are common sounds and the prenasalized ones are not limited to

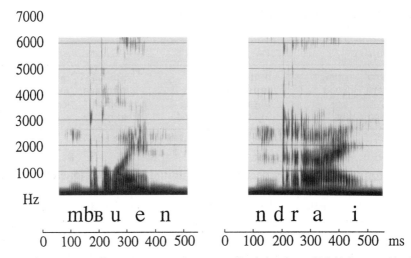

Figure 4.17 Spectrograms illustrating contrasting prenasalized alveolar and bilabial stops with trilled release in Kele in the words **ndrai** '(your) blood' and **mbʙuen** 'its fruit'.

Table 4.12. Words illustrating bilabial and alveolar prenasalized stops with trilled release in Kele.

Prenasalized bilabial		Prenasalized alveolar		Alveolar	
mbʙuen	'it's fruit'	**ndrikei**	'leg'	**riuriu**	sp. of insect
mbʙulei	'greens'	**ndruin**	'his/her bone'	**raman**	'red'
mbʙuin	'her vagina'	**ndrileŋ**	'song'	**rarai**	sp. fish

particular vowel contexts, the prenasalized instances are virtually the only occurrence of any bilabial trills in the world's languages, and are usually still limited in their occurrence to the narrow set of environments in which they developed (Maddieson 1989b, Demolin 1988). Apart from a few exceptions which remain unexplained in Nias (Catford 1988b), and the special case of Luquan Yi fricative vowels (see chapter 9), all bilabial trills historically developed from a sequence of a prenasalized bilabial stop followed by a relatively high back rounded vowel, i.e. a sequence such as **mbu**. These segments remain prenasalized and contain a short oral stop phase which is released into a trill that occupies much of the anticipated duration of the following vowel. In languages such as Na?ahai, where the trilled release is in complementary distribution with a simple prenasalized bilabial stop, the bilabial trill articulation is equally open to being regarded as a modification of **u** that occurs after a prenasalized bilabial stop as to being regarded as a modification of **mb** that occurs before **u**.

Table 4.13 shows the results of measurements on prenasalized bilabial stops with trilled release in three Austronesian languages and the Camerounian language Nweh. The duration of the oral stop closure before the trill is exactly comparable to that in prenasalized voiced stops in other languages, where it is

Table 4.13 Mean measurements of prenasalized bilabial stops with trilled release in three Austronesian languages and in Nweh (1 speaker each, number of tokens in parentheses after language name)

	DURATION OF NON-NASAL ([b]) CLOSURE	DURATION OF PERIOD IN TRILL	FREQUENCY RATE OF TRILLING
Kurti (*n* = 37)	33.8 ms	37.6 ms	26.8 Hz
s.d.	5.0	3.5	2.8
Na?ahai (*n* = 22)	30.7 ms	45.6 ms	22.1 Hz
s.d.	1.2	3.7	1.8
Uripiv (*n* = 14)	33.8 ms	37.3 ms	27.2 Hz
s.d.	12.8	4.5	3.8
Nweh (*n* = 15)	33.1 ms	44.1 ms	23.1 Hz
s.d.	8.12	3.73	2.1
Mean across languages	32.85	41.15	24.8

usually on the order of 30 ms. The closure period in the trill is considerably shorter, resulting in the duration of the period from the release of one closure of the trill to the release of the next being only a little longer than the stop closure. Most interestingly, the rate of trill vibration for the lips is only slightly slower than that observed in apical trills despite the larger mass of the lips. This point will be taken up in chapter 7.

The use of a trill as a modification of the release of a coronal stop occurs in a number of languages. Stops of this kind are reported in Austronesian languages such as Malagasy (Dyen 1971), Fijian (Milner 1956) and several of the Admiralty Islands languages in addition to Kele. The Fijian case is reportedly a trill following a voiced prenasalized post-alveolar stop. But in a study of 11 speakers of Fijian, Maddieson (1991) observed that trilling was in fact very rare at the release of this stop. The major distinguishing characteristic is rather that the place of articulation is postalveolar.

4.4 Nasalized Consonants

There are two major types of nasalized consonants. One type is a nasalized click. Since the click-producing mechanism of the velaric airstream operates in front of the velic opening, pulmonic air may quite freely pass through the nasal passage simultaneously with the production of a click, resulting in a nasalized click. A variety of different laryngeal settings may also be employed, so that this nasal accompaniment to the click can be voiced, voiceless, breathy, and so on. A separate chapter is devoted to clicks, and these nasalized clicks will be discussed there.

Table 4.14 Nasalized and non-nasalized voiceless glottal approximants in Kwangali

h̃oh̃o	'devil's thorn'	hompa	'chief'
h̃uh̃wa	'fowl'	huma	'bite'
muh̃o	'kind of spear'	muhona	'master'
koh̃i	'beneath, under'	ruhunga	'feather'

The second major type of nasalized consonants are oral continuants (fricatives and approximants) produced with a lowered velum so that air is also free to pass out through the nasal passage. These types of segments occur most often as allophonic variants of their non-nasalized counterparts in positions where nasality spreads from a nasal consonant or a nasalized vowel in the neighbourhood. The segments said to be involved are usually voiced. For example, standard accounts and our own observations of Yoruba agree that the voiced approximants **w** and **j** are nasalized when they precede a nasalized vowel. In some languages a nasal segment can be accompanied by anticipatory nasalization, potentially of several preceding syllables, as occurs in Guarani (Gregores and Suarez 1967, Lunt 1973). (Guarani also has been variously analyzed as having inherently nasalized morphemes or a set of nasalized vowels, and nasalization also spreads from these. The facts are phonologically complex and a full presentation will not be attempted here). In the course of this spreading of nasalization, nasalized voiced continuants and approximants are phonetically derived. Gregores and Suarez note that the nasalized counterparts of the voiced fricatives **v** and **ɣ** are the voiced approximants **ʋ̃** and **ɰ̃**.

Languages clearly differ in the degree to which nasalization spreads to and through adjacent segments and the direction of the spread, and hence in the number and kind of surface nasalized segments that occur, as has been shown by Cohn (1990, 1993). The acoustic consequences of a lowered velum are also not uniform for segments of different types. There is very little auditory difference between nasalized and non-nasalized voiceless fricatives and approximants; and it seems likely that articulatory assimilation of voiceless sounds to adjacent nasal or nasalized segments is more common than is usually reported. We believe that in Yoruba, for example, the voiceless approximant **h** is usually also nasalized before a nasalized vowel, although this is not noted in descriptions of the language. Nasalization of **h** is clearly demonstrated in Central Igbo in a kymogram tracing published by Carnochan (1948), and in Sundanese in data published by Cohn (1993). We are less sure that the nasalized voiced and voiceless labiodental and alveolar fricatives reported for Igbo by Green and Igwe (1963) actually have simultaneous nasal airflow, rather than being elements that occur with nasalization of the following vowel – the device of marking the consonants as nasalized being employed, as noted by Williamson (1969), to identify the limited set of consonants that can begin syllables with nasalized vowels.

However, nasalized voiceless approximants do occur contrastively in some

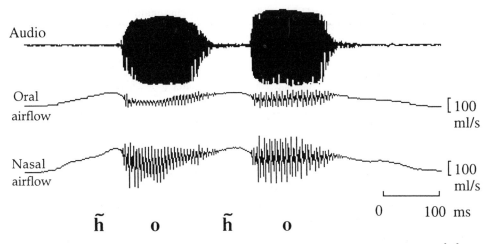

Figure 4.18 Aerodynamic records of voiceless glottal fricatives in the Kwangali word **hoho** *nhonho* 'devil's thorn'.

Southern Bantu languages. Both Kwangali and ThiMbukushu, two Kavango languages spoken in northern Namibia, have clear contrasts between **h** and **h̃**. Near-minimal pairs from Kwangali are shown in table 4.14. Aerodynamic data for the first word in table 4.14 are shown in figure 4.18. During the initial and the intervocalic consonant there is both oral and nasal airflow. In both cases the peak velocity in the nasal airflow is greater than that in the oral airflow. It is also evident that there is a great deal of nasal airflow throughout both vowels. These vowels are both phonologically **o** (there are no contrastively nasalized vowels in this language), but they are phonetically **õ**. In all the words containing **h̃** that we recorded it was clear that the following vowel was also nasalized. The nasalization might therefore be thought of as a property of the syllable as a whole, much as it might be in Yoruba. But in Yoruba nasalized vowels contrast with oral vowels after oral consonants and nasalized semivowels occur only before nasalized vowels. In Kwangali there are no phonologically nasalized vowels; these vowels occur only in the context of nasals and nasalized consonants, which must include **h̃**.

Nasalized continuants have been claimed to be contrastive segments in a number of languages apart from Igbo. Boyeldieu (1985) argues for interpreting **w̃** as a phoneme in Lua. Stringer and Hotz (1973) describe Waffa as having a nasalized voiced bilabial fricative **β̃**. This segment contrasts with **β, m** and the sequence **mb** (treated as a single unit by Stringer and Hotz). Examples illustrating these sounds in Waffa, taken from Stringer and Hotz's work, are given in table 4.15. Stringer and Hotz do not comment on vowel nasalization, but they do not report nasalized vowels to be phonemic in Waffa.

Ohala (1975) offers persuasive reasons for believing that voiced nasalized

Table 4.15 Words illustrating voiced bilabial segments in Waffa, including the nasalized fricative

	INITIAL		MEDIAL	
mb	mbúume	'stamens'	jámbáa	'banana'
β	βaíni	'close by'	óoβə	(type of yam)
β̃	β̃atá	'ground'	jaáβ̃ə	'reed skirt'
m	mátee	'now'	kamə	'round taro'

fricatives are difficult to produce, since to generate friction at the oral constriction while air is flowing out through the nasal passage requires a high volume of airflow and voicing limits airflow through the glottis. These antagonistic factors presumably account for alternations between non-nasalized fricatives and nasalized approximants such as those reported in Guarani. We do not have direct evidence that Waffa β̃ is actually fricative, rather than approximant, in nature but there is good evidence that a nasalized fricative occurs in UMbundu. According to Schadeberg (1982), UMbundu has a 'voiced nasalized labial continuant' which he symbolizes with ṽ. He classifies this segment as an obstruent, and after commenting on Ohala's observation indicates that it is a fricative; additionally he points out that it is distinct from the approximant w̃, which also appears in the language in certain predictable environments. His analysis of the patterns of nasalization in UMbundu leads him to posit ṽ as one of a set of four underlying nasalized consonants, namely ṽ, l̃, h̃, j̃. These occur preceded and followed by phonetically nasalized vowels, but the nasalization of the vowels is treated as the result of a spreading of nasality from the consonants. Underlying nasalized vowels also occur, but the pattern of spreading of nasalization from these is different, and nasalization of consonants cannot be accounted for in this way. Hence ṽ is both a phonetic and phonological segment in UMbundu.

A third and minor type of nasalized consonant is a stop produced with a lowered velum. Nasalized stops can only be produced if the oral closure is further back (or lower) than the velic opening, that is, in the pharyngeal or glottal regions. If the closure is in front of the velic opening it will, of course, result in a nasal consonant rather than a nasalized stop. Nasalized glottal stops occur in Sundanese, though in contexts where their nasality is predictable (Robins 1957).

4.5 Conclusion

The aerodynamic and acoustic consequences of a lowered velum depend very much on whether or not there is a concurrent oral or glottal occlusion. In accord with this, we follow traditional phonetics and make a strict distinction between nasals and nasalized sounds. Only when a lowered velum is combined with a forward oral occlusion are members of the class of consonants we call nasals produced. Accompanying any other articulation a lowered velum produces a nasalized sound. In traditional phonetic classification the major consonant manner classes consist of those based on degree of stricture, i.e. stops, fricatives, and approximants, *plus* nasals. In this classification these classes form a mutually exclusive set. A segment cannot be both a nasal and a stop; similarly it cannot be both a nasal and a fricative or a nasal and an approximant. The significance of these classes is shown by the fact that the great majority of the world's languages include members of each class, whereas nasalized consonants are comparatively rare in the world's languages, and frequently are only derived surface segments. In nasalized sounds, the major manner class of the segment is determined by the degree of stricture of the oral articulation. Although nasality is an accompanying feature, a nasalized fricative, say, is still a fricative acoustically as well as in terms of distributional privileges and syllabification. Although what we call nasals have been called 'nasal stops' by others, they are not straightforwardly the nasalized equivalents of plosives in the same way that ṽ and j̃ are the nasalized equivalents of v and j. Nasals are acoustically continuant, characterized by a steady state. And they are often distributed in a way that is parallel to liquids and other sonorants, rather than to stops.

Nonetheless, the same articulatory property, a lowered velum, distinguishes nasals from plosives as distinguishes nasalized fricatives and approximants (and vowels) from their non-nasalized counterparts. In articulatory terms a single classificatory feature [nasal] is all that a phonetic theory requires to account for both nasals and nasalized segments. Furthermore, there is no need for more than the indication of the presence or absence of nasality. At least as far as consonants are concerned, we need to indicate only whether the velic aperture is open or closed, since there is no evidence that degrees of opening are linguistically relevant. (A possible counterexample with respect to nasalized vowels in Palantla Chinantec will be discussed in chapter 10). We recognize that nasals are characterized by the [stop] value of the feature Stricture; they are distinguished from stops by being [+nasal], a specification that applies also to nasalized consonants.

Using the same feature may appear to overlook the differences between nasals and nasalized fricatives, nasalized approximants and nasalized glottal stops that we have stressed above. However, there are very close relationships between nasals and nasalized segments, especially in assimilatory rules, that require expression. Nasalized segments often occur contiguous to nasals, and in a few languages, such as Niaboua (Bentick 1975), nasals occur in place of voiced plosives in the environment of nasalized vowels. Nonetheless, nasalized consonants have the distributional properties of their non-nasalized counterparts, whereas nasals do not pattern in the same way as (non-nasal) stops. The task for a linguistic phonetic theory is thus to express the articulatory and

temporal relationships between nasals and nasalized segments while account-
ing for the differences in their distributional patterns and markedness that are
based on their acoustic nature. We would consider nasals to be distinguished
from stops by being sonorant, giving an acoustic definition to this property.
Nasals and nasalized vowels and approximants are all [+ sonorant], but fricatives are obstruents and the acoustic signature of their obstruency is poorly
compatible with nasality. The similarities between nasals and nasalized consonants arise from articulatory considerations, whereas the differences arise
from acoustic considerations.

The other major theoretical requirement concerning nasality is to express the
relationship between movements of the velum, movements of oral articulators
and changes in laryngeal setting. For the most part these are simply matters of
relative timing. Although the timing of velic opening and closing movements
are often quite closely coordinated with a distinct oral gesture for a consonant
(or vocal tract configuration for a vowel), the velic aperture is often held open
for the duration of several oral articulatory gestures or configurations.
Equally, a single oral configuration (e.g. an oral closure) may be maintained
while velic position is changed. We do not see phonetic evidence of any special
binding of the components of such gestural sequences in certain cases (i.e.
prenasalized stops, etc.) as opposed to those cases where contiguous segments
which share common articulatory features are adjoined in free combination. In
each case, it is simply necessary to express the temporal relationship of the
independent movements.

The independence of velic movements has, of course, been recognized in
earlier phonological traditions, e.g in the Firthian prosodic school (Robins
1957), but this fact needs to be incorporated into an overall statement of
the combinatory possibilities. This can be formally represented by assigning
nasality to a separate phonological tier (Halle and Vergnaud 1980) in a multi-
tiered representation, or to a separate node in a feature tree (Sagey 1990,
Ladefoged 1988, 1992). These formalisms enable lack of temporal coordination
between movements of the velic and other articulators to be directly represented. They also express the fact that nasality can be a component of segments
of different manners. This fact was not formally captured by Clements' (1985)
proposal to group [nasal] with other manner features in a manner node,
since the combinatory possibilities between manners must be stipulated
additionally.

Besides capturing the formal relationships, a phonetic theory must also provide for an expression of the actual timing and magnitude of velic movements.
Phonetic implementation rules of this kind lie outside the scope of this chapter,
but work by Moll and Shriner (1967), Vaissière (1983) and Cohn (1990) indicates that timing patterns of velic movement in English can be generated from
underlying binary specifications of nasality and information on prosodic and
segmental context.

5

Fricatives

Fricative sounds are those in which a turbulent airstream is produced within the vocal tract. We will restrict the discussion in this chapter to the articulatory gestures required for central fricatives. Lateral fricatives will be discussed in chapter 6. Secondary articulations will be discussed in the chapter on multiple articulations. Forms of **h**, **ɦ** in which a turbulent airstream is produced at the glottis are also sometimes classed as fricatives (e.g. by Jones 1956, Bronstein 1960), but it is more appropriate to consider them in the chapter on vowels.

The gesture forming the constriction in many fricatives has a greater degree of articulatory precision than that required in stops and nasals. Making the articulatory closure for a stop involves simply moving one articulator so that it is held against another. It usually does not make much difference to the sound if the target position, which is above the upper surface of the vocal tract, is a few milllimeters higher so that there is a tight closure, or lower so that the closure is formed more gently. A stop closure will produce more or less the same sound as long as it is complete, irrespective of whether there is firm or light articulatory contact. But in a fricative a variation of one millimeter in the position of the target for the crucial part of the vocal tract makes a great deal of difference. There has to be a very precisely shaped channel for a turbulent airstream to be produced. Moreover, in a stop closure the strength of the closure does not have to be constant throughout the gesture. But in many fricatives, particularly sibilants, an exactly defined shape of the vocal tract has to be held for a noticeable period of time. These demands result in a fricative such as **s** having a greater constancy of shape in varying phonetic contexts, in comparison with the corresponding stops **t**, **d** and the nasal **n** (Bladon and Nolan 1977, Subtelny and Oya 1972, Lindblad 1980, Byrd 1994).

Table 5.1 Terms and symbols for principal categories of fricatives

1) Non-sibilants

	Labio-dental	Linguo-labial	Inter-dental	Coronal	Palatal	Velar	Uvular	Pharyngeal	Epiglottal
Bilabial									
ɸ β	f v	θ̪ ð̪	θ̬ ð̬	↓ ↓	ç ʝ	x ɣ	χ ʁ	ħ ʕ	ʜ ʢ

2) Coronal sibilants and non-sibilants

	Dental	Alveolar	Flat Post-alveolar (Retroflex)	Domed Post-alveolar (Palato-alveolar)	Palatalized Post-alveolar (Alveolo-palatal)	Closed Post-alveolar (Hissing-hushing)	Sub-apical palatal (Retroflex)
Plain	θ ð	θ̬ ð̬	ɻ̝				
Sibilant	s̪ z̪	s z	ʂ̬ ẓ	ʃ ʒ	ɕ ʑ	ŝ ẑ	ʂ ʐ

Fricative sounds may be the result of turbulence generated at the constriction itself, or they may be due to the high velocity jet of air formed at a narrow constriction going on to strike the edge of some obstruction such as the teeth. We will call the latter type sibilants, a term which has been used for a few centuries (e.g. by Holder 1669, and many phoneticians after him). More recent terms for these sounds include strident (Jakobson, Fant and Halle 1952, Chomsky and Halle 1968) and obstacle fricatives (Shadle 1985, Shadle, Badin and Moulinier 1991). In other fricatives, such as θ, ð, the turbulence is produced at the constriction itself.

Further exemplification of the distinction is given in table 5.1, which provides an overview of the terms and symbols we will use in this chapter. Some of these terms and symbols are used in slightly unconventional ways. We have distinguished between dental and interdental fricatives by the use of a diacritic to indicate a more forward articulation in the case of the latter sounds. We have used ɻ̝ for a post-alveolar retroflex fricative. Following Catford (1983) and the practice of phoneticians in the former Soviet Union we have used ŝ, ẑ for what we will describe as closed post-alveolar sibilants. We have also included within the table the IPA symbols ɕ, ʑ, which are traditionally called alveolo-palatal fricatives, but which we will regard as palatalized post-alveolar sibilants. The terms for the places of articulation in table 5.1 are not exactly the same as those listed in chapter 2. At the end of the chapter we will discuss how the data suggest a more elaborate descriptive framework.

We will begin by considering gestures made with the lips, and then those involving the tip and blade of the tongue in the dental and alveolar regions. We will next discuss all the sibilant gestures that can be made, starting with those in which the constriction is near the upper teeth, and then considering alveolar and post-alveolar sibilants. We will then continue with the non-sibilants, work-ing through the possibilities within the mouth to those within the pharynx. During the course of the chapter we will also discuss the acoustic structures of fricatives. The acoustic structure of fricatives seems to vary widely from indi-vidual to individual, but this really reflects only the unfortunate fact that we do not yet know what it is that we ought to be describing. We do not know how to sum up what is constant, and what is linguistically and perceptually most relevant in acoustic terms. As we do not yet have an adequate model for the acoustics of fricatives, we are in a position comparable to having to de-scribe vowels without having the notion of formants, or at least peaks in the spectrum. Our best guess is that what matters for fricatives (more especially for sibilant fricatives) is the overall intensity, the frequency of the lower cut-off point in the spectrum, and something corresponding to the center of gravity and dispersion of the spectral components above a certain threshhold. We will follow Lindblad's (1980) suggestion that "the cut-off frequency is a correlate of the shade of auditory brightness along the scale of sibilance," and we will also take note of the spectral width associated with different fricatives.

5.1 Non-sibilant Anterior Fricatives

We noted the difficulty of finding examples of a contrast between bilabial and labio-dental stops and nasals in the discussion of places of articulation in chap-ter 2. It is a lot clearer that these places contrast among fricatives. Several lan-guages spoken in West Africa contrast bilabial and labiodental fricatives. Examples from Ewe, which contrasts voiced and voiceless sounds of this kind, are shown in table 5.2. As we also noted in chapter 2, labiodental fricatives are more common than bilabial ones, and the latter in many cases are allophones of bilabial stops. This allophonic variation produces intervocalic distinctions between voiced bilabial and labiodental fricatives in many Bantu languages. In some of these languages further changes have led to a situation in which un-conditional contrasts between the two can be found. Examples from Tsonga were given in table 2.2 above.

Bilabial fricatives, like bilabial stops, are made with a gesture that involves a lowering of the upper lip in addition to the larger and more significant

Table 5.2 Words and phrases illustrating Ewe bilabial and labiodental fricatives

é ɸá	'he polished'	é fá	'he was cold'
èβè	'the Ewe language'	èvè	'two'
é ɸlè	'he bought'	é flɛ́	'he split off'
èβló	'mushroom'	é vló	'he is evil'

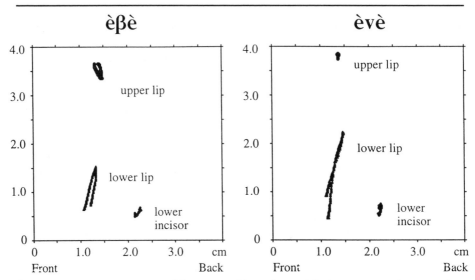

Figure 5.1 Movement trajectories of the upper and lower lips and the lower incisors during production of the Ewe words èβè 'people' and èvè 'two'. Each panel represents the mean of ten repetitions (see Maddieson 1993 for further details).

movement of the lower lip. In labiodentals ordinarily only the lower lip moves. Movement patterns for the lips in the two words on the second line of table 5.2 spoken by a speaker of the Aŋlo dialect of Ewe from Kpando are shown in the two panels of figure 5.1. This figure shows the trajectory taken by receivers placed on the outer surface of the upper and lower lips and on the lower incisors. For β, in the left panel, the upper lip moves down and back and the lower lip moves up and back. (Note that the receivers do not meet due to the need to mount them where they will not interfere with natural speech.) The release of the constriction lies in a plane a little behind that of the movement towards constriction. For v, in the right panel, the lower lip makes a larger excursion, reaching a higher and more retracted position than is reached in β. The upper lip remains stationary and takes no part in the articulation. It is in a slightly higher position throughout the articulation of the word èvè than it is during any part of the word èβè. For this speaker, the upper lip height in èvè is similar to that seen in eké 'sand', suggesting that there is some coarticulatory lowering of the upper lip during the vowels surrounding the β in èβè. The lower incisor trace shows that in neither case is there much raising of the jaw, although there is some retraction.

Sequences of frames from side-view cine-films of speakers of several European languages published by Bolla and his co-workers at the Institute of Phonetics in Budapest indicate that broadly similar movement patterns are found in the labiodental fricatives of the speakers of Finnish, German, Russian, Polish and English. The upper lip remains in a static position while the lower lip is raised and retracted. In these photographs, it can also be seen that the lower lip is positioned below the upper incisors at the peak of the gesture.

In addition to Ewe, some of the neighboring languages such as Siya and Logba also contrast bilabial and labiodental fricatives. In these languages, as illustrated by the photographs published in Ladefoged (1968), and by our more recent video recordings (Maddieson 1995), the lips are narrowed for β by being compressed in the vertical direction. There is no sign of any form of rounding through the corners of the lip having been brought forward. In v the upper lip does not move so that it is usually in a higher position than in β, in which there is a downward movement. Ladefoged (1990) suggested that the upper lip was actively moved upward in the labiodental fricatives, but our recent fieldwork (Maddieson 1995) has shown that this is not the case. Another language, Isoko, which contrasts a labiodental fricative v with a labiodental approximant ʋ also has a higher upper lip position for the fricative v than for the approximant ʋ, as shown in figure 9.33, again presumably not because the upper lip is actively raised, but because it is lowered for the approximant. We will discuss this articulation when we consider semivowels in chapter 9.

The contrast between bilabial and labiodental fricatives also occurs in a number of Southern Bantu languages. In these languages there is sometimes a slight lip protrusion when making the bilabials ɸ, β. We investigated contrasts as produced by three speakers of Kwangali, and three speakers of RuGciriku, two Bantu languages in the Kovango group, spoken in Namibia and Southern Angola. Both these languages contrast voiced bilabial and labiodental fricatives, but do not have voiceless sounds of this kind. Both voiced and voiceless bilabial and labiodental fricatives also occur in Venda; we recorded a single speaker of this language. In all these languages the contrast was made by drawing the lower lip back over the lower teeth for the labiodental, and (for some speakers) bringing the corners of the lips forward to make a more slightly rounded version for the bilabial (the latter gesture was present in only three of our seven speakers). Ladefoged (1990b) discusses some of the implications of this use of different techniques for making the contrast between bilabials and labiodentals, but, as we noted, he was wrong in believing that the majority of speakers of West African languages such as Ewe and Siya have an active upward movement of the upper lip in the labiodentals.

Labiodentals may also be produced with less retraction of the lower lip than the articulations we have been discussing. From our own observations of speakers of English we know that the lower lip may be positioned so that the narrowest constriction is between a part of the inner surface of the lip and the front surface of the incisors.

Figure 5.2 shows spectrograms of the Ewe words in the second line of table 5.2. The speaker was conscious of the reason for recording these words, and consequently the fricatives are somewhat longer than usual. The second formant transition has an earlier onset and moves to a lower frequency for the bilabial fricative. There are differences in the spectra of the two fricatives,

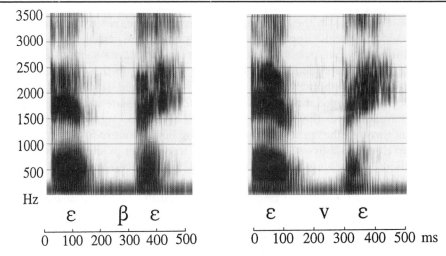

Figure 5.2 Spectrograms of Ewe bilabial and labiodental voiced fricatives in èβè 'people' and èvè 'two'.

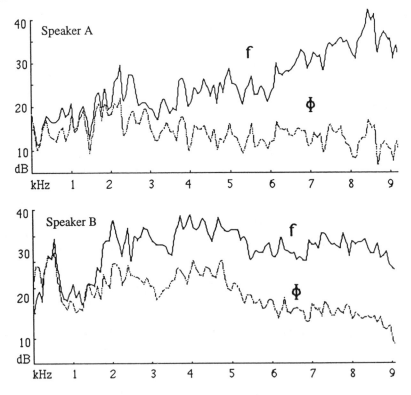

Figure 5.3 Means of 30 FFT spectra made at 5 ms intervals throughout the Ewe fricatives φ and f as produced by two speakers during the words in the first row of Table 5.2. The mean noise on the part of the recording immediately adjacent to each word has been subtracted from each spectrum.

which are more evident in the voiceless fricatives shown in figure 5.3. Above about 2 kHz **f** has distinctly greater energy than **ɸ**.

The existence of linguo-labial gestures in some of the languages spoken in Vanuatu was pointed out in chapter 2. Linguo-labial fricatives in Tangoa were exemplified along with the stops in table 2.2. We do not know of any languages other than those in Vanuatu that use linguo-labial articulations for fricatives.

Non-sibilant dental and interdental fricatives occur in many languages, but we do not know of any that contrast them. Nevertheless because some languages may consistently use one, and others the other, we have separated the two possibilities in table 5.1, using the symbols **θ, ð̪** for the interdental gestures. Examples of possible differences between languages are provided by Navarro Tomas (1968), who describes (and diagrams) Spanish **θ** as in **θiŋko** *cinco* 'five' as being interdental with the tongue "beneath the edges of the teeth", and Balasubramanian (1972), who provides palatographic data showing that Tamil **ð** as in **pʰɑːðɪ** 'half' is dental.

There is evidence that dialects of English differ in this respect. Textbooks teaching the pronunciation of the RP dialect of British English (e.g. Jones 1956, Gimson 1970, Roach 1983) diagram **θ, ð** as being typically made with the tip of the tongue behind the upper front teeth, in a gesture which we will call dental, whereas those teaching American English from a Western US perspective (e.g. Prator and Robinett 1985) describe these sounds as interdental. We investigated 28 native Californian college students and 28 British university students and staff speaking with a wide variety of English and Scottish accents. Nearly 90 percent of the Californian speakers produced **θ** as in *think* as shown in figure 5.4, with the tip of the tongue protruded between the teeth so that the turbulence is produced between the blade of the tongue and the upper incisors. Only 10 percent of the British speakers made this sound in this way; 90 percent of them used an articulation with the tip of the tongue behind the upper front teeth.

Interdental fricatives are, of necessity, laminal; the constriction is between

Figure 5.4 The tip of the tongue protruded between the teeth in **θ** as in *thief* as pronounced by a speaker of Californian English.

the blade of the tongue and the lower edges of the upper incisors. Dental fricatives can be apical or laminal, but we do not know of any consistent linguistic
use of these two possibilities. Jespersen (1897–9) considered the difference to be
partially determined by dental idiosyncrasies. He suggests that if there are
spaces between the teeth the tip of the tongue will be raised so that there is a
closure between the tongue and the upper teeth, and the friction will occur in
the spaces between the teeth; but if the teeth are close together, the tip of the
tongue will be down so that a laminal fricative is produced. In our survey of
British speakers we tried to find whether the gestures for the dental fricatives
were made with the tip or the blade of the tongue. This was often a difficult
question to answer, but it seemed that the constriction was usually between
the edge of the tip of the tongue and the upper teeth.

A similar difference to that between British and American dialects has been
observed between several Shandong dialects of Chinese by Sung (1986). Where
the majority of dialects in this group have sibilants, Rongcheng and Qingdao
have developed dental nonsibilant fricatives, and Jiaonan has taken the change
still further and uses interdental fricatives. The speakers of this latter dialect
are well known for the way in which they actually protrude the tongue between the teeth.

Both the American and British varieties of θ and ð are non-sibilant fricatives,
with the turbulence being produced at the interdental or dental constriction.
Non-sibilant fricatives of this kind can also be made further back, with the
tongue near the front part of the alveolar ridge. The IPA does not provide a
symbol specifically for non-sibilant alveolar fricatives. Following the principles used in the previous chapter, we will use θ̠ and ð̠ with the diacritic indicating a more retracted articulation. In Icelandic both θ̠ and ð̠ are definitely alveolar non-sibilant fricatives, the former being laminal, and the latter usually
apical. Figure 5.5, based on data in Pétursson (1971), shows the pronunciation
of θ̠ as in θ̠akið̠ 'roof', and ð̠ as in vað̠an 'whence'. In each case the constriction
is in the alveolar region, and the teeth are fairly far apart so that it is clear that
they do not form an obstruction.

A voiced alveolar fricative ð̠ sometimes occurs as an allophone of the alveolar stop **d** in formal Danish, in phrases such as 'læð̠ə foɣɪð̠ (*lade foged*) 'barn
keeper'. Jespersen (1897–9) describes this Danish sound as a laminal alveolar
fricative, made with the tip of the tongue behind the *lower* front teeth. However, the constriction in present-day Danish ð is often so weak that there is
little audible friction, and the sound might be better classified as an
approximant. Bauer, Dienhart, Hartvigson and Jakobsen (1980) note that "only
in very distinct Danish – as from the stage of the Royal Theater – do we get a
fricative."

It is possible to form a non-sibilant fricative using the teeth themselves as the
only constriction. Passy (1899) describes a fricative in the Shapsug dialect of
Adyghe which has "the lips fully open, the teeth clenched and the tongue flat,
the air passing between the teeth; the sound is intermediate between ʃ and f"

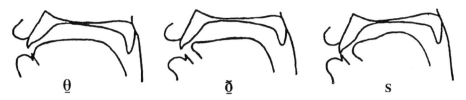

Figure 5.5 Tracings from x-rays of Icelandic non-sibilant alveolar fricatives θ̠ as in θ̠akið 'roof', and ð̠ as in vað̠an 'whence', compared with the sibilant alveolar s as in sunnar 'proved' (based on Pétursson 1971).

(Passy 1899: 110, our translation). This sound was noticed independently by Catford who comments that "the Adyghe bidental fricative is, in fact, a variant of x, occurring for the x in such words as xə 'six' and daxe 'pretty' in the Black Sea sub-dialect of Shapsug" (Catford, personal communication). A convention for transcribing bidental sounds with the dental diacritic both above and below a Coronal symbol has been proposed by Duckworth, Allen, Hardcastle and Ball (1990).

5.2 Sibilants

The more usual fricatives in the dental and alveolar regions are the sibilant fricatives s̠, z̠, s, z. In these fricatives the principal source of the sound is the turbulent airstream produced when the jet of air created by the dental or alveolar constriction strikes the teeth, which form an obstacle downstream from the constriction itself. We see, therefore, that at some points within the vocal tract it is possible to form two different constrictions, one that will produce a sibilant fricative, and one that will produce a non-sibilant fricative. Icelandic, in fact, has both a sibilant and a non-sibilant alveolar fricative. The right-hand part of figure 5.5 shows the Icelandic sibilant fricative s. Pétursson (1971), describing the difference between what we have called the non-sibilant and sibilant voiceless alveolar fricatives says: "The first important difference is that θ̠ is articulated with the blade of the tongue, but for s the tip is raised. The place of articulation is more advanced for θ̠ than for s. The shape of the tongue is different for the two consonants; for θ̠ it is flat, for s it has a characteristic curve. The alveolar constriction is also different: for θ̠ it is large, for s it is a narrow channel." (Our symbols and translation.) An apical/laminal distinction is thus playing a role in this distinction, but it is not the only one. Note also that although both these fricatives have constrictions near the alveolar ridge, in the sibilant fricative the teeth are also close together.

It is also possible to produce sibilant fricatives with a dental constriction, in the same region as that used for the non-sibilant θ sounds. Indeed, the sibilant s is regularly described as a voiceless dental fricative in many well-known languages (e.g. Cantonese: Hashimoto 1972; Standard Chinese: Chao 1968; Swedish: Elert 1964). It is often difficult to be sure whether sibilants in this area are dental or alveolar. But Bright (1978) has pointed out that a considerable number of the languages of California contrast ʂ with ş. He notes that Karok has minimal word-pairs like **şúːf** 'creek' vs **ʂúːf** 'backbone', describing the sound at the beginning of the first of these words as being "a very far-forward, apico-dental sound ... pronounced by younger speakers as θ." The sound at the beginning of the second word is described as being "apico-alveolar," and further identified as a "retracted ess". We interpret this as an apical post-alveolar in our terms. This contrast also appears in Luiseño in words such as **şúkat** 'deer' vs **ʂukmal** 'fawn'.

English **s** usually has a constriction in the middle of what we refer to as the alveolar region (i.e. the forward part of the alveolar ridge). It can be formed either by the tip of the tongue, or by the blade with the tip behind the lower front teeth. Bladon and Nolan (1977) point out that there is considerable disagreement among authorities as to which is the most common articulation. In their own videofluorographic study of eight speakers of different forms of British English, they found that seven of these speakers had a laminal **s**. In her investigation of 20 English speakers, Dart (1991) found that 52.5 percent of the tokens had laminal articulations and 42.5 percent had apical articulations. The differences in the part of the tongue used are probably due to individual anatomical characteristics. The amount of protuberance of the alveolar ridge, and the relation between the lower jaw and the upper teeth, affect the gesture that is required to produce the acoustic structure necessary for **s**. Indeed, McCutcheon, Hasegawa and Fletcher (1980) have shown that even the location of the rugae (the ridges on the roof of the mouth) have an effect on how an individual chooses to form the constriction for **s**. There are, of course, articulatory regularities that are constant. All speakers of English pronounce this sound with the upper and lower teeth close together, making it a strident fricative; and there is always a narrow groove in the tongue directing a jet of air towards the teeth. For many speakers the lower lip is also involved in directing the airstream towards the edge of the upper teeth. The constriction must be close to the teeth, but the precise channel location, and the apical-laminal distinction are not of particular importance in the characterization of the general, cross-speaker, properties of English **s**.

Perhaps the most remarkable but least remarked feature of the articulatory gesture for English **s** is the deep pit which may occur in the center of the tongue. The articulatory constriction forming the jet of air consists of a groove, 5–10 mm long, running in the posterior-anterior direction. Behind this groove there is often a wide pit, extending out to the sides of the tongue. Some English speakers produce **s** in a word such as *saw* with the center of the tongue depressed several millimeters below the level of the sides of the tongue, as can be seen in figure 5.6, which is based on x-ray and palatographic data reported by

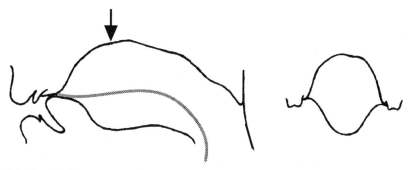

Figure 5.6 The articulatory gesture for s as in *saw,* as pronounced by Peter Ladefoged. The solid line indicates the position of the center of the tongue as known from x-rays; the grey line indicates the positions of the side of the tongue as indicated by palatograms. The coronal section on the right gives a transverse view of the shape of the tongue at the point indicated by the arrow on the sagittal section on the left (based on data in Ladefoged 1957).

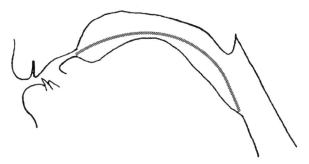

Figure 5.7 Tracings from an x-ray photograph of David Abercrombie, another speaker of British English (RP dialect), taken during the pronunciation of s as in *saw.* The grey line indicates the position of the sides of the tongue. The solid line shows the center of the tongue, as outlined by a radio opaque marker.

Ladefoged (1957). For this speaker (Peter Ladefoged) at a point about 20 mm behind the tip of the tongue the midline is 12 mm below the sides. This particular utterance may have had a slightly exaggerated articulation in that the x-ray picture was taken during a very slow pronunciation of the word *saw;* but it neither sounded nor felt in any way atypical.

The fact that there is a deep hollow in the center of the tongue is often hard to determine from x-ray pictures in which the midline of the tongue has not been explicitly marked. Bladon and Nolan (1977) do not comment on the possibility, perhaps because they chose to mark the sides rather than the center of the tongue, fearing that a strip down the center of the tongue might affect the pronunciation. We did not notice anything unusual in the speech of any of our subjects who were being photographed while they had a thin line of barium sulphate down the midline of the tongue. Figure 5.7 shows the gesture used by another speaker, David Abercrombie, whose dentition is such that the crucial part of the tongue could be clearly seen. This speaker produced s with a more laminal articulation than that shown in figure 5.6, with the center of the tongue approximately 10 mm below the sides of the tongue. Hardcastle (1974), in his survey of instrumental investigations of lingual activity in speech, notes that "if the central line of the tongue is outlined, it is possible to measure the depth of a groove, for instance in the articulation of [s]." His "simplified tracing from an X-ray photograph taken during the author's [Australian English] articulation of [s]" does not have a scale, but it appears that at a point below the soft palate there is a groove which is at least 17 mm deep. Stone (1991) illustrates a subject with a groove 6–8 mm deep at the point at which the coronal sections were obtained. Similar gestures have been observed in other languages. From other comments in the text, it is likely that the "characteristic curve" mentioned by Pétursson (1971) in his description of Icelandic s quoted above is a hollowing of this kind. We do not know the proportion of all s sounds that involve a hollowing of the tongue just behind the constriction, but it is probably more common than has been previously reported.

The more posterior sibilant in English, symbolized ʃ in the IPA tradition, has been variously described. Jones (1956), Abercrombie (1967), Ladefoged (1993), and Prator and Robinett (1985) call it a palato-alveolar fricative. Bronstein (1960) describes the tongue position in much the same way as Jones, but uses the term alveolo-palatal. Most of the authors note that the constriction in ʃ is wider as well as being further back than in s. Both Jones and Bronstein say that most people make this sound with the tip of the tongue up, but that some speakers have the tip of the tongue down behind the lower front teeth. Borden and Harris (1980) somewhat eccentrically describe English ʃ as palatal. Hockett (1958) describes it as a lamino-alveolar or lamino-domal surface spirant, involving "a close approximation of a whole area, from side to side and from back to front."

English ʃ is similar to s in that for both sounds the teeth are close together, making them strident fricatives. There are several differences between them: the constriction is further back and wider for ʃ; the part of the tongue immediately behind the constriction for ʃ is raised (or domed), as opposed to being hollowed for s; and ʃ has added lip rounding or protrusion. It should be noted that the secondary articulation of lip rounding is a feature of ʃ in some languages, such as English and French, but it is not found in many other languages, such as Russian.

The articulation of ʃ in 'Shaw' as produced by Peter Ladefoged is illustrated in figure 5.8. The constriction is in what we have called the post-alveolar region, that is, on the center of the alveolar protruberance. It is clearly further back than the alveolar s illustrated in figure 5.6, in which the constriction is on the flat part of the alveolar ridge, just behind the upper incisors. The front of the tongue is raised, with the center being above the level of the sides.

In a palatographic survey of 164 students at the University of Edinburgh,

Figure 5.8 The articulatory position for ʃ as in *shaw*, as pronounced by Peter Ladefoged. The solid line indicates the position of the center of the tongue as known from x-rays; the grey line indicates the positions of the side of the tongue as indicated by palatograms. The coronal section on the right gives a transverse view of the shape of the tongue at the point indicated by the arrows on the sagittal section on the left (based on data in Ladefoged 1957).

Ladefoged (1957) reported that "for every speaker the articulation of the voiceless fricative in *sip* involves the formation of a narrower channel (which is usually also further forward) than that in *ship*." The wider channel in ʃ results in the jet of air striking the teeth at a lower velocity in ʃ than in s. In addition, all the speakers described in Ladefoged (1957) produced ʃ with the sides of the tongue raised higher up towards the hard palate than for s, with, presumably, concomitant raising of the center of the tongue as shown for the speaker in figure 5.8. The degree of lip rounding was not recorded for these subjects, but, as we have noted, English ʃ is typically somewhat rounded. The acoustic structure of sibilant fricatives will be considered later, but we may note here that both the lower velocity of the airstream, and the lengthening of the vocal tract by added lip rounding, will cause ʃ to have a lower pitch than s.

Consideration of the articulatory characteristics that we have observed lead us to define ʃ as a post-alveolar domed sibilant. By domed we mean to denote the raising of the front of the tongue that occurs, irrespective of whether an apical or laminal articulation is used. This doming is equivalent to a small amount of palatalization. We will regard the phrase palato-alveolar sibilant as an exactly equivalent specification, denoting a comparatively wide constriction in the post-alveolar region near the center of the alveolar protruberance, with concomitant raising of the front of the tongue. We will distinguish between palato-alveolar and alveolo-palatal sibilants, using the latter term as an alternative specification for the post-alveolar palatalized sibilants that we will describe in Standard Chinese. We will avoid Borden and Harris's use of the term palatal, reserving that for sounds made further back in the mouth.

English ʃ is also like s in that both sounds can be made with the tip of the tongue up or down. In a survey of 16 speakers of Californian English we found that 8 of them raised the tip of the tongue above the plane between the upper and lower incisors when saying the word 'saw' and 8 of them (not all the same 8) raised the tip of the tongue for 'Shaw' (or 'Shah', the two words are homophones in Californian English). In each case the remaining 50 percent produced what we would judge to be laminal articulations. It appears that the apical-laminal distinction is not relevant in the formation of the English sibilants, and speakers are free to vary this aspect of their production. On the other hand, the eight speakers of 'O'odham studied by Dart (1991, 1993) were much more consistent in producing an apical/laminal difference between their contrasting sibilants s and ʂ than differences in other aspects, such as the constriction location.

We will now consider Standard Chinese (Mandarin), which has a number of sibilant fricatives made in the alveolar and post-alveolar regions. Relevant examples are given in table 5.3, together with words illustrating the other fricatives of the language. We have given standard IPA transcriptions, with the initial consonants each followed by just the vowel **a**. From a phonetic point of view there is nothing other than a normal transition between the initial consonant and the following vowel in all these cases. But the usual Chinese Pinyin orthographic forms have *ia* where we have **a** in the palatalized post-alveolar (alveolo-palatal) column. This reflects one possible interpretation of the phonological status of the alveolo-palatal sounds, that is, that they are the result of assimilation of alveolar sibilants to a following high front vowel.

Figures 5.9 and 5.10 show data for alveolar s, post-alveolar (retroflex) ʂ, and palatalized post-alveolar (alveolo-palatal) ɕ as produced by three speakers of Standard Chinese (based on Ladefoged and Wu 1984). The first point to note is that for all three sounds for all three speakers the upper and lower teeth are fairly close together, so that these three sounds are all clearly sibilant fricatives. In each of the sounds the tongue forms a differently shaped channel for the air; but the main source of acoustic energy is always the turbulence that arises when this air passes between the nearly clenched teeth.

Table 5.3 Words illustrating contrasts among Standard Chinese fricatives and affricates. All the words shown have high level tone (Tone 1)

LABIODENTAL	ALVEOLAR	FLAT POST-ALVEOLAR (RETROFLEX)	PALATALIZED POST-ALVEOLAR (ALVEOLO-PALATAL)	VELAR
fa 'to issue'	sa 'let out'	ʂa 'sand'	ɕa 'blind'	xa 'sound of laughter'
	tsa 'take food with tongue'	tʂa 'to pierce'	tɕa 'to add'	
	tsʰa 'to wipe'	tʂʰa 'to stick in'	tɕʰa 'to dig finger-nail into'	

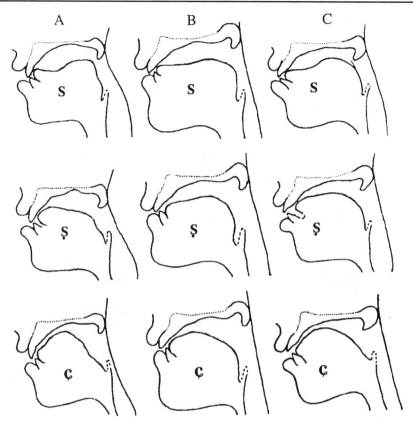

Figure 5.9 Tracings from x-rays of three speakers producing Standard Chinese sibilant fricatives, based on Ladefoged and Wu (1984).

As the top row of figure 5.9 shows, all three speakers produced s with the tip of the tongue; in all three cases there is a hollowing of the tongue such that the tongue is concave with respect to the roof of the mouth, although the hollow does not appear to be as deep as that for the English speakers reported above. The palatograms show that speakers B and C make this sound with a narrow slit, with a width of 4.5 mm for speaker B and 3.75 mm for speaker C. Speaker A made this sound with the narrowest channel on the teeth, so palatographic data is not available for this measurement. The height of the slit is about 1 mm for speakers A and B, and even less for speaker C. These measurements of the width and height of the constriction are similar to those for English s reported by Subtelny and Mestre (1964) and Subtelny and Oya (1972).

The position of the point of greatest constriction is slightly different for each speaker. For speaker A it is on the teeth, for speaker B slightly behind the teeth, and for speaker C still further back, so that it is on the front part of the alveolar

A   B   C

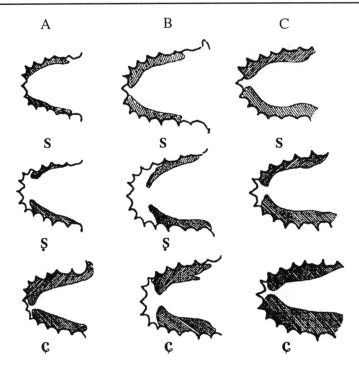

S   S   S

ṣ   ṣ

ç   ç   ç

Figure 5.10 Palatograms of the same words illustrated in Figure 5.9, based on Ladefoged and Wu (1984).

ridge. Given these data, it seems that this sound does not have a very exact place of articulation (in the sense of the precise location of the constriction in relation to the anatomical features of the roof of the mouth). This again agrees with the data for English s as described above. In Chinese, as in English, s must have a constriction located close to the teeth; and this constriction must form a narrow channel directing air towards the teeth at a high velocity. But the speaker's individual dentition and mouth shape will determine where the constriction is in relation to the alveolar ridge. For each of the speakers in figure 5.9 the constriction is at a similar distance from whatever narrowing provides the obstacle – the gap between the lower and upper teeth for speakers A and C, but probably the gap between the lower lip and the upper teeth for speaker B.

   The Standard Chinese so-called retroflex ṣ is shown in the middle rows of figures 5.9 and 5.10. This gesture is plainly very different from that in the retroflex stops discussed in chapter 2. It does not involve the tip of the tongue being curled up and backwards into the palatal region, as in the Dravidian sub-apical retroflex stops, nor does it have the apical post-alveolar shape that occurs in the Hindi retroflex stops shown in figure 2.5. In our Standard Chinese data, all three speakers produce the constriction for this sound with the upper surface of the tip of the tongue, making it a laminal rather than an apical post-alveolar. The constriction is at about the same place for all three speakers, further back than in s, so that it is nearer to the center of the alveolar ridge. Both the height and the width of the channel are greater than in s, but the width varies considerably, from 18.5 mm for speaker A to 5 mm for speaker C. The location and width of the constriction are thus very comparable with those for English ʃ. The front of the tongue is fairly flat for speakers A and C, and slightly hollowed for speaker B, rather than being slightly raised towards the hard palate as it is in ʃ. Because the part of the tongue immediately behind the constriction is not domed as it is for ʃ, we have termed this sound a flat post-alveolar sibilant. A further point to note about this gesture is that no part of the tongue is touching the lower teeth, as occurs in the articulation of s. Instead the tongue is drawn slightly back, so that there is a sublingual cavity. Perkell, Boyce and Stevens (1979) have shown that a cavity of this type has a significant acoustic effect, producing a comparatively low frequency spectral peak. Additional x-ray data in other publications (Zhou and Wu 1963, Ohnesorg and Svarny 1955) all show substantially the same gesture, confirming the notion that Standard Chinese ʂ is a (laminal) flat post-alveolar sibilant. The traditional description of this sound as a retroflex is inappropriate as a description of its articulation.

The third sibilant in Standard Chinese, ɕ, is usually termed an alveolo-palatal sound. The tongue has a very different position in this sound from that in any of the other sounds we have been considering, as may be seen from the data in the bottom rows of figures 5.9 and 5.10. There are some similarities to English ʃ, but both the blade and the body of the tongue are higher in the mouth, forming for each speaker a comparatively long, flat, constriction. The extent of this constriction may be estimated from the palatograms in figure 5.10. For all three speakers there was contact between the sides of the tongue and the palate high in the mouth all the way back to the molar teeth. It is possible that some of the turbulence may be formed along the wall of this long constriction, as suggested by Shadle (1985) for palatal and velar fricatives. But it is also apparent that these speakers raise the lower jaw so that the upper and lower teeth are close together, making the Standard Chinese ɕ a strident fricative.

For none of the speakers is the constriction for ɕ in exactly the same place as in either of the other two Chinese sibilants. From a comparison between the palatograms and the x-ray tracings in figure 5.9 it is apparent that the narrowest channel occurs near the front part of the alveolar ridge for speakers A and C, and notably farther back for speaker B. The palatograms show that it is consistently farther back than in s but not quite as far back as in ʂ. The difference between ʂ and ɕ is small, so that it might be possible to consider both of them as having constrictions in the post-alveolar region, as in English ʃ. However, all phoneticians who are familiar with both English and Chinese invariably note that English ʃ is not the same as Chinese ɕ, the major difference being in the degree of raising of the front of the tongue. We referred to ʃ as a domed

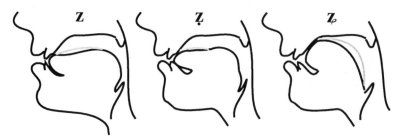

Figure 5.11 The articulatory gestures involved in Polish fricatives, based on x-ray data given by Puppel, Nawrocka-Fisiak and Krassowska (1977).

post-alveolar (palato-alveolar). It is therefore appropriate to refer to ¢ as a palatalized post-alveolar, with the IPA term alveolo-palatal being a possible alternative. We are thus making a distinction between three post-alveolar sibilant gestures: flat post-alveolar (retroflex) ş; domed post-alveolar (palato-alveolar) ʃ, and palatalized post-alveolar (alveolo-palatal) ¢.

There are a number of other fricatives that have to be compared with these English and Standard Chinese sounds. The Polish fricatives exemplified in table 5.4 have many similarities but also some differences from the Standard Chinese sibilants. A great deal of data on the acoustic structure of the Polish fricatives has been given by Kudela (1968). Additional data can be found in Jassem (1962). We will concentrate here on the articulatory gestures required for these sounds, relying largely on the descriptions by Puppel, Nawrocka-Fisiak and Krassowska. (1977). They use the symbols s z š ž ś ź for sounds which we symbolise by ş z̦ ¢ z̦ ş z̦. (Throughout the following discussion we will use our symbols not theirs, even when directly quoting from them.) Diagrams based on their x-ray tracings of the voiced sounds are shown in figure 5.11. Again it is clear that these three pairs of sounds are all strident fricatives with the teeth close together.

The authors note that:

> The Polish sounds ş and z̦ belong to dentalized sounds, i.e. those which are articulated in the alveolar region but with the blade of the tongue being very close to the inner side of the upper front teeth. Thus, the hissing effect is very strong. However, the English counterparts are articulated more in the purely alveolar region. Thus, in English, the tongue is more retracted for the articulation of these sounds.

From their diagrams it is clear that the sounds are ş and z̦ and not s and z, and thus differ from the corresponding sounds in English and Standard Chinese.

In describing ş and z̦ Puppel et al. say: "The narrowing is made by the tip of the tongue and the blade of the tongue, and the alveolar ridge. The narrowing, as compared with that for ş and z̦, is a bit more open. The lips are protruded

Table 5.4 Words illustrating contrasts among Polish sibilants

Dental			Flat post-alveolar (retroflex)			Palatalized post-alveolar (alveolo-palatal)		
koṣa	*kosa*	'scythe'	**kaṣ a**	*kasza*	'kasha, groats'	**baça**	*Basia*	'Barbara' (dim.)
koẓa	*koza*	'goat'	**gaẓa**	*gaa*	'gauze'	**baẓa**	*bazia*	'catkin'

and slightly rounded.... The Polish ṣ and ẓ consonants are articulated more in the alveolar region. They also belong to those sounds which are slightly dentalized." We would also point out the more complex obstruction caused by the close approximation of the upper lip with both the lower lip and the lower teeth in these sounds, making them somewhat rounded.

We do not know what Puppel et al. mean when they say that these sounds are "slightly dentalized." Nor, judging from the illustrations, do we consider the tip of the tongue to be involved in making the constriction. But the tip of the tongue is slightly retracted from the lower teeth, so that there is a small sublingual cavity. These sounds seem to us to be produced in a similar way to the Standard Chinese laminal post-alveolar (retroflex) sibilants. They differ in that Standard Chinese ṣ is not rounded (except before rounded vowels and semivowels) and has a larger sublingual cavity. These two differences tend to cancel one another, in that the addition of lip rounding or the introduction of a larger sublingual cavity both have very similar effects, thus making these Polish and Chinese sounds auditorily very similar.

The third pair of Polish fricatives, ç and ʑ, involve an articulatory gesture which is very similar to that in the Standard Chinese sound for which we have used the symbol ç. Puppel et al. describe the Polish sounds as follows: "The sounds are produced with the body of the tongue in the front position. The tongue is tense and the lips are spread. The air escapes through a very narrow channel made between the post-alveolar region of the palate and the middle of the tongue ... the lips are slightly spread." When Puppel et al. specify that the body of the tongue is in the front position, they presumably mean that the sound is palatalized. From the illustrations in figure 5.11 it is clear that the gesture for Polish ʑ is very similar to those for Chinese ç (at least for speakers A and C in figure 5.9).

The well known Dravidian and Indo-Aryan languages of India also have apical or laminal retroflex sibilants. An example of a Tamil sibilant that we would symbolize as ṣ is shown in figure 5.12 (based on x-ray data in Svarný and Zvelebil 1955). The articulation appears to be further back than the post-alveolar sibilants in Standard Chinese and Polish. But, as we have remarked before, there are no absolute landmarks in the vocal tract, so it is difficult to compare articulatory data from one person with that from another, just as it is difficult to compare acoustic data from different individuals. We will classify

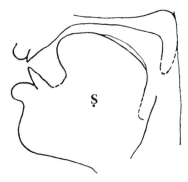

Figure 5.12 The articulatory gesture involved in Tamil ṣ in paṣa as indicated by x-ray data given in Svarny and Zvelebil (1955).

Table 5.5 Words illustrating contrasts among Toda sibilants

LAMINAL ALVEOLAR	APICAL POST-ALVEOLAR	LAMINAL POST-ALVEOLAR	SUB-APICAL PALATAL
ko:s̪ 'money'	**po:s̠** 'milk'	**po:ʃ** 'language'	**po:ṣ** (place name)

Tamil ṣ as a laminal post-alveolar, but reserve judgment on whether it really is equivalent to the Standard Chinese and Polish sounds that we have symbolized in the same way.

One of the most remarkable sets of sibilant contrasts occurs in another Dravidian language, Toda, which was well described by Emeneau (1984), and has recently been studied by Shalev, Ladefoged and Bhaskararao (1994). The analysis presented here is based on the same fieldwork as reported in this latter work, but differs from its conclusions in some details. Toda has four different articulatory gestures for sibilant fricatives, whereas the other Dravidian languages have only three. Words illustrating the Toda contrasts are shown in table 5.5.

Figures 5.13–5.16 show the palatograms, linguograms and sagittal reconstructions of the four sibilants from one speaker. The pictures were reproduced life size, and lined up so that the front incisors are in line with the incisors on the sagittal section (which, since it was traced from a dental impression of the speaker's mouth, was also life size). Like many of the Toda, this speaker has a deep palate. As the shape of the palate is known from the dental impressions, the height of the contact at the sides can be observed on the palatograms. We have used this information to make a rough estimate of the position of the center of the tongue (shown by a grey line). Note that the dark marks on the speaker's front teeth in these photographs are betel juice stains, and are not the result of tongue contact.

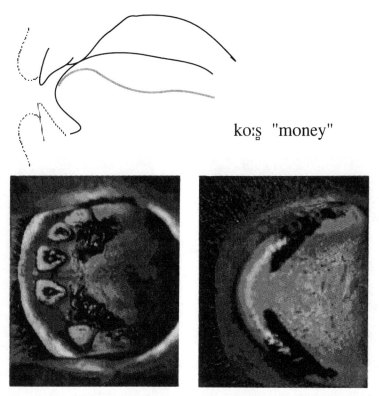

koːṣ "money"

Figure 5.13 Palatographic and linguographic records of the Toda word **koːṣ** 'money'. The solid lines on the sagittal section show the known shape of the palate and the observed position of the sides of the tongue. The grey line indicates estimated positions of the lips and the center of the tongue.

Toda ṣ has a laminal alveolar articulation. Emeneau (1984) describes it as being "post-dental (pre-alveolar)", and we agree in that the constriction might be said to be closer to the teeth than in English **s**, but it is in the alveolar region. What is most remarkable about this sound is that it is clearly laminal, but nevertheless there is only a narrow part of the blade of the tongue contacting the roof of the mouth. Similar narrow contact areas on the blade of the tongue were observed for all three subjects for whom we have palatographic records. The sides of the tongue touch the hard palate well above the level of the molar teeth. We do not know whether the center of the tongue is hollowed, but from the fact that the distance between the points of contact on the alveolar ridge is slightly smaller than the distance between the comparable points on the tongue, and from direct observation of the production of this sound, we believe that the tongue is slightly grooved, so that it might be in the position shown in the diagram.

The laminal contact for ṣ contrasts with the apical contact for ṣ in the same

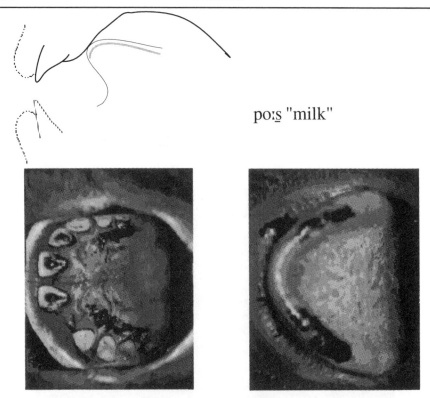

po:ṣ "milk"

Figure 5.14 Palatographic and linguographic records of the Toda word **po:ṣ** 'milk'. The solid lines on the sagittal section show the known shape of the palate and the observed position of the sides of the tongue. The grey line indicates estimated positions of the lips and the center of the tongue.

language. This sound, which is illustrated in figure 5.14, is an apical sibilant. The two sounds also differ in that ṣ has a wider channel for the airstream, and is articulated slightly further back, on the center of the alveolar ridge, making it post-alveolar. The contact areas at the side of the mouth are closer to the molar teeth, indicating a generally lower position for the tongue. There may also be some hollowing of the tongue in this sound, but it is not as extensive as in ṣ.

The third Toda fricative, ʃ, is a laminal post-alveolar, i.e. a palato-alveolar sibilant, with more contact of the tongue with the palate than either of the preceding sibilants, as can be seen in figure 5.15. The laminal tongue constriction is similar to that in Toda s, but involves a narrower channel, with the tongue sides being much higher in the mouth. The tongue is domed up towards the roof of the mouth, in a way somewhat similar to that in English ʃ.

The final sibilant in Toda is ṣ, a sub-apical palatal fricative, a genuinely retroflex gesture, as illustrated in figure 5.16. It is rather different from the Tamil gesture seen in figure 5.12. The contact is between the underside of the

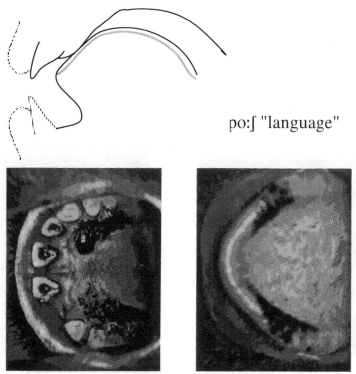

po:ʃ "language"

Figure 5.15 Palatographic and linguographic records of the Toda word **po:ʃ** 'language'. The solid lines on the sagittal section show the known shape of the palate and the observed position of the sides of the tongue. The grey line indicates estimated positions of the lips and the center of the tongue.

tip of the tongue (so that it is not all visible in the linguogram) and a point on the roof of the mouth behind the post-alveolar region.

So that all these Toda sibilant fricatives might be compared, the tongue positions shown in the preceding diagrams have been superimposed in figure 5.17. The major point to note is that only one of these sounds, the sub-apical palatal (retroflex) sibilant, can be readily described in terms of the modal possibilities for places of articulation that were listed in chapter 2. Each of the others involves subtle distinctions in tongue shape relative to the teeth. We have described each of these fricatives in articulatory terms, but they do not all exemplify the modal possibilities associated with these terms.

The situation in Caucasian languages is also very complex, although for these languages Catford (1983 and personal communications) has given excellent accounts of some of the phonetic data available. Catford (ms in preparation) has described what we would call five different primary articulatory gestures (i.e. without considering secondary articulations, or different

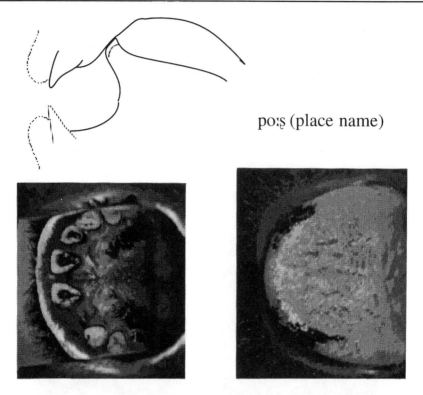

poːṣ (place name)

Figure 5.16 Palatographic and linguographic records of the Toda word **poːṣ** (place name). The solid lines on the sagittal section show the known shape of the palate and the observed position of the sides of the tongue. The grey line indicates estimated positions of the lips and the center of the tongue.

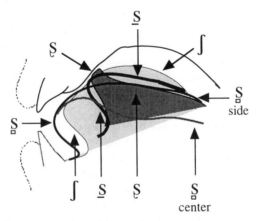

Figure 5.17 A composite diagram of Toda tongue positions in sibilant fricatives. In the case of ṣ the center and sides of the tongue have been shown separately. The position of the center and sides is taken to be much the same for the other sounds, and only one tongue line is shown for each of them.

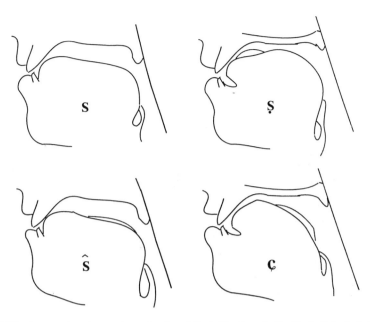

Figure 5.18 The four contrasting gestures for the sibilant fricatives in the Bzyb dialect of Abkhaz, based on x-ray tracings from Bgazhba (1964) and interpretive comments by Catford (ms in preparation).

states of the glottis) for sibilant fricatives in North West Caucasian languages, such as Ubykh and Abkhaz. Four of these sounds, s ʃ ʂ ç, are similar to sounds that we have symbolized this way in other languages. The fifth sound, which Catford symbolizes as ŝ, he describes as "acoustically and physiologically between a typical s and a typical ʃ," calling it a "hissing-hushing sound." He goes on to say: "In its production the tip of the tongue rests against ... the lower teeth (as for a laminal ş), but the main articulatory channel is at the back of the alveolar ridge (as for a lamino-post-alveolar ʃ)." It is therefore like ʃ (and ʂ and ç) in that its constriction is in the post-alveolar region; but it is like laminal s in that the tip of the tongue rests against the lower teeth so that there is no sublingual cavity.

Figure 5.18 shows the four contrasting gestures in the Bzyb dialect of Abkhaz, based on x-ray tracings in Bgazhba (1964) and the interpretive comments in Catford (ms in preparation). The constriction for s (at the top left of the figure) is in the alveolar region, on the front part of the alveolar ridge. The blade of the tongue is close to the alveolar ridge, and the tip of the tongue is on the floor of the mouth. The three other sounds all have constrictions on the middle of the alveolar ridge, in what we are calling the post-alveolar region. ç has the front of the tongue raised, making it a laminal palatalized post-alveolar (alveolo-palatal) sibilant. ʂ is made with the tip of the tongue, so it is an apical

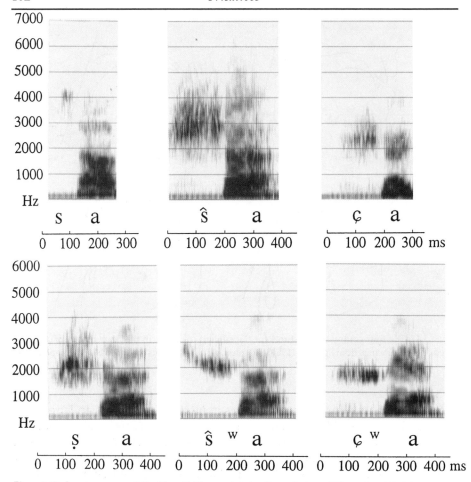

Figure 5.19 Spectrograms of Ubykh syllables containing the voiceless sibilants in table 5.6.

Table 5.6 Words illustrating contrasts among Ubykh sibilants

	LAMINAL DENTI–ALVEOLAR	LAMINAL CLOSED POST–ALVEOLAR	LAMINAL POST–ALVEOLAR	APICAL POST–ALVEOLAR
PLAIN VOICELESS	**saːba** 'why'	**ŝa** 'three'	**çaça** 'mother-in-law'	**ṣa** 'head'
PLAIN VOICED	**za** 'one'	**ẑaẑa** 'kidney'	**ʑawa** 'shadow'	**ẓa** 'firewood'
ROUNDED VOICELESS		**aŝʷa** 'white'	**çʷa** 'sea'	
ROUNDED VOICED		**aẑʷan** 'it boils'	**aʑʷan** 'it roasts'	

post-alveolar (retroflex) sibilant. Both these sounds on the right of the figure have a sublingual cavity that is not present in ŝ, in which the tip of the tongue is in a position similar to that in s, but the constriction made by the blade is further back. Because of the absence of the sublingual cavity in ŝ, we have termed this sound a laminal closed post-alveolar sibilant.

The four contrasting gestures for sibilant fricatives also occur in Ubykh, as illustrated by the words in table 5.6. Spectrograms of the voiceless sibilants in this table are shown in figure 5.19. The s (at the top left) in this particular set of matched tokens was not particularly loud. The frequency components with greatest amplitude are around 4000 Hz. There was probably more energy at higher frequencies. The laminal closed post-alveolar ŝ has energy centered nearer 3000 Hz in its unrounded form. When it is labialized (as in the middle of the bottom row), the energy is more tightly constrained in a lower region, around 2000 Hz. The other laminal post-alveolar, ç, has energy in an even lower region, around 2500 Hz when unrounded, and well below 2000 Hz when rounded. Lastly, the apical post-alveolar ş (at the left of the bottom row) has the lowest frequency of all the unrounded sibilants, with its center at only a little above 2000 Hz. As may be seen from the examples in the bottom row, adding rounding causes the fricative energy to be contained in a narrower band.

Catford (ms in preparation) also has a similar description of the acoustic data, based on his analysis of a number of the Caucasian languages. The general pattern is one in which the lower cut-off frequency gets lower as the cavity in front of the constriction gets bigger. In the languages he examined, ŝ generally had a higher cut-off frequency and a higher range than the other post-alveolars. Catford's data suggest that ʃ, which does not ocur in Ubykh and Abkhaz, differs from ş and ç by having a broader frequency range and perhaps by an intermediate cut-off frequency. Among the unrounded fricatives, ş has the lowest cut-off and the lowest range. The rounded sibilants have both lower cut-off frequencies, and considerably smaller ranges.

There may be sibilant fricatives in which the primary articulatory constriction is as far back as the palatal region. The descriptions are not completely clear, but what might be regarded as voiceless palatal sibilants may occur in Gununa-Kena (Gerzenstein 1968), and voiced palatal sibilants in Muinane (Walton and Walton 1967) and Cofan (Borman 1962). We neither have nor know of instrumental data on these languages. Although some palatal fricatives may, like the sibilants, have a high pitched sound, they are not obstacle fricatives and are therefore not what we would call sibilants.

In summary, the seven articulatory gestures for sibilants in table 5.1 will accommodate all the sibilants we have been discussing, but only with some difficulty. On some occasions we need to make clear whether we are decribing apical or laminal sibilants, as shown in table 5.7. The first sound listed, ş, is the same in both table 5.1 and table 5.7. Following Bright (1978), we regard the dental sibilant as being apical. In general, specification of the apical/laminal

Table 5.7 Types of sibilants

		"Place of articulation"	Exemplifying languages
1	ş	apical dental	Chinese, Diegueño, Polish
2	s	apical or laminal alveolar	English, Ubykh
3	s̻	laminal alveolar	Toda
4	ʂ	laminal flat post-alveolar	Chinese, Polish, Ubykh
5	s̱	apical post-alveolar	Diegueño, Toda
6	ʃ	apical or laminal domed post-alveolar (palato-alveolar)	English
7	ʃ̻	laminal domed post-alveolar	Toda
8	ɕ	laminal palatalized post-alveolar (alveolo-palatal)	Chinese, Polish, Ubykh
9	ŝ	laminal closed post-alveolar ('hissing-hushing')	Ubykh
10	ʂ	sub-apical palatal (sub-apical retroflex)	Toda

distinction is not necessary (and may even be misleading) for the next possibility, the alveolar sibilant **s** listed in the second row. As we saw in languages such as English, some speakers have apical **s**, and others laminal **s**. But in Toda the alveolar sibilant ş is always laminal, and for that reason we have added a specific symbol in the third row of table 5.7. The next row begins the listing of the post-alveolar sibilants. The sibilants in the fourth row are traditionally called retroflex in descriptions of Chinese and Polish; but they are usually laminal, whereas retroflex consonants of other kinds and in other languages are usually apical. For this reason we call the Polish and Chinese sounds laminal (flat) post-alveolar sibilants, and avoid the term retroflex in their description. There are, however, true retroflex sibilants. Toda might be said to have two retroflex sibilants, an apical post-alveolar ş, listed in the fifth row, which contrasts with a sub-apical palatal ş, listed in the tenth row.

The domed post-alveolar ʃ in the sixth row can be apical or laminal in English. In Toda, however, it must be laminal. A more specific symbol for the Toda sound can be formed with the laminal diacritic added to the symbol ʃ as shown in the seventh row of table 5.7. Both the apical and the laminal post-alveolar domed sibilants are sometimes called palatoalveolars, whereas the sibilant in the eighth row, ɕ, may be called alveolo-palatal. The three sibilants ş, ʃ, ɕ differ from one another by increasing amounts of raising of the part of the tongue immediately behind the constriction. The sibilant in the ninth row, ŝ, differs from the others in that the tip of the tongue rests against the lower teeth so that there is no sublingual cavity. The final sibilant in the table, ş, is perhaps the most different from all the others from an articulatory point of view, in that it is a sub-apical sound.

5.3 Posterior Non-sibilant Fricatives

Most of the fricatives in the dental, alveolar and post-alveolar regions are of the sibilant, obstacle, type. But, in addition to the non-sibilant alveolar fricatives of the θ

Table 5.8 Words illustrating Margi palatal and velar stops, fricatives, and approximants

| | PALATAL | | VELAR | |
	VOICELESS	VOICED	VOICELESS	VOICED
STOP	càŋ°á 'cat'	ɟadʼí 'hump of a cow'	kákádə̀ 'book'	gàlí 'spear'
FRICATIVE	çà 'moon'	jàɟàɗə̀ 'picked up'	xá 'big water pot'	ɣàfə́ 'arrow'
APPROXIMANT		jà 'give birth'		

type that we described earlier, there are also non-sibilant fricatives further back in this region. A non-sibilant apical post-alveolar (retroflex) fricative occurs in some forms of English. This sound, which we symbolize by ɻ̣ is the fricative counterpart of the retroflex approximant ɻ. It is the usual pronunciation of *r* in words such as *red roses* in South African English as spoken in the Eastern Cape. Note that in this dialect ɻ̣, which is a post-alveolar non-sibilant fricative, contrasts with ʒ, which is a post-alveolar sibilant fricative, in words such as *drive* vs. *jive*. The non-sibilant fricative ɻ̣ differs from the sibilant fricatives z and ʒ in the position of the jaw and the shape of the articulatory constriction. The non-sibilant fricative does not have the lower jaw raised so that the teeth are close together; and the constriction is wider so that it does not produce a high velocity jet of air striking an obstacle. A post-alveolar non-sibilant fricative ɻ̣ also occurs in some forms of Edo, where it contrasts with an approximant ɹ (Ladefoged 1968). We will illustrate sounds of this type in chapter 7.

Phonological contrasts involving voiceless palatal fricatives are fairly rare; less than 5% of the languages of the world include ç in their inventory (Maddieson 1984a). The voiced palatal fricative ʝ is even more rare. But the Chadic languages Margi and Bura have – at least on the surface – not only both the voiced and voiceless palatal fricatives ç, ʝ but also contrast these with a voiced approximant j, as well as with voiced and voiceless velar stops, and voiced and voiceless velar fricatives. In the phonology of Margi the palatal fricatives are the palatalized counterparts of the velar fricatives (Maddieson 1987). Margi words illustrating all these sounds are shown in table 5.8. The voiced velar fricative ɣ is often more like an approximant than a true fricative.

It is not clear whether the vocal tract shapes in palatal fricatives are equivalent to the overall shapes in the corresponding stops, with the difference being simply that there is a narrow constriction for the fricatives, and a complete closure for the stops. We do not have any physiological data on these Margi sounds; but x-ray data for other languages indicate that palatal stops and fricatives may differ considerably in the position of the root of the tongue. Figure 5.20, based on x-ray data in Bolla (1980), shows that Hungarian ç and ɟ have the root of the tongue more advanced than ç and ʝ. This may be because the stops (and the nasal ɲ) require an articulatory gesture in which the tongue has to be raised considerably higher, as if the aim were to push the tongue through the

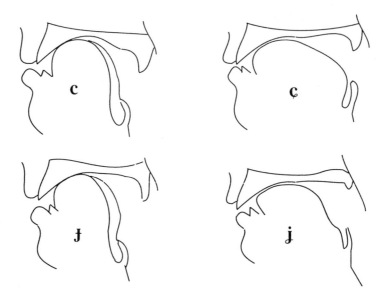

Figure 5.20 X-ray tracings of Hungarian palatals (after Bolla 1980). Note that the root of the tongue is more advanced for the stops on the left-hand side, than for the palatal fricative ç and approximant j on the right.

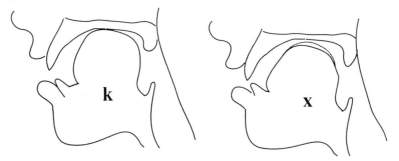

Figure 5.21 A comparison between a voiceless velar stop and a voiceless velar fricative in Standard Chinese (based on data in Zhou and Wu 1963).

roof of the mouth, as we noted in chapter 2.

There are data on several languages containing velar fricatives, indicating that the vocal tract shape is much the same in the stops and in the fricatives. The differences in the overall vocal tract shape are less dramatic than those for the palatal gestures, perhaps because the gesture for a velar stop requires a less extreme tongue movement than that required in palatal stops. A comparison between Standard Chinese x and k (based on data in Zhou and Wu 1963) is shown in figure 5.21.

Velar fricatives contrast with uvular fricatives in a number of languages (e.g. in the

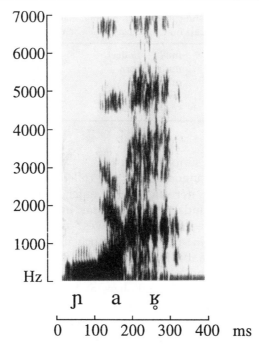

Figure 5.22 Voiceless uvular fricative trill ʁ̥ in Wolof (after Ladefoged 1968).

Amerindian languages Haida, Tlingit, Wintu and Pomo, and in many Caucasian languages). We do not have any phonetic data of our own on any of these languages, but we think it likely that uvular fricatives may have much the same vocal tract shape as uvular stops. There is, however, a complication in the case of uvular fricatives in that the shape of the vocal tract may be such that the uvula vibrates. An example of a trilled uvular fricative in Wolof is presented in figure 5.22. Uvular trills are discussed in chapter 7.

As we noted in chapter 2, pharyngeal fricatives are not as common as might be supposed from the literature, as most of the sounds to which this label is attached (e.g. in Arabic and Hebrew) are actually what we would call epiglottal rather than pharyngeal in place. There is, however, a clear case of a language with a pharyngeal fricative that contrasts with an epiglottal fricative in Agul. Examples of the contrasts in the Burkikhan dialect of Agul were given in table 2.9, repeated here as table 5.9. Spectrograms illustrating these contrasts are shown in figure 5.23. The first and second formants come very close together in the pharyngeal fricative, with the first formant having a very high value (well above 1000 Hz at the maximal pharyngeal position for the fricative). The first formant then falls during the early part of the following vowel. The epiglottal fricative is both noisier (having a greater intensity relative to the surrounding vowels) and more like a simple noise source producing energy in

Table 5.9 Words illustrating contrasting pharyngeal and epiglottal fricatives, and epiglottal plosives, in the Burkikhan dialect of Agul (data from S. Kodzasov, personal communication)

VOICED PHARYNGEAL FRICATIVE	muʕ	'bridge'	muʕar	'bridges'
VOICELESS PHARYNGEAL FRICATIVE	muħ	'barn'	muħar	'barns'
VOICELESS EPIGLOTTAL FRICATIVE	mɛʜ	'whey'	mɛʜɛr	'wheys'
VOICELESS EPIGLOTTAL	jaʔ	'center'	jaʔar	'centers'
STOP	sɛʔ	'measure'	sɛʔer	'measures'

the formant frequencies of the surrounding vowels.

The sounds in Semitic languages that are called pharyngeal fricatives are often neither pharyngeals nor fricatives (Laufer and Condax 1979, 1981). Catford describes these sounds as approximants; in fact he goes on to say that they are "often wrongly described as fricatives," a sentiment with which we agree. He is clearly correct in saying that in much, if not most, casual colloquial Arabic (as opposed to citation forms produced for the benefit of linguists) these sounds are not fricatives. In our experience there is audible local turbulence in the sound that Catford symbolizes as ħ, but, as he notes, it is very seldom apparent in what he symbolizes as ʕ.

We would also suggest that these Semitic fricatives might more properly be called epiglottal rather than pharyngeal. Catford (1977b) describes a gesture that we regard as truly pharyngeal in which "the part of the pharynx immediately behind the mouth is laterally compressed, so that the faucal pillars move towards each other. At the same time the larynx may be somewhat raised." He considers this to be "the most common articulation of the pharyngeal approximants." There are, however, several

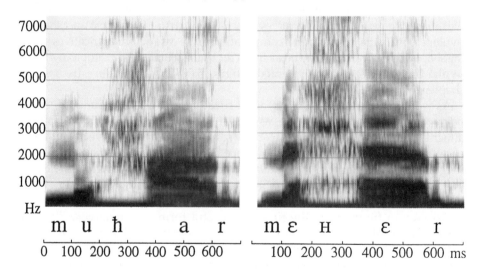

Figure 5.23 Spectrograms of the Agul words **muħar** 'barns', and **mɛʜɛr** 'wheys' spoken by a male speaker of the Burkikhan dialect.

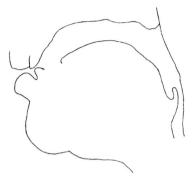

Figure 5.24 A voiceless epiglottal fricative ʜ (before u:) in Arabic (from data in Bukshaisha 1985).

instrumental records indicating that these gestures are more usually made in the epiglottal region, rather than in the upper part of the pharynx. A typical gesture as indicated by x-rays is as shown in figure 5.24 (from data in Bukshaisha 1985). The diagrams based on x-rays in Al-Ani (1970) for Iraqi Arabic and Ghazeli (1977) for Tunisian Arabic also show that there is a constriction near the epiglottis. Laufer and Condax (1981), using fiberoptic data, describe a gesture in which the epiglottis has a more active role. In their work on Hebrew (and in later work on Palestinian Arabic, Laufer, personal communication) they conclude that the constriction "in no way involves the tongue." Instead it is "made between the epiglottis and the posterior pharyngeal wall, and may involve contact between the epiglottis and the arytenoids." This may be somewhat of an over-statement in that a more recent x-ray study by Boff Dkhissi (1983) concludes that the movement of the epiglottis is not independent from that of the root of the tongue; rather the two elements work together in forming the constriction. In so far as these sounds are epiglottal rather than pharyngeal fricatives, they might better be symbolized ʜ, ʕ, rather than ħ, ʕ.

Gestures involving the epiglottis occur in a number of other languages, in addition to the Semitic languages discussed above. We noted above and in chapter 2 that the Burkikhan dialect of Agul contrasts these sounds with pharyngeal fricatives. Catford (1983) says that this language "has no fewer than seven pharyngeal and laryngeal sounds: pharyngeal ħ and ʕ, 'deep pharyngeal' [which we would call epiglottal] or 'emphatic' ʜ, ʕ, and the corresponding stop ʡ, and glottal h and ʔ." There are x-ray studies of some of these fricatives in other Caucasian languages. Figure 5.25 shows tracings (also reproduced by Catford) from x-rays by Gaprindashvili (1966) and Bgazhba (1964) showing the difference between fricatives in the epiglottal region in Dargi and in the middle or upper part of the pharynx in Abkhaz.

It may be that, instead of two distinct regions, pharyngeal and epiglottal, there is actually a range of possible gestures made in this one general area. The most anterior of these would be the gestures described by Catford (1977b) as involving the faucal pillars and the part of the pharynx immediately behind the oral cavity. A slightly more

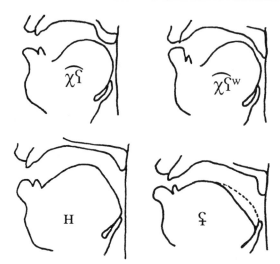

Figure 5.25 Upper pharyngeal constrictions (extending into the uvular region) in Abkhaz (top row, based on Bgazhba 1964), and epiglottal constrictions in Dargi (bottom row, based on Gaprindashvili 1966).

retracted gesture can be exemplified by Danish *r*. This sound is sometimes considered (e.g. by the International Phonetic Association 1949) to be a form of uvular ʁ, but it actually involves a weak constriction much nearer to the middle of the pharyngeal continuum. In contemporary Danish these sounds are usually approximants rather than fricatives, but in a very distinct, more old-fashioned, pronunciation a turbulent airstream is formed in the vicinity of the constriction associated with a low back vowel. This is closer to the glottis than the constriction near the faucal pillars in the upper part of the pharynx described by Catford (1977b), but it is distinctly above the level of the epiglottis.

Gestures involving constrictions that may be even closer to the larynx occur in Khoisan languages, where they are used in the production of so-called 'strident' vowel sounds (Ladefoged and Traill 1984, Traill 1985). There are phonological and phonetic reasons for considering these Khoisan gestures as phonation types rather than as fricatives of the kind we have been considering in this chapter. They are additive components that affect the vowels rather than forming in themselves a consonantal gesture; and they often involve a concomitant laryngeal gesture. Nevertheless they are definitely fricative sounds, with a turbulent airstream being produced by a constriction within the vocal tract, just above the vocal cords. X-ray tracings (from Traill 1985) showing the articulations used by two speakers of !Xóõ are given in figure 5.26. Traill notes that the epiglottis is hard to specify in these tracings from frames in a cine-x-ray film, as it was usually vibrating. Accordingly it might be appropriate to describe these sounds as epiglottal fricative trills.

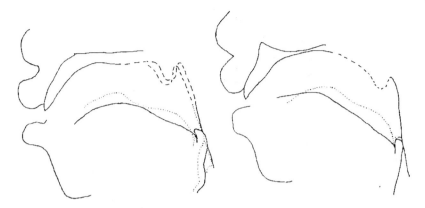

Figure 5.26 X-ray tracings of two speakers of !Xóõ producing epiglottal articulations accompanying vowels of an **u** type (dotted line) and of an **a** type (solid line) (after Traill 1985).

Finally in this survey of possible fricative gestures, we must consider some more complicated possibilities. Shona has so-called 'whistling fricatives' in which there is extreme lip rounding combined with a laminal alveolar gesture. These sounds are discussed further in chapter 10, when we consider multiple articulations. Some dialects of Swedish have a fricative that has been said to have two or even three articulatory constrictions (Abercrombie 1967). We do not, however, think it is correct for more than one of these constrictions to be considered a fricative articulation. There is good data available on the Swedish sibilant fricatives (Lindblad 1980) allowing us to consider these sounds in detail.

Swedish has four phonologically distinct fricative gestures. The contrasting sounds are sometimes symbolized **f, s, ç, ɧ**; in addition, in Standard Swedish, there is a retroflex fricative ʂ, which is, phonologically, the sequence /rs/. The first two of these, **f, s**, do not need extensive comment; **f** is labiodental **f**, and **s** is dental ʂ. The other two, **ç, ɧ**; are more difficult to describe. The basic descriptive problem is one of geographical, social, and stylistic variation. According to Lindblad (1980), the most common usage is for **ç** to be a "predorsoalveolar fricative." His further comments and sketches based on x-rays indicate that **ç** is similar to the Polish gesture that we symbolized in the same way, which we called a palatalized post-alveolar sibilant. Lindblad notes that variations of this phoneme in Swedish include an affricate **tç** or **tʃ**, and a palatal fricative **ç** similar to that in German *ich*.

The fourth Swedish fricative, usually symbolized by **ɧ**, is the most interesting. Lindblad describes two common variants of Swedish **ɧ**. The first, for which he uses a different symbol, he calls a highly rounded, labiodental, velar or velarized fricative. A redrawn version of his x-ray tracing is shown in figure 5.27. Lindblad suggests that the source of friction is between the lower lip and the upper teeth, and it certainly appears to be so from his x-ray. He also demonstrates that the upper lip is considerably protruded in comparison with its position with that in the gesture for **i**. In addition to these

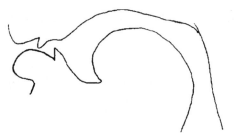

Figure 5.27 Swedish ɧ, a highly rounded, labiodental, velar or velarized fricative (based on data in Lindblad 1980).

Figure 5.28 Lindblad's (1980) pronunciation of an alternative form of Swedish ɧ on the left, and his pronunciation of German x on the right.

anterior gestures, Lindblad notes that the "tongue body is raised and retracted towards the velum to form a fairly narrow constriction. (The presence of this constriction is constant, but not its width or location, which vary considerably.)" The posterior constriction in this variety of ɧ is not great enough to be itself a source of turbulence, so that, although this sound may have three notable constrictions, one in the velar region, one labiodental, and a lesser one between the two lips, only the labiodental constriction is a source of friction.

The second common variant of Swedish ɧ, illustrated in figure 5.28, is described by Lindblad as a "dorsovelar voiceless fricative" pronounced with the jaw more open and without the lip protrusion that occurs in the other variety. Lindblad suggests that the difference between this sound and the more usual velar fricative x is that the latter "is formed with low frequency irregular vibrations in the saliva at the constriction" (Lindblad 1980, our translation). We infer from his descriptions and diagrams that this variant of ɧ has less friction, and may be slightly further forward than the velar fricative x commonly found in other languages. Lindblad claims that between the extreme positions of the labiodental ɧ and the more velar ɧ, "there are a number of intermediate types with various jaw and lip positions, including some with both anterior and posterior sound sources." As we note in chapter 10, we doubt that it is possible to produce turbulence at two points in the mouth simultaneously for ordinary linguistic purposes.

5.4 Acoustic Differences among Fricatives

Some aspects of the acoustics of fricatives have been noted above, but here we will attempt a more general summary. There have been surprisingly few studies of the acoustics of fricatives. One of the most comprehensive works on the English fricatives is still that of Hughes and Halle (1956). In their discussion of **f, s, ʃ** as spoken by three speakers, they note that there are great discrepancies among the spectra of a given fricative as spoken by different speakers, but the differences among the spectra are consistent for a single speaker. Hughes and Halle found very varied spectral characteristics for **f, v**, but more specific spectral properties for the sibilants, with **s, z** being characterized by spectral peaks at higher frequencies than **ʃ, ʒ**. In their more recent study, Shadle, Moulinier, Dobelke and Scully (1992) come to a similar conclusion. Hughes and Halle (1956) did not investigate English **θ, ð**, and there is still a lack of published acoustic data on these sounds, with only small amounts of data having been reported by Shadle et al. (1992). It seems that in the case of the pairs **f, θ** and **v, ð** in English, the inconsistencies between speakers are so great that it may be profitless to try to characterize the acoustic spectra of the fricatives themselves. Shadle et al. (1992) note that the generally accepted view is still that of Harris (1958) who suggested that the principal difference between these fricatives lies in the formant transitions.

Lindblad (1980), whose articulatory investigations of Swedish fricatives were described above, also provided two different kinds of acoustic data on Swedish fricatives. One is the analysis of a subset of these fricatives as they occur in different phonetic contexts, and as spoken by different individuals. The other is an analysis of a wider range of Swedish fricatives as spoken by himself as an illustration of archetypal productions ('cardinal' versions) of these sounds. His analysis of **s, ç** and **ʂ** as spoken by five different speakers is reproduced here in a slightly modified form in figure 5.29. There are large variations among the speakers, but it is true that for each of them **ʂ** has the lowest cut-off frequency, **ç** the next, and **s** the highest. There are also very considerable contextual effects, as may be seen from figure 5.30, which shows these same fricatives as pronounced by two of the speakers in a variety of vowel contexts. For any one vowel context the spectral relations among **s, ç, ʂ** are similar to those described above when they occurred before **ɑː**. But the variations in the spectrum of each of these fricatives before different vowels are enormous. Figures 5.29 and 5.30 provide good evidence of the difficulty of characterizing fricatives in terms of their spectra.

Lindblad's demonstrations of his own pronunciations of some of the fricatives that occur in different Swedish dialects are shown in figure 5.31. He notes that these sounds may be characterized to a great extent by the frequency of the lower edge of the band of fricative noise. For the three sibilants **s, ʂ, ʃ** on the left of the figure, this frequency gradually descends. (It is somewhat surprising that it should be lower in **ʃ**, than in **ʂ**.) In the palatalized post-alveolar sibilant **ç** in the lower left of the figure there is a less

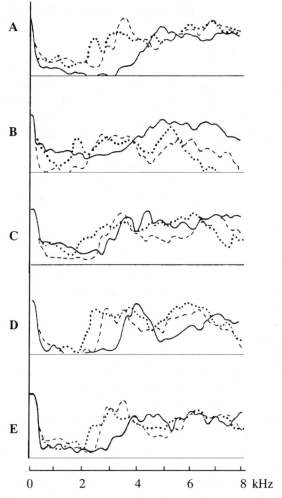

Figure 5.29 Spectra of Swedish s (solid line), ç (dashed line), and ʂ (dotted line) before ɑː as produced by five speakers designated A–E (after Lindblad 1980).

sharp lower frequency cut off, as there is in the palatal fricative ç opposite it on the lower right side; ç differs from ɕ by having a higher mean spectral energy. The rounded fricatives in the upper right part of the figure have a strong low frequency peak. Both ʃʷ and ɥ also have a low frequency peak, as well as a considerable amount of energy in the region just above 4 kHz.

The technique of investigating the acoustics of fricatives by using a single speaker to produce a wide range of fricatives, employed by Lindblad for Swedish, enables speaker-dependent variables to be controlled. Studies of this

A   B

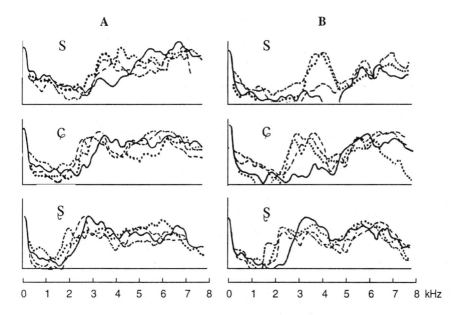

0   1   2   3   4   5   6   7   8   0   1   2   3   4   5   6   7   8 kHz

Figure 5.30 Spectra of Swedish s, ç, and ʂ before iː (solid line), yː (dashed line) and before uː (dashed and dotted line) as produced by two speakers A and B (after Lindblad 1980).

kind include Strevens (1960), Jassem (1962), and Shadle (1985). Shadle analyzed sustained productions of the fricatives ɸ, f, θ, s, ʃ, x as spoken by three male and three female "phoneticians or speech researchers familiar with the phonemes." She again found "tremendous variation in spectral shape" between speakers. However, in her later work she and her co-authors note that "simple measures such as frequency range for high amplitude regions are likely to be highly variable," and have shown that it is possible "to locate low amplitude but consistent spectral peaks, and to discover their cavity affiliation." (Shadle, Baudin and Moulinier 1991: 44).

A comparison of a larger range of sounds is presented by Jassem (1968), who considered the acoustic structure of a number of fricatives in different languages. Spectra of 12 of these sounds are reproduced in figure 5.32. When considering Jassem's findings, it must be remembered (as he himself emphasizes) that the data represent fricatives as produced by only a single speaker; but, nevertheless, this speaker (Jassem) is "well acquainted with these sounds through contact with languages in which they occur and/or through exhaustive phonetic training" (Jassem 1968). There is little more that we need say about ɸ, f, θ, apart from noting their comparatively flat spectrum. All the sibilants have a relatively sharp low frequency cut off that is higher in frequency in proportion as the sibilant is more front in articulation (as we have noted above). The palatal fricative ç in Jassem's spectra seems to be similar to the alveolo-palatal fricative ç in Lindblad's pronunciation shown in figure 5.31, being marked by a particularly strong localized spectral peak. Conversely, the alveolo-

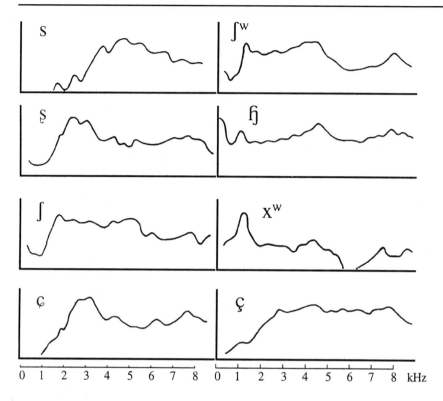

Figure 5.31 The sibilant fricatives that occur in different Swedish dialects as prononounced in their 'cardinal' versions by Lindblad (1980). (Lindblad uses different symbols, here turned into their IPA equivalents.)

palatal fricative ç in Jassem's spectra seems to be similar to the palatal fricative ç in Lindblad's, being relatively flat. The more back fricatives, x, χ, ħ, have a spectral peak that decreases in frequency as the place of articulation approaches the glottis, and additional peaks in the higher part of the spectrum.

5.5 Laryngeal Settings and other Modifications of Fricatives

The majority of fricatives are voiceless and we have used voiceless examples in most of the previous discussion, with fewer mentions of their voiced counterparts. The greater frequency of voiceless fricatives in the world's languages may be due to the fact that the strong low-frequency energy that results from voicing tends to mask the lower-amplitude frication noise in the higher frequency range. However, many languages contrast

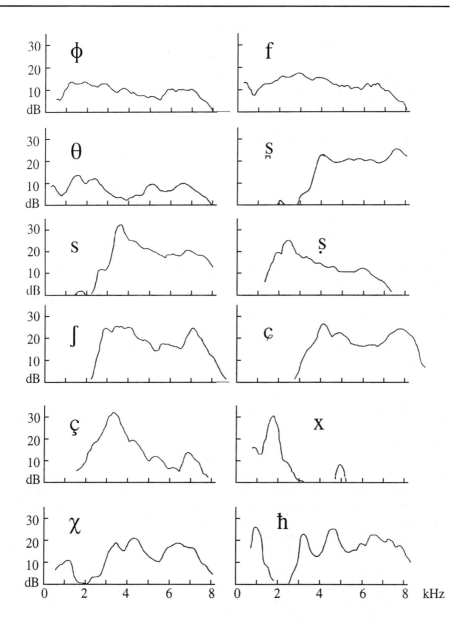

Figure 5.32 Spectra of 12 fricatives as produced by Jassem (1968).

voiced and voiceless fricatives, and there are a few that have a three-way contrast in laryngeal timing. Many speakers of Burmese, for example, have voiced, voiceless unaspirated and aspirated fricatives, as exemplified in table 5.10, which differ from one another in voice onset time. The articulatory and acoustic differences among these sounds are similar to those between voiced, voiceless unaspirated and aspirated stops.

Fricatives rarely occur with non-modal types of voicing. As we discussed in chapter 3, Korean has a variety of stiff voice that characterizes what are sometimes called fortis consonants. In addition to the stops, there is a fricative, **s***, in this series. (The * denotes a fortis articulation.) Hausa has a form of **s** that may be laryngealized, but is usually ejective, as we will discuss below. Apart from these two languages, only four languages with laryngealized fricatives are listed in Maddieson (1984a), and none of them has more than one such sound. A voiceless laryngealized fricative ş is reported in Southern Nambiquara (Price 1976) and Siona (Wheeler and Wheeler 1962), which may well be similar to the Korean **s***. Wapishana (Tracy 1972) has ẕ, and Sui (Li 1948) has ɣ̰. There are no languages listed with breathy voiced fricatives. However, voiced fricatives in Wu dialects produce the same tonal effects as the stops with breathy release. It is therefore likely that they share this characteristic with the stops.

All the fricatives we have been discussing so far have used the pulmonic airstream mechanism, but glottalic egressive (ejective) fricatives also occur. Yapese, Tlingit, Hausa, and Amharic are among the languages that have ejective fricatives. Words illustrating pulmonic and ejective fricatives in Tlingit are shown in table 5.11.

Hausa ejective fricatives are illustrated in figure 5.33, which shows a spectrogram of the Hausa phrase **s'úns'àː jéː nè** 'They are birds'. Both examples of ejective **s'** are accompanied by a rising movement of the closed larynx, followed by its subsequent return to its normal speech position. This up-and-down movement is probably responsible for the movement of the point of articulation in the gesture which causes a variation of the pole frequency associated with the fricative noise. The variations in frequency can be clearly seen in the medial **s'** and are also evident in the initial **s'**. We have seen similar variations in ejective **s'** in other languages. The upward movement of the glottis in an ejective is achieved by raising the hyoid bone. This action will also produce an upward and forward movement of the body of the tongue. The resulting more forward articulation of the **s'** will have a higher frequency, as the cavity in front of the constriction will be smaller. When the larynx falls, the reverse process occurs, and the pole frequency is lowered. Figure 5.33 also shows that there is an interval of about 40 ms between the end of the medial fricative noise and the release of the glottal stop, and a further short interval before the vocal folds start vibrating.

The occurrence of prenasalized fricatives is noted in chapter 4 and lateral fricatives are discussed in chapter 6.

Table 5.10 Words illustrating contrasts among Burmese fricatives

VOICED	VOICELESS UNASPIRATED	VOICELESS ASPIRATED
zà	**sà**	**sʰà**
'lace'	'to be hungry'	'letter'

Table 5.11 Words illustrating contrasts among Tlingit pulmonic and glottalic egressive (ejective) fricatives in verb stems from Story and Naish (1973)

	ALVEOLAR	VELAR	LABIALIZED VELAR	UVULAR	LABIALIZED UVULAR
PULMONIC	**saː**	**xaːt**	**xʷaːs**	**χeːt**	**χʷaːl**
	'be narrow'	'stick out from'	'hang'	'multiply'	'shake, tremble'
EJECTIVE	**s'aː**	**x'aːt**	**xʷ'aːs'k**	**χ'eːt'**	**χʷ'aːs'**
	'claim' (property)	'file'	'be numb'	'gnaw, chew'	'become bald'

5.6 Phonological Features for Fricatives

We will now consider how all these fricatives can be classified within each language in terms of features. We will start by considering the features that are necessary to classify fricatives as distinct from other sounds. Then, assuming the validity of the distinction between sibilants and non-sibilants within

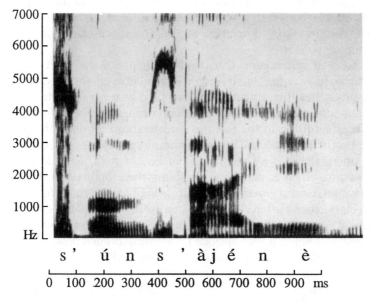

Figure 5.33 A spectrogram of the Hausa phrase **s'úns'àː jéː nè** 'They are birds'.

the class of fricatives, we will go on to assess the adequacy of the place features discussed in the previous chapter for making further distinctions among fricatives.

In traditional distinctive feature terms there is no single property that characterizes fricatives; they are distinguished from other classes of sounds by the feature values [+ continuant] and [– sonorant]. Other phonological feature theories (e.g. Ladefoged 1992, Steriade 1993a,b) have proposed an Aperture or Stricture feature. Ladefoged uses the terms [stop], [fricative], and [approximant], for three principal values in a multi-valued continuum, whereas Steriade defines Aperture as having just three phonologically relevant possibilities (notated A_0, A_f and A_{max}) which are similar to Ladefoged's principal values. Most feature theories allow for a further distinction among fricatives. Both from a phonological and from a phonetic point of view, the appropriate division is into sibilant (obstacle) and non-sibilant (non-obstacle) fricatives. We can see no reason for grouping **f**, **v** along with **s**, **z**, **ʃ**, **ʒ** and the other sibilant fricatives, as proposed by Chomsky and Halle (1968) on the basis of purported similarities of constriction length. It is far preferable to divide fricatives into sibilants and non-sibilants as indicated at the beginning of this chapter in table 5.1.

The further differentiation of fricative sounds involves what is traditionally called the place of articulation. As we noted in the last chapter, the place features can be thought of as specifying the direction of the movement, and the shape of the moving articulator. For many non-sibilant fricatives, the direction of the movement and the general cavity shape is much the same as in the corresponding stop. However, the extent of the movement and its temporal organization is always very different; fricative transitions are slower than those for the corresponding stops. Fricatives require the specification of a separate, intrinsic, timing pattern.

The places of articulation discussed in chapter 2 can be used in a fairly straightforward way for classifying the articulatory gestures in most non-sibilant fricatives. But, for sibilant fricatives (and also for sibilant affricates) further distinctions are made by using different shapes of the articulator. We propose that, in addition to the features Fricative and Sibilant, the phonological classification of fricatives will require a feature specifying these different tongue shapes. Among alveolars we have noted that some of them have a deep groove in the tongue, whereas others do not. This suggests that there might be a feature Shape, with possible values flat and grooved. This feature might also be used for distinguishing post-alveolar sibilants, in which there are two further values, domed and palatalized. Chinese and Polish so-called retroflex **ʂ** is a laminal flat post-alveolar; Toda and (for some speakers) English palato-alveolar **ʃ** is a laminal domed post-alveolar; and Chinese and Polish alveol-opalatal **ɕ** is a laminal palatalized post-alveolar. The four possibilities for the Shape feature, grooved, flat, domed and palatalized, form a mutually exclusive set. There is also another possibility among post-alveolar sibilants which specifies not the shape of the tongue behind the point of maximum constriction, but whether or not there is a sublingual cavity. It is hard to consider this as another value of the feature Shape, as it could be combined with any of the four values. We suggest that there is a separate feature Closed.

We speculate that these additional variations in tongue shape are not used contrastively in stops (although they may be redundantly present) because their effect on the acoustic signal is too small. Place information in a stop is signaled by the adjoining transitions and the release burst, that is, only at the margins of the segment. However, in a fricative, in addition to that provided by the transitions, place information is provided by the spectrum of the noise throughout the duration of the segment, even though providing good quantitative descriptions of this information remains a challenge to phoneticians. As a result, more subtle variations in articulatory posture can be perceived. This is all the more the case with sibilants, as differences in the angle at which the air strikes the obstacle and the velocity of the airflow can cause large spectral differences. The distinctions required for describing fricatives are thus more elaborate than those which will adequately characterize stop contrasts. The consequence of this fact is that there is no uniform transformation between the vocal tract shape of a fricative and that for a stop, even if the primary place is the same.

6

Laterals

In this chapter we will review all of the various types of segments which have a lateral component. Laterals are usually defined as those sounds which are produced with an occlusion somewhere along the mid-saggital line of the vocal tract but with airflow around one or both sides of the occlusion. We will define laterals slightly differently; they are sounds in which the tongue is contracted in such a way as to narrow its profile from side to side so that a greater volume of air flows around one or both sides than over the center of the tongue. In most laterals there is in fact no central escape of air, but our definition does not require the presence of a central occlusion, and will allow for some central airflow.

The common types of laterals, voiced lateral approximants, have traditionally been grouped with rhotics (r-sounds) under the name of 'liquids'. The core membership of the class of rhotics is formed by segments in which there is a single or repeated brief contact between the tongue and a point on the upper surface of the vocal tract, i.e. principally apical trills, taps and flaps. Laterals and rhotics are grouped together because they share certain phonetic and phonological similarities. Phonetically they are among the most sonorous of oral consonants. And liquids often form a special class in the phonotactics of a language; for example, segments of this class are often those with the greatest freedom to occur in consonant clusters (for more discussion of these similarities see Bhat 1974). Furthermore, quite a few languages have a single underlying liquid phoneme which varies between a lateral and a rhotic pronunciation. We note the validity of the liquid grouping but have chosen to devote separate chapters to laterals and rhotics. Rhotics and related sounds are discussed in chapter 7. We will also discuss the relation between laterals and rhotics in that chapter.

Our review of laterals will begin by discussing the articulatory and acoustic properties of the most frequent type of lateral, a voiced lateral approximant, before turning to other types of lateral segments, such as fricatives. A final section will discuss the issues concerning linguistic representation of laterals that are raised by our analysis of their phonetic nature.

6.1 Voiced Lateral Approximants

Most lateral segments in the world's languages are made with an occlusion in the dental/alveolar region (Maddieson 1984a). Palatographic and x-ray studies of several languages have shown that in many cases the occlusion is limited to a few millimeters on the alveolar ridge in the area behind the incisors and perhaps extending to the premolars. It does not extend back to the molar regions but instead the body of the tongue is relatively low in the mouth behind the closure, permitting lateral air escape as far forward as the front of the palatal region. Figure 6.1 compares the articulatory position for l with that for t for a German and a Standard Chinese speaker by means of palatograms and sagittal x-ray tracings from Wängler (1961) and Zhou and Wu (1963) respectively. The contact indicating sealing of the closure around the sides of the palate seen in the palatograms of t in the lower half of the figure is missing in the palatograms of l. The x-rays indicate that, although the tongue tip makes contact at a fairly similar location for t and l, the profile of the tongue behind the closure differs, so the tongue is lower in the mouth below the front palate area for the lateral. Note that the jaw is also more open for l than for t. This low position facilitates the lateral escape of air. Similar differences in the tongue profile can be seen in published data on a number of other languages with dental or alveolar stops and laterals. In the German l there is also a much wider pharynx than is seen in the stop.

Though this articulatory pattern of a quite limited medial closure restricted to the front of the mouth is common for dental and alveolar laterals, it is by no means universal. The area of contact may extend further back in the mouth than occurs in the examples in figure 6.1, meaning that the lateral escape is located further back. It is also possible for the closure at the front to be incomplete. Balasubramanian (1972) includes palatograms of the long alveolar lateral l of Tamil which show a more extended lateral contact on the right-hand side of the palate. Bolla (1981) shows bilateral contact back to the third molars for a Russian speaker. Figure 6.2 shows retracings of three palatograms of a Gonja speaker (from Painter 1970) producing alveolar laterals. In each case, these laterals are produced with a small escape channel at the front to the left of the medial line. The main lateral escape is further back. In figure 6.2 (a) it is on the left in the mid-palatal region. In figure 6.2 (b) and (c) the escape around the

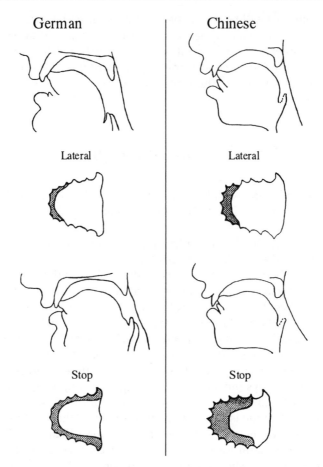

Figure 6.1 X-ray tracings and palatograms comparing articulatory positions for l and t in German and Standard Chinese (based on data in Wängler 1961, and Zhou and Wu 1963 respectively).

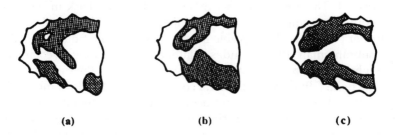

Figure 6.2 Palatograms showing contact area for three repetitions of l by a Gonja speaker (based on data in Painter 1970).

oral obstruction is further back in the mouth than the palatogram is able to show.

Dynamic palatographic records of a British English speaker published by Dent (1984) show contact maintained along the edges of the palate above the molar teeth and on both sides of the alveolar ridge in most instances of l, but during production of an l in the cluster sl a small central escape channel in the alveolar region remains open. Dent notes that this absence of medial closure occurs sometimes with two out of her three subjects but that the percept remains that of an authentic lateral. So we see that laterals do not always have complete central closure. However, even when they have some central airflow they have a larger escape channel further back in the mouth. Note that these laterals with no central closure are in syllable-initial positions, not in final position. We will return to the question of laterals without a central closure below, in connection with the vocalization of postvocalic laterals.

First let us review what articulatory gestures are used in the production of laterals of the common voiced approximant type. We will do this by reference to the point of most forward contact of the tongue (the traditional place of articulation) and to the part of the tongue that is involved. We will also discuss some questions concerning the shape of the remainder of the tongue where this is known. As in previous chapters, we will begin by examining the differences between typical productions of contrasting lateral segments within a language and then building a composite picture of the range of contrasts that seems possible. The terminology for places of articulation will be that developed in earlier chapters.

There are fewer places at which laterals are produced and fewer contrasts between laterals than is the case with stops or fricatives. The largest number of contrasting simple voiced lateral approximants known to occur in a language is four, as found in our own work on Kaititj (see below) and reported from several other Australian languages such as Pitta-Pitta (Blake 1979), Diyari (Austin 1981) and Arabana (Hercus 1973). Kaititj has laminal dental, apical alveolar, apical post-alveolar and laminal post-alveolar laterals. Examples of words containing these are given in table 6.1.

The number of languages which contrast simple voiced lateral approximants at three places of articulation is also relatively small, and many of these are also languages of Australia. Examples are Nunggubuyu, Alawa and Bardi.

Table 6.1 Words illustrating contrasting laterals in Kaititj

	LAMINAL DENTAL l̪		APICAL ALVEOLAR l		APICAL POST-ALVEOLAR ɭ		LAMINAL POST-ALVEOLAR l̠	
INITIAL	l̪inp	'armpit'	lubiɻ	'thigh'	ɭaɻiŋk	'hit'	lukuŋk	'light (fire)'
MEDIAL	al̪uŋ	'burrow'	aluŋk	'chase'	aɭat	'sacred board'	alil̠k	'smooth'
FINAL	al̪bal̪	'smoke'	irmal	'fire saw'	aɭdimaɭ	'west'	kural̠	'star'

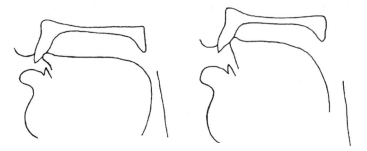

Figure 6.3 Cine x-rays of apical dental and apical alveolar laterals in Albanian: ļ in ha**ļ**a 'aunt', l in **pala** 'pair' (based on data in Bothorel 1969–70).

These languages lack the palatal lateral found in languages like Pitta-Pitta. The Papuan language Mid-Waghi, which will be discussed below, also has three places for laterals, as do a number of languages from other parts of the world, including Khanty (Gulya 1966) and Argentinian dialects of Mapuche (Key 1978). Languages with two laterals are much more frequently encountered; detailed articulatory phonetic information is available on some of these languages. Several of these throw interesting light on the role of tongue profile in contrasting articulatory gestures.

Cine x-ray studies (Bothorel 1969–70) indicate that Albanian has a distinction between what might be labeled apical dental and apical alveolar laterals. Tracings of these are given in figure 6.3. Note that besides the different location of the 'place of articulation' there are several other differences between l in *pala* and ļ in *halla* in this figure. The back of the tongue is retracted for ļ so that a narrowed pharynx results, and the body of the tongue lies lower in the mouth than for l. The speaker represented in Dodi (1970) seems to have less of a place difference than the two speakers examined by Bothorel, but does show the difference in tongue profile. The Albanian laterals indicate that the dental vs alveolar place contrast can occur with the 'enhancement' of different tongue body positions but without differing by one being laminal and the other apical.

Laminal post-alveolar (palato-alveolar) laterals occur in limited surface contrast with apical alveolar laterals in the dialect of Breton spoken at Argol (Bothorel 1982). Cine x-rays of these sounds are shown in figure 6.4. The particular token of the apical lateral shown in this figure has a somewhat more forward position than those before other vowels, and the tongue partly contacts the teeth. It was selected in order to show the two contrasting laterals of the language in similar vowel environments. The laminal post-alveolars occur only after an actual or historical i and consequently have some similarities of tongue position to the high front tongue position for i. However, they cannot

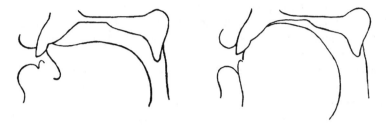

Figure 6.4 Cine x-rays of apical dental and laminal post-alveolar (palato-alveolar) laterals in Breton, Argol dialect: l̪ in sa̪la:n 'salads', l̺ in buta̪ladu 'bottles' (based on data in Bothorel 1982).

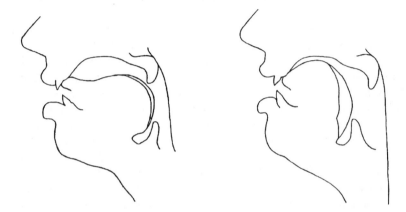

Figure 6.5 Cine x-rays of apical alveolar and laminal alveolar laterals in Russian: l̺ak 'varnish', l̪ina 'line' (based on data in Koneczna and Zawadowski 1956). The laminal articulation is the phonologically palatalized counterpart of the apical lateral.

be regarded as simply the result of coarticulation since they do not necessarily occur next to an actual **i** vowel, as the example we have chosen shows.

The Breton laminal post-alveolar lateral tongue shape is in some respects quite similar to that seen in cine x-rays of the Russian 'soft l' (Koneczna and Zawadowski 1956, Fant 1960, Jazić 1977, Bolla 1981, 1982), although in the Russian sound the contact is further forward. This Russian laminal lateral is commonly referred to as a palatalized version of the apical 'hard l', but as the example in figure 6.5 shows, for many speakers the primary articulation itself differs from that seen in the non-palatalized counterpart. For some speakers of Russian, the contrast can be described as between an apical and a laminal alveolar. For others, the contrast is between an apical alveolar and a laminal dental. In addition, there are differences in the position of the body of the tongue. The apical lateral in figure 6.5 has some raising of the back of the tongue and considerable narrowing of the pharynx. For the laminal lateral in figure 6.5 the highest point of the tongue is under the back of the palate and the pharynx is wide. In this case, tongue backing occurs with the segment that Stevens, Keyser and Kawasaki (1986) would call [- distributed], that is, with the one we would classify as [- laminal].

In Bulgarian there is also a difference in primary place of articulation between the two laterals. These are normally treated as differentiated by presence or absence of palatalization, but in our view, the difference is really in the primary articulation, as in Russian. In the Bulgarian case, both the laterals are laminal. The cine x-rays and palatograms we have seen (Stojkov 1942, 1961), as well as the verbal descriptions by Stojkov, make it clear that Bulgarian l is a laminal dental. Except before front vowels, the front of the tongue is low behind the occlusion and the back of the tongue is raised toward the velum. Its palatalized counterpart is laminal post-alveolar (palato-alveolar), and the body of the tongue is generally higher in the mouth, particularly in the front (although it seems less high than in the Breton case cited above).

The x-ray study by Jazić (1977) contrasts Russian and Serbo-Croation l's and their palatalized counterparts. For Serbo-Croation lʲ the occlusion is palato-alveolar, with the tongue body high and the pharynx wide. Serbo-Croatian l has a low tongue profile but still a relatively wide pharynx, similar to that seen in the German and Breton x-rays in figures 6.1 and 6.4. Thus, phonological palatalization is not always accompanied by a big difference in pharynx width.

The extent to which different tongue profiles of the types seen in the contrasting laterals of Albanian, Breton, Russian, Bulgarian and Serbo-Croatian can be chosen independently of the tongue tip and blade activity is unclear. It seems reasonable to suppose that the choice of laminal or apical articulation restricts the freedom of position for the tongue body to some degree, and that raising the front of the tongue favors laminal articulation, whereas lowering it favors apical articulation. The data we have seen suggests that wide pharynx and raised tongue front usually accompany the laminal articulations, but the Bulgarian data shows that this is not invariably the case. The tongue profile may be more variable when the articulation is apical, but raising of the back of the tongue and/or narrowing of the pharynx are not uncommon. But there is unfortunately too little data available from too few languages to be sure how generally these observations apply. It would be nice to know, for example, if the tongue profile differences in Russian laterals are replicated in Diegueño (Langdon 1970). This is also a language with laterals with two types of articulation, in one of which "the apex [of the tongue] is raised to touch the alveolar ridge" while in the other "it is lowered to touch the back of the lower teeth with the blade contacting the alveolar ridge." However, Diegueño lacks the general phonological division of consonants into plain and palatalized classes which characterizes Russian and several of the other languages we have discussed here. We do not know if laminal alveolar or post-alveolar laterals occur without an accompanying raising of the tongue front which might be characterized as some form of 'palatalization'. Our examination of spectrograms of the

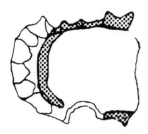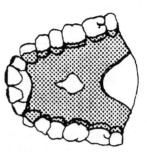

Figure 6.6 Palatograms of apical alveolar and laminal palatal laterals in Spanish, Standard Peninsular Castilian dialect (after Navarro Tomás 1968).

Diegueño laminal lateral suggest that it is a palato-alveolar articulation, with a raised tongue position.

The pre-palatal laminal laterals we have been discussing so far can be distinguished from dorsal palatal laterals. Laterals of the latter type are found in Italian in contrast with apical alveolars, as well as in Spanish and a number of other languages. In these palatal laterals, contact is made between the tongue dorsum and the hard palate. Bladon and Carbonaro (1978) show the occlusion for Italian ʎ being made about two-thirds of the way back on the hard palate. In those dialects of Spanish which have a palatal lateral (principally those of European Spanish), the articulation seems to be a little further forward. The contact area is quite extended, as may be seen in figure 6.6 based on palatograms of Spanish l and ʎ in Navarro Tomás (1968). A tracing of an x-ray of Spanish ʎ in Straka (1965) shows the tongue tip not making any contact with the teeth (as in the palatogram in figure 6.6), whereas one in Quilis (1963) shows an extension of the contact area all the way from the palate to the teeth.

Contrasts involving sublaminal post-alveolar (retroflex) laterals appear in Tamil, Malayalam, Toda and other Dravidian languages in which stops at this place of articulation occur. Most Dravidian languages have only two places of articulation for laterals, instead of the six or seven places they have for stops. Svarný and Zvelebil (1955) publish palatograms and x-rays documenting the fact that Tamil and Telugu contrast apical alveolar and sub-apical retroflex laterals, with a tongue shape for the retroflex lateral very similar to that for the corresponding stops shown previously in figure 2.7. The contact for the retroflex lateral is on the hard palate, hence these sounds could be considered as produced with the 'apical' variety of the palatal place of articulation. Outside the Dravidian language family contrastive sub-apical retroflex laterals are not known for certain to occur, but, to judge from a sketch of the articulators in Gulya (1966), this type of retroflex lateral may occur in Khanty, in contrast

Table 6.2 Words illustrating laterals in Mid-Waghi

Laminal dental	Apical alveolar	(Dorsal) velar
aḻa aḻa	**alala**	**aʟaʟe**
'again and again'	'speak incorrectly'	'dizzy'

with both palatal and alveolar laterals. We assume that the retroflex laterals of the Australian languages are likely to be sub-apical since, as noted above in chapter 2, the corresponding stops seem to be produced in that fashion, whereas those of the Indic languages with retroflex laterals, such as Panjabi, are apical post-alveolars.

It used to be said that only coronal sounds could be lateral (Chomsky and Halle 1968), or that laterals occurred only at the dental, alveolar, retroflex and palatal places of articulation (Ladefoged 1971). However, velar laterals also occur contrastively. Velar laterals, not always of the voiced approximant type, appear in Melpa and Mid-Waghi in contrast with laterals at other places of articulation (Ladefoged, Cochran and Disner 1977), and in Kanite (Young 1962) and Yagaria (Renck 1975) as the only lateral segments. These are all languages of New Guinea, but velar laterals are reported also in Kotoko and possibly also occur in other East Chadic languages (Paul Newman, personal communication) and Hagège (1981) reports a voiced velar lateral in Comox. Words illustrating the three contrasting laterals which appear in Mid-Waghi, laminal dental, apical alveolar and (dorsal) velar, are shown in table 6.2. The acoustic character of these examples is discussed below.

The precise location of the contact and of the lateral escape channel for the velar cannot be recorded by direct palatography since the closure is too far back, but with an open vowel before and after a velar lateral it is possible to see both the central velar closure and the lateral opening simply by looking into the speaker's mouth. For the Mid-Waghi speakers we recorded, it was possible to see that the tongue was bunched up in the back of the mouth with the tip retracted from the lower front teeth. The body of the tongue was visibly narrowed in the central region, and presumably also further back where it could not be seen. The only articulatory contact was in the back of the velar region in much the same position as for a velar stop and, according to the speaker, air escaped around both sides of this contact in the region of the back molars. In addition, the auditory impression created by the brief stop closure which sometimes occurs before the lateral is clearly velar. In his account of Comox, Hagège (1981) gives a similar description of this sound. He notes that the back of the tongue makes quite firm contact with the back of the velum and the sides of the tongue are lowered so that there is only weak friction and the sound is an approximant.

Trager and Smith (1956) claim that velar laterals also occur in certain varieties of American and Scottish English, but no other observers have agreed with

Table 6.3 Places of articulation for lateral approximants and examples of languages using them

DENTAL		ALVEOLAR		POST-ALVEOLAR		PALATAL		VELAR
APICAL	LAMINAL	APICAL	LAMINAL	APICAL	LAMINAL	SUB-LAMINAL	LAMINAL	
1	2	3	4	5	6	7	8	9
	Kaititj	Kaititj			Kaititj	Kaititj		
	Mid-Waghi	Mid-Waghi						Mid-Waghi
	Panjabi			Panjabi				
	Malayalam					Malayalam		
Albanian		Albanian						
		Russian	Russian					
	Italian						Italian	

this claim. It seems likely that they were referring to what we would call velarized alveolar laterals, or possibly to laterals without a central occlusion which we will discuss later.

Production of uvular or epiglottal (pharyngeal) laterals by narrowing the tongue and using a medial occlusion formed with the uvula or the epiglottis respectively is not inconceivable; however, no such sounds are known to occur in any natural human language. Bilabial and labiodental approximants can be produced with a central occlusion and lateral airflow, but these seem to be indistinguishable from the corresponding central approximants. (In fact, for many English speakers the labiodental fricatives **f** and **v** are produced as what might by some definitions be lateral segments, since they have a closure in the midline.) Note that since we define laterals as involving narrowing of the tongue, these labial articulations are not laterals by our definition. On the other hand, laterals can be produced by an articulation involving the tongue and the upper lip. Linguo-labial laterals sound quite distinctive, but none of the languages that have developed this place of articulation (illustrated for stops and fricatives in chapter 2) has employed it in the production of lateral segments as far as we know.

We therefore have indications that there are nine 'places of articulation' used for lateral approximants, as summarized in table 6.3. Of these nine places, eight participate in pairs that can be distinguished by the apical/laminal feature operating independently of other aspects of the place feature system, as described in chapter 2. Distributional facts concerning laterals in Australian languages (Dixon 1980) provide good evidence for treating the apical/laminal distinction as a separate feature. For example, in those languages with four laterals only the two apical laterals may appear as the first element of a medial consonant cluster.

Voiced approximant lateral segments seem to be prone to considerable variation in their production, both from individual to individual and from one phonetic context to another. In a palatographic and linguographic study of 20 English speakers and 21 French speakers, Dart (1991) found a wide variety of

Figure 6.7 Tracings of frames from x-ray film of l + ʒ in the phrase *belles jambes* spoken by a speaker of French (based on data in Rochette 1973). The speaker was a 23-year-old male native of Paris.

articulations for l within the dental/alveolar region, with somewhat greater variation among English speakers than among French speakers. She also noted that there is a strong tendency for l to be apical. Even in French, in which t, d, n are usually laminal dental, about 85 percent of the speakers produced l as an apical alveolar.

Contextual variations among laterals have been well documented in many languages. In English, for example, l is subject to considerable assimilatory effect from adjacent voiceless consonants (especially from preceding stops), considerable coarticulatory effect of adjacent vowels, and considerable variation attributable to effects of position in the syllable and morpheme (Lehiste 1964, Giles and Moll 1975, Bladon and Al-Bamerni 1976, Dent 1984, Gartenberg 1984, Sproat and Fujimura 1993). Large within-speaker variation in the articulatory position for French l in various consonant sequences are documented by Rochette (1973). These include even sublaminal palatal (retroflex) productions in the sequences l + ʒ and l + f. The production of an l + ʒ sequence is illustrated in figure 6.7. The heavy outline shows the steady state position for the l, which is maintained for about 60 ms. The lighter traces show phases of the release, as the tongue tip is lowered towards the position for ʒ and the lips are protruded in anticipation of the rounding that usually accompanies this fricative in French.

The resonant nature of laterals and their somewhat vowel-like acoustic structure seem to make coarticulated variation in their production quite noticeable, more so than might be the case with other classes of segments. The degree of variability seems to depend in part on tongue position; laterals with a high tongue body position such as palatals or laminal post-alveolars show less variation than laterals with a lower tongue body position. For example, Italian l shows much more variation, measured acoustically by variation in F2, with respect to both following and preceding vowel context than does ʎ

(Bladon and Carbonaro 1978). Somewhat similarly, the laminal post-alveolar (palato-alveolar) lateral in Catalan varies less than the apical alveolar lateral, according to both dynamic palatographic and acoustic studies carried out by Recasens (1984a, b).

As we mentioned earlier, laterals may also be produced without a complete medial occlusion. Extremes of this process may be seen in languages such as English and Portuguese where completely unoccluded 'laterals' occur in postvocalic positions. In some forms of British English, such as that spoken in London and much of southeast England, two quite different types of laterals must be distinguished. For syllable initial /l/ the tip of the tongue touches the alveolar ridge and the tongue is narrowed so that there is no contact at one or both sides. In syllable-final /l/ there is no alveolar contact and the tongue tip may be behind the lower front teeth. But there may still be a narrowing of the tongue so that, by our definition, this segment is still a lateral. It seems as if the situation is similar in Portuguese. Feldman (1972) shows that the final allophone of /l/ in certain varieties of Brazilian Portuguese is produced with no occlusion but with a marked raising of the tip of the tongue towards the alveolar ridge, where initial allophones of /l/ would have a contact. This vestigial tongue-raising gesture, together with raising of the back of the tongue produces a segment which is acoustically very similar to ʊ, and for some speakers of Brazilian Portuguese merges with that segment. Laterals of this type are likely to become simply vowels or semivowels with the passage of time (as they have in Polish and some forms of Southern British English), but as long as the tongue narrowing gesture remains they are still correctly classed as laterals.

6.2 Acoustic Characteristics of Voiced Lateral Approximants

Canonical voiced lateral approximants are characterized acoustically by well-defined formant-like resonances. The first formant is typically rather low in frequency. The second formant may have a center frequency anywhere within a fairly wide range depending on the location of the occlusion and the profile of the tongue. The third formant has typically a relatively strong amplitude and high frequency; and there may also be several closely spaced additional formants above the frequency of F3. When a lateral is adjacent to vowels an abrupt change in formant location can often be observed both when the medial closure for the lateral is formed and when it is released, particularly if the articulation is apical. Laminal and dorsal laterals may have somewhat slower transitions from and to adjoining vowels. These properties can be seen by examining the spectrograms in figures 6.8 (Arrernte) and 6.9 (Mid-Waghi) below.

The first formant of lateral segments is uniformly low – typically below 400

Table 6.4 Formant frequencies (in Hz) of Arrernte laterals

	n	F1	F2	F3	F3–F2
LAMINAL DENTAL	40	391	1811	2891	1080
APICAL ALVEOLAR	75	386	1677	3162	1484
APICAL POST- ALVEOLAR	37	368	2132	3278	1146
LAMINAL POST-ALVEOLAR	34	376	2324	3096	772
'PALATALIZED RETROFLEX'	26	415	2282	3290	1008

Hz for male speakers. Fant (1960) and Bladon (1979) have suggested that F1 varies inversely with the cross-sectional area of the lateral passage. If this were so then laminal Coronal and Dorsal laterals would be expected to share a higher F1 (since the body of the tongue is raised and the lateral passage consequently more constricted) and apical and sub-apical laterals would share a lower F1. Note that this grouping of laterals on acoustic grounds has no parallel with the groupings established by acoustic properties of stops or nasals. We find at best partial confirmation of Fant and Bladon's theoretical claims in real language materials. We have measured the formants in a large number of laterals in words spoken by one female speaker of Arrernte. Spectrograms of representative tokens of the four coronal laterals in intervocalic position, together with the special retroflex lateral variant which occurs in clusters with stops are shown in figure 6.8. Measured formant values are shown in table 6.4. The apical post-alveolar has a significantly lower F1 than other laterals and the laminal dental and 'palatalized retroflex' (which also appears to have a laminal articulation) have the highest F1's. However, the apical alveolar and the laminal post-alveolar have similar F1 values and do not follow the theoretical expectations. (The other formant frequencies in table 6.4 will be discussed later in this section.)

Data from some other languages also offer no support for the idea that laminal laterals uniformly have a higher F1. The laminal post-alveolar lateral of Breton has a lower range of F1 than the apical alveolar (Bothorel 1982), and the palatalized lateral of Bulgarian has an F1 100–150 Hz lower than the plain (apical) lateral (Tilkov 1979). Vages, Ferrero, Magno-Caldognetto and Lavagnoli (1978) show a mean F1 of 500 Hz for l and of 280 Hz for ʎ for ten speakers of Italian. The two laterals of Russian are, however, shown as having the same F1 by Zinder, Bondarko and Berbitskaja (1964), contra Fant (1960).

We would anticipate a high F1 for velar laterals following Fant and Bladon. And, in fact, in our materials from Mid-Waghi (one speaker) and Melpa (two speakers) the highest F1 in a lateral segment is observed in the velar lateral. The relatively high F1 for the velar lateral can be seen in the spectrograms of the three contrasting laterals in Mid-Waghi given in figure 6.9. It may also be noted that the velar laterals in Mid-Waghi are occasionally 'prestopped'. There

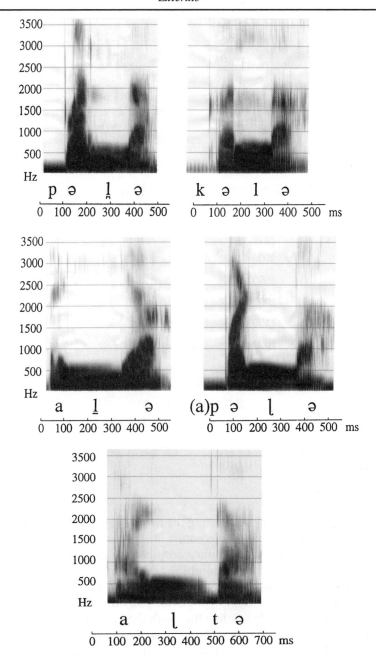

Figure 6.8 Spectrograms of the four (non-labialized) coronal laterals of Arrernte and the variant, traditionally considered a 'palatalized retroflex' which occurs in clusters before stops. The words are **pələ** 'spit', **kələ** 'all right', **aḻə** 'boomerang', **apəɭə** 'father's mother' (initial vowel not shown), **aɭtə** 'day'.

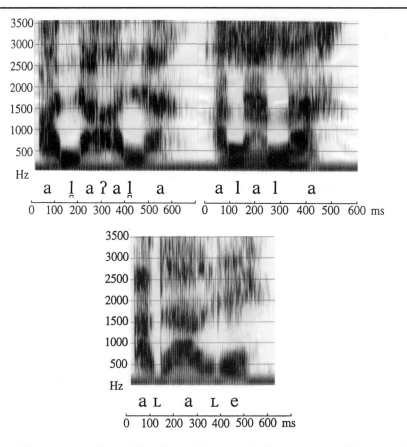

Figure 6.9 Spectrograms of laminal dental, apical alveolar and velar laterals in Mid-Waghi (see Table 6.2 for glosses).

is a brief velar stop closure preceding the first velar lateral in figure 6.9, but the second is entirely approximant in nature.

For laterals without a secondary constriction involving the back of the tongue, the frequency of the second formant seems to be inversely related to the volume of the oral-pharyngeal cavity behind the articulatory occlusion (Bladon 1979). Measurements of F2 for the four laterals of Kaititj and Alyawarra, given in table 6.5, together with the F2 measurements on Arrernte in table 6.4 confirm this pattern. The pattern of relative height of F2 is generally similar for all three speakers. It is lowest in the apical alveolar, intermediate in the laminal dental and apical post-alveolar (retroflex) cases, and highest in the case of the laminal post-alveolar (palato-alveolar) laterals, which have the smallest cavity behind the closure. When F2 is similar the laminal dental and apical post-alveolar are presumably distinguishable by the decidedly higher F1

Table 6.5 F2 (in Hz) in laterals of two additional Arandic languages

	KAITITJ (MALE)	ALYAWARRA (FEMALE)
LAMINAL DENTAL	1350	1750
APICAL ALVEOLAR	1225	1425
APICAL POST-ALVEOLAR	1300	1800
LAMINAL POST-ALVEOLAR	1800	2250

Table 6.6 F2 (Hz) in laterals differing in velarization. Data from Zinder, Bondarko and Berbitskaja (1964), Tilkov (1979) and Dodi (1970)

	RUSSIAN	BULGARIAN	ALBANIAN
VELARIZED	900	1000	950
CONTRASTING LATERAL	2200	1800	1550

of the dental, as well as by different durations and transitional characteristics. In general, as table 6.4 and figure 6.9 show, F2 and F3 are closer together in laminal laterals than in apical ones.

In Melpa and Mid-Waghi the lowest F2 is again found in the apical alveolars, but F2 is lower in the velar laterals than in the laminal dental type, contrary to expectation. This may be seen for Mid-Waghi in figure 6.9. However, note that F2 is much higher in these velar laterals than it is in *velarized* alveolars (i.e. those in which the back of the tongue is partially raised toward the velum). Values for Albanian, Bulgarian and Russian velarized and non-velarized laterals are given in table 6.6. Although one must be cautious in comparing data across different subjects, it does seem that F2 is lowest in apical laterals with an additional narrowing at the back. F2 will be lower the narrower this constriction becomes, as for the production of high back vowels.

6.3 Other Types of Laterals

The most common laterals are voiced and approximant, as discussed above; but there are also a number of other possibilities. Lateral articulations can be accompanied by most of the different laryngeal settings discussed in chapter 3 and they can occur with various types of stricture. We will discuss these various possibilities in this chapter, and some of the interactions between phonation type and manner that are commonly observed among laterals. Lateral clicks will be discussed in chapter 8, together with other clicks.

Variations in phonation type

Lateral articulations can have different types of phonation, in that they may be voiced, voiceless, breathy voiced, or laryngealized. As we noted earlier, most lateral approximant segments are voiced, but voiceless lateral approximants occur as contrastive segments in languages such as Burmese, Tibetan, Klamath, Iaai, Kuy and some dialects of Irish. We know of few languages in which voiceless lateral approximants contrast with their voiced counterparts at other than the dental or alveolar places of articulation, but Toda has voiced and voiceless sub-apical palatal (retroflex) laterals. Examples of these Toda laterals are given in table 6.7. A voiceless apical post-alveolar (retroflex) lateral occurs in Iaai (Ozanne-Rivierre 1976, Maddieson and Anderson 1994), contrasting with its voiced counterpart, and with a pair of voiced and voiceless dental laterals. As seems to be the usual pattern for languages with voiceless lateral approximants, there are also voiceless nasals in Iaai, but this pattern does not hold true for Toda.

In some instances, linguists have chosen to regard voiceless lateral approximants as phonemically composed of either **l** + **h**, as in Purnell's (1965) analysis of Mien (Yao), or of **h** + **l**, as Smith (1968) does for Sedang, but we believe these segments are in no way distinct from other voiceless lateral approximants. (We do not rule out the occurrence of clusters of **h** + **l** or **l** + **h**, but simply note that transcriptions such as **hl**, **lh** are often equivalent to **l̥**).

In the case of a substantial number of other languages the available descriptions do not specify if the voiceless laterals occurring in them are approximant or fricative in nature. Perhaps this is because there is a widespread tradition of regarding all voiceless laterals as fricatives, with turbulence necessarily resulting from the air passing through the lateral aperture (cf. Pike 1943). However, we draw a distinction between voiceless laterals that are articulated with an aperture comparable in area to that of voiced lateral approximants and those produced with a more constricted aperture, comparable to that of other fricatives. We will discuss lateral fricatives more fully below; at this point we would only like to point out that voiceless lateral approximants are distinguishable acoustically from voiceless lateral fricatives in a number of different ways. Maddieson and Emmorey (1984) compared Burmese and Tibetan, which have voiceless lateral approximants, with Navajo and Zulu, which have voiceless lateral fricatives. Their measures showed that the voiceless

Table 6.7 Words illustrating contrasting laterals in Toda

	ALVEOLAR		RETROFLEX	
VOICELESS	ka**l̥**	'study'	pa**ɭ̥**	'valley'
VOICED	ka**l**	'bead'	pa**ɭ**	'bangle'

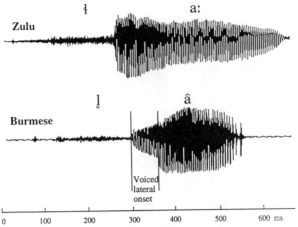

Figure 6.10 Waveforms illustrating differences between a voiceless lateral fricative in the Zulu syllable ɬaː and a voiceless lateral approximant in the Burmese syllable l̥â. The lower amplitude and the
anticipation of the voicing in the approximant are apparent.

Table 6.8 Devoicing and frication of final laterals in Melpa

	LAMINAL DENTAL		APICAL ALVEOLAR		VELAR	
MEDIAL	kialt̪im	'fingernail'	lola	'speak improperly'	paʟa	'fence'
FINAL	waɬ	'knitted bag'	baɬ	'apron'	raʟ̥	'two'

approximants typically have a lower amplitude of noise, a greater tendency to
anticipate the voicing of a following vowel, and a concentration of energy
lower in the spectrum than voiceless fricative laterals do. Waveforms of tokens
from Burmese and Zulu illustrating some of these differences are given in figure 6.10. The distinction between Burmese and Tibetan as opposed to Navajo
and Zulu is quite clear, but in other cases it is difficult to decide whether a
voiceless lateral should be described as an approximant or a fricative. Taishan
Chinese, which was also included in Maddieson and Emmorey's study, is usually described as having a voiceless dental lateral fricative, which varies with a
central dental fricative, θ. The measurements showed that the lateral variant in
this language was intermediate between the clearer cases.

We do not know of a language with a minimal contrast between voiceless
lateral approximant and fricative but both types can appear in the same language. Hupa (Golla 1970) has the allophone l̥ after h in the word tʃʼahl̥ 'frog' as
well as the fricative ɬ, e.g. in miɬ 'when'. It is not unusual for lateral
approximants to become substantially devoiced in clusters with voiceless segments, or in final position. All three lateral segments in Melpa and Mid-Waghi
devoice in final position, as noted in the Melpa examples given in table 6.8, but
in these languages the results of this devoicing process are best described as
lateral fricatives.

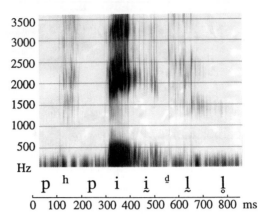

Figure 6.11 Spectrogram of the Montana Salish word **ppi̬l̬** (in a narrow transcription [pʰpii̬ᵈl̬l̥]) 'pint'.

Table 6.9 Words illustrating contrasting alveolar laterals in initial position in Montana Salish

Voiceless fricative	ɬáqʃəlʃ	'sit down!'
Voiced approximant	láqʼi	'sweatbath'
Laryngealized approximant	l̬láts	'red raspberry'
Ejective affricate	tɬʼáqʼ	'hot'

Voiced laryngealized lateral continuants occur in several languages, such as Tiddim Chin, Nez Perce, Chemehuevi, Haida, Sedang, Klamath. These last two languages have a three-way contrast of voice quality in laterals, having voiced, voiceless and voiced laryngealized lateral approximants. Montana Salish has modally voiced and laryngealized voiced lateral approximants, as well as laterals of other types. Examples from Montana Salish are given in table 6.9, which also illustrates the lateral ejective which we will discuss later. A laryngealized lateral from Columbian Salish was illustrated in figure 4.2.

In Montana Salish, the lateral approximants, including the laryngealized laterals, tend to be prestopped, and to become devoiced in final position and before voiceless consonants. Thus, as shown in figure 6.11, a laryngealized lateral, which, phonologically, is the final consonant in the word, may be produced as a creaky voiced vowel, followed by a brief stop, a creaky lateral, and finally a voiceless lateral approximant.

This prestopping can also occur in Montana Salish when there is a sequence of identical laterals, as in the example in figure 6.12, which shows the sequence of consonants in the middle of the word **pʼəllitʃʼtʃ** 'turned over'. Note that these laterals are produced with a considerable amount of (non-distinctive) frication, indicating that the lateral escape channel is very narrow. In the narrow transcription in figure 6.12, the symbol ꞎ has been used. The first of these

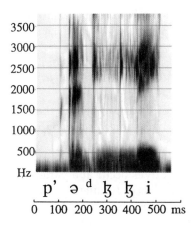

Figure 6.12 The sequence of lateral consonants in the first part of the Montana Salish word **p'əllitʃ'tʃ** 'turned over'. In the narrow transcription beneath the spectrogram the prestopping is indicated by a raised ᵈ.

two laterals has a stop closure preceding it, and a burst as this closure is released, similar to that seen in figure 6.10. The second lateral does not have a similar closure interval, but there is a transient in the spectrum, closely resembling that produced by the release of a stop. It is much stronger than the transient produced at the onset of the following vowel by the release of the central closure of the tongue. Exactly how this transient is produced is not clear to us at the moment, but it must involve a very brief obstruction of the lateral escape channel. This would be facilitated by the fact that the channel is already constricted so that only a small movement is required. Furthermore, the constricted airflow will result in an elevated intra-oral air pressure, compared to an approximant production. A very brief closure would therefore impound pressure immediately. Such discontinuities indicate that, in these cases at least, the sequences consist of two separate consonants rather than long consonants.

Breathy voiced laterals occur in a number of languages, notably those that also have breathy voiced stops. Hindi is often considered to have a phonemic contrast of plain and breathy voiced lateral approximants, though Ohala (1983) suggests that l̤ should be regarded as a sequence **lh** principally because breathy voiced liquids and nasals are limited to medial position. Dixit (1975) showed that although vocal cord vibration continues throughout this segment, there is also a glottal opening gesture. This gesture starts after the oral closure for the lateral is formed, and peaks some 40 ms after the release. In broad terms, this relative timing pattern is similar to that seen for breathy voiced consonants of other types in intervocalic position, hence we consider l̤ a genuine lexical segment of Hindi. Although they have not been studied in such detail in any other language, breathy voiced laterals occur in several other Indo-Aryan languages and in several languages in the Wu and Yue groups of Chinese dialects, for example in Rongxian (Tsuji 1980).

Variations in stricture

Although laterals are most often approximant, they can also occur with other types of stricture. We have had some discussion of lateral fricatives in a preceding section. In addition to the production of laterals with frication as allophonic variants, as in the Melpa and Montana Salish cases mentioned there, contrastive lateral fricatives occur at a variety of places and with different phonation types. They are most frequently voiceless. In addition to the occurrence of lateral fricatives alone, a stop closure can be released into a homorganic lateral fricative, with the combination being considered to form a lateral affricate under the same kind of conditions that would lead to a decision to consider a stop released into a central fricative to be an affricate. In the affricates the stopped portion of the segment is not itself lateral (it could not be a stop otherwise); but the stop is released by lowering some portion of the sides of the tongue, rather than the center. Like lateral fricatives, lateral affricates are more commonly voiceless than voiced, and are frequently ejective. Because these classes of sounds are closely related, we will discuss them together.

A stop closure can also be combined with an approximant lateral. Such combinations usually involve what we would consider a sequence of sounds, as in English words such as *melt, weld, puddle, shuttle*. Clusters consisting of homorganic approximant laterals and stops in either order occur widely in the world's languages. Because the articulatory adjustment required to pass from a lateral to a homorganic stop or vice-versa is a minimal one, these sequences can be closely bound together at the level of articulatory organization. A special term, lateral plosion, is used to describe the release of a plosive directly into a lateral by lowering one or both sides of the tongue. In a small number of languages prestopped laterals have been analyzed as units. In Arabana and Wangganuru (Hercus 1973) **d̪l** and **dl** occur as allophones of the (laminal) dental and apical alveolar lateral approximants. These variants occur in word-medial positions after the initial stressed syllable in words which begin with a consonant. Although the distributional pattern of these elements may justify their treatment as single units from the phonological point of view, we know of no evidence in this case that they are phonetically distinct from stop + lateral clusters. We have noted above the allophonic prestopping of laterals in Montana Salish, where there are special phonetic characteristics to observe. We are not aware of any languages for which it has been proposed that a lateral + stop sequence should be analyzed as a single segment, i.e. as a 'prelateralized stop' parallel to the prenasalized stops discussed in chapter 4.

Laterals can also be flaps or taps. We will illustrate these at the end of this section. We do not know of any segment that we would call a lateral trill; and of course lateral nasals are a contradiction in terms in that there cannot be a lateral oral air escape and simultaneously no oral escape. A nasalized lateral is, however, occasionally encountered, and examples were given in chapter 4.

Lateral fricatives and affricates

Perhaps the best-known example of a language with a lateral fricative is Welsh. This segment, a voiceless alveolar lateral fricative, alternates with a voiced alveolar lateral approximant under specific morphological conditions, but because of loanwords the two segments now contrast. A voiceless approximant occurs in clusters after an initial voiceless stop. Examples are given in table 6.10. Ball and Müller (1992) provide measurements on ɬ and l for two speakers of Welsh. In initial and medial positions ɬ is about twice as long as l and has no anticipatory voicing. The fricative ɬ has a higher second formant than l and considerable noise concentrated in the frequency range between about 5000 and 7000 Hz.

Lateral fricatives occurring at different places of articulation occur in Bura, which is unusual in having a contrast between voiceless lateral fricatives at two places of articulation, apical alveolar and palatal. We will use the symbol ʎ̥ for the voiceless palatal lateral fricative. There is also a voiced apical alveolar lateral fricative, and an alveolar lateral of the more usual voiced approximant type. Spectrograms of these four sounds are given in figure 6.13.

Hoffman (1957) and Ladefoged (1968) give examples of an additional lateral, a voiced palatal lateral approximant, making Bura a language with five lateral segments. The two voiceless lateral fricatives differ in that the main noise concentration in the palatal is centered in a higher frequency region than it is in the alveolar. A similar distinction is found between the apical alveolar and laminal post-alveolar voiceless lateral fricatives of Diegueño. A voiced lateral segment described by Shafeev (1964) as a 'prepalatal fricative' occurs in Pashto. This would appear to be the voiced counterpart of the Diegueño segment. As noted above, the Taishan dialect of Chinese has a voiceless apical dental lateral fricative, which for many speakers can vary with a central dental fricative, θ. Gowda (1972) describes a voiced apical post-alveolar lateral fricative in Ao (Naga). We have not heard this sound but the description seems quite clear.

Table 6.10 Words illustrating laterals in Welsh (from Thomas 1992)

Voiceless fricative		Voiced approximant		Voiceless approximant	
ɬond	'full'	loːn	'road'	tl̥uːs	'pretty'
miɬdir	'mile'	xwildro	'revolution'	kl̥iːst	'ear'

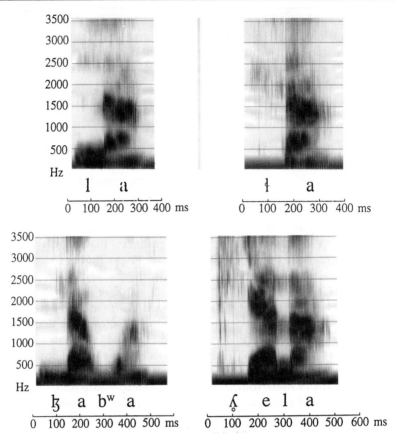

Figure 6.13 Spectrograms of four laterals in Bura. The words are **la** 'build', **ɬa** 'cow', **ʒabʷa** 'beat' and **ʃela** /ʎela/ 'cucumber'.

We therefore know, so far, of dental, alveolar, post-alveolar (apical and laminal) and palatal places of articulation for lateral fricatives.

We can exemplify contrasts between lateral approximants, fricatives and affricates from Zulu. Words illustrating six contrasting types of laterals in this language are given in table 6.11. So that all the occurring lateral consonant types of Zulu are represented, lateral clicks are also included in this table, but further discussion of these is postponed until chapter 8.

There are seven different laterals illustrated in table 6.11, but the Zulu alveolar lateral affricate occurs only as an allophone of the voiceless lateral fricative ɬ after a nasal. Spectrograms illustrating the five lateral sounds ɬ, t͡ɬ, ʒ, l, kʟ̥' spoken by a male speaker of Zulu are given in figure 6.14. For some speakers the alveolar affricate may be produced as an ejective, but the token we show is pulmonic. For this speaker the spectrum of ɬ appears to have a greater amount

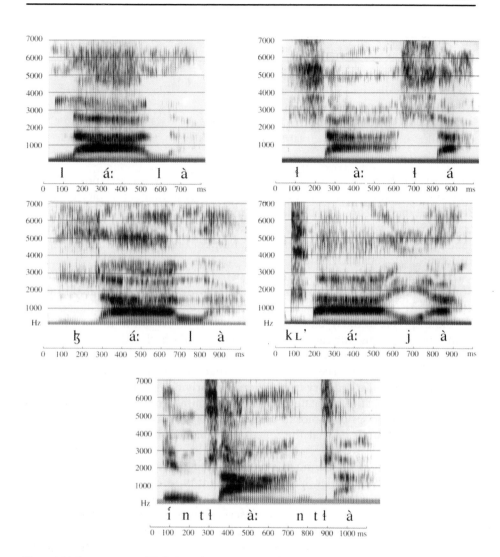

Figure 6.14 Spectrograms of Zulu lateral approximants, fricatives and affricates.

Table 6.11 Words illustrating lateral consonant types in Zulu

	Voiceless		Voiced	
Alveolar approximant			lálà	'lie down'
Alveolar fricative	ɬàɬá	'cut off'	ɮálà	'play'
Alveolar affricate	ínt͡ɬànt͡ɬà	'good fortune'		
Velar ejective affricate	kʟ̝̊'ájà	'push in between'		
Alveolar click	k‖ók‖a	'narrate'	g‖álà	'stride'

Table 6.12 Non-geminate lateral segments in Archi (from Kodzasov 1977)

	PLAIN		LABIALIZED	
VOICELESS PRE-VELAR AFFRICATE	kʟan	'hole'	kʟʷijt'u	'seventeen'
PRE-VELAR EJECTIVE AFFRICATE	kʟ'al	'lamb'	kʟʷ'as	'to murder'
VOICELESS PRE-VELAR FRICATIVE	ʟob	'sheath'	ʟʷalli	'large ravine'
VOICED PRE-VELAR FRICATIVE	naʟdor	'home'		
VOICED APICAL APPROXIMANT	lapʰ	'much, very'		

of energy in the region below 2000 Hz than occurs in the fricative portion of kʟ. The voiced fricative ɮ has a noise spectrum similar to that of its voiceless counterpart; it has a considerably lower amplitude of voicing than the voiced approximant l and lacks any strong low frequency resonance that might be labeled the first formant. Thus, the large number of laterals in Zulu are clearly differentiated from each other.

The velar lateral ejective affricate illustrated in figure 6.14 is an unusual sound. In Ladefoged (1971) this segment was described as a palatal lateral ejective affricate (on the grounds that velar laterals were not believed to be possible speech sounds). However, there seems no reason to doubt that both components of this affricate are really velar in place of articulation, and we have described it this way in table 6.11 above. As Doke (1926) observed, when a homorganic nasal precedes this element that nasal is ŋ. We add that when a vowel precedes, the auditory impression is clearly of a velar closure. The fricative component of this affricate is auditorily reminiscent of the velar fricative x but is lateral. Hence our choice to transcribe this affricate as kʟ', using the raising diacritic to indicate that the voiceless velar lateral ʟ is fricative in these circumstances.

Zulu is not unique in having this type of exotic lateral. A set of several velar, or more precisely pre-velar, laterals of different types are reported to occur in Archi. These are all fricatives or affricates. Archi also has a Coronal lateral approximant of the more usual type, described as being apical. Examples from Kodzasov (1977) are given in table 6.12. (From the distribution of the pre-velar lateral fricatives it seems very likely that the voicing in these fricatives is allophonic, although Kodzasov reports voiced and voiceless pre-velar lateral fricatives as being separate phonemes.)

We have heard recordings of these sounds but have not observed their production. Kodzasov gives the following description:

> In the production of lateral fricated sounds the tip of the tongue is passively lowered to the lower teeth while the body of the tongue is raised to the palate, forming an extended obstruction covering both the velar and palatal regions. . . . In their articulation and auditory quality the Archi laterals are similar to palatalized velars (Archi speakers perceive Russian soft x as a lateral fricative) (pp. 225–6, our translation).

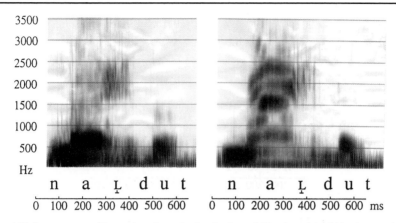

Figure 6.15 Spectrograms illustrating the voiced velar lateral fricative of Archi in the word **naʟdut** 'blue' as produced by two male speakers. The second speaker is an adolescent; frication of the lateral is even stronger in his speech than in that of the adult male.

Table 6.13 Words illustrating contrasts among laterals in Tlingit

VOICELESS FRICATIVE	ɬaa	'melt'
EJECTIVE FRICATIVE	ɬ'aa	'suck'
VOICELESS AFFRICATE	tɬaa	'be big'
VOICED AFFRICATE	dƛaa	'settle (of sediment)'
EJECTIVE AFFRICATE	tɬ'aak'	'be wet'

According to Kodzasov's description the closure for these sounds is more forward than that for the Zulu affricate. The auditory impression is of very strong frication. As may be seen in the spectrograms shown in figure 6.15, the resonance of the second formant is relatively high in frequency and quite close to that of the third formant. Both have strong amplitude. A non-ejective velar lateral affricate may also occur in Axluxlay (Stell 1972) but the description is somewhat unclear.

The most common lateral sound made with a glottalic airstream mechanism is an ejective affricate; ejective lateral fricatives are less frequent but do occur in a number of languages. Contrasts between voiceless pulmonic lateral fricatives and ejective lateral fricatives have been reported, but only in a few languages of North America, for example in Tlingit. This language is unusual in that it has laterals of five distinct types but none of them is a voiced lateral approximant of the common type. The examples of verb stems in table 6.13 from Story and Naish (1973) illustrate the contrasts between laterals in Tlingit. Place of articulation is not clearly indicated in the sources we have seen but is fairly certainly alveolar.

Navajo also has five contrasting alveolar laterals. It does not have the ejective fricative reported for Tlingit, but it has segments similar to the other

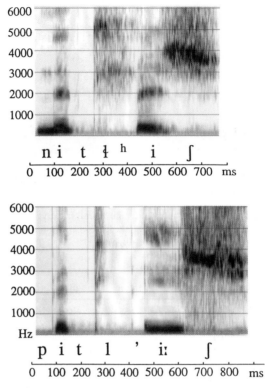

Figure 6.16 Navajo voiceless aspirated lateral affricate **tɬʰ** in **nitɬʰiʃ** *nitlish* 'it has arrived' and the ejective lateral affricate **tɬ'** in **pitɬ'iːɬ** *bitl'iish* 'his snake'.

four Tlingit laterals plus the more usual alveolar lateral approximant **l** (Sapir and Hoijer 1967). In Navajo the voiceless lateral affricate has a long period of frication which McDonough and Ladefoged (1993) considered to be equivalent to aspiration. Figure 6.16 shows the contrast between this pulmonic aspirated lateral affricate and the ejective lateral affricate. There is a long fricative portion in the aspirated lateral affricate **tɬʰ**, with only a very small interval for the aspiration. (Both the increase in length of the fricative and the small interval for the aspiration are similar to those in the other aspirated affricates in Navajo.) The ejective lateral affricate has a noticeable but short fricative period, as the source of frication is necessarily supraglottal. The duration of the frication is governed by the amount of air trapped above the glottis; it would be physiologically impossible to make it as long as in the pulmonic affricate in the upper part of the figure. In the Navajo lateral ejectives we have recorded, the glottal closure is often released and then re-made. This produces a spike on the spectrogram, as immediately above the ['] symbol in figure 6.16. There is then a short interval in which there is a glottal stop, which is finally released as the

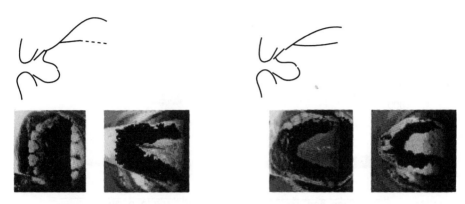

Figure 6.17 Palatograms, linguograms and inferred sagittal view of the lateral ejective affricate in the word 'bone' **mitʃ'a** as spoken by two male Hadza speakers. The position of the tongue body is shown by a dashed line for speaker 1 as the mouth was not open sufficiently and the extent of contact cannot be seen (from Sands, Maddieson and Ladefoged 1993).

voicing in the vowel begins. For some speakers this interval was filled with two or three pulses of a creaky voice phonation.

The third lateral affricate in Navajo, transcribed **dʒ** here, is often only weakly fricated. The stop closure is usually voiceless and only about 40 ms of the following lateral is voiceless. This is similar to the voice onset time measured after unaspirated velar stops (McDonough and Ladefoged 1993: 154). The remainder of the lateral is voiced and approximant. The segment might well therefore be transcribed **dl** (or **dl̥**). The length of the approximant lateral segment in **dl** pronunciations of this unaspirated lateral 'affricate' in Navajo is similar to that of the lateral segment **l** occurring alone.

We have so far noted lateral affricates at alveolar and velar places. Lateral ejective affricates that are best described as palatal or palato-alveolar in place occur in Iraqw, Sandawe and Hadza. Palatograms and linguograms of two Hadza speakers are shown in figure 6.17. Speaker 1 shows a broad contact over the post-alveolar and palatal regions in the palatogram, with the tongue contact area extending from the back of the tongue blade to the tongue front. Speaker 2 has a narrower contact which is better described as laminal post-alveolar.

We thus see that the world's languages use a wide range of lateral segments in which there is a more constricted aperture than that found in the common lateral approximant sounds. In a number of languages lateral fricatives vary with lateral affricates, and the affricates sometimes vary between ejective and pulmonic pronunciations (as in Zulu), showing that these various types of constricted laterals have close interrelationships. Nonetheless, it is possible to find languages which clearly show their contrastivity.

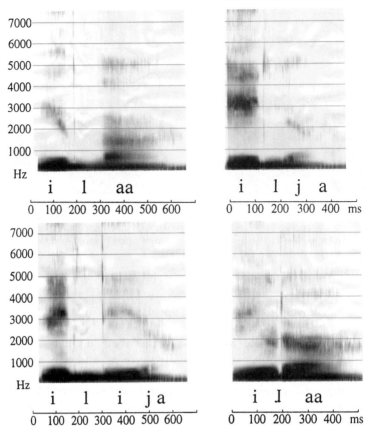

Figure 6.18 Spectrograms of the KiChaka words **ilaa** 'to lie down', **ilja** 'to eat', **ilija** 'to cry' and **iɹaa** 'to dress oneself' illustrating major allophones of approximant l and the lateral flap ɹ. The speaker is female.

Lateral flaps and taps

The final type of laterals that we must consider are those made with very rapid gestures, that is, lateral flaps and taps (the difference between these two types of articulation will be discussed in the next chapter, and we will not consider their distinction here). We have recorded lateral flaps in several languages. For example, one occurs in KiChaka in contrast with what seems to be only one other lateral phoneme, albeit one which has rather varied allophones. In addition to the apical alveolar lateral flap ɹ, the KiVunjo dialect of KiChaka has a lateral approximant which is most typically laminal dental. In most vowel contexts this has a rather low F2 suggesting possibly some velarization, but before **i** it becomes a palato-alveolar or palatal lateral with a considerably higher F2. Before **j** a laminal alveolar lateral with some palatalization occurs. The

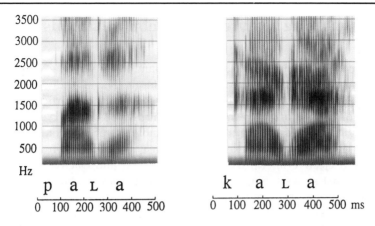

Figure 6.19 Velar lateral taps in the Melpa word **paʟa** 'fence' and the Kanite word **kaʟa** 'dog'. Both speakers are male.

KiChaka apical alveolar lateral flap ɭ also varies acoustically depending on segmental context, but less than l does. The three major allophones of l and the flap ɭ are shown in the spectrograms in figure 6.18. Note the lowering of the second formant throughout the initial i in **ilaa**, compared to the more localized lowering before ɭ.

Elugbe (1978) suggests that alveolar lateral taps occur in Ghotuo and Abua (as well as a number of other Nigerian languages for which he has only secondary data). In these languages there is a contrast between an alveolar lateral approximant of normal duration, and an alveolar lateral of brief duration that forms part of a series of lenis consonants in the phonological structure of these languages. Elugbe states that the formant frequencies of both the laterals are the same; however, in the one published pair of spectrograms in his article this does not seem to be the case. In particular, F2 seems lower in the brief lateral than it is in the longer one. We are therefore not sure if the two articulatory gestures are the same in the location of their target.

We also have seen and heard production of an apical post-alveolar lateral flap in 'O'odham, and Balasubramanian (1972) demonstrates that the non-geminate sublaminal lateral in Tamil is usually produced as a flap. Lateral flaps thus probably occur at all the places which have apical or sublaminal articulations. In addition, the intervocalic velar laterals that occur in Kanite and Melpa can be very brief and hence could be described as taps. We have used the same symbol for these as for velar approximant laterals. The spectrograms in figure 6.19 indicate that the articulatory closure lasted only 20–30 ms. Observation of the articulations as the speakers pronounced these words showed that the same narrowing of the tongue occurred in the velar region as in the case of the Mid-Waghi velar laterals discussed in section 6.1 above.

6.4 The Feature Description of Laterals

Table 6.14 complements table 6.3 by listing languages which exemplify contrasts among the manners of articulation in laterals. The table does not include all of the types of laterals that we have discussed, omitting particularly differences of phonation apart from the simple contrast of voicing. We believe that the majority of the missing contrasts in this table are accidental. For example we have not listed a language exemplifying the contrast between voiced lateral fricatives and ejective lateral fricatives, but voiced and ejective central fricatives do contrast so we see no reason that such a contrast should not also appear among laterals. The only gap we believe is non-accidental is the contrast between voiceless lateral fricatives and voiceless lateral approximants, which we have marked with asterisks. All of the languages mentioned in this table have been discussed earlier in this chapter.

Table 6.15 combines information from tables 6.3 and 6.14 and adds further examples of languages with laterals at different places of articulation. The places at which lateral flaps can occur are limited. But apart from this restriction, we know of no other constraints on the relations between places and manners among laterals. The table is presented primarily as a summary of the data we have discussed in this chapter, and the gaps that occur do not indicate the impossibility of such segments. These tables show that many of the place and manner properties that distinguish other types of segments also apply to laterals. We especially note that since lateral segments occur at places of articulation that are Coronal or Dorsal in terms of the scheme proposed in chapter 2,

Table 6.14 Languages exemplifying contrasting types of lateral segments

	VOICELESS AFFRICATE	EJECTIVE AFFRICATE	VOICED FRICATIVE	VOICELESS FRICATIVE	EJECTIVE FRICATIVE	VOICED APPROX.	VOICELESS APPROX.	VOICED FLAP
VOICED AFFRICATE	Tlingit	Tlingit		Tlingit	Tlingit			
VOICELESS AFFRICATE		Tlingit	Archi	Navajo Archi	Archi	Archi		
EJECTIVE AFFRICATE			Archi Zulu	Navajo Archi	Tlingit	Navajo		
VOICED FRICATIVE				Archi Zulu		Zulu		
VOICELESS FRICATIVE					Tlingit	Navajo Zulu	****	
EJECTIVE FRICATIVE								
VOICED APPROX.							Burmese	KiChaka
VOICELESS APPROX.								

Table 6.15 Languages exemplifying contrasting places of articulation among lateral segments

| | DENTAL | | ALVEOLAR | | POST-ALVEOLAR | | PALATAL | | VELAR |
	APICAL 1	LAMINAL 2	APICAL 3	LAMINAL 4	APICAL 5	LAMINAL 6	SUBAPICAL 7	LAMINAL 8	9
VOICED APPROXIMANT	Albanian	Kaititj	Albanian	Russian	Panjabi	Bulgarian	Malayalam	Italian	Mid-Waghi
VOICELESS APPROXIMANT			Burmese		Iaai				
VOICED FLAP	Taishan	KiChaka					Tamil		
VOICELESS FRICATIVE		Kabardian	Zulu		'O'odham	Diegueño		Bura	Archi
VOICED FRICATIVE			Zulu		Ao	Pashto			Archi
VOICELESS AFFRICATE			Navajo						Archi
VOICED AFFRICATE			Tlingit						
EJECTIVE AFFRICATE		Kabardian	Navajo						Archi
EJECTIVE FRICATIVE		Tlingit							

it is inappropriate to constrain the feature Lateral so that lateral segments are limited to the Coronal region alone. Laterals are not necessarily Coronal.

Phonetic feature inventories traditionally include a feature Lateral. At first glance it seems as if this feature is one which unambiguously has only binary values. An articulation is either lateral or not. However, the situation with laterals is not the same as that with nasals, where we argued that a single binary feature gave an appropriate phonetic classification for the position of the velum. Whereas we know of no linguistic contrast among nasals based on varying degrees of width of the velic opening, there are important differences among laterals based on the size of the lateral escape aperture. Laterals can be either approximant or fricative. Although this distinction often correlates with voicing – approximants being voiced and fricatives being voiceless – it cannot be predicted from it, since voiced and voiceless fricative laterals contrast, as do voiced and voiceless approximant laterals. Hence degree of stricture – approximant or fricative – must be specified with respect to the lateral aperture. The location of this aperture, except perhaps for velar laterals, is at a different position on the upper surface of the vocal tract from that for the maximal constriction, which is traditionally recognized as the place of articulation for the lateral. The manner specification describing the lateral aperture thus does not apply to the action at the articulatory target region which defines the place of the lateral segment.

Moreover, as we noted above, it is not necessarily true that laterals are produced with a central contact, nor is it appropriate to limit the term lateral to approximants and fricatives. Hence, to describe phonetic detail, including important allophonic variation in some languages, the type of central stricture also needs to be specified. In a sense, then, we are arguing that laterals are segments with two articulations. One governs the location and type of stricture of the central articulation and the other governs the location and size of the lateral aperture. Admittedly, there are probably few instances where advantage is taken of the degrees of freedom implied by recognizing two articulations. Lateral fricatives (and the fricative phase of lateral affricates) will normally be produced with a central closure since this will facilitate narrowing of the lateral escape aperture. Most research indicates that lateral approximants also usually have a central closure. Nonetheless we need to be able to provide a description of (at least) lateral approximants with and without central closure and laterals with a central closure with and without a fricative escape. In considering the production of laterals, it is important to bear in mind that the place of articulation for a lateral and its degree of stricture result from two separate articulatory components.

7

Rhotics

7. 1 What are Rhotics

This chapter describes the class of sounds that are sometimes labeled 'rhotics', or more informally, 'r-sounds'. Most of the traditional classes referred to in phonetic theory are defined by an articulatory or auditory property of the sounds, but the terms rhotic and r-sound are largely based on the fact that these sounds tend to be written with a particular character in orthographic systems derived from the Greco-Roman tradition, namely the letter 'r' or its Greek counterpart *rho*. The International Phonetic Alphabet provides a wide selection of symbols based on plain, rotated, turned or otherwise modified lower-case and capital versions of the letter 'r', including r, ɾ, ɹ, ɽ, ɻ, ʀ, ʁ, ɭ. Brief definitions of the sounds represented by these symbols are given in table 7.1.

The most prototypical members of the class of rhotics are trills made with the tip or blade of the tongue (IPA r). These central members of the class show phonological relationships to the heterogeneous set of taps, fricatives and approximants which form the remainder of the class. In addition to tongue tip and blade articulations, trills and other continuants made at the uvular place are also classed as rhotics. (As we noted in chapter 4, bilabial trills also occur but they are not part of the class of rhotics.) It is not therefore the manner of articulation that defines this group of sounds. Neither is there a particular place involved, as both Coronal and Dorsal articulations are included. Consequently an issue for phoneticians is whether the class membership is based only on synchronic and diachronic relationships between the members of the

Table 7.1 Symbols for some rhotic consonants

DEFINITION	SYMBOL
VOICED DENTAL OR ALVEOLAR TRILL	r
VOICED DENTAL OR ALVEOLAR TAP OR FLAP	ɾ
VOICED DENTAL OR ALVEOLAR APPROXIMANT	ɹ
VOICED POST-ALVEOLAR FLAP	ɽ
VOICED POST-ALVEOLAR APPROXIMANT	ɻ
VOICED UVULAR TRILL	R
VOICED UVULAR APPROXIMANT	ʁ
VOICED DENTAL OR ALVEOLAR LATERAL FLAP	ɺ

class, or whether there is indeed a phonetic similarity between all rhotics that has hitherto been missed. This similarity might be auditory or acoustic, rather than articulatory. The issue has been particularly discussed by Lindau (1985), and the following account will draw quite heavily on the data and ideas in that paper, as well as further materials collected by Inouye (1991a, b).

Phonologically, rhotics tend to behave in similar ways. In particular, rhotics often occupy privileged places in the syllable structure of different languages. They are not uncommonly the only consonants allowed as second members of clusters in the syllable onset, or as first members of clusters in coda position. More generally, we may say that in languages with consonant clusters, rhotics tend to occur close to the syllable nucleus (Lindau 1985). Frequently they share this privileged position with lateral approximants, and/or nasals. The affinity between rhotics and vowels is apparent in a number of other ways as well. Rhotics are quite likely to have syllabic variants, or to merge in various ways with contiguous vowels. Such processes, operating diachronically, are a particularly fertile source of phonetic differences between dialects of the same language. Hence the familar division of varieties of English into 'rhotic' and 'non-rhotic' types, depending on whether or not historic postvocalic /r/'s in pre-pausal and preconsonantal positions are retained in pronunciation. Somewhat parallel variations occur in other Germanic languages, including German, Danish, and Swedish. Further evidence of the rhotic-vowel affinity is the fact that vowels before /r/'s tend to lengthen, as in Swedish, and to be 'colored' in their quality by the following /r/. Acoustic modifications of vowels before /r/'s are known from French and Danish with their uvular r-sounds, as well as in Standard Swedish with its apical r-sound. Most important as evidence that they belong in a single class, at least from a phonological point of view, is the fact that rhotics of one type often alternate with other rhotics. In Farsi, /r/, which is a trill in initial position, has a tap allophone in intervocalic position and a voiceless trill variant in word-final position. In Fula, a trill is realized as an approximant ɹ before a consonant, as a trill elsewhere. In Palauan /r/ is generally a tap in intervocalic and postvocalic environments but an approximant in initial position; the contrasting orthographic 'rr' is most commonly an approximant with some frication, but its range of variation encompasses trills (Inouye 1991b).

Thus, the rhotics form a heterogeneous group from the phonetic point of view, exhibiting a wide variety of manners and places of articulation. We find rhotics that are fricatives, trills, taps, approximants, and even 'r-colored' vowels, as well as articulations that combine features of several of these categories. The most common places of articulation are in the dental-alveolar area, although post-alveolar (retroflex) /r/'s are not unusual, and in some languages /r/'s have a uvular articulation. We will define and illustrate the range of these types, paying particular attention to the possibilities that seem to occur contrastively. Following this discussion, we will return to the question of whether an auditory or acoustic property can be held to unify the various disparate members of the group.

Following conventional notions of the membership of the class as being primarily those sounds that are written with some variant of the letter 'r', it is apparent that rhotics are quite common in the languages of the world. About 75 percent of all languages contain some form of an /r/ phoneme (Maddieson 1984a). These languages mostly have a single /r/, and it is most commonly some form of trill, but 18 percent of languages with /r/'s contrast two or three rhotics. Languages with multiple rhotics are especially common in the Australian language family.

7. 2 Trills

The primary characteristic of a trill is that it is the vibration of one speech organ against another, driven by the aerodynamic conditions. One of the soft moveable parts of the vocal tract is placed close enough to another surface, so that when a current of air of the right strength passes through the aperture created by this configuration, a repeating pattern of closing and opening of the flow channel occurs. This movement has been modeled by McGowan (1992). In its essentials this is very similar to the vibration of the vocal folds during voicing; in both cases there is no muscular action that controls each single vibration, but a sufficiently narrow aperture must be created and an adequate airflow through the aperture must occur. The aperture size and airflow must fall within critical limits for trilling to occur, and quite small deviations mean that it will fail. As a result, trills tend to vary with non-trilled pronunciations. So with trills, as with voicing, there is a potential conflict between an acoustic definition (more than one period of actual vibration) and an articulatory definition (positioning of the articulators in a configuration such that, given the right aerodynamic conditions, vibration would occur). In this chapter we will consider trills to be sounds made with an articulatory configuration

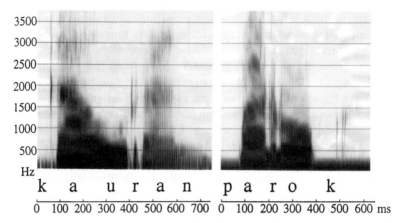

Figure 7.1 Spectrograms of apical trills in the Finnish word **kauran** 'oats (genitive)' and the Russian word **porok [pa'rok]** 'threshold'. Both speakers are female.

appropriate for vibration, regardless of whether vibration actually occurs. Although a vibratory pattern can be sustained for as long as a sufficient airflow is available, acoustic trills in linguistic use usually consist of two to five periods (geminate occurrences may be longer). We have noted that the first closure in a trill often has a slightly longer duration than following ones.

Trills are much more easily produced if the vibrating articulator has relatively small mass, hence the most common trills involve the tongue tip vibrating against a contact point in the dental/alveolar region, or the uvula vibrating against the back of the tongue. In fact by far the most common type of trill is one involving the tongue tip. We will discuss trills of this general type at some length, using them to illustrate some of the general characteristics of trills, before going to on talk of ones made at other places of articulation. Figure 7.1 shows spectrograms of voiced apical trills in Finnish and Russian. Apical trills typically consist of two to three periods of vibration – these examples both have two – but may contain only one or have more than three. Each period consists of a closed phase during which the articulators are in contact, succeeded by an open phase in which they are slightly apart. On the spectrograms the closed phases appear as light areas, as the formant energy is absent or weak. The open phase between these two closures, which is vowel-like in its acoustic structure, appears as a dark area with concentrations of energy in characteristic formant regions. The closed phases of these trills last on the order of 25 ms each. The open phases have roughly similar duration, so that each complete cycle occupies about 50 ms. There would thus be about 20 of these cycles in a second, and we can say that these particular trills have a frequency of vibration of about 20 Hz. In Lindau's study, the mean rate of vibration for apical trills produced by a total of 25 speakers of Edo, Degema, Ghotuo, Kalabari, Bumo, Spanish, and Standard Swedish was 25 Hz (range 18–33 Hz, s.d. 4.5).

As noted earlier, trills are very sensitive to small variations in the articulatory and aerodynamic conditions obtaining during their production. We will discuss some of the resulting variation in production using illustrative data from Italian. Spectrograms of six words containing trills are shown in figure 7.2. Pronunciations by two female speakers are represented. The top row illustrates word-initial trills. For speaker A on the left, the trill in **rana** 'frog' contains two contacts with an open phase between them, but there are two other features to notice. First, the contacts are preceded by a short approximant or vowel-like sound of about 50 ms duration. Secondly, after the contacts there is another approximant interval, lasting over 50 ms, with a similar formant structure to that seen in the open phase. This is part of the consonant duration, as the tongue does not move away from the consonantal position until it ends. The end of the consonant is indicated by an abrupt upward transition of the third formant, as well as a significant upward shift in F1. The approximant phases flanking this trill indicate that the tongue was not consistently held close enough to the upper surface of the mouth for trilling to be sustained. Approximant phases at the end of trills occurred on some occasions in all the languages with trills studied by Lindau (1985). By contrast, the initial trill in speaker B's pronunciation of **rosso** 'red' contains five very short closures, including an initial one before phonation begins, and there is no delay of the transition to the vowel following the last closure release. As a result the total acoustic duration of the initial consonants in these two words is very similar, although their detailed phonetic structure is quite different.

In Italian, single and geminate forms of most consonants contrast in intervocalic position (a contrast between stops was illustrated in chapter 2). The single/geminate opposition also applies to trills. The second and third rows of figure 7.2 illustrate these single and geminate intervocalic trills in the minimal pair **karo** 'expensive' and **karro** 'wagon, cart'. In **karo**, speaker A has a very short trill consisting of only one contact and no other components, speaker B shows one clear contact followed by a less complete occlusion with frication. The geminate trills in **karro** show multiple contacts followed by one or more periods in which the articulatory closure is not completed but the articulator is still oscillating sufficiently to produce a diminution of the amplitude. For speaker A the trill consists of three closures, a partial occlusion during which formant structure remains visible, and an extended approximant articulation, indicated by the low amplitude and the low frequency of the third formant. The end of the consonant can be recognized by the point at which the third formant begins to rise. Its total duration is about 200 ms. (The end of the final vowel is strongly laryngealized, giving a visual impression of another trill in the spectrogram.) For speaker B the trill ends as a fricative. There are also noticeable differences in the formant transitions, which are particularly apparent in the single trills. Speaker B has a greater increase in F2, and a lowering of F3, suggesting a more retracted position of the tongue.

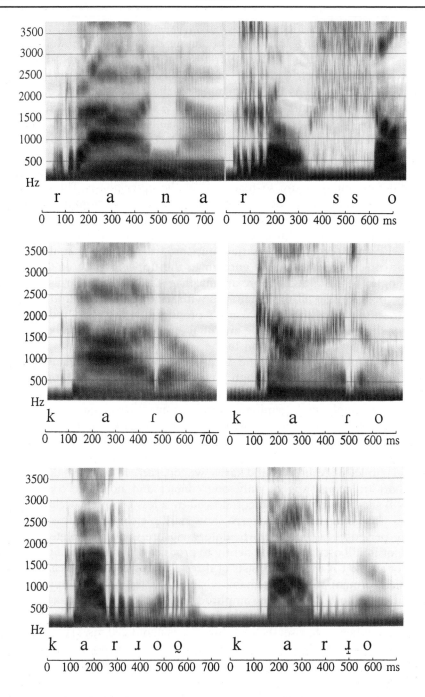

Figure 7.2 Initial, medial single and medial geminate alveolar trills from two speakers of Standard Italian. See text for discussion.

Variations of the types that we have described in Italian are also apparent in the trills of other languages, although the single/geminate distinction adds to the complexity in the Italian case. In repetitions of the words **karo** and **karro** from a total of five speakers of Standard Italian we found none of the intervocalic single trills to have more than two contacts. The geminate trills showed no fewer than three contacts and up to seven. The distinction is also signaled by the length of the preceding vowel, which is much shorter before a geminate, as in **rosso** and **karro**, than before a single consonant, as in **rana** and **karo.**

A further variant of a voiced trill, as Lindau also pointed out, is one in which vocal fold vibration ceases during one or more of the brief occlusions. This can sometimes be seen more easily in examination of a waveform. Figure 7.3 shows a spectrogram of the Finnish word **koiran** 'dog (genitive)'. An expanded waveform of the portion containing the trill is also shown at eight times the time scale of the spectrogram. This particular trill contains two contacts of the tongue, indicated by the arrows linking the waveform and spectrogram. During the first, but not the second, the vocal fold vibration dies away. This absence of voicing cannot be due to active changes in the laryngeal setting. Voicing occurs during the open phase between the closures, and it is not possible to alternate voluntary movements with sufficient rapidity. Hayes (1984) suggests that, in Russian, r's that are adjacent to voiceless obstruents regularly show this devoicing in closures, with voiced open intervals. Although only a small amount of data is shown, this result might suggest that a slightly more open glottis throughout the trill is associated with the occurrence of voiceless closures. The devoicing in such cases is presumably aerodynamically driven, in that the rapid variations in oral pressure associated with a trill may result in moments in which the transglottal pressure drop is insufficient to sustain vocal fold vibrations. However, since the closures are of such short duration it is necessary to assume that the vocal tract walls are held in a stiff position so that there is very little compliance.

Although apical trills all use the same active articulator, they vary across speakers and languages in the location of the contact on the upper surface, and in some languages different places of articulation are contrastive for apical trills. An x-ray tracing of the apical trill of Peninsular (Iberian) Spanish in Quilis and Fernández (1964) shows a contact just above the gum line of the upper teeth, which could be labeled postdental. In Russian, Skalozub (1963) shows a post-alveolar trill as typical for r, but a dental contact for the palatalized trill rʲ. This difference is illustrated by the palatograms in figure 7.4 from one of the speakers she studied. Variations in the shape of the tongue behind the forward contact are also apparent in this figure, which shows much greater lateral contact for the palatalized trill. Skalozub reports that the post-alveolar trill had typically 3–4 contacts, whereas rʲ often has only one. The raising of the blade and front of the tongue that is required for the palatalization may make it more difficult to maintain the aerodynamic conditions for trilling. Variation in

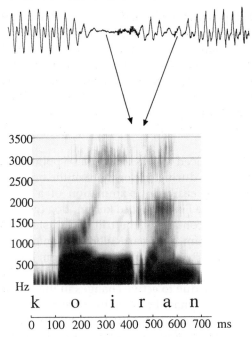

Figure 7.3 Spectrogram of the Finnish word **koiran** 'dog (genitive)' spoken by a female speaker from Helsinki, with expanded waveform of the apical trill showing devoicing of the first closure interval.

place of contact can also be inferred from acoustic records. Lower spectral peaks are likely to indicate more retracted articulations. Lindau noted a difference of this type between the Chicano Spanish of Los Angeles and other forms of Spanish from Argentina, Colombia, and Mexico. These display a much higher third spectral peak than the Chicano Spanish, indicating a more dental place of articulation. Lindau suggests that the low third spectral peak in Chicano Spanish may be due to influence from English.

Some Dravidian languages have more than one tongue tip trill. In careful speech (perhaps influenced by the orthography) some speakers of Malayalam contrast **kaṟi** 'soot' and **kari** 'curry' by making the first of these words with a more advanced alveolar trill, and the second with a more retracted alveolar trill, which is almost a retroflex sound. Ladefoged, Cochran and Disner (1977) provide spectrograms of these two trills, showing that the more forward trill has a higher locus for the second formant (at approximately 1750 Hz in comparison with 1250 Hz). The more retracted trill has a lower third formant, as is commonly found in apical post-alveolar sounds. Other speakers of Malayalam use an alveolar tap in the first word and an alveolar trill in the second (Velayudhan 1971, Kumari 1972, Yamuna 1986). We will discuss this variety of Malayalam in section 7.6 below. It is perhaps worth noting that both these rhotics are phonologically related to stops in Malayalam.

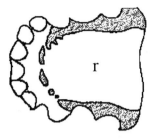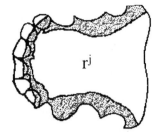

Figure 7.4 Palatograms of **r** and **rʲ** in **paˈra** 'time' and **paˈrʲa** 'soar, hover (past part.)' spoken by a female speaker of Russian (after Skalozub 1963).

Table 7.2 Words illustrating contrasting apical trills in Toda

	FRONTED ALVEOLAR		ALVEOLAR		RETROFLEX	
PLAIN	**kaɾ**	'border'	**kaɾ**	'juice, sap'	**kaɽ**	'pen for calves'
	eːɾ	'to plough'	**eːr**	'male buffalo'	**meːɽ**	'to drive buffalo'
PALATALIZED	**paɾʲ**	'to gallop'	**karʲ**	'to laugh'	**poɽʲ**	'funeral rice'

Another Dravidian language, Toda, is the only language we know of that has rhotics at three places of articulation which are all trilled. All three contrast in postvocalic positions (Spajić, Ladefoged and Bhaskararao 1994). Words illustrating these three segments are given in table 7.2.

The words in the first row of table 7.2 are illustrated by the spectrograms on the left of figure 7.5 and by the palatograms and linguograms in figures 7.6–7.8. We have recordings of 12 speakers of Toda, together with palatographic and linguographic records of three of them producing these rhotic sounds. Two of the three speakers clearly produce the word meaning 'pen for calves' in the third column with an apical or even sub-apical retroflex articulation, as illustrated in figure 7.8. This column in the table has been labeled accordingly. The word for 'juice' in the second column is produced with an apical contact on the front part of the alveolar ridge at the base of the teeth. This column is therefore labeled 'alveolar'. In the standard work on Toda phonology (Emeneau 1984), the trill in the first column is described as post-dental. Our palatograms may show a slightly more forward contact, hence the label 'fronted alveolar' for this column, but there is very little visible difference in the articulatory position of the trills in the first and second columns, as shown in figures 7.6 and 7.7. However, the acoustic records indicate that this trill has a different shape of the tongue behind the contact area.

The spectrograms of the Toda trills on the left of figure 7.5 throw more light

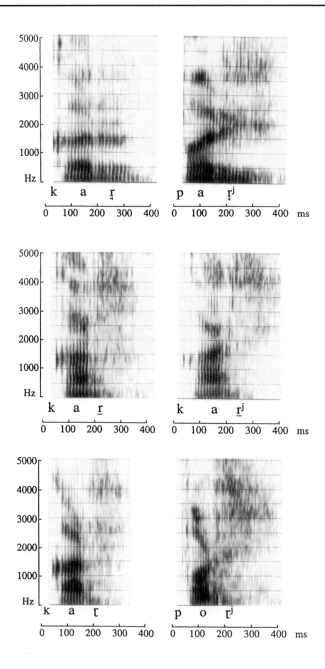

Figure 7.5 Spectrograms of the trills in six Toda words illustrating word-final rhotics. The six words are those in rows one and three of table 7.2. Plain forms are on the left, palatalized forms on the right.

on how these two sounds differ. They suggest that the major distinguishing feature of the first trill in the table is the effect on the preceding vowel, which is higher (indicated by the lower first formant) throughout its duration. One might have expected this lower F1 to be due to a higher tongue position, but there is little indication of this in the palatogram in figure 7.6. Another possibility is that this sound is produced with the root of the tongue fronted. We have somewhat speculatively symbolized this trill with the IPA diacritic for an advanced tongue root [̟], although we do not have any data beyond the spectrograms to substantiate this interpretation. There is usually an audible high front vowel-like offglide after this trill and a greater tendency for acoustic trilling to cease early during its production so that it terminates as an approximant (often with some frication). This is similar to the variation noted for the palatalized rhotic in Russian. We therefore regard this as a form of palatalized alveolar trill, noting, however, that the sides of the tongue do not make contact with the hard palate in the way that is characteristic of a high front semivowel and typically found in palatalized sounds, including the Russian rʲ illustrated in figure 7.4. Emeneau (1984) describes this sound as a dental flap, and it may have been so at the time of his fieldwork in the 1930s, but our video and acoustic recordings show that a trill is the typical pronunciation.

As shown in table 7.2, all three of the Toda trills can also have distinctive palatalization. The spectrograms on the right of figure 7.5 show movements of the formants towards those typical of a high front vowel before each of the three palatalized trills. There is also an offglide with a great deal of energy in the higher frequencies. In this figure the lowering of the frequencies of the higher formants before the retroflex trill is also evident.

The other well-known class of trills is that in which it is the uvula rather than the tongue tip which vibrates. Uvular trills occur in some conservative varieties of Standard French and Standard German, although most speakers of these languages use uvular fricatives or approximants rather than trills. We have also heard uvular trills in Southern Swedish and in some varieties of Italian and Russian where the standard form of these languages would have an apical trill. They are rare outside Western Europe, but do occur at least in Abkhaz and in some varieties of Ashkenazic Hebrew.

Delattre (1971) showed in x-ray studies of several speakers of French and German that the uvular trills are produced by an initial movement of the tongue root backwards followed by an upward movement toward the uvula, which is also moved forward to a position where trilling can occur. These movements can be followed in the series of tracings of successive frames from x-ray films shown in figure 7.9.

There are variations in uvular trills similar to those in apical ones. Spectrograms of the word ʀas 'breed' spoken by a male speaker of Southern Swedish are shown in figure 7.10. In the first repetition of this word, four contacts occur; in the second there are only two contacts, including an initial one, but there is then an approximant phase before the vowel begins.

kaɽ

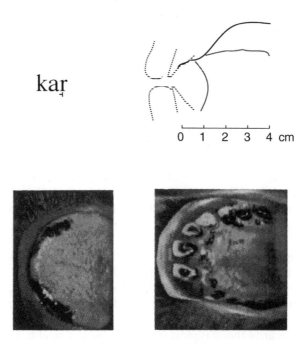

Figure 7.6 Palatogram, linguogram and reconstructed tongue position of the trill in the Toda word **kaɽ** 'border of cloth'. The dark marks on the teeth in this and the following Toda palatograms are stains, and do not reflect tongue contact.

There is a consistent distinction in the spectral domain between uvular and apical trills, with the uvular trills showing a much higher third resonance (between 2500 and 3000 Hz in these examples). There may also be a durational difference: in Lindau's (1985) data intervocalic uvular trills tended to be longer than the apical ones, often consisting of four to six periods.

The uvula might be expected to vibrate somewhat faster than the tip of the tongue, due to its smaller mass, but we cannot show this to be so from the available data. Although Lindau reports that the mean rate of vibration for uvular trills is higher than that for apical trills (her three speakers of Southern Swedish who consistently produced trills had a mean vibration rate of 30.5 Hz), the range (29–33 Hz, s.d. 2.5) is contained within the range observed for apical trills reported earlier. Conversely, Ladefoged, Cochran and Disner (1977) report a mean rate of 26.2 Hz for uvular trills for two speakers (one a Southern Swedish speaker, the other a speaker of a prestige dialect of Italian with uvular trills) compared with 28.6 Hz for apical trills (ten speakers of diverse languages). Trill rates for apical and uvular trills therefore seem to be

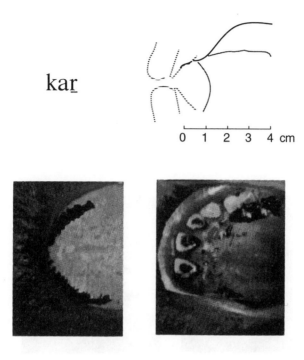

kar̠

Figure 7.7 Palatogram, linguogram and reconstructed tongue position of the trill in the Toda word **kar̠** 'juice'.

very similar, with any differences perhaps dependent on speaker characteristics rather than on the use of different articulators. To control for speaker differences it would be necessary to examine a language which uses both apical and uvular trills, although we are not sure that any such language now exists. Older speakers of Eastern dialects of Occitan (Coustenoble 1945, Bouvier 1976) may still maintain a contrast between lingual and uvular trills, deriving from the Latin contrast of single vs geminate **r**'s, in words such as **gari** 'cured' vs **gaʀi** 'oak tree'. We do not know of any articulatory or acoustic measurements on such speakers' trills.

It is interesting to note that the bilabial trill releases of prenasalized stops discussed in chapter 4 have a similar rate of vibration to other trills, despite the fact that the lips have a larger mass than either the uvula or the tongue tip. Ladefoged, Cochran and Disner (1977) report a mean rate of 29.3 Hz for prenasalized bilabial trills (five speakers), while Maddieson (1989b) reports a mean rate of 24.8 Hz (four speakers). The range is thus very similar to that observed in apical and uvular trills. As the various non-linguistic uses of

kaɽ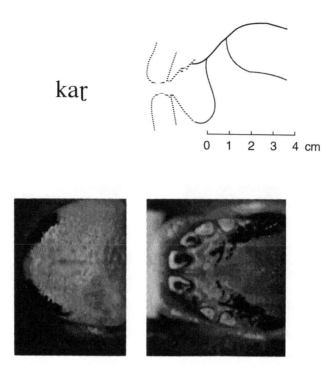

0 1 2 3 4 cm

Figure 7.8 Palatogram, linguogram and reconstructed tongue position of the trill in the Toda word **kaɽ** 'pen for calves'.

bilabial trills illustrate, the rate of lip vibration can be varied over a wide range. In the English-speaking world both the relatively high frequency labial trill of the disrespectful 'Bronx cheer' or 'raspberry' and the low frequency trill conventionally written 'brrr' and indicating shivering cold are familiar. Frequency variation is controlled by changing the degree of lip spreading and the compression of the lips so that differing amounts of the mass of the lips are actually involved in the vibration. Because bilabial trills in linguistic use are almost always released into high rounded vowels, as noted in chapter 4, lip width is somewhat constricted and the resulting trill rate is intermediate in the potential range.

The only regularly occurring trill we know of that is made with the blade of the tongue is the Czech 'ř'. This trill is typically made with the laminal surface of the tongue against the alveolar ridge. Short (1987) describes this sound as "a rolled post-alveolar fricative (never the sequence of [r] plus [ʒ] attempted by

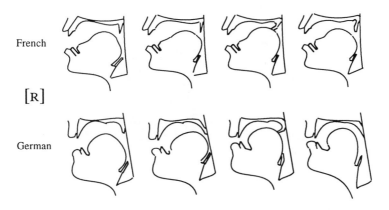

Figure 7.9 Frames traced from x-ray films of German and French intervocalic uvular trills (after Delattre 1971). The second frame in each row, shows retraction of the tongue, and the third frame in each row shows backward movement of the tongue root followed by tongue body raising and fronting of the uvula.

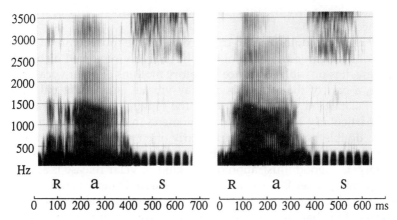

Figure 7.10 Spectrograms of uvular trills in two repetitions of ʀas 'breed' spoken by a male Southern Swedish speaker from Helsingborg.

non-Czechs . . .)." We agree with his description that it is (often) 'rolled', although we would use the term trilled. He is also correct in noting that the frication is not of the ʒ type. But in our observation this sound is usually a sequential combination of a trill and a fricative. The frication is not like that of ʒ (with which this sound contrasts) but has a distinctive whistle-type of relatively narrow-band noise. It is often partially voiceless. Some speakers produce just the fricative, without a trill component (this variant will be described below), but others, perhaps most, Czech speakers have a trill at the beginning.

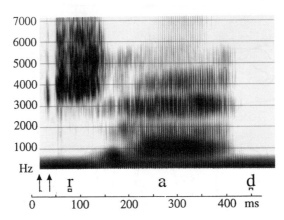

Figure 7.11 A spectrogram of the Czech word ꭇaḍ *řad* 'order'. The closure phases of each of the two vibrations of the blade of the tongue are indicated by arrows.

A spectrogram of the Czech word ꭇaḍ *řad* 'order' is shown in figure 7.11. In this utterance there were two vibrations of the blade of the tongue, which were themselves fairly fricative, followed by a fricative during which voicing commences.

As we have noted, tongue tip trills are by far the most common type of trill, uvular trills are rarer and bilabial trills have a very restricted distribution. Beyond these, it is possible to induce vibratory motions of other vocal organs. For example, a part of the tongue body may vibrate against the palatal or velar surface. Palatal and velar vibrations of the tongue body are sporadically produced, particularly as transitional phenomena in the release phase of Dorsal stops. A 'double burst' is seen particularly often at the release of a velar stop; this could be said to be a brief trill, but it never appears to be a required articulatory target. A good illustration of this kind of velar release is seen in figure 7.2 above, in Speaker B's pronunciation of **karro**. Other examples can be seen in the Toda spectrograms in figure 7.5. The strident vowels of !Xóõ, which will be discussed in chapter 9, are produced with trilling of the epiglottis. Trills of the velum or uvula on an ingressive airstream produce one of the major types of sounds in snoring.

7.3 Taps and Flaps

Another class of rhotic sounds are those which invariably have a single short closure. These are called taps and flaps, and are generally apical. Many linguists, including Lindau (1985), do not make any distinction between these two terms. However, Ladefoged (1968) has suggested that it is useful to

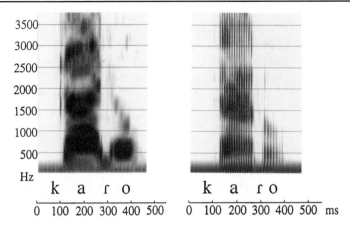

Figure 7.12 Spectrograms showing taps from a female speaker of Peninsular Spanish and a male
Spanish speaker from Peru in the word **karo** 'expensive'.

distinguish between them. The distinction now proposed is that a flap is a
sound in which a brief contact between the articulators is made by moving the
active articulator tangentially to the site of the contact, so that it strikes the
upper surface of the vocal tract in passing; a tap is a sound in which a brief
contact between the articulators is made by moving the active articulator directly towards the roof of the mouth. Both types are usually coronal. Thus
flaps are most typically made by retracting the tongue tip behind the alveolar
ridge and moving it forward so that it strikes the ridge in passing. Taps are
most typically made by a direct movement of the tongue tip to a contact location in the dental or alveolar region.

A tap, usually described as dental, occurs in intervocalic position in most
varieties of Spanish in words such as **karo** 'expensive'. Quilis (1981) measured
the mean closure duration of this segment as 20 ms. Two productions of **karo**
are illustrated by the spectrograms in figure 7.12, the one on the left spoken by
a female Peninsular Spanish speaker and the one on the right by a male Peru-
vian Spanish speaker. In the first of these, there is a marked rise in the second
formant as the consonant is formed, but no comparable rise occurs in the second utterance, suggesting that the place of articulation may differ somewhat
between the two. Note that in the second of these utterances, although the
sound is described as voiced, there is no vocal fold vibration during the short
closure. This is a not unusual feature of this type of sound, and parallels the
observation made concerning trills.

Most speakers of American English produce similar brief closures for the
well-known flap allophone of post-stress pre-syllabic alveolar stops in words
such as *city*, *latter* and *ladder*. A clear difference between this American English
flap and the Spanish tap can be seen in the x-ray films of Monnot and Freeman

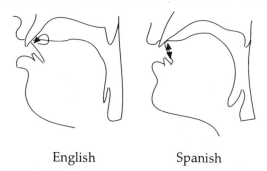

English   Spanish

Figure 7.13 X-ray tracings of the articulation of American English alveolar flap and Spanish dental tap, in the words *water* and *Iberica* respectively (after Monnot and Freeman 1972). The direction of movement is indicated by arrows.

(1972). Tracings from the closure phase of these sounds are shown in figure 7.13. The English speaker has a preparatory raising and retraction of the tongue tip during the preceding vowel, which is apparent in earlier frames of the film (not reproduced here). The tongue is then moved forward to make the contact which is captured in the frame illustrated here, after which it returns to the floor of the mouth. The Spanish tap does not involve any substantial anticipation, but instead has a quick upward and downward movement confined to the tongue tip. (Monnot and Freeman do not state where the speakers used in this study were from. It was carried out in California but the Spanish speaker was probably Iberian.) Recasens (1991) shows that the tap in Catalan has similar formant transitions going into and out of the consonant. English flaps often have detectably different transitions before and after the contact.

A considerable proportion of the linguistic literature does not make the distinction between tap and flap that is illustrated here, hence it is often uncertain which of these two types of movements occur in particular languages.

7.4 Fricative and Approximant /r/'s

The family of rhotics also includes members in which there is no contact, but instead only an approximation between the articulators. In some instances the typical production is accompanied by friction, in others an approximant is produced. A fricative alveolar rhotic occurs in the KiVunjo dialect of KiChaka (Davey, Moshi and Maddieson 1982), and a fricative uvular rhotic is the most common production of 'r' in French, as shown in the x-ray films by Simon (1967). A spectrogram of this typical French pronunciation is shown in figure 7.14.

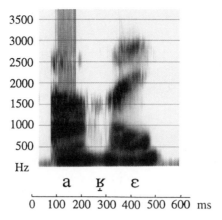

Figure 7.14 Spectrogram of the word *arrêt* 'stop' pronounced with a uvular fricative by a female speaker of Standard French.

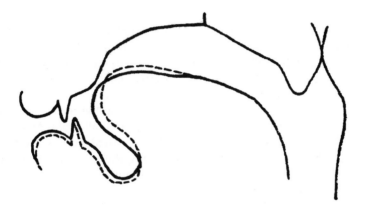

Figure 7.15 Mid-saggital section of the Czech rhotics in the words **paɹa** and **maɹa** based on palatographic and linguographic data (after Hála 1923). Solid line indicates ɹ, dashed line ɹ.

As noted above, some speakers of Czech have a trill with a fricative component whereas others have only a fricative. Palatograms and linguograms of ɹ published by Hála (1923) show a narrow open channel at the center of the mouth which is narrower and formed further forward than that for the contrasting approximant ɹ which also occurs in Czech. Based on this data, Hála infers that for speakers of this type the mid-saggital shape for the two Czech rhotics is as in figure 7.15.

An alveolar approximant rhotic is typical of Southern British English; this segment may appear only in prevocalic positions. A uvular approximant is common in Standard German, especially in non word-initial positions (a uvu-

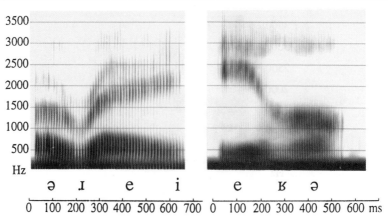

Figure 7.16 Spectrograms of rhotic approximants in a Southern British pronunciation of *array*, and a Standard German pronunciation of *Ehre* 'honor'.

lar fricative or trill is more likely to occur initially). Examples of these two segments are illustrated by the spectrograms in figure 7.16.

There is also an approximant rhotic in most varieties of American English. For some speakers this is alveolar or post-alveolar in its articulation, but a more complex articulation occurs in the so-called 'bunched r'. This sound is produced with constrictions in the lower pharynx and at the center of the palate, but with no raising of the tongue tip or blade (Uldall 1958). As no phonetic symbol has been proposed for representing this articulation, we will continue to use the symbol ɹ. A spectrogram illustrating the bunched 'r' in the word *sorrow* is shown in figure 7.17. Most striking about this sound is the very low frequency of the third formant (in other contexts paralleled by lowering of the second formant). All nine Californian English speakers studied by Lindau (1985) had a lowered third formant, similar to that in figure 7.17.

The American English ɹ also has syllabic variants, as in the word *herd*. Figure 7.18 shows the articulatory position for ɹ in this word as spoken by six speakers of Midwestern American English traced from x-ray films. The constrictions in both the low pharynx and at the mid-palatal region for "bunched r" and the absence of any tongue tip raising can be seen in these images. Several of these speakers, particularly those numbered 2, 4, and 5, also show considerable narrowing of the lip aperture. When there are constrictions in the lower pharyngeal region or in the palatal region, acoustic models of vowel production predict a relatively low third formant, close to the second formant (Fant 1968). Both second and third formants are also lowered by lip rounding.

Other speakers of American English use a more or less retroflex articulation for ɹ, which is also combined with a constriction in the lower pharynx, as well as lip rounding (Delattre and Freeman 1968). This articulatory combination also produces a low third formant. Thus it seems that speakers of American

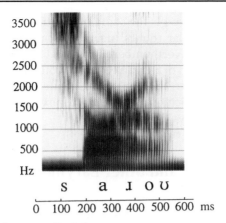

Figure 7.17 Spectrogram of American English *sorrow* saɹoʊ.

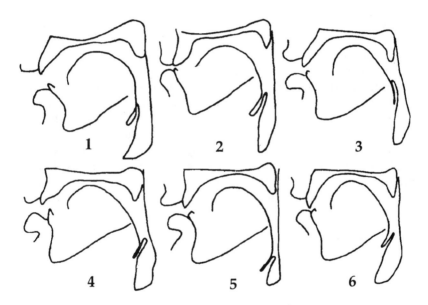

Figure 7.18 Articulatory position for syllabic 'bunched r' from six speakers of American English (after Lindau 1985).

English combine several articulatory mechanisms to produce a low third formant for whichever variant of this segment they employ.

Considering these varieties of rhotic approximant ɹ, and rhotic sounds found in other dialects of English, we can exemplify nearly all the different forms of rhotics we have been discussing simply by reference to this one language. Alveolar fricative ɹ is the standard rhotic in some urban South African English dialects. Uvular rhotics (usually fricative ʁ, but occasionally the trill ʀ) are a marker of the Northumberland dialect spoken in the North West of England and of the English of Sierra Leone. In Scottish cities such as Edinburgh and Glasgow the norm is an alveolar tap ɾ. Despite stage caricatures of Scottish speakers, it is only in the Scottish Lowlands (for example in Galashiels) that an alveolar trilled r is the most common form.

7.5 Voicing and other Laryngeal Contrasts

Apical trills are most often voiced but a number of languages have a contrast between voiced and voiceless trills. Breathy voiced and laryngealized voiced trills also occur. Based on data presented by Smith (1968), Sedang is an example of a language with three laryngeal settings for trills. Smith prefers to interpret voiceless and laryngealized trills as clusters of /r/ preceded by /h/ and /ʔ/ respectively, but this analysis is not supported by anything other than reasons of economy.

As noted above, voiced apical trills often contain portions without vocal cord vibration, but the intervals between the closures are always voiced. From the acoustical point of view, therefore, voiceless trills are likely to differ from their voiced counterparts primarily in having voiceless portions between the closures. These sounds occur, for example, in Chechen-Ingush, Nivkh, Irish, and several of the Edoid languages of Nigeria. The contrast between word-final voiced and voiceless trills from a male speaker of Ingush is shown in the spectrograms in figure 7.19. Lindau observed a slightly slower mean rate of vibration for the voiceless trill than for the voiced trill for three speakers of Edo

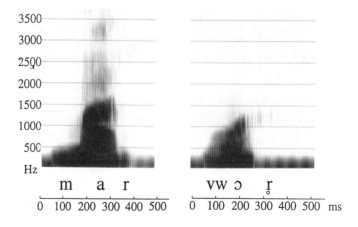

Figure 7.19 Spectrograms of the Ingush words **mar** 'husband' and **vwor̥** 'seven'

who used trills, namely 22.5 Hz, but this is well within the range of variation seen for the voiced apical trills. A different Edo pronunciation will be illustrated in section 7.6 below.

Contrasting voiceless rhotics of other types, such as approximants, may also occur in a few languages, for example Scottish Gaelic, Hmar (Tibeto-Burman), Konda (Dravidian) and Yaygir (Australian). We do not know the exact production of these sounds, however. Voiceless allophones of rhotics are quite common, especially in utterance-final positions, and after voiceless stops.

7.6 Contrasts between Rhotic Types in the Same Language

The great majority of the world's languages have only a single type of rhotic sound in their inventory, but there are a number with more than one. We have already discussed the three trills in Toda, but it is more usual to find contrasts among rhotics that involve the contrast of type, rather than place. We have also already illustrated the occurrence of both trills and taps in Spanish. These two sounds contrast only in intervocalic position, where the trill historically derives from a sequence *rt or *rd. It therefore has some of the character of a geminate. In a number of languages in which, unlike Spanish, there is regularly a distinction between single and geminate consonants, the single and geminate rhotics differ in just the way that the Spanish segments do. Single rhotics are taps, and geminates are trills. Some varieties of Arabic, as well as Afar (Parker and Hayward 1985) and Shilluk (Gilley 1992) are among the languages which conform to this pattern. Elsewhere, for example in Finnish, even single rhotics are trilled and geminate rhotics are just longer trills, with in this case 6–8 contacts (Inouye 1991a).

Most native speakers of Hausa have a contrast between two rhotics (Newman 1980). One is an alveolar trill in words such as **bárá:** 'servant'. This contrasts with a post-alveolar rhotic, pronounced as either a flap or an approximant, in words like **báɽà:** 'begging'. When the trill is pronounced with a single contact (as often happens in normal speech, cf. Ladefoged 1968: 30) and the post-alveolar rhotic is a flap then the contrast between **bárá:** 'servant' and **báɽa:** 'begging' can be mainly one of place rather than manner. Palatograms and deduced articulatory gestures for these two words produced in this fashion are shown in figure 7.20. Spectrograms of the same two words by another speaker who uses a post-alveolar approximant ɻ rather than a flap are shown in figure 7.21.

As with the other consonants of Hausa, the rhotics appear in single and geminate forms. The lengthened trill has a greater number of contacts, as in Italian or Finnish, but the geminate equivalent of the flap is a relatively long retroflex approximant, marked by a low third formant, terminating with a

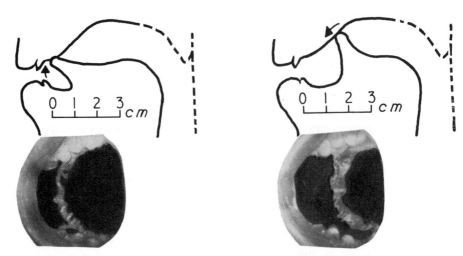

Figure 7.20 Palatograms (retouched) and deduced tongue positions in Hausa ɾ and ɽ in the words **bárà:** and **bárɽà:** spoken by a male speaker from Zaria (from Ladefoged 1968).

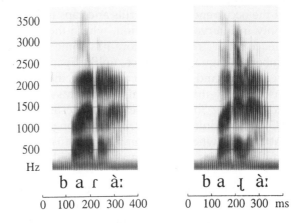

Figure 7.21 Spectrograms of the minimal pair **bárà:** 'servant' and **báɽà:** 'begging' contrasting Hausa ɾ and ɽ spoken by a male speaker from Kano.

brief more constricted phase. The four contrasting types are illustrated in the spectrograms in figure 7.22.

Many Australian languages have two rhotics which, like those in Hausa, differ both in place and manner. Spectrograms and waveforms of a contrasting pair of words of Arrernte are shown in figure 7.23. The word on the left has an alveolar trill. In this token there are two complete contacts, followed by a third oscillation of the articulator that does not reach complete closure. Its presence can be detected by observing an attentuation of the acoustic energy,

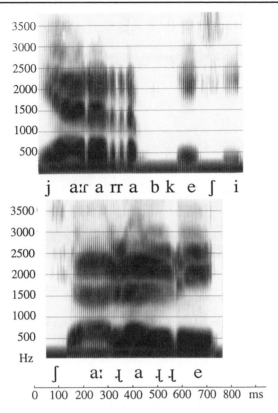

Figure 7.22 Spectrograms of words containing single and geminate Hausa rhotics. The utterances are *yaa rarrabkee shi* 'he flogged him' and *shararree* 'swept'.

visible in both the spectrogram and the waveform. The contrasting approximant in the second word has considerable duration, strong amplitude throughout, and considerable energy in the 2000–2500 Hz range. This segment is usually described as post-alveolar. Segments of these two types are common to the majority of Australian languages.

It is significant that the number of rhotics in Australian languages is generally limited to two. Many Australian languages have four coronal stops, four coronal nasals and four coronal laterals. These are divided into an apical pair and a laminal pair, with laminal dental, apical alveolar, apical post-alveolar and laminal post-alveolar places. However, this proliferation of coronal contrasts does not extend to the rhotics. In descriptions of Australian languages the two rhotics are usually both described as apical. For example, Morphy (1983: 18) notes that in Djapu "the apico-alveolar rhotic is realized as a tap or a trill, while the apico-postalveolar rhotic is a retroflex continuant." Dixon's (1980) survey reports that "in the typical Australian pronunciation of /ɻ/ the

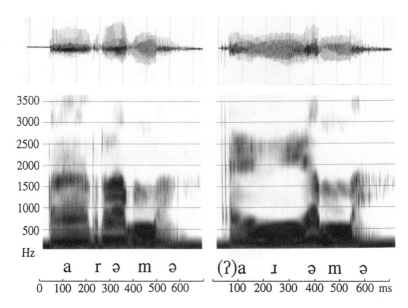

Figure 7.23 Waveforms and spectrograms of the Arrernte words **arəmə** [ɐrəᵇmə] 'louse' and **aɻəmə** [ʔɐɹəᵇmə] 'sees' illustrating the contrasting rhotics of the language. (Note the voiced stop-like onset to the nasals, see chapter 4.)

tip of the tongue is turned back, almost as far as for the retroflex /ɖ/, /ɳ/ and /ɭ/." (Butcher's work in progress on Australian languages shows from palatograms and linguagrams that the 'retroflex' stops can be sublaminal.) The fact that in a linguistic area where laminal consonants are so common, rhotics do not take part in the apical/laminal opposition, suggests that the major types of rhotics (most obviously trills and flaps) are not easily made with larger articulatory organs.

A smaller number of the Australian languages have three rhotics (Dixon 1980:140). In addition to having the the two usual Australian rhotics, Pitta-Pitta, Diyari, Arabana, and Kurtjar are among those having an alveolar flap, Murinhpatha has an alveolar approximant, Warlpiri a post-alveolar flap and Yaygir a voiceless alveolar trill. The three rhotics of Warlpiri are illustrated by the two words in figure 7.24. The word **paɻari** 'rainbow' illustrates the approximant and the trill; **pu ɽuru** 'hairstring' the flap and the trill. The trills in both these examples have only very weak trilling with some associated frication. In contrast the flap has lower amplitude during the brief closure and a quite marked burst at its release. In initial position, the flap is often preceded by a brief prothetic vowel-like segment, as in figure 7.25. This segment assists in setting up the acoustic cues for the flap, which thus become comparable in both initial and intervocalic environments.

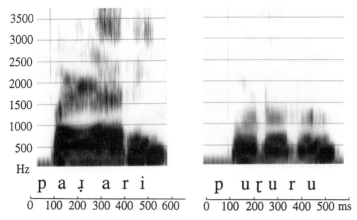

Figure 7.24 Spectrograms of rhotics in Warlpiri in the words **paɻari** 'rainbow' and **puɽuɽu** 'hairstring'.

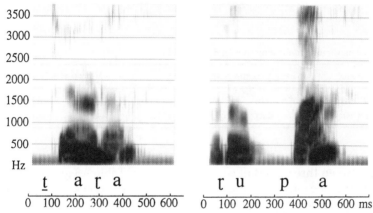

Figure 7.25 Spectrograms of flaps in initial and medial position in Warlpiri in the words **ʈaɽa** 'sleep' and **ɽupa** 'windbreak'.

As we noted earlier, the two rhotics of Malayalam differ by being trills at different places for some speakers. Other speakers have a distinction between alveolar tap and trill. Yamuna (1986) measured the mean duration of the closure in the tap in his speech as 25 ms. Individual closure durations in the trill were shorter, but trills divided into two acoustic types, those with only one closure (mean 16 ms) and those with more than one closure. For the latter type the mean duration of the total trill was 47 ms.

Some languages in the Edoid group have three contrasting rhotic sounds. In Edo itself they have been described as voiced and voiceless trills, and a voiced approximant (e.g. Elugbe 1973, Amayo 1976), all of them alveolar. However, Ladefoged (1968) described these sounds as a voiced fricative ɹ a voiced approximant ɹ, and a voiceless fricative ɹ̥ in other words, as representing a

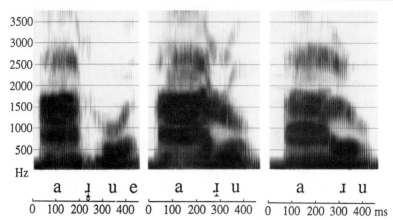

Figure 7.26 Spectrograms of the Edo words in the second line of table 7.3 spoken by a male speaker from Benin City.

Table 7.3 Words illustrating contrasting alveolar rhotics in Edo

VOICELESS FRICATIVE		VOICED FRICATIVE		VOICED APPROXIMANT	
ḁ̀ɹ̊à	'burial ceremony'	aɹa´	'caterpilar'	áɹába	'rubber'
ḁ̀ɹ̊ue	'circumcision'	aɹu´	'eye'	àɹu	(name of a village)

contrast between three types of continuant rhotics. Table 7.3 gives examples of words contrasting these sounds and figure 7.26 shows spectrograms of the words in the second line of the table. These spectrograms and others we have examined show that the approximant ɹ has a very lax articulation, causing only a small reduction in intensity. The voiced fricative ɹ̠ clearly has a closer articulation, as there is a greater amplitude drop, yet there is actually very little frication. The difference between these two voiced sounds does involve a difference in the degree of stricture, but they might be considered to be more open and more closed approximants, rather than an approximant and a fricative. We note that while ɹ̥ is voiceless when it occurs in utterance-initial position, in its most frequent intervocalic position it is generally breathy voiced, as in this figure. We note also that ɹ̠ and ɹ̥ show a marked lowering of the higher formants, whereas the higher formants are unperturbed for ɹ although the constriction results in a significant lowering of the first formant. This suggests that there is also a difference in place of articulation between ɹ and the other two rhotics of Edo.

7.7 Relationship to Laterals

Before turning to the issue of the unity of the class of rhotics, we will briefly discuss the relationship between rhotics and laterals. Sounds of these two classes are often grouped together into a larger class known as 'liquids'. They have a member in common – the lateral flap. This is articulated like the flaps described earlier in this chapter, by drawing the tongue tip back and making a brief ballistic contact in passing (usually) in the post-alveolar region. However, during this gesture one side of the tongue remains low so that air can flow continuously through a lateral escape channel (the higher side of the tongue may or may not make a firm enough contact to seal off airflow on the opposite side). The resulting sound is auditorily reminiscent of both r and l. Some of the reports of alternations between r and l in a variety of languages may be attributable to different perceptions of what is in fact a consistent articulation, particularly when the conditioning environment is said to be vowel environment, as in Nasioi (Hurd and Hurd 1966), Barasano (Stolte and Stolte 1971), and Tucano (West and Welch 1967). In general, back vowels seem to predispose toward the production (or perception) of lateral variants, and front vowels toward rhotic variants. In Chumburung (Snider 1984), the phoneme l has a rhotic variant which occurs medially in words with narrowed pharynx (retracted tongue root) vowels.

In other languages, Korean for example, it is much clearer that there are two distinct articulations involved. Further, in Korean it is the position within a syllable that determines this variation; r occurs in syllable-onset position and l in syllable-coda position (Cho 1967). In yet others the lateral and rhotic pronunciations vary freely, as in several of the West African languages surveyed in Ladefoged (1968). In Japanese, Shimizu and Dantsuji (1987: 16) note that

> Some Japanese use both a lateral approximant [l] and a flap [r] as completely free variants. Some Japanese use a lateral approximant [l] in the word initial position and use a flap [r] in the intervocalic position. Some use a lateral approximant [l] in each position. Others use a retroflex voiced stop [ɖ] in addition to these sounds.

Thus there are patterns of alternation between rhotics and laterals that associate these two classes together. As noted earlier, there are also distributional similarities between rhotics and laterals. The most typical members of these classes are relatively sonorous, but both classes include sounds that are far from being so.

7.8 Factors underlying the Unity of
Rhotics as a Class

Given the articulatory variation in both place and manner between different types of rhotics, it is difficult to imagine a single articulatory property that would unify the class. Instead, a unifying property might be sought in the acoustic domain. Based on data mainly from English, Ladefoged (1975) and Lindau (1978) suggested a lowered third formant as a common acoustic factor. This would be manifested in the relatively steady-state formant structure of approximant and other continuant rhotics, and, in trills, in the formant structure of the brief intervals between the closures of the trill, as well as in the transitions to and from the consonant in any adjoining vowel.

A lowered third formant is a well-justified specification for the various articulations of American English ɹ, including that in figure 7.17. Some of the approximant rhotics in other languages also share this property. All four speakers of Izon examined by Lindau showed a considerably lowered third formant very similar to that of American English and many of the Italian speakers we have examined also show a relatively low third formant. The third formant lowers in all six of the Toda trills shown in figure 7.5. But other rhotics have high third formants. For example, the Hausa retroflex approximant in figure 7.21 has a third formant at the same level as that in the surrounding **a** vowels, and the Czech fricative rhotic in figure 7.11 has a third formant near 3000 Hz. Uvular r-sounds in figure 7.10 from Swedish, in figure 7.14 from French and in figure 7.15 from German all show a third spectral peak over 2500 Hz, although otherwise they are somewhat different from each other. The Arrernte retroflex approximant shown in figure 7.23 also has a high third formant.

These differences in the location of formants in the approximant r-sounds are important cues to the constriction location. Uvular r-sounds have a high third formant, sometimes close to the fourth formant. Dental r-sounds also have a relatively high third formant, as illustrated in the Spanish spectrograms in figure 7.13, though not as high as the uvulars (Fant 1968). A lowered third formant signals a particular set of articulatory configurations. It is thus not a good candidate for a property that unifies the rhotic class.

But if the phonetic correlate is not the proposed lowered third formant, is there any property that makes us recognize all these different sounds as rhotics? Lindau suggests that "there is no physical property that constitutes the essence of all rhotics. Instead, the relations between members of the class of rhotics are more of a family resemblance." She argues for a series of step-by-step connections. Thus the uvular trill used in Southern Swedish and the American English approximant do not seem to have much in common. However, there are striking similarities between trills at different places. The similar pulsing patterns in apical and uvular trills could explain the changes from tongue-tip trills to uvular trills that has occurred historically in French, German, and Southern Swedish. Once the r-sound is established as uvular, it often weakens, and there is free variation between uvular trills, fricatives, and approximants. All uvular rhotics have similar spectral shapes in that they have some spectral peak in the area of a high third formant. Dental trills and approximants also have fairly high third formants. That there is an acoustic similarity between these rhotics is demonstrated in some areas in Sweden on the border between the areas that use tongue tip /r/'s and uvular /ʀ/'s. In these areas, members of the same family may use either front or back r-sounds, and other family members never notice the difference (Ohlsson, Nielsen and Schaltz 1977).

There is also acoustic similarity between trills and taps and flaps. From an acoustic point of view, a trill is not unlike a series of taps. Particularly in intervocalic position, trills may be reduced to a single period (sometimes referred to in the literature as a 'one-tap trill'). In a number of cases we have observed that frication and trilling may co-occur. This may result in fricative-approximant variants as noted in French, Edo and other languages. Several of the trills illustrated in section 7.2 were produced with one or more closures followed by an open phase that is prolonged into an approximant instead of further alternations of shorter openings with closures. This instability in the production of trills, leading to trills with a prolonged open phase, could explain why trilled r-sounds vary with, or change into, approximants.

In this way, according to Lindau, each member of the rhotic class resembles some other member with respect to some property, but it is not the same property that constitutes the resemblance for all members of the class. Trills and taps are alike in having short closure duration, the open phase of a trill resembles an approximant in the presence of formants, and tongue-tip trills and uvular trills resemble each other in their pattern of rapid pulses. Rhotics produced with the same constriction location(s) are alike in the distribution of spectral energy.

Such family resemblances explain well several of the synchronic alternations and diachronic changes that connect different types of rhotics to each other, but equally close resemblances also extend to many sounds that are not traditionally considered members of the rhotic class. Sounds with similar constriction locations are likely to have similar spectral properties whether or not they are 'rhotic'. Taps, flaps and trills all have similarities to stops because they all involve closure, and, indeed, often alternate with them. Fricative rhotics have obvious similarities to other fricatives. And so on. Although there are several well-defined subsets of sounds (trills, flaps, etc) that are included in the rhotic class, the overall unity of the group seems to rest mostly on the historical connections between these subgroups, and on the choice of the letter 'r' to represent them all.

8

Clicks

Clicks are stops in which the essential component is the rarefaction of air enclosed between two articulatory closures formed in the oral cavity, so that a loud transient is produced when the more forward closure is released. The means of moving the air in the production of clicks is called the velaric airstream mechanism. It is always ingressive, and cannot be used for sounds other than stops and affricates.

Clicks are a regular part of the consonant systems of many of the languages spoken in Southern Africa. They are most common in the Khoisan languages such as !Xóõ, !Xũ and Nama, in which they are very frequent. Over 70 percent of the words in a !Xóõ dictionary (Traill 1994) begin with a click. They also occur, with a far lower frequency, in a number of Bantu languages of Southern Africa, such as Zulu, Xhosa, RuGciriku and Yei, and in three East African languages, Dahalo, a Cushitic language of Kenya, and Sandawe and Hadza, two languages spoken in Tanzania. In all these languages the proportion of words with clicks is much smaller. In a vocabulary of Sandawe containing approximately 1200 entries (Kagaya 1993) only about 25 percent of the words contain clicks, and the entire set of Dahalo words containing clicks amounts to only about 40 (Maddieson, Spajić, Sands, and Ladefoged 1993). Clicks do not occur in any ordinary languages outside Africa, although they are familiar as extralinguistic signals in many societies. They were also reported in Damin, the auxiliary language formerly used by Lardil speakers in Australia, which is constructed somewhat on the lines of a language game (Hale and Nash, unpublished).

The sequence of events in the production of a simple alveolar click is illustrated in figure 8.1, which is based on x-ray tracings of a !Xóõ speaker published in Traill (1985). For simplicity, we describe it in terms of four phases: (1) A body of air is enclosed by raising the tip of the tongue to form a closure in the

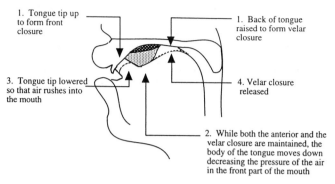

1. Tongue tip up to form front closure

1. Back of tongue raised to form velar closure

3. Tongue tip lowered so that air rushes into the mouth

4. Velar closure released

2. While both the anterior and the velar closure are maintained, the body of the tongue moves down decreasing the pressure of the air in the front part of the mouth

Figure 8.1 The articulatory sequence involved in production of an alveolar click in !Xóõ. The dark shaded area shows the cavity enclosed when the closures are formed. The light shaded area shows the cavity just before the release of the anterior closure. The dashed lines show the lowered tongue positions corresponding to steps 3 and 4.

front of the mouth, and by also raising the back of the tongue to make a velar closure on the soft palate. (2) The air in the cavity between the two closures is rarefied by the downward movement of the center of the tongue, while both the back and the tip of the tongue maintain contact with the roof of the mouth. (3) The tip and blade or side of the tongue move down, releasing the forward closure so that air rushes into the mouth to equalize the air pressure, producing a sharp transient. (4) The closure formed by the back of the tongue is released.

The presence of a posterior closure is an essential component of a click, and every click has both a tip or blade (or lip) action determining the type of click, and also an accompanying velar or uvular articulation. Beach (1938) coined a pair of terms for these two aspects of the articulation of a click. He calls the first, the location and release of the front closure, the click *influx*. From our point of view the click influx determines what we call the click type. The velar or uvular articulation and other accompanying properties were in Beach's terminology the click *efflux*. We will not use this term, but will instead use the expression click accompaniment to describe properties of the back oral articulation together with any pulmonic activity, laryngeal setting, or nasal airflow that accompanies the click.

8.1 Articulatory Properties of Click Types

Because no language is known to use more than five click types we will regard any click as belonging to one or other of only five types: bilabial, dental, alveolar, palatal and lateral. We symbolize these five click types as ⊙, | !, ǂ, ‖,

Table 8.1 Articulatory phonetic classifications by different authors of the |, !, ǂ, and ‖ click types. The O click type is not included in this table as it is always described as bilabial by those authors who refer to it.

SOURCE	LANGUAGE			!	ǂ	‖
This paper	all	dental	alveolar	palatal	lateral
Beach (1938)	Nama	dental affricative	alveolar implosive	denti-alveolar implosive	lateral affricative
Bleek and Lloyd (1911)	|Xam	dental	cerebral	palatal	lateral
Doke (1926)	Zulu	dental	palato-alveolar		post-alveolar lateral
Doke (1937)	ǂKhomani	dental with friction	palato-alveolar instantaneous	alveolar instantaneous	lateral with friction
Köhler (1981)	Kxoe	dental	palatal retroflex	alveolar	lateral
Maddieson (1984a)	Nama	dental affricated	alveolar	palato-alveolar	alveolar lateral affricated
Maddieson (1984a)	Zulu	alveolar affricated	palato-alveolar		alveolar lateral affricated
Sagey (1986)	Khoisan	+ coronal + anterior + distributed - lateral	+ coronal - anterior - distributed - lateral	+ coronal + anterior + distributed - lateral	+ coronal - anterior - distributed + lateral
Snyman (1975)	Zhuǀ'hõasi	denti-alveolar	palatal	alveolar	lateral
Taljaard and Snyman (1990)	Zulu	apico-lamino-dental	apico-palatal		lateral apico-alveo-palatal

respectively. Although the click types are given labels that refer primarily to place of articulation, these terms cover several aspects of the front articulation. Each should be considered a shorthand description for a range of articulatory and acoustic characteristics that tend to occur together and which jointly define a family of clicks that are considered to belong to the same type. We will note the differences in the articulation of these types, both between languages and between speakers within languages in the following discussion. Comparatively few languages use all five types of clicks. Dahalo and SiNdebele are examples of languages that use only one (dental); Southern Sotho also uses only one, but in this case it is alveolar. Zulu, and Xhosa are among the Bantu languages that use three (dental, alveolar, and lateral). Sandawe and Hadza also use three. Nama, !Xũ and many of the other Khoisan languages use four (all except the bilabial). Only Southern Khoisan languages such as !Xóõ and |Xam use five.

In the history of the study of these sounds there has been an enormous diversity in the articulatory descriptions offered for what we consider to be the same type of click. Some of the principal descriptive labels that have been used are summarized in table 8.1. The variation among descriptions of these types is such that we and writers such as Snyman (1975) give precisely the opposite names for ! (our alveolar, their palatal), and ǂ (our palatal, their alveolar); other authors offer yet other names for these two sounds. Similarly, what we call dental, Maddieson (1984a: 297) calls alveolar in Zulu, and our alveolars are his palato-alveolars. There are several reasons for this variation in naming. The maximum occlusion during a click is more extensive than the occlusion that exists just before the release; judgments on the place of articulation will vary according to whether place is based on the maximum occlusion or a later timepoint. Also, auditorily similar click types can be produced by different speakers using somewhat different articulations. Finally, different authors stress different aspects of the articulations, for example, adding comments on the abrupt or fricated nature of the release.

The articulatory positions for the five types of clicks in !Xóõ are illustrated in figure 8.2, which is based on cine-radiology data from Traill (1985). In the original data the lips are visible only in the case of the bilabial click. Outlines of the lips have been added to each of the other clicks, with their positions based on those of the lower teeth, which are visible on the records of all the clicks. In each case the left-hand diagram shows the the maximal occlusion, when the cavity enclosed by the tongue is at its smallest, while the right-hand diagram indicates the position just before the anterior closure was released.

We will consider the moments of maximal closure (the left-hand diagrams) first. There are smaller differences among the click types at this time than there are just before the release. The left-hand diagrams are rather similar, except for the bilabial click. In all of the four lingual click types, the tongue contacts much of the upper surface of the oral cavity. The most significant difference among them at this time is that the anterior margin of the enclosed body of air is somewhat further from the front of the mouth for the alveolar and palatal clicks than for the dental and lateral types.

The diagrams on the right of the figure show that the differences in articulatory positions among the click types are greater just before the release. The differences between the two columns reflect the considerable tongue movements required to produce the rarefaction of the air in the cavity, which forms the basis of the velaric airstream. A more retracted location of the anterior

Bilabial

Dental

Alveolar

Palatal

Lateral

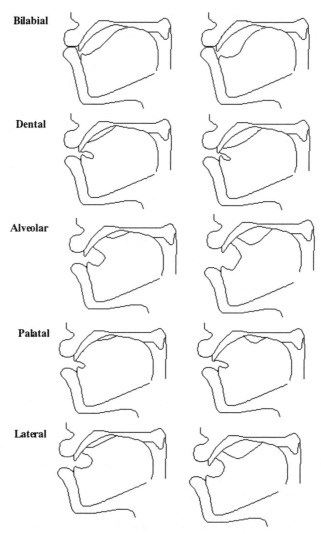

Figure 8.2 The positions of the vocal organs at the onset of the click closure (left column), and just before the release of the click closure (right column) in the five click types of !Xóõ, based on cine-radiology data published in Traill (1985).

margin of the cavity continues to distinguish alveolar and palatal clicks from the dental and lateral types. A different grouping emerges from examining the lowest point of the center of the tongue just before release. This is lower for the alveolar and lateral click types than for the dental and palatal types.

The distinctive acoustic characteristics of any click type are determined by the location of the closure at the moment of release, not the location of the closure at its maximum extent. For this reason, in the articulatory labels we provide for the click types, we emphasize the articulatory position just before the release. It is these points in the articulation that we will consider in most detail, noting the location of the rearward edge of the anterior closure, especially just before the closure is released. Note that this emphasis means that static palatograms are of limited use in determining the place of articulation for clicks, since they show the entire area contacted at any point during the click. However, they do serve to indicate limits within which the articulation falls. Accompanying linguographic data can also provide valuable information on the part of the tongue making contact. In the following paragraphs the articulation of each click type will be considered in turn.

As noted above, clicks of the bilabial type occur only in Southern Khoisan languages. They are illustrated in the top row of figure 8.2. In most forms of this click the lips are together, but not rounded or protruded unless there is labialization. The regular gesture is one of lip compression rather than the puckering of the lips normally associated with a kiss. In some productions the lower lip may articulate against the upper teeth as the click is released, thus increasing the turbulent airflow associated with the release of the click.

The dental click type (illustrated in the second row of figure 8.2) occurs in more languages than any other type. In the particular token illustrated in the figure, the release involves only the tip of the tongue. We do not know what part of the tongue was involved in the frame of the film immediately prior to this, but usually both the tip and blade of the tongue are used to make the front closure, so we would classify this click type as typically having a laminal articulation. Louw (1977) suggests that speakers of Nama and Zulu as well as most speakers of Xhosa use an articulation "with the tip of the tongue being sucked away from the upper front teeth." He may be considering the term 'tip of the tongue' to encompass what we would term the blade. The linguogram of a Zulu speaker in Doke (1926) certainly shows a relatively broad laminal contact on the tongue for |. However, Louw notes one group of Xhosa speakers who "press the tip of the tongue against the lower teeth and suck the front part of the tongue . . . away from the upper teeth." These speakers clearly use a laminal articulation and, in comparison with them, the other speakers Louw is describing might be said to have a more apical articulation. Doke (1925) suggests that the dental click type may be produced with an interdental articulation in !Xũ ; and we have ourselves observed some speakers of Sandawe and Hadza who protrude the tip of the tongue between the teeth. Thus, as with dental sounds of other classes, the specific articulation used for a dental click may vary in place of contact and tongue shape.

When the clicks of this type are formed, the front closure may extend as far back as the post-alveolar region, so that it might seem preferable to call these denti-alveolar or even denti-palatal clicks. But, as we noted earlier, the crucial point in the description of a click type is the position at the moment of release. In the clicks that are being classified as dental, the closure at the time of the release usually involves at least part of the blade of the tongue, and is usually on the teeth and the anterior part of the alveolar area, making them clearly laminal dental or laminal denti-alveolar. It is also characteristic of clicks of this type that the front release is accompanied by noise; hence they are often described as affricated (see table 8.1 above).

The third row in figure 8.2 shows the articulation for the click transcribed as !. Clicks of this type differ from the dental clicks in that they are always produced with a more abrupt, non-affricated, front release. But their place of articulation may be somewhat varied and different aspects emphasized, resulting in their being given various names. Clicks of this type were for many years conventionally called 'palatal', but we have chosen to call them alveolar as the contact just before release is usually confined to a location well in front of the palatal region, although it may certainly be post-alveolar. Traill (1985) prefers the term postdental on the grounds that most of the considerable number of speakers of Khoisan languages that he has examined have smoothly sloping palates without an alveolar ridge, making it difficult to separate articulatory regions behind the teeth. An alternative would be to call these sounds simply apical clicks on the grounds that by far the majority of clicks of the ! type are made with the tip of the tongue contacting the roof of the mouth at the moment of release of the closure. But this is not true for all speakers; our linguograms show that some speakers of Hadza and Sandawe have a laminal articulation in which the tip of the tongue does not touch the roof of the mouth.

Clicks of the ! type are often post-alveolar in place of articulation; hence the occurrence of terms such as retroflex and cerebral in the ! column of table 8.1. (In fact, the symbol ! derives from adding the dot diacritic used to indicate retroflex by scholars of Indian languages to the slash used to represent dental clicks.) Both apical post-alveolar and sub-apical post-alveolar varieties occur, but we do not know of any contrasts between click types with these different articulatory positions. Rather, these seem to be variants within the same language, as in the palatograms in figure 8.3 (re-drawn from Traill 1985: 103). These show single articulations of words containing initial ! produced by five different speakers·of !Xóõ. Note the inverted curve for the first two speakers (marked by the arrow). The contact in the center of the mouth is further back than at the sides. This kind of contact area is produced by the tip of the tongue curling back as it touches the roof of the mouth, in a sub-apical articulation. Similar contact areas have been found in studies of the retroflex consonants in Malayalam (Dart 1991). As for the other three speakers' articulations, 3 and 4 might be best described as alveolar, while speaker 5's pronunciation is post-alveolar but lacks any indication of sub-apical articulation. These five palatograms thus illustrate three articulatory strategies for producing the same click type. Similar variations are apparent in production of the ! click type in Zulu and Xhosa. Doke (1927: 127) and Beach (1938: 82) both publish palatograms of a single speaker using both laminal postalveolar and sub-apical variants of !.

Doke (1925: 148) described a sub-apical retroflex click in !Xū and implies

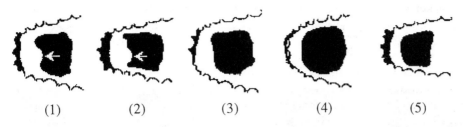

(1)   (2)   (3)   (4)   (5)

Figure 8.3 Palatograms of ! produced by five speakers of !Xóõ (based on Traill 1985: 103). In this figure the contact area is shown in white.

that this retroflex click type contrasts with the alveolar type. Jan Snyman, the most experienced investigator working on this language (Snyman 1970, 1975, 1978, 1980) does not note any such contrast, but consistently transcribes the words that Doke writes with a retroflex click as simply containing clicks of the ! type. No linguists working on other Khoisan languages report a contrast between alveolar and retroflex places for clicks. It seems most likely that some of Doke's speakers used a retroflex click, but no contrast existed then or exists now between this sound and a non-retroflex form of the ! click. It is certainly possible that retroflex clicks may be the favored form of pronunciation of ! in some languages, but we do not believe that it is a contrastive possibility.

We have studied the production of the ! click type in Sandawe and Hadza. These languages also demonstrate substantial variability in the production of these sounds. In both languages, clicks of the ! type were especially noted to vary a great deal in terms of how forcefully they were produced by speakers. In some instances, the amplitude of the release was very low, as if the click were produced with very little suction (for more details, see Sands, Maddieson and Ladefoged 1993). A notable allophonic variation of the click type occured for a number of speakers. In these instances, the tongue tip makes contact with the bottom of the mouth after the release of the front click closure. The release of the front closure and the contact with the bottom of the mouth is one continuous, ballistic movement, with the underside of the tip of the tongue making a percussive sound as it strikes the floor of the mouth. This version of the ! click is thus similar to the sound sometimes made by speakers of non-click languages trying to imitate the sound of a trotting horse and is the articulation which Tucker, Bryan and Woodburn (1977) characterized as a flapped palato-alveolar click. The only parallel variant reported from any Southern African languages with clicks concerns an individual !Xũ speaker who used what Doke called a palato-alveolar flapped click. The tongue-front is "flapped smartly to the floor of the mouth, the under-side making a resounding 'smack' behind the lower front teeth and on the floor of the mouth" (Doke 1925: 163).

Palatograms, linguograms and inferred sagittal sections of the front articulation of the ! clicks for two speakers of Hadza are shown in figure 8.4. In

Speaker 1

ŋ!

Speaker 2

ŋ!

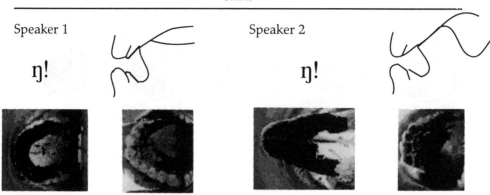

Figure 8.4 Palatograms, linguograms and inferred sagittal view of the alveolo-palatal click in the word 'cut' ŋ!eʔe 'cut' as spoken by two male Hadza speakers.

comparison with the !Xóõ clicks shown in figure 8.3, it is possible that the back closure does not extend as far forward in Hadza, meaning that the cavity enclosed may be larger. As in other languages, the front closure of these ! clicks in Hadza tends to be made at a less anterior place of articulation than the | click, and is typically more apical. This is certainly the case for speaker 1, but speaker 2 shows more similarity in his articulations for | and !. Our linguograms for speaker 2 show front closure contact on the tongue to be similar in length and location for both | and !, but the dental click differs in the shape of the area in the middle of the tongue which did not make contact with the roof of the mouth. In the dental click, this area is tapered toward the front, whereas ! displays a more rectangular shape for the corresponding area. Neither of these two Hadza speakers nor the three speakers of Sandawe for whom we have palatographic records have a sub-apical articulation.

We have noted, as have Sands (1991), Traill (1992) and Ladefoged and Traill (1994), that writers on clicks have described the ! click type in a large number of different ways. In the preceding paragraphs we noted that for some speakers in some languages this click may involve a laminal articulation, whereas for others it is apical or sub-apical. We suspect that the laminal articulation of ! can occur only in languages that do not have a contrasting palatal click ǂ of the type we will discuss below. Except for Traill's data on !Xóõ, we do not have any data (cine-radiology or dynamic palatography) which show the place of articulation on the roof of the mouth at the moment of the release of the click. Considering all the varieties of ! clicks that have been observed, many of them being differences among individual speakers of the same language, we think it best to use the term alveolar to describe these clicks, noting, however, that it should not be interpreted too specifically. We should also note that in each of the languages we have investigated with a ! click, at least some speakers make this sound with an apical (or sub-apical) contact in the alveolar region. In the

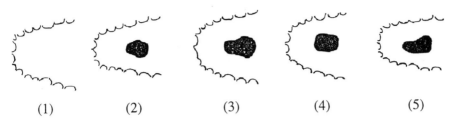

(1)   (2)   (3)   (4)   (5)

Figure 8.5 Palatograms of the palatal clicks of five !Xóõ speakers, after Traill (1985). Contact area is shown in white.

Khoisan languages of Southern Africa it is always made in this way, and for these languages ! can be considered simply as an apical click.

The ‡ click type shown in the fourth row of figure 8.2 has been called denti-alveolar (Beach 1938) or alveolar (Doke 1925, Köhler 1981). These descriptions seems to us to focus on the wrong aspect of the articulation, and we will refer to it as palatal. This, as table 8.1 shows, is a return to the term used by Bleek and Lloyd (1911) and other early writers such as Krönlein (1889). It is true that the tip and blade of the tongue are in contact with the teeth and alveolar ridge, but the forward edge of the click cavity is much further back; and this is the relevant factor. Traill's cine-radiology data also demonstrate how the location of the click cavity alters during the production of this click. Comparison of the left and right sides of figure 8.2 shows that the contact made by the blade of the tongue moved further back while the suction was being developed. This is a common but by no means invariable feature of this click type (see Traill 1985: 127). At the moment of the release of the click, there is no doubt that ‡ should be described as a palatal sound.

The other striking aspect of the ‡ click type is the small size of the cavity between the two closures during the maximal occlusion. The short length of this cavity in the sagittal plane and its shallow depth can be seen in figure 8.2. Palatograms of five !Xóõ speakers in Traill (1985), which formed the basis for figure 8.5, as well as a palatogram of a Nama speaker in Beach (1938: 77) make clear that the cavity is also narrowed by extensive contact along the lateral margins. The cavity in this click type before expansion is thus the smallest of any type even being zero for speaker one. Because this cavity is so small a comparatively small movement of the tongue will create a sufficient volume change to produce the negative pressure required in a click.

The lateral click type in the last row of figure 8.2 is also somewhat varied in its place of articulation. The most significant aspect of this click type is, of course, the lateral release, which is usually made by moving one side of the tongue at the level of the molar teeth. There are no reports of a sublaminal version of this click, but the place may be dental, alveolar or post-alveolar. In the Southern African languages the central closure is usually apical alveolar, as

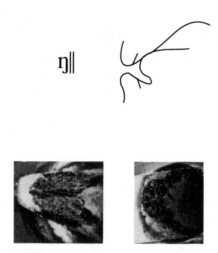

Figure 8.6 Palatogram and linguogram of a lateral click in the word ŋǁaʔa 'scavenge' as spoken by a male Hadza speaker (speaker 2 in Figure 8.3 above).

in figure 8.2, and the lateral click ǁ has a similar front closure just before release to that in the ! click; but in Sandawe and Hadza the articulation is similar to that in the palatal lateral ejective cʎ̥', which these languages also have. Indeed, the lateral click in these two languages might well be regarded as a lateral version of the ǂ click, rather than of the ! click. A palatogram and linguogram of a Hadza lateral click type are shown in figure 8.6. The extensive strictly laminal contact on the tongue is very apparent. Whether the articulation is apical or laminal, lateral clicks in all languages that have been studied have an affricated front release. It is perfectly possible to produce a non-affricated release (as in a sound used by many English speakers to signal approval or surprise), but this does not seem to be used in natural languages.

Apart from differences in the place of articulation and the apical/laminal parameter, the four lingual click types differ in the rate of movement of the front articulatory release. In all the languages that we have heard, the dental and lateral clicks are affricated, whereas the alveolar and palatal clicks are sharply released. In figure 8.2 it can be seen that the affricated click types are those which have a cavity before expansion that is relatively long in the sagittal plane.

We follow Traill (1985) in emphasizing that, for languages that have both alveolar and palatal clicks, the major articulatory distinctions among ǀ, !, ǂ, ǁ are not in the place of articulation on the roof of the mouth, but in the part of the tongue used. In these languages, two of the clicks, !, ‖, are apical and two |, ǂ are laminal. The two apical click types are those in which cavity expansion is achieved by greater lowering of the center of the tongue. The distinction between the two apical clicks is that ! is central and ‖ lateral. The tongue tip contact on the roof of the mouth can be anywhere from the dental to the post-alveolar region. There is a distinction in traditional place of articulation terms between the two laminal clicks |, ǂ. The laminal closure for | is on the teeth and the teeth ridge (in so far Khoisan speakers can be said to have an alveolar ridge; as we have noted, most have very flat palates). The closure for the other laminal click, ǂ, always extends further back into the palatal region. In coming to these conclusions, Traill (1985) was discussing a particular language, !Xóõ, but his findings seem equally applicable to the other click languages that have |, !, ‖, ǂ. Many of the descriptions of clicks in these languages are inadequate because they do not pay sufficient attention to the apical/laminal distinction. Note, however, that the apical/laminal distinction is independent of the affrication of the release.

8.2 Acoustic Properties of Click Types

In the past there have been few attempts to describe clicks from an acoustic perspective. The most important are Kagaya's (1978) study of Naron, and Sands' (1991) study of Xhosa. These authors have described the click types in terms of the general shape of the acoustic spectra of their releases and whether or not they are associated with noise (affricated). The account that follows is based on Ladefoged and Traill (1994). The most convenient way to introduce a discussion about the acoustic properties of clicks is to consider the differences in the waveforms, shown in figure 8.7. We will concentrate on the acoustic structure of the waveform that occurs at the release of the anterior closure. This waveform is determined by the place and manner of the click release, and by the cavity and walls of the vocal tract anterior to the posterior closure. The relevant acoustics of the release of the posterior closure will not be discussed here. They are similar to the releases that occur in other velar and uvular consonants.

There are obvious differences among the waveforms in their duration and noisiness. Click releases, like those of other stops, can be considered to have two acoustic components; a transient which occurs when the articulators come apart, and a noise associated with turbulent flow between the articulators. The transient is due to the rapid rate of change of vocal tract shape; it produces a wave that is like an impulse response of the vocal tract cavity at that time. The wave forms of the alveolar and palatal clicks (in the lower part of the figure 8.7) are dominated by the transient response; they are not accompanied by significant amounts of turbulent noise after the release. The bilabial, dental and

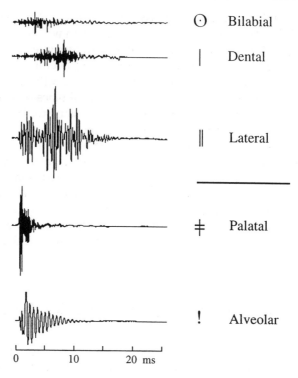

$$\begin{array}{ll}
\odot & \text{Bilabial} \\
| & \text{Dental} \\
\| & \text{Lateral} \\
\ddagger & \text{Palatal} \\
! & \text{Alveolar}
\end{array}$$

0   10   20 ms

Figure 8.7 Waveforms of the noise bursts for the five !Xóõ click types. The two waveforms in the lower part of the figure are dominated by the transient response, those in the upper part have considerable turbulent noise after the release.

lateral click releases (in the upper part of the figure) are longer and noisier. These differences correspond to the clear auditory differences between these two classes; the abruptly released clicks provide an intense but brief stimulation of the auditory nerve, whereas the noisy clicks provide a sharp onset followed by sustained stimulation. This makes the clicks !, ǂ more like the plain stops **t, k** whereas the noisy clicks ☉, |, ǁ are more like the affricates **pɸ, ts, kx**. In the noisy clicks, the tongue (for the dental and lateral clicks) and the lips (for the bilabial click) move more slowly when the front closure is broken and the negative pressure is equalized. Hagman (1977) suggests in his Nama grammar that the affrication of dentals is due more to the fact that the release is made by pulling the tongue away from an irregular surface formed by the teeth, between which there may be gaps, so that the resulting aperture is created in a somewhat piecemeal fashion. This seems an interesting and plausible suggestion, and accounts for the fact that it is difficult to produce a non-affricated dental click, whereas it is much easier to produce non-affricated lateral and bilabial ones. In the abrupt (palatal and alveolar) clicks, the front of the tongue moves very fast when the anterior closure is broken, so that the impulse response of the chamber is accompanied by almost no noise.

A feature that can also be seen in figure 8.7 is the crescendo and decrescendo of the noise. For the noisy clicks, after the anterior closure is released, the noise increases in intensity until it reaches a maximum, after which the noise decreases in intensity. This gives a measure of the speed with which the anterior part of the tongue or the lower lip moves away from its point of articulation. For the noisy clicks this is relatively slow, so that the duration of the fricative portion is about 30 ms; for the abrupt clicks the duration of this portion is about 6 ms.

Another acoustic feature of the abruptly released clicks ! and ǂ, visible in the waveforms are the damped oscillations, initiated by the transient energy. The noisy clicks have a more random waveform. The waveform of the alveolar click has damped oscillations with a frequency of about 1200 Hz. The palatal click has less clearly visible damped oscillations, with a frequency over 3000 Hz, reflecting the fact that the cavity for the palatal click is smaller than that for the alveolar, as may be seen in figure 8.2.

The spectra of clicks can be divided into three classes, dependent on the general distribution of energy. The dental and palatal clicks have more energy above 2.5 kHz, and the alveolar and lateral clicks have more below it. The spectra of the bilabial click are partly reminiscent of those for the dental click, with a high frequency peak at 3700 Hz, but in addition there is a wide band of intense lower frequencies between about 900 and 1500 Hz. There are two regions of spectral energy because the bilabial click is the only click in which the initial transient and the following noise burst are in different regions.

Finally, in our consideration of the acoustics of clicks, we must emphasize the importance of their intensity. Clicks stand out from the sounds around them. This is partly due to their usually being preceded by silence or low level voicing, and often followed by a voiceless accompaniment. But it is more because many of the clicks contain a great deal of energy compared with the surrounding sounds. As the illustrations in the later part of this chapter will show, they often have a peak to peak voltage ratio that is more than twice that of the following vowel, meaning that they have at least 6 dB greater intensity. (It may be helpful to remember that if one sound is 5 dB greater than another, and has approximately the same frequency components, then it sounds about twice as loud as the other.) This is an important acoustic feature that distinguishes clicks from other consonants. The clicks |, !, ǂ, ‖ are nearly always more intense than the following vowel. Only the bilabial click normally has much less intensity than the following vowel; but it is, nevertheless, at least as intense as s, the strongest of the other voiceless consonants. As a class clicks are probably the most salient consonants found in a human language. They are easier to identify than non-click consonants, and are virtually never confused with non-click consonants (Ladefoged and Traill 1994). They thus form a robust and perceptually salient class.

8.3 Click Accompaniments

Clicks must involve two closures. So far we have been discussing only the sound that is caused by the release of the anterior closure, the so-called influx. We will now consider the range of sounds associated with the posterior closure and with the laryngeal and oro-nasal settings during clicks. These variations are called the accompaniments or, in older terminology, the 'effluxes' of the clicks. It should be emphasized that they are a necessary part of any click. There cannot be a click without an accompaniment of some kind, and our transcriptions of individual clicks, as opposed to click types, will always include a way of symbolizing this part of the sound. The posterior closure is usually in the velar region, so that most clicks include a velar plosive **k** or **g** or a velar nasal **ŋ** as one of their attributes.

There are three types of variations in the accompaniments of clicks: (1) those associated with activities of the larynx; (2) those associated with the oro-nasal process; and (3) those associated with the place and manner of release of the back closure. Nguni languages such as Zulu and Xhosa use only the first two of these possibilities. The Khoisan languages use all three. We will begin a more detailed study of click accompaniments by considering data from Xhosa, in which there are five different accompaniments for each click. These clicks may be accompanied by a voiceless, or an aspirated, or what we will call a breathy voiced velar plosive **k**, **kʰ**, **g**; in addition there may be a voiced velar nasal **ŋ**, or a breathy voiced velar nasal **ŋ** Xhosa clicks have one of three possible anterior releases, dental, alveolar or lateral. Accordingly this language has 15 contrasting clicks as shown in table 8.2.

We can see a number of points about these different accompaniments by considering the waveforms for the alveolar clicks, which are shown in figure 8.8. The voiceless click in the top row has a small amount of aspiration; but it is clearly distinct from the aspirated click in the second row, which has a voice

Table 8.2 Words illustrating contrasting clicks in Xhosa

	DENTAL	ALVEOLAR	LATERAL
VOICELESS	ukúk|ola 'to grind fine'	ukúk!oɓa 'to break stones'	úk||olo 'peace'
ASPIRATED	úkuk|ʰóla 'to pick up'	ukúk!ʰola 'perfume'	ukúk||ʰoɓa 'to arm oneself'
BREATHY VOICED	úkug|óɓa 'to be joyful'	ukúg!oba 'to scoop'	ukúg||oba 'to stir up mud'
VOICED NASAL	ukúŋ|oma 'to admire'	ukúŋ!ola 'to climb up'	ukúŋ||iɓa 'to put on clothes'
BREATHY VOICED NASAL	ukúŋ|ola 'to be dirty'	ukúŋ!ala 'to go straight'	ukúŋ||oŋ||a 'to lie on back knees up'

onset time (VOT) of about 125 ms. The click in the third row may be called breathy voiced, and transcribed with a voiced velar symbol with a dieresis under it; but figure 8.7 shows that in the velar plosive accompaniment in the third row there is no vocal fold vibration during the closure. The breathy voiced clicks in Xhosa (and in the neighboring languages such as Zulu) are part of the set of depressor consonants, which are marked by the lowering of the tone on the following vowel (Traill, Khumalo and Fridjhon 1987). The breathy voice in these depressor consonants in Bantu languages such as Zulu and Xhosa is not accompanied by strong breathy voice during the release of the closure as it is in Indo-Aryan languages such as Hindi or Marathi.

The clicks in the fourth row occur almost at the end of the accompanying velar nasal, as do the clicks in the fifth row. The clicks in these two rows are distinguished by the fact that the breathy voiced nasal in the fifth row is a depressor consonant, lowering the tone. Unlike the situation in the case of the accompanying velar stop in the third row, in this case there is sufficient transglottal pressure difference to keep the vocal folds vibrating throughout the click and the following vowel. The breathy voice vibrations are evident in the waveform, which also has a lower fundamental frequency. Again the breathiness is not as strong as it is in the breathy voiced nasals in, for example, Marathi.

There are additional click accompaniments in the Khoisan languages. Nama has clicks accompanied by a glottal stop and clicks with a voiceless nasal accompaniment, which will be discussed below. As it also has three of the possibilities mentioned so far – the nasal, voiceless unaspirated and aspirated accompaniments – there are five different forms of each of the anterior releases. Nama has four types of anterior release (the three in Xhosa and a palatal type), so that there are 20 distinct clicks as shown in table 8.3. Ladefoged and Traill (1984) have given a full account of these Nama clicks.

The clicks in the first, second and fourth rows have similar accompaniments to those in Xhosa, except that, in some dialects of Nama, the aspirated release may be accompanied by velar friction. The third row contains clicks with accompanying voiceless nasal airflow. This property has been discussed elsewhere (Ladefoged and Traill 1984) under the label delayed aspiration. When a vowel precedes clicks with this accompaniment that vowel is nasalized or a short transitional nasal segment is heard (Beach 1938 : 86–7), but in utterance-initial position these clicks are difficult to distinguish from the aspirated (velar affricated) clicks in the second row. The voicing delay (VOT) is very similar. The auditory distinction that is most noticeable is that the aspirated clicks have a very obvious velar release – it is clear that they are accompanied by k^h or even k^x – whereas the velar release is virtually inaudible when there is a voiceless nasal accompaniment. This is because there is no build up of pressure behind the velar closure in these clicks.

The aerodynamic records in figure 8.9 (taken from the same series as that reported in Ladefoged and Traill 1984) show how the contrast is produced for

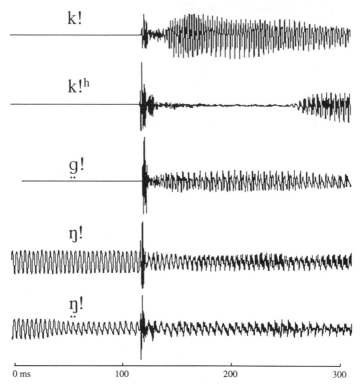

Figure 8.8 Waveforms illustrating the five click accompaniments in Xhosa with alveolar clicks.

the words **k|ʰo** 'play music' and **ŋ|ʰo** 'push into', spoken as citation forms. For the aspirated click (which was, in this case, slightly affricated) on the left of the figure, pressure is built up behind the velar closure during the formation of the click. Then the anterior click release and the velar release occur at almost the same moment (as is the case for most clicks, other than those with a nasal accompaniment, and special cases to be discussed later). There is a rapid flow of air out of the mouth, which falls as the vowel begins. In the click with de-layed aspiration on the right of the figure, very little pressure is built up behind the velar closure. This is because, as can be seen in the nasal airflow record, there is voiceless nasal airflow starting just before the click release. When the velar closure is released there is a comparatively small oral airflow, which in-creases slowly as the nasal airflow diminishes. The clicks in the third row of table 8.3 do not have an audible velar release, because the pressure that might have been built up behind the velar closure has been vented through the nose. Instead of having an aspirated velar stop **kʰ** as an accompaniment (as is the case of the clicks in the second row of table 8.2) the clicks in the third row are

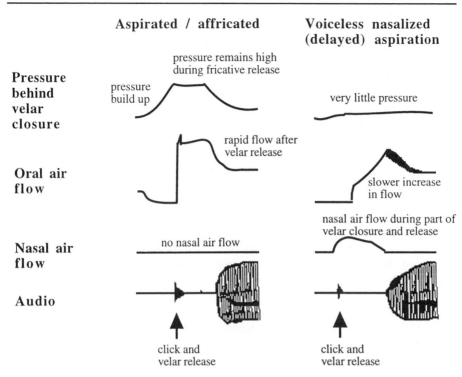

Figure 8.9 Aerodynamic records (retouched) illustrating the difference between the aspirated (velar affricated) and voiceless aspirated nasalized (delayed aspirated) clicks in the Nama words k|ʰo 'play music' and ŋ̊|ʰo 'push into', pronounced as citation forms. Only the beginning of each word is shown.

Table 8.3 Words illustrating contrasting clicks in Nama. All these words have a high tone

	DENTAL	ALVEOLAR	PALATAL	LATERAL
VOICELESS UNASPIRATED	k|oa 'put into'	k!oas 'hollow'	k‡ais 'calling'	k||aros 'writing'
VOICELESS ASPIRATED	k|ʰo 'play music'	k!ʰoas 'belt'	k‡ʰaris 'small one'	k||ʰaos 'strike'
VOICELESS NASAL	ŋ|ʰo 'push into'	ŋ!ʰas 'narrating'	ŋ‡ʰais 'baboon's arse'	ŋ||ʰaos 'special cooking place'
VOICED NASAL	ŋ|o 'measure'	ŋ!oras 'pluck maize'	ŋ‡ais 'turtledove'	ŋ||aes 'pointing'
GLOTTAL CLOSURE	k|ʔoa 'sound'	k!ʔoas 'meeting'	k‖ʔais 'gold'	k‖ʔaos 'reject a present'

accompanied by a voiceless velar nasal ŋ. We will provide further documentation on the airstream mechanisms involved in our discussion of the clicks of !Xóõ below.

The clicks in the last row are accompanied by a glottal stop. During the glottal closure there is no increase in pharyngeal pressure. However, aerodynamic records show that at the release of the click there is some nasal airflow, indicating that the velum is clearly lowered at this time. The voiceless nasal release was first noted by Beach (1938). It is possible that it is caused by a raising of the closed larynx while the velum is down. (Note that if the larynx had been raised while the velo-pharyngeal port was closed, then a pharyngeal pressure increase would have been observed.) Clicks of this type do not occur as phonological contrasts in Xhosa or other Nguni languages, but Lanham (1964) notes that the voiceless unaspirated stop in Xhosa may be followed by a glottal stop.

We have so far discussed seven ways (five in Xhosa and two others in Nama) in which the posterior component (the accompaniment) of a click can be varied. Several additional accompaniments occur in !Xóõ. Words illustrating the complete set of !Xóõ clicks (including some sequences of clicks and other consonants) are give in table 8.4. As we have noted, !Xóõ has five types of click articulation; there are bilabial, dental, alveolar, lateral, and palatal clicks. Each click has one of 17 possible accompaniments, which are exemplified in the table.

Waveforms for the alveolar click series are shown in figures 8.10 and 8.11. These words were recorded at Lokalane in the Kalahari Desert, in a free field, about a kilometer away from the settlement. The slight background noise which is evident during voiceless closures is the unavoidable sound of the wind in the trees. In order to get visually comparable waveforms we used representative utterances made by one speaker in a single recording.

We should note here that linguists are not agreed on the most appropriate way of symbolizing click accompaniments (Köhler, Ladefoged, Traill, Snyman and Vossen 1988). The symbols used in table 8.3 (and in all similar tables in this book) are an attempt at a systematic approach in accordance with the principles of the International Phonetic Association (1989). Every click involves a back closure, but since it may be either velar or uvular in place this aspect of a click must be written separately. This is done by writing a symbol for a velar or uvular consonant before the symbol for the click type. (The ordering of symbols does not indicate that the articulatory gestures are necessarily ordered in the corresponding way.) Other features of the click, such as presence or absence of voicing, as well as presence or absence of nasal air flow are indicated by choosing between, k, g, ŋ, N and so on. We have observed the following possibilities: k, g, ŋ, ŋ̊, ŋ, ʔŋ, q, ɢ. The click itself is symbolized using the IPA (1989) approved symbols. Different releases of the posterior closure are noted when necessary by an additional symbol after the symbol for the click. Possibilities include aspiration ʰ, affrication ˣ, and a glottal release either in the form of a glottal stop ʔ, or with a glottalic airstream mechanism forming an ejective '. These symbols are placed superscript in accordance with the IPA convention that superscript symbols represent shades of sounds, rather than separate segments.

We have not yet discussed the first accompaniment listed in table 8.4, a modally voiced velar plosive, because it does not occur in Nama or Xhosa. But it occurs in !Xóõ and in many other Khoisan languages. As may be seen from the waveform in the top row of figure 8.10, there is a noticeable period of voicing before the release of the click. As often happens in fully voiced velar stops, regular voicing for the vowel does not begin for 10–20 ms after the release of the accompanying velar closure. The second click shown in figure 8.10 has the voiceless unaspirated accompaniment; it is the same as the click in Nama which we have already discussed. The voiceless unaspirated click in row (2) of figure 8.10 has a vowel onset very similar to that in the voiced click above it, but it has no voicing during the closure. The !Xóõ voiceless aspirated click in line (3) is also similar to that found in Nama. The duration of the aspiration is fairly extensive, well over 100 ms in this example.

The clicks in lines (4) and (5) have uvular accompaniments. In these clicks, the back of the tongue is in the uvular region at the time of release of the posterior closure. Clicks with this type of release are found in only a very few languages such as !Xóõ and ǁAni (Vossen 1986). We have followed a convention of regarding a velar accompaniment as the unmarked case, and have usually referred to the clicks we have been considering as, e.g., voiced, rather than voiced velar. When there is a uvular accompaniment it will be specifically mentioned. The voiced uvular plosive accompaniment (4) and the voiceless unaspirated uvular plosive accompaniment (5) are the direct counterparts of the velar accompaniments (1) and (2). However, there is less voicing for the voiced uvular, and slightly more aspiration for the voiceless unaspirated uvular. The release of the uvular closure also occurs slightly later with reference to the release of the anterior click closure. Traill (1985: 126) notes that the velar release is so soon after the click that it is not audible, but the uvular release is a separate event. Perhaps because it is difficult to sustain voicing throughout a uvular stop, voiced clicks of the form ɢ! are often prenasalized and might be transcribed as ɴɢ!. In some tokens, by the time of the release of the click there is no voicing, and it is not until about 30 ms later that vocal fold vibrations can be seen. Ladefoged and Traill (1984) transcribed clicks of this form as ɴ!ɢ, noting, however, that the nasalization can be very short and that this click may be regarded as the voiced counterpart of q!.

!Xóõ has the voiced velar nasal (in row 6) that we have discussed above in relation to Nama, and also two other nasal accompaniments in rows (7) and (8) in figure 8.10. Row (7) shows a voiceless velar nasal accompaniment in which there is a strong nasal airflow. Spectrograms show that in this sound the release of the anterior closure (the click) occurs towards the end of the voiceless nasal, about 20 ms before the voicing commences.

A glottalized nasal accompaniment is exemplified by the word in row (8).

Table 8.4 Words illustrating clicks and clusters involving clicks in !Xóõ

	BILABIAL	DENTAL	ALVEOLAR	LATERAL	PALATAL
1	gʘòō (type of worm)	g|áā 'work'	g!àā 'accompany'	g‖àā 'beg'	g‡àa 'exploit'
2	kʘôō 'dream'	k|àā 'move off'	k!àā 'wait for'	k‖āā 'poison'	k‡àā 'bone'
3	kʘʰoū 'ill fitting'	k|ʰáa 'be smooth'	k!ʰàn 'inside'	k‖ʰàā 'other'	k‡ʰàa 'stamp flat'
4	ɢʘòo 'be split'	ɢ|áa 'spread out'	ɢ!ą́ā 'brains'	ɢ‖àa 'light up'	ɢ‡àa 'depress'
5	qʘóu 'wild cat'	q|àa 'rub with hand'	q!ą̄e̱ 'hunt'	q‖áā 'thigh'	q‡âa 'conceal'
6	ŋʘọ̀ō 'louse'	ŋ|āa 'see you'	ŋ!āā 'one's peer'	ŋ‖áā 'grewia berry'	ŋ‡àa 'peer into'
7	ŋʘâʔā 'be close together'	ŋ̊|û̠ʔi 'be careful'	ŋ̊!âʔm 'evade an attack'	ŋ̊‖âʔm 'be damp'	ŋ̊‡û̠ʔā 'be out of reach'
8	ʔŋʘâje 'tree'	ʔŋ|àa 'to suit'	ʔŋ!ą̀n 'lie horizontal'	ʔŋ‖àhā 'amount'	ʔŋ‡âū 'right side'
9	ŋʘʰòō 'smeared with dirt'	ŋ̊|ʰáa 'look for spoor'	ŋ̊!ʰài 'fall'	ŋ̊‖ʰáa 'carry'	ŋ̊‡ʰàa 'ahead'
10	kʘˣóā 'walk slowly'	k|ˣâā 'dance'	k!ˣáa 'go a distance'	k‖ˣàa 'scrape'	k‡ˣáa 'mind out'
11	gʘkxàna 'make fire with sticks'	g|kxáā 'splatter water'	g!kxàn 'soften'	g‖kxáʔn 'calf muscle'	g‡kxáʔā 'sneeze'
12	kʘ'q'óm 'delicious'	k|'q'àa 'hand'	k!'q'áa 'spread out'	k‖'q'âā 'grass'	k‡'q'âū 'neck'
13	gʘq'óō 'fly'	g|q'àā 'chase'	g!q'áā 'cry incessantly'	g‖q'áā 'tumor'	g‡q'àa 'ground to powder'
14	gʘhòō 'sp. bush'	g|hâa 'stale meat'	g!hàa 'thorns'	g‖hàā 'bone arrow tip'	g‡háa 'cut'
15	kʘʔòo 'be stiff'	k|ʔâa 'die'	k!ʔáā 'be seated' [pl.]	k‖ʔàa 'not to be'	k‡ʔāa 'shoot you'
16	qʘ'ûm 'close mouth'	q|'án 'small' [pl.]	q!'àma 'stickgrass'	q‖'úɲa 'turn one's back'	q‡'àn 'lay down' [pl.]
17	—	ɢ|hâô 'put into'	ɢ!hâɲa 'grey haired'	ɢ‡hâē 'push away'	—

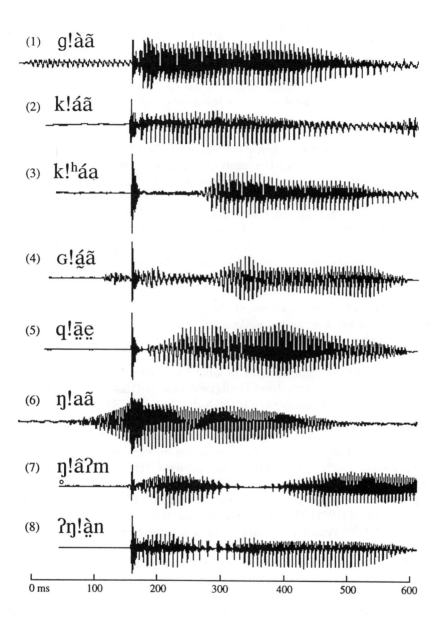

(1) g!àã

(2) k!áã

(3) k!ʰáa̱

(4) ɢ!á̰ã

(5) q!ā̰ḛ

(6) ŋ!aã

(7) ŋ̊!âʔm

(8) ʔŋ!a̱̰n

0 ms 100 200 300 400 500 600

Figure 8.10 Waveforms showing the first eight alveolar clicks in !Xóõ in table 8.4.

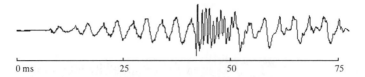

Figure 8.11 The waveform of a preglottalized nasal click and the first few periods of the vowel in ʔŋ!àn. The time scale has been expanded so that the individual periods can be seen more easily.

The preglottalized nasal is not evident in the particular token shown in figure 8.10. (As we have noted, all the examples in this figure are taken from a single recording of one speaker, resulting in this one not being as typical as we would have wished.) The glottalization can be seen in another token of the same word shown in figure 8.11. The preglottalized nasal is usually very short (about 50 ms) with the click burst occurring near the middle of the nasal. The irregularities in the first three or four glottal pulses are evident in the waveform in figure 8.11, which is shown on a slightly expanded scale. In this case the click occurs about 30 ms into the nasal, and the waveform for the vowel appears as soon as the high frequencies associated with the click can no longer be seen.

The remaining click accompaniments in !Xóõ are shown in figure 8.12. Row (9) shows the voiceless aspirated velar nasal accompaniment (delayed aspiration) which is also found in Nama. In these clicks, after the release of the anterior closure there is a long period of voicelessness (about 250 ms in the citation forms such as those in the figure 8.12), in the latter part of which weak aspiration may become more evident. Ladefoged and Traill (1984) note that the clicks with voiceless nasal aspiration in !Xóõ are similar to those in Nama, but they could not hear a voiceless velar nasal in citation forms; it is also not visible on the waveforms or in spectrograms of these sounds. The !Xóõ sounds also differ from the corresponding sounds in Nama, in that the !Xóõ nasal often remains voiceless even when the click is preceded by a vowel, although Traill (1994) notes that voicing is present in more rapid speech styles.

The puzzle of what goes on in the silent 250 ms after the click has now been explained by Traill (1991). He has shown that the velum is lowered so that the pressure behind the velar closure can be vented through the nose. But, unlike the similar Nama sound, there may be no audible voiceless velar nasal because there is no egressive airflow. Instead of a passive venting of the pressure behind the velar closure, there is an active pulmonic ingressive airstream mechanism, drawing air inwards. This !Xóõ click is probably unique among the sounds of the world's languages in that, even in the middle of a sentence, it may have ingressive pulmonic airflow. (It has been claimed by Fuller (1990) that ingressive pulmonic phones occur in Tsou, but this claim has been disputed by Ladefoged and Zeitoun (1993).)

Row (10) illustrates the voiceless velar affricate accompaniment. This click contrasts with the voiceless aspirated click in row (3) of figure 8.10 in that

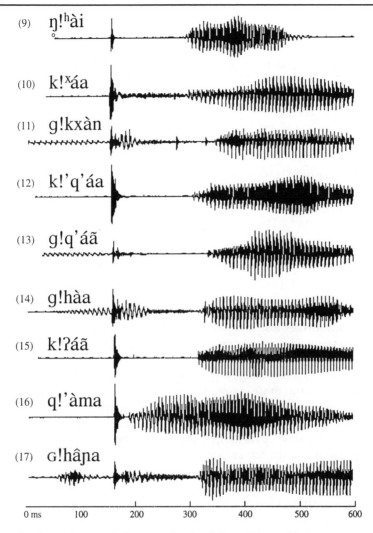

Figure 8.12 Waveforms showing the last nine alveolar clicks in !Xóõ in table 8.4.

the velar release is much more fricative. This can be demonstrated by data in which there are accompanying records of the pressure of the air in the pharynx, as in figures 8.13–8.18. These records were made using techniques described by Ladefoged and Traill (1984). It may be seen that in the accompaniment with a fricative constriction, the pressure behind the posterior closure may remain comparatively high for more than 140 ms after the click.

As argued by Traill (1992), the clicks in the next few rows are best regarded as sequences of consonants. The click in row (11) has voicing during the closure and for two or three periods after the release of the click. Other tokens of

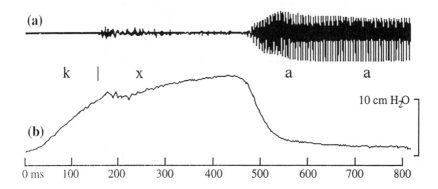

Figure 8.13 (a) Audio waveform and (b) pharyngeal pressure in a dental click with a voiceless velar affricate accompaniment.

this click are more like those in figure 8.14, which shows a dental click which can be transcribed as **g|kx**. Both in the dental click in figure 8.14 and in the corresponding alveolar click **g!kx** in figure 8.10 there is ample evidence of friction. After the release of the click there is a considerable pressure build up during **k**, followed by a fricative portion **x**. Clicks such as those in row (11) are sequences involving a voiced click with an accompaniment as in row (1) of figure 8.10, followed by a voiceless velar affricate. Sometimes the velar closure is not maintained after the anterior click release, and there is a click with a voiced (velar) accompaniment, followed by a voiceless velar fricative, so that the sequence is **g|x** rather than **g|kx**.

The click in row (12) is even more complex. In this particular dialect of !Xóõ it consists of a voiceless velar ejective released just after the release of the click, followed by the immediate formation of a uvular closure for an ejective that is released just before the vowel. This sequence can be more easily understood by reference to the dental click with the same accompaniment shown in figure 8.15. As can be seen, the pressure builds up towards the end of the closure of the click much more rapidly than seen in the previous figure. We infer that this is because the glottis is closed and the larynx is being rapidly raised. Then the releases of the anterior closure of the click and of the velar closure occur in close succession. They are followed by the immediate formation of another dorsal closure, this time at the uvular place, and a continued glottalic airstream mechanism, producing a uvular ejective.

Row (13) illustrates the voiced counterpart of this sequence. It consists of a voiced click followed by a uvular ejective. Similar articulations occur in the dental click **g|q'** shown in figure 8.16. During the click closure there is very little increase in pharyngeal pressure (as is normal in a voiced click), but afterwards there is a large increase in the pharyngeal pressure, which goes up to 20 cm H_2O. The uvular ejective is released

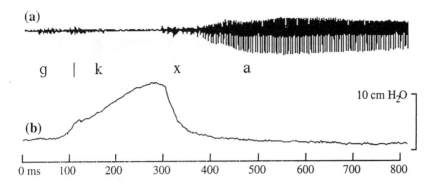

Figure 8.14 (a) Audio waveform and (b) pharyngeal pressure in a voiced dental click followed by a voiceless velar affricate.

the pharyngeal pressure, which goes up to 20 cm H_2O. The uvular ejective is released immediately before the onset of the vowel. The timing of the articulations of clicks of types (13) and (14) makes it quite clear that these are sequences of a voiced or a voiceless click followed by a uvular ejective rather than unitary segments. This notion is further supported by the fact that !Xóõ has a uvular ejective in its consonant inventory making these sequences more plausible. A similar point has been made recently by Traill (1992).

The accompaniments in both rows (12) and (13) are pronounced with more velar friction in other dialects of !Xóõ. Instead of the sequence of two ejectives k|'q' illustrated in figure 8.15, there is a single ejective affricate with a less uvular quality, more appropriately transcribed as k!X'; and instead of the prevoiced version g|q', there is a sequence that could be transcribed gk!X'. These more affricated dialectal pronunciations correspond to the standard pronunciation in Zhu|'hõasi, as will be illustrated later.

Row (14) in figure 8.12 illustrates the click g!h. In this alveolar click there is voicing throughout the closure, and for a few periods after the release of the click. It is this continuation of the voicing that prevents a salient voiced velar release. Pharyngeal pressure records of a dental click of this kind are shown in figure 8.17. Again the voicing is apparent right through the closure. After the click the pharyngeal pressure drops rapidly, and there is little evidence of friction during the interval before the voicing for the vowel begins. There seems to be some variability in the way that this sound is produced. Traill (1985: 148) regarded it as a voiced click accompanied by voiceless nasal airflow, but it now appears that the oral air flow may have the more rapid acceleration found with k|ʰ, rather than the more slowly rising oral air flow that occurs when air is also flowing out through the nasal cavity. Traill also notes that he did not have any evidence of nasal venting. We will consider clicks of this type as generally sequences, involving a voiced click of type (1), followed by aspiration, as shown by the sequence of symbols g| and h. But on

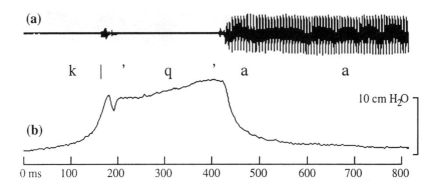

Figure 8.15 (a) Audio waveform and (b) pharyngeal pressure in a voiceless dental click with an ejective accompaniment, followed by a uvular ejective.

occasions when the voicing ceases before the release of the click, the conditions will be right for a voiceless velar aspirated release, and we may regard it as a sequence of the form **gk|ʰ**.

Row (15) illustrates the click with an accompanying glottal stop in !Xóõ. As we have seen, there is a similar click in Nama. The glottal closure is formed during the velar closure for the click, and is released considerably later. The velar release is not audible, as it occurs during the glottal closure, without any pressure build up. Our pharyngeal pressure records for both Nama and !Xóõ show that the air pressure in the pharynx does not increase during clicks of the type shown in (15), so this is not an ejective accompaniment. As the example in figure 8.12 shows, the delay before the onset of voicing for the vowel is very similar to that in (9) with a voiceless aspirated nasal accompaniment, but the onset of the following vowel is more abrupt. The VOT is also very similar in (10), the voiceless velar affricated click, **k!ˣ**, in which the interval between the release of the posterior closure and the vowel is accompanied by considerable velar friction.

The click in row (16) is the uvular counterpart to (15), the voiceless velar plus glottal stop; but whereas the velar plus glottal stop does not involve an upward movement of the larynx, in the case of the uvular plus glottal stop accompaniment there is an upward movement of the larynx, making this an ejective accompaniment. As can be seen in figure 8.18, which shows a comparable dental click, the uvular plus glottal closure accompaniment has an increase in the pharyngeal pressure both during and, more sharply, after the release of the anterior click closure. There is a noticeable burst when the uvular closure is released about 15–20 ms after the release of the click, which is perceptible as a separate event. In the case of the dental click in figure 8.18, the ejective release is followed by a period of comparable length to the VOT in (15) before the glottal stop is released and voicing commences. The token illustrated in figure 8.12 has

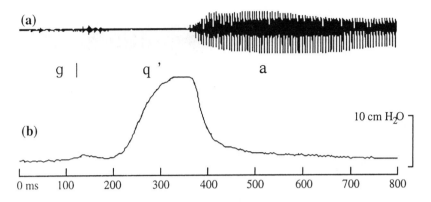

Figure 8.16 (a) Audio waveform and (b) pharyngeal pressure in a voiced dental click followed by a uvular ejective.

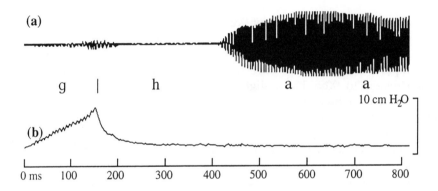

Figure 8.17 (a) Audio waveform and (b) pharyngeal pressure in a voiced dental click followed by aspiration.

a far shorter VOT.

Row (17) in table 8.4 and figure 8.12 is the uvular counterpart to (14); it consists of a voiced uvular plosive accompaniment, followed by aspiration. As can be seen in table 8.4, only three of the five clicks have been found with this possibility. As noted above, this accompaniment usually has a brief uvular nasal onset. In figure 8.12 the higher amplitude voicing seen prior to the 100 ms time marker is probably due to such a short nasal component. Lower amplitude voicing persists through the next phase of the click before the releases of the front closure and back closures in rapid succession. The release is followed by strong voiceless aspiration which may have accompanying velar friction or uvular trilling.

(a)

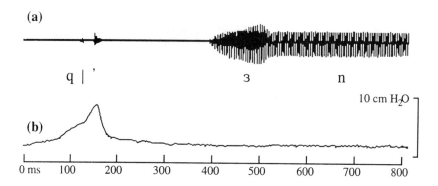

$q \mid \text{'}$ 3   n

10 cm H$_2$O

(b)

0 ms   100   200   300   400   500   600   700   800

Figure 8.18 (a) Audio waveform and (b) pharyngeal pressure in a dental click with a uvular ejective accompaniment.

Zhu‖'hõasi, which is a dialect of !Xũ , is another Khoisan language for which there is a considerable amount of published data (Snyman 1970, 1975, 1978, 1980). In this chapter we will use data from our own field recordings, which are comparable to those we have for !Xóõ. This language, which is only re-motely related to !Xóõ, has a slightly smaller number of clicks than !Xóõ. It does not have bilabial clicks, and also has fewer click accompaniments. Examples of contrasts involving the alveolar click are shown in table 8.5, and in figures 8.19 and 8.20.

Most of the clicks illustrated in figure 8.19 are similar to those in !Xóõ, and need little further discussion. The main differences are in VOT, with the Zhu‖'hõasi examples having more voicing and less aspiration. In addition, unlike the situation in !Xóõ, the VOT is much shorter for the aspirated click in row (3) and the click with glottal stop accompaniment in row (6) than for the click with voiceless aspirated nasal accompaniment in row (5). We do not know if these differences in timing reflect real differences between the two languages or if they are simply due to a difference in the rate of speech or to the particular speakers that were recorded on the different occasions.

Figure 8.20 shows the remaining Zhu‖'hõasi clicks in table 8.5. Again they are largely similar to the corresponding clicks in !Xóõ, except for differences in timing, which may be due to the individual circumstances of the recordings. However, this is not always the case. In row (7) there is a click in Zhu‖'hõasi that we transcribed as **g!ˠ** There is a similar click in !Xóõ in row (11) of figure 8.12; we transcribed the !Xóõ click as **g‖kx**, a voiced click followed by a voiceless velar affricate, noting at the time that there may be no velar closure after the anterior closure has been released, so that this may be **g!kx** or **g!x**. In Zhu‖'hõasi the comparable click is not only always fricative, but is also usually (but not always) voiced throughout. We do not know of any language that contrasts the !Xóõ clicks **g!kx** or **g!x** with the typical Zhu‖'hõasi click **g!ˠ**, although one might be considered a sequence of a voiced

Table 8.5 Words illustrating Zhu|'hōasi alveolar clicks

1	g!à	'rain'
2	k!ábî	'roll up a blanket'
3	k!ʰánî	'palm tree'
4	ŋ!àmà	'road'
5	ŋ!ʰānà	'walking stick'
6	k̥!ʔàbú	'rifle'
7	g!ˠàré	'cut open an animal'
8	k!ˣárá	'cough up from throat'
9	k!ˣˀàm	'tighten a bow string'
10	g!hánî	'tie'
11	gk!ˣˀàrú	'leopard'
12	ŋŋ̥!ʰàm	'spider'

click followed by a voiceless velar affricate or fricative, and the other a voiced click with a velar fricative accompaniment.

Another difference between the dialect of !Xóõ represented in figure 8.12 and Zhu|'hōasi is that the former has clicks such as **k!'q** and **g!q'**, whereas Zhu|'hōasi has clicks such as **k!ˣˀ** and **gk!ˣˀ**, illustrated in rows (9) and (11) in figure 8.20. We noted above that in other dialects of !Xóõ the clicks **k!x'** and **gk!ˣˀ** occurred instead of **k!'q'** and **g!q'**. No language that we know of contrasts clicks of the form **k!'q'** and **k!ˣˀ** or the voiced counterparts **g!q'** and **gk!ˣˀ**. We should also note a sequence that does not occur in !Xóõ, but does occur in Zhu|'hōasi, as exemplified in row (12), a voiced velar nasal and voiceless aspirated velar nasal. This is another example of the complex voicing clusters that occur in these languages. (The particular token illustrated in figure 8.20 has only very weak voicing.)

We are now in a position to try to summarize the complete range of click accompaniments. The number of possible accompaniments is fairly considerable, as can be seen from table 8.6, which lists symbols and a short description for 21 accompaniments, together with one or more languages in which each occurs. As we have noted, some of these accompaniments might be better regarded as involving sequences of consonants. Khoisan languages have no constraint forbidding voiced and voiceless sequences of obstruents within a single cluster. All these sequences are included here so as to give a more complete overview of possible sounds involving clicks.

There are problems in trying to draw up a list such as that in table 8.6, in that it is not easy to say when two sounds in different languages should be regarded as phonetically the same. This is an issue that has plagued phoneticians for many years. It is at the heart of the International Phonetic Association's difficulty in trying to decide which symbols need to be represented on its chart (Ladefoged 1990). If two sounds contrast phonologically in a single language, of course they must have distinct phonetic qualities. But if two seemingly different sounds never occur in the same language, how can one

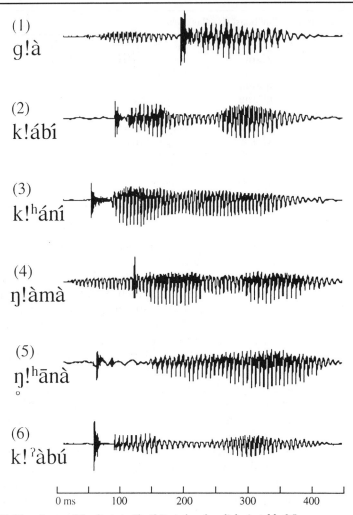

(1)
g!à

(2)
k!ábí

(3)
k!ʰání

(4)
ŋ!àmà

(5)
ŋ̥!ʰānà

(6)
k!ʔàbú

0 ms   100   200   300   400

Figure 8.19 Waveforms of the first six Zhuǀ'hõasi alveolar clicks in table 8.5.

decide whether they are indeed different?

The first six items in table 8.6 present no problems in this respect, but it is worth considering why phoneticians have no difficulty in recognizing that there are six different sounds although they do not all contrast in a single language. The first four are all contrastive in two of our exemplifying languages, !Xóõ and Zhuǀ'hõasi. The fifth and sixth, the clicks with breathy voiced plosive and breathy voiced nasal accompaniments, occur only in Nguni languages here exemplified by Xhosa. As we noted earlier, the description of these sounds as being breathy voiced is largely a phonological designation of them

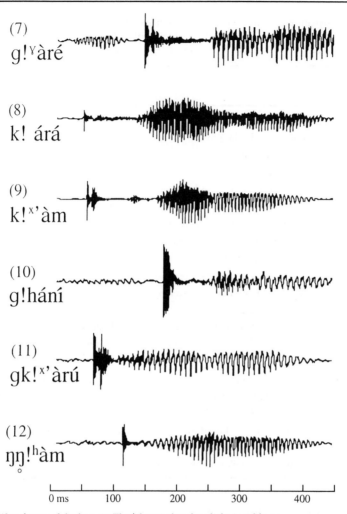

Figure 8.20 Waveforms of the last six Zhu|'hōasi alveolar clicks in table 8.5.

as being tone depressors (Traill, Khumalo, and Fridjhon 1987). Accordingly, the breathy voiced velar plosive accompaniment might be considered as simply the Nguni variant of the voiced velar plosive accompaniment, as these languages do not have this possibility. But there are two points against this interpretation. Firstly, this solution is not available in the case of the breathy voiced velar nasal accompaniment, as there is a contrasting voiced velar nasal accompaniment in these languages. This makes it evident that a breathy voiced accompaniment has to be recognized as distinctive for some clicks. Secondly, these languages also contrast voiced velar plosives and breathy voiced velar plosives in the non-click

Table 8.6 A systematic representation of clicks and their accompaniments, here shown with the alveolar click !. In other clicks the symbol ! would be replaced by one of the symbols ʘ, |, ‖, ǂ. The example languages are chosen from Xhosa, Nama, !Xóõ, and Zhu|'hõasi (a dialect of !Xũ)

Symbol	Description: Alveolar click plus: –	Example languages
1 ɡ!	Voiced velar plosive	!Xóõ, Zhu|hõasi
2 k!	Voiceless unaspirated velar plosive	all four
3 k!ʰ	Aspirated velar plosive	all four
4 ŋ!	Voiced velar nasal	all four
5 ɡ̤!	Breathy voiced velar plosive	Xhosa
6 ŋ̤!	Breathy voiced velar nasal	Xhosa
7 ŋ̥!ʰ	Voiceless aspirated velar nasal (delayed aspirated)	Nama,!Xóõ, Zhu|'ɦõasi
8 k!ˀ	Voiceless velar plosive and glottal stop	Nama,!Xóõ, Zhu|'ɦõasi
9 k!ˣ	Voiceless affricated velar plosive	!Xóõ, Zhu|'ɦõasi
10 ɡ!h	Voiced velar plosive followed by aspiration	!Xóõ, Zhu|'ɦõasi
11 ɡk!ˣ	Voiced velar plosive followed by voiceless velar fricative	!Xóõ, Zhu|'ɦõasi
12 k!ˣ'	Affricated velar ejective	Zhu|'ɦõasi
13 ɡ!kˣ'	Voiced velar plosive followed by voiceless affricated ejective	Zhu|'ɦõasi
14 ŋŋ!ʰ	Voiced velar nasal followed by voiceless aspirated velar nasal	Zhu|'ɦõasi
15 ŋ̥!	Voiceless velar nasal	!Xóõ
16 ʔŋ!	Preglottalized velar nasal	!Xóõ
17 ɢ!	Voiced (optionally prenasalized) uvular plosive	!Xóõ
18 q!	Voiceless unaspirated uvular plosive	!Xóõ
19 k!'q'	Voiceless velar ejective, followed by uvular ejective	!Xóõ
20 ɡ!q'	Voiced velar plosive, followed by uvular ejective	!Xóõ
21 ɢ!h	Voiced uvular plosive, followed by aspiration	!Xóõ

consonant series. This also makes it plausible to consider the voiced velar plosive accompaniment and the breathy voiced velar plosive accompaniment as potentially contrastive. It seems as if the first six accompaniments are all potentially contrastive and therefore they must be considered as phonetically distinct sounds.

A different problem arises in the case of the seventh item, the voiceless aspirated nasal accompaniment. There is instrumental evidence showing that these sounds differ in Nama and !Xóõ. Ladefoged and Traill (1984) showed that in Nama there is a voiceless velar nasal with a pulmonic egressive airstream. Traill (1991) showed that in !Xóõ there is also a voiceless velar nasal, but an ingressive pulmonic airstream. Moreover these differences have phonological implications, in that the Nama voiceless aspirated nasal clicks show some voicing assimilation when they occur intervocalically so that they have a voiced velar nasal onset, but the !Xóõ sounds are less likely to show such an assimilation. Nevertheless we have decided to regard these two click accompaniments as being phonetically the same at some classificatory phonetic level, on the grounds that no language could use the difference between them to form phonological contrasts. Considering the amazingly small (to our ears) contrasts that languages do use, this is an act of faith on our part. And we would be happy to be proved wrong.

Items (7) through (14) all occur in Zhu|'hõasi as contrasting sounds, and are plainly phonetically distinct (at least to speakers of Zhu|'hõasi). Similarly items (15) through (21) all occur in !Xóõ. The only question is whether any of those listed as occurring in !Xóõ but not in Zhu|'hõasi could in fact be identified with any of the Zhu|'hõasi items. We have already discussed some cases in which this can be done. Items (12) and (13) in Zhu|'hõasi, **k!x'** and **gk!x'**, are comparable with items (19) and (20) in !Xóõ, **k!'q'** and **g!q'**, in the sense that the Zhu|'hõasi forms occur in !Xóõ as dialectal variants of the forms listed for !Xóõ. Another pair of items that are fairly similar are (14), **ŋŋ!ʰ**, the voiced velar nasal followed by a voiceless aspirated velar nasal in Zhu|'hõasi, and (15), **ŋ!**, the voiceless velar nasal, in !Xóõ. There are no strong arguments for regarding these non-contrasting sounds as distinct at a phonetic classificatory level. But, just as we held in the case of the different voiceless aspirated nasal accompaniments that they were not likely to be used contrastively, so we simply offer it as our opinion that the opposite is true in these cases: these pairs of sounds are sufficiently distinct to justify classifying them as different phonetic items that are potentially contrastive.

The other items, (16) through (21), occur in !Xóõ, but have no counterparts in Zhu|'hõasi. The preglottalized velar nasal accompaniment does not occur outside !Xóõ; and Zhu|'hõasi also lacks all the contrastive uvular accompaniments.

Table 8.6 shows that if we include possible sequences involving more than one segment, then there might be 5 x 21 = 105 ways of beginning a word with a click. As we have seen in table 8.4, 83 of these actually occur as phonologically contrastive items in !Xóõ. If we consider items (10, 11, 13, 14, 19, 20, 21) to be sequences, then there are still 14 x 5 = 70 phonetically distinct click segments, 55 of which occur in !Xóõ. We should also note the limits of the list that we have given in table 8.6. When we consider the wide variety of click accompaniments that do occur, then a number of other possibilities must be considered as just accidental gaps that might have occurred but are not attested. Combinations using additional phonation types would be possible. We should also consider other airstream mechanisms that might be used. It is comparatively easy to produce a voiced velar implosive while producing a click. In fact, it is probably easier for most non-Khoisan phoneticians to say **ɠ!a** than it is to say **g!q'a**. But implosives never occur as click accompaniments.

Some clicks are complex articulations; but many are simple sounds, judging from the fact that they are fairly easy to produce. Almost any child can, and probably does, make bilabial, dental and lateral clicks as extralinguistic noises. Nor have we found any real difficulty in teaching students to integrate these sounds into syllables, although many have difficulty in avoiding nasalizing clicks and the adjoining vowels. In our experience, most clicks are much easier to teach people to make than ejectives or implosives. Considering also their perceptual salience, it might seem as if they should be highly favored consonants in the world's languages. Their desirability is evidenced by the fact that they were readily borrowed from Khoisan into the neighboring Nguni languages. Their ready acceptance and retention was no doubt facilitated by their phonetic qualities. Indeed, we cannot explain why these easy to make and perceptually optimal consonants are found in so few languages. It is only the addition of diverse complex accompaniments that provides real phonetic challenge. !Xóõ words such as ŋ̊ǃʰài, 'fall', with a voiceless pulmonic ingressive nasal, and complex sequences of clicks and ejectives such as that in kǁ'q'âã, 'grass' are among the most difficult articulations that we know of in common words in the world's languages. But most people can easily learn to say simple !Xóõ words such as kǀàa, 'move off,' so that it is surprising that plain clicks do not occur in more languages.

9

Vowels

In this chapter we will consider the kinds of vowel sounds that occur in the world's languages. But before we do this we should try to define what we mean by a vowel. In many linguistic descriptions sounds are classified as either vowels or consonants. The original intuition behind this classification was that vowels are sounds that may be pronounced alone, but consonants must be sounded with a vowel. In many languages the sounds called vowels can form a word by themselves, but the sounds called consonants must be accompanied by a vowel. The phonetic basis of the distinction between vowels and consonants is not straightforward. An important contribution on this topic was made by Pike (1943) who began by splitting segments in another way. He first of all made a distinction between vocoids and contoids, with a vocoid being defined as a central resonant oral. He then went on to define a vowel as a syllabic vocoid. In practice this is very similar to the definition given by Chomsky and Halle (1968) in the latter part of *The Sound Pattern of English*. Their definition is that a vowel is a segment with the features [+ syllabic, – consonantal], with [– consonantal] sounds being defined as those that do not have a central obstruction of the oral tract. In many ways this is functionally equivalent to the later practice of autosegmental phonologists in defining a vowel as a [– consonantal] segment attached to a V slot. Whichever definition is used it is equivalent to saying that a vowel is defined by features that ensure that there are no major strictures in the vocal tract; and that it is syllabic.

We know what we mean by there being no obstructions in the vocal tract, but what, from a phonetic point of view, do we mean by syllabic? There is no phonetic parameter that can be used to define syllabicity in articulatory, or physiological terms. When Pike proposed his definition, he suggested that syllables correspond to the valleys between peaks in structural degree. Thus the

English word *pit* forms a single syllable because there is a more open degree of stricture between two regions of greater stricture. However, the word *split* on this definition would have two syllables, as **s** has lower stricture than **p**. This conflicts with the intuitive sense of what constitutes a syllable, and with the behavior of **s** in other positions. An earlier proposal was that of Stetson (1951), who claimed that each syllable is associated with the particular kind of respiratory activity that Stetson called a 'chest pulse'. We now know that syllables are not necessarily associated with a chest pulse (Ladefoged 1967), but phoneticians have not been able to suggest an alternative definition of the physiological properties of a syllable. The best that we can do is to suggest that syllables are 'necessary units in the organization and production of utterances' (Ladefoged 1982). This is a neurophysiological, or cognitive view of the syllable, making the syllable a phonological rather than a phonetic unit. Syllables are identifiable as the primary elements over which the rhythmic patterns of language can be observed, or the primary domain over which sequential constraints apply, or coarticulatory adjustments can be made. Vowels are defined by the physiological characteristic of their having no obstruction in the vocal tract, and by their function within a phonologically defined syllable. At the end of the chapter we will consider semivowels, which we will take to be sounds that are like vowels in that they have no obstructions in the vocal tract, but unlike vowels in that they are not syllabic.

9.1 Major Vowel Features

Many of the features required for linguistic descriptions of vowels have been established for some time. An excellent summary of their application to the world's languages was given by Lindau (1978). The discussion here will follow a similar framework; we will summarize our differences at the end of the chapter.

The basic parameters of most vowel systems are the three scales whose endpoints are traditionally called high and low, front and back, and rounded and unrounded. Figure 9.1 shows the location of a set of reference vowels, the cardinal vowels described by Jones (1956), within the space defined by these dimensions. In our examination of the vowels of the world's languages we will continue to use the traditional terms high/low and back/front, and we will refer to these dimensions as Height and Backness. These terms were originally proposed as descriptions of actual articulatory characteristics of vowels, and taken to specify the highest point of the tongue. However, although we will use the traditional articulatory labels, we do not mean to imply that we necessarily think that these terms can be directly interpreted as indicating the shape of the vocal tract, as it is not at all clear that the classes of vowels defined by tongue body positions are the same as those defined by the traditional use of these

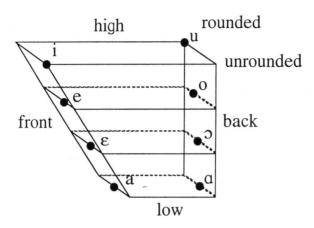

Figure 9.1 The primary Cardinal Vowels displayed in terms of the major dimensions of vowel quality.

terms. The mean position of the tongue in the saggital plane during nine American English vowels as produced by five speakers is as shown on the left of figure 9.2 (based on data and calculation of means by factor analysis as described in Harshman, Ladefoged and Goldstein 1977). Dots have been placed on the highest point of the tongue in each vowel, and the resulting spacing of vowels is given on the right of the figure. As can be seen, the tongue height of **u** is below that of ɪ, that of ʊ is below that of ɛ and the tongue height of **o** is below that of æ. Traditional descriptions of English vowels would classify **i, ɪ, u, ʊ** all as high vowels, but with ɪ, ʊ lower than **i, u;** **o** as mid and æ as low. Diagrams showing the height of the center of the tongue body (as advocated by Fischer-Jørgensen 1985) would reveal much the same relationships as in figure 9.2.

There are a number of alternative possible ways of quantifying the position of the tongue in vowels. The most well known is that used by Stevens and House (1955) and Fant (1960), who point out that, from an acoustic phonetic point of view, the most important articulatory characteristics of vowels are the position of the point of maximum constriction of the vocal tract, and the cross-sectional area of the vocal tract at that point. Figure 9.3 shows the vowels in figure 9.2 arranged in this way. The groupings in this figure do not form any obvious natural classes from a linguistic point of view.

There is an interesting possible compromise between the two characterizations we have considered so far. In this view each vowel is characterized in terms of the distance of the highest point of the tongue from the roof of the mouth, as shown in figure 9.4. For the front vowels below the hard palate this is effectively the same as the position of the highest point of the tongue as in figure 9.2. For the back vowels it is somewhat different, especially as it must be remembered that the height of the soft palate is directly correlated with the height of the vowel, so that the low vowels are in fact closer to the roof of the

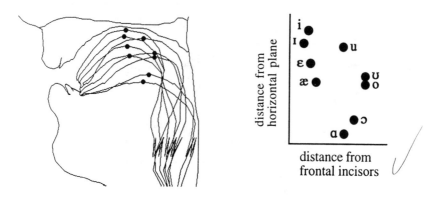

Figure 9.2 The mean tongue positions in American English vowels. The points show the locations of the highest point of the tongue with reference to the tips of the frontal incisors and a horizontal plane parallel to the upper molars.

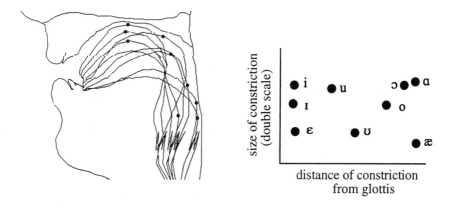

Figure 9.3 The mean tongue positions in American English vowels measured in terms of the size of the constriction, and the distance of the constriction from the glottis, as suggested by Stevens and House (1955) and Fant (1960).

mouth than appears in the figure, which shows only one position of the soft palate. The line along which this distance was measured for the back vowels is shown in figure 9.4.

However, even this representation of the articulation of vowels is not as close to the usual linguistic representation of these vowels as is that provided by the acoustic data. Figure 9.5 compares data on the mean frequencies of the first two formants in these same vowels with the articulatory representation of figure 9.4. In this figure the frequency values are scaled so that equal distances along either axis more nearly correspond to equal perceptual distances (using the Bark scaling techniques proposed by Schroeder, Atal and Hall 1979). The

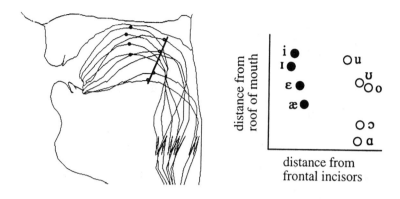

Figure 9.4 The mean tongue positions in American English vowels measured in terms of the distance of the highest point of the tongue from the roof of the mouth. The lowering of the soft palate that takes place in low vowels has been taken into account in the placement of the points on the right of the figure.

frequency of the first formant, F1, is plotted against the difference between the frequencies of the second and first formants, F2–F1, and the scale on the ordinate is double that on the abscissa, so as to give appropriate prominence to F1 and make the plots more in accord with the auditory judgments of professional phoneticians. The origin of the axes is to the top right of the plot. The acoustic representation corresponds more closely to the auditory phonetic description in terms of height and backness than the articulatory plots in figures 9.2–9.4. Note, for example, the way in which the low vowels æ and ɑ have approximately the same height, and the vowels u and ʊ are slightly forward as they are in American English. There are some notable discrepancies between the acoustic plot and the traditional linguistic classification. In particular the vowels ɪ and ʊ, which are traditionally classed as high, are acoustically closer to the mid- vowels ɛ and o rather than to i and u. But this plot does place the expected vowels at the appropriate corners of the space.

Recognition that the placement of vowels on an auditory chart such as the one in figure 9.1 is supported more readily by acoustic than by articulatory measurements does not mean that articulatory scales can be discarded in the phonetic description of vowels. The first and second formant frequencies do not reflect only the properties that are described as Height and Backness. In fact, many articulatory adjustments contribute to the values of these acoustic parameters, one of the most important being the effect of lip rounding. As will become clear at several points in the remainder of this chapter, formant values often distinguish between pairs of vowels which would be said to have the same Height and Backness. It is important therefore to pay attention to both articulatory and acoustic aspects of vowels.

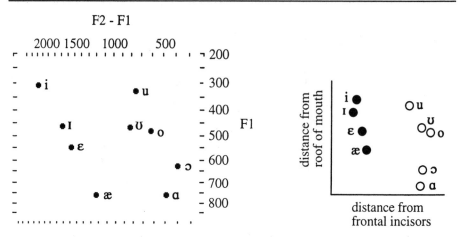

Figure 9.5 A comparison of an acoustic representation and an articulatory representation of a mean set of American English vowels.

Vowel height

All languages have some variations in vowel quality that indicate contrasts in the vowel height dimension. Even if a language has only two phonologically contrastive vowels, the differences will always be in this dimension rather than the front-back dimension. Thus, in native vocabulary, the Chadic language Margi has ɨ, a and the Australian language Arrernte has ə, a. Among the Caucasian languages, Ubykh and Abkhaz have only two phonological vowel heights, with the contrasts usually represented as ə and a (Catford 1977b). None of these two-vowel languages make any phonological use of the front-back, or the rounding, dimensions in their vowel systems. The same is true of some of the other Caucasian languages, such as Kabardian, which have three phonologically contrastive vowels (not, as far as Kabardian is concerned, zero, one or two as suggested by Kuipers 1960, Anderson 1978 and Halle 1970 respectively).

In all these cases of languages that have only height differences, there are also very obvious differences in the front-back dimension, so that to the casual observer it might appear as if the language used a wider range of vowel qualities. Figure 9.6 shows the distribution in the F1/F2 space of over 100 tokens of Arrernte /ə/ spoken by a female speaker. The formants were measured from spectrograms at the vowel mid-point in word-medial CVC syllables with stops. The data points are mostly plotted with symbols that indicate the preceding consonant, as there is some correlation between the preceding consonant and the vowel formants.

However, although figure 9.6 shows that there is much variation in the acoustic quality of the ə vowels, this variability is for the most part

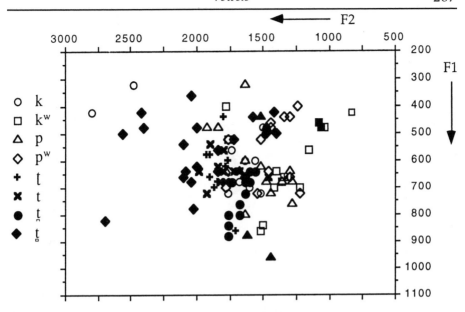

Figure 9.6 Scatter of values of F1 and F2 for /ə/ in Arrernte.

uncorrelated with particular consonant environments. The tendency for the mid-point of the vowel to be influenced in any consistent way by the place of a preceding consonant is quite weak, as is shown by the plot in figure 9.7. This shows the mean for each of the consonant environments for which ten or more tokens were measured. As is apparent, the means lie very close together in figure 9.7.

As another example, figure 9.8 is a formant plot of the allophones of some Kabardian vowels analyzed by Choi (1991). As is shown by the location of the points on the chart, this language has a wider range of vowel qualities than is indicated by the use of just three symbols that represent only differences in vowel Height, but only certain consonant environments show significant effects on the vowel formants. The main variations within each vowel type occur because the approximants **j** and **w** (and labialized consonants) have assimilatory effects on the neighboring vowels, and because uvular and pharyngeal consonants (absent in Arrende) have marked lowering effects. All these different qualities are predictable allophones of the three vowels, **i, ə, a**. It is also clear, as Choi (1991) points out in discussing this analysis, that Catford (ms in preparation) (and many linguists in the fomer Soviet Union) are correct in recognizing **a** as a third vowel. In Choi's view **a** is a long vowel that could be written **a:**, but it is a separate phoneme, and cannot be considered to be an allophone of ə as suggested by Kuipers (1960) and Halle (1970).

Variations in vowel quality often involve all three of the primary dimensions, Height, Backness, and Rounding. This sometimes makes it difficult to

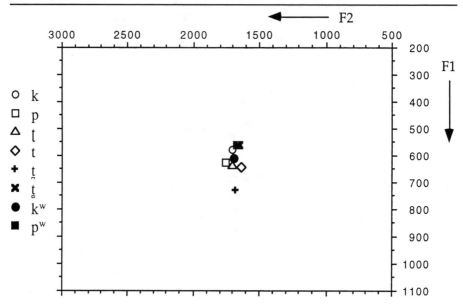

Figure 9.7 Mean position of values of F1 and F2 for /ə/ in Arrernte for ten or more tokens sorted according to preceding consonant context.

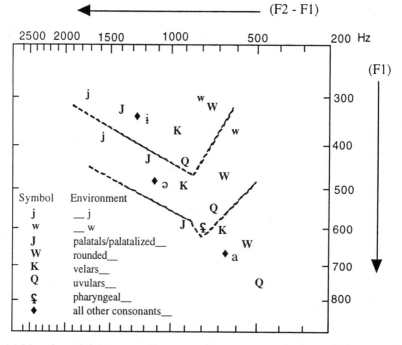

Figure 9.8 Mean formant frequencies of the three Kabardian vowels in different contexts as produced in connected speech by three speakers (based on data in Choi 1991). The symbols indicate the formant frequencies of the steady-state portion in the contexts shown.

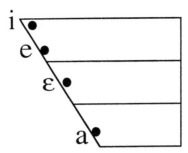

Figure 9.9 The relative phonetic qualities of the four front unrounded vowels of Danish, based on Uldall (1933).

Table 9.1 Words illustrating four degrees of vowel height in Danish

vilə	'wild (pl)'	viːlə	'rest'	viːðə	'know'
menə	'remind'	meːnə	'mean (vb)'	veːðə	'wheat'
lɛsə	'load'	leːsə	'read'	veːða	'wet (vb)'
masə	'mass'	maːsə	'mash'	vaːðə	'wade'

decide how many distinct levels of Height there may be in a particular language. Bearing this in mind, we will consider how many levels of Height are used in the world's languages. Some linguists (e.g. Chomsky and Halle 1968) have suggested that there are only three (although, of course, these linguists recognize other dimensions which they use for representing what we regard as simply variations in Height). Jones's (1956) Cardinal Vowel scheme makes reference to four particular levels of the Height dimension, but has provision for more possibilities. The full set of vowel symbols recommended by the IPA (1989) implies that there are seven levels. We doubt that any language uses this full range; but there are clearly more than three levels of the auditory property Height.

Evidence for the possibility of more than three contrasting vowel heights comes from Danish, in which there are four front vowels that contrast simply in vowel height. Examples are shown in table 9.1. It is noteworthy that at each of these four vowel heights there is also a contrast between a short and a long vowel, which do not differ appreciably in quality. These vowels are even more interesting because it is quite clear that they are not equidistant. Uldall (1933) represents them as shown in figure 9.9. There is a much larger gap between the vowels represented here by ɛ and a than there is between the vowels i and e. This raises the possibility that there might be a language with five vowel heights.

Traunmüller (1982) has suggested that the Bavarian dialect spoken in Amstetten, Austria, might be such a language. In his analysis this language has

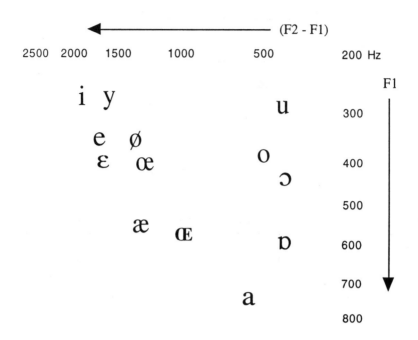

Figure 9.10 The mean formant frequencies of the long vowels of eight speakers of the Amstetten dialect of Bavarian (data from Traunmüller 1982).

four front unrounded, four front rounded and four back rounded vowels, in addition to the low central vowel **a**. Traunmüller conducted a controlled study in which he recorded a number of speakers of this dialect, and measured the acoustic characteristics of the 13 long vowels so as to obtain an indication of the traditional Height and Backness values. The mean formant frequencies of eight of his speakers (as reported by Disner 1983) are shown in figure 9.10. We have not ourselves investigated the vowels of this dialect of Austrian German, and so we cannot say whether there are any other factors involved which might lead to it being possible to describe this language as having fewer than the five vowel heights that are apparent in figure 9.10.

Front-back variations in vowels

The languages of the world make much more limited use of the front-back and rounded-unrounded dimensions, which usually support no more than binary oppositions. There are not many cases of a language with three vowels that contrast just by being front, central and back, with all other features remaining

Table 9.2 Words illustrating high vowels in Nimboran (based on Anceaux 1965)

	FRONT	CENTRAL	BACK
	di	**'undɨ**	**dɯ**
	'wood'	'banana'	'child'
	ki	**kɨ**	**kɯ**
	'woman'	'faeces'	'time, day'
	kip	**kɨp**	**'pakɯp**
	'fire'	'lime'	'lid'

Table 9.3 Words illustrating contrasting front, central and back vowels in Nweh (from Ladefoged 1971)

	FRONT	CENTRAL	BACK	
ROUNDED	**nty**		**mbu**	
	'advise'		'corners'	HIGH
UNROUNDED	**mbi**	**mbɨ**		
	'cowries'	'dog'		
	mbe	**ntsə**	**mbɤ**	
	'knife'	'water'	'ivory'	MID

the same. One possibility is Nimboran, a Papuan language. Anceaux (1965) describes this language as having six vowels which he symbolizes **i, e, a, o, u, y**. He notes that "all vowels are unrounded and voiced. They contrast in tongue height and tongue placement." The vowel **i** "is a voiced high close front unrounded vocoid." His **y** (for which he says "the symbol … has been chosen quite arbitrarily and for practical reasons only") he describes as "a rather tense voiced high close central unrounded vocoid." We would transcribe this vowel as **ɨ**. He describes his **u** as "a voiced high close back unrounded vocoid," which we would transcribe as **ɯ**. It would therefore appear as if there were three high unrounded vowels contrasting only in backness in this language. Examples (from his data, but in our transcription) are shown in table 9.2.

There are a number of other cases such as that in Nweh (Ngwe), illustrated in table 9.3, where it is certainly convenient to postulate the existence of a category central, which is neither front nor back. The situation in Nweh is complicated by the fact that Dunstan (1964) has shown that the surface vowel **y** is underlying **ɨ**, and the surface vowel **ə** is underlyingly **ɤ**, so the surface contrast between the mid vowels **e, ə,** and **ɤ** does not involve a three-way phonological opposition. But even taking this into account there is still a phonological contrast between front **i**, central **ɨ**, and back **u** and **ɤ**.

Another language which can be said to have a three-way contrast in the front-back dimension is Norwegian, described by Vanvik (1972) as having

Table 9.4 Words illustrating contrasting front, central and back rounded vowels in Norwegian

	FRONT	CENTRAL	BACK
HIGH, ROUNDED	**byː** 'town'	**bʉː** 'shack'	**buː** 'live'

Table 9.5 Words illustrating Swedish high front vowels varying in lip position. y has (horizontal) lip rounding and protrusion; ʉ has (vertical) lip compression

PROTRUSION	COMPRESSION	NEUTRAL
ryːta 'roar'	**rʉːta** 'window pane'	**riːta** 'draw'

three high rounded vowels as shown in table 9.4. Consideration of a number of very different cases, such as Nweh and Norwegian, leads us to conclude that it is probably appropriate to recognize a front-back dimension containing three major phonetic categories: [front], [central] and [back]. There are also phonological reasons for saying that in languages with systems containing five vowels, and in many of those with systems containing seven vowels, the lowest vowel is neither front nor back, and should be regarded as central. This is often the position taken in descriptions of the vowels of Italian. It is arguable that a similar situation obtains in English with respect to the starting points of the diphthongs in *high* and *how*. For many people these diphthongs have the same, or very similar, starting points. A generalization is lost if the inadequacies of the feature system do not allow one to say that both these diphthongs start with a low central vowel.

A rather unusual acoustic correlate of the front-back parameter occurs in a variety of i in Swedish, which differs from the more usual varieties of i in that it is made with the constriction even further forward. This effect can be achieved by slightly *lowering* the body of the tongue while simultaneously raising the blade of the tongue (Ladefoged and Lindau 1989), and we suggest that this may occur in the usual Stockholm Swedish pronunciation of this vowel. Acoustically this pronunciation is characterized by having a very high F3, and an F2 which is *lower* than that in e. This provides another instance of the need to consider acoustic and articulatory facts together in the analysis of vowels. This Swedish vowel is illustrated in table 9.5.

Lip position

The great majority of the world's languages have a predictable relationship between the phonetic Backness and Rounding dimensions. Front vowels are usually unrounded and back vowels are usually rounded. However, as shown

Table 9.6 Words illustrating the vowels of Vietnamese

	FRONT	BACK	
		UNROUNDED	ROUNDED
HIGH	**ti**	**tɯ**	**tu**
	'bureau'	'forth'	'to drink'
MID-HIGH	**te**	**tɤ**	**to**
	'numb'	'silk'	'soup bowl'
MID-LOW	**té**	**ʌŋ**	**tɔ**
	'to fall down'	'favor'	'large'
LOW	**æŋ**	**tɑ**	
	'to eat'	'we/our'	

above for Bavarian German, front vowels with a rounded lip position also occur. In addition, back vowels without lip rounding can be found, sometimes
simply because a language has relaxed the linkage between Backness and
Rounding (as for the high back vowel of Japanese), but also on occasion because rounded and unrounded vowels are independently contrastive within
the class of back vowels, as in the Turkic languages Chuvash and Yakut. Vietnamese has some notable contrasts between back rounded and unrounded
vowels, as shown in table 9.6.

Rounding and Height are also related in that higher vowels are usually more
rounded than lower vowels. All of these matters concerning lip position can be
illustrated with the data in figure 9.11, which shows the lip position of the ten
vowels of Iaai taken from a videotape of a speaker pronouncing isolated
words. Each vowel in this figure is represented by the frame with the maximal
gesture of the lips for the vowel. The three high vowels **i, y, u** illustrate a rounding contrast independent of backness. The four higher mid-vowels **e, ø, o, ɤ**
extend this independence to include a back unrounded vowel. The lip aperture
is markedly smaller for the two high rounded vowels (**i, y**) than for the two
higher mid-rounded vowels (**ø, o**), and the rounded low vowel **ɔ** has an even
greater aperture. The three more open vowels **æ, a, ɔ** all have relatively open
lip positions. Nonetheless, the lips are visibly rounded for **ɔ** in a way that is not
so for **æ** and **a**.

There are exceptions to this general relationship between Height and
Rounding. Sometimes the deviations are comparatively small, as in the case of
RP British English **ɔ**, which has been described by Jones (1956) as having lips
"more closely rounded than for Cardinal **ɔ**." But in other languages there is a
considerable discrepancy between the Height and the degree of rounding. In
Assamese there are two low back vowels, one of which sounds like British
English **ɑ** as in 'father', and probably has similar tongue and lip positions to
that vowel. The other Assamese low back vowel has a slightly different tongue
position – more like that of British English **ɔ** as in 'caught' – but is accompanied
by close lip rounding like that in Cardinal **u**.

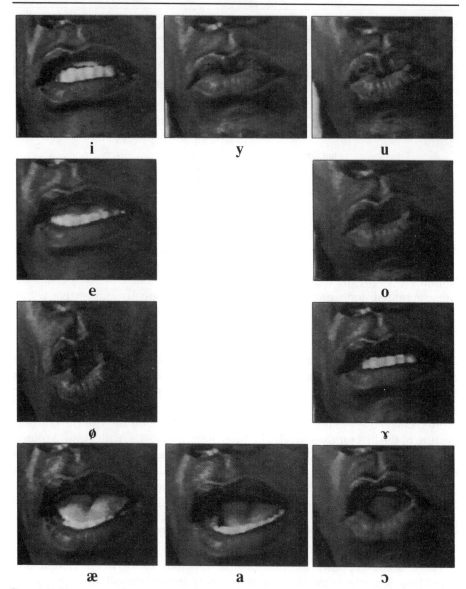

Figure 9.11 Lip positions for ten vowels of Iaai.: i in ʈii 'tea', y in yy 'dispute', u in kaluu 'fall down', e in eeʈ 'fishing net', ø in møøk 'ill', o in oʈ 'lobster', ɤ in ɤʈ 'cooking pot', æ in mææk 'heavy', a in aaʈ 'wounded person', and ɔ in ʈɔɔŋ 'oven'.

Apart from the small number of 'over-rounding' cases such as Assamese, most languages have vowels which can simply be classified as rounded or unrounded. Even in Assamese, the rounding of ŋ seems to be of the same nature as in other vowels. However, there have been suggestions that there could be more than one distinct type of rounding gesture. A possible case occurs in Swedish, in which there are three vowels which are all high and are all front, but which have different lip gestures. Examples of these vowels are shown in table 9.5. The symbol ʉ in this table is used to specify a high front vowel, rather than a high central vowel, which is its defined IPA value (and which is the value it has in transcribing Norwegian vowels in table 9.4). The precise quality of this vowel has been an issue for many years (Sweet 1877, 1879, Malmberg 1951, 1956). As Malmberg (1951) notes: "This vowel has caused trouble for phoneticians for a long time ... It may perhaps be best characterized by saying that it combines the half-close tongue position of e with a very special labialization (the lips are not protruded as much as for y but are contracted in a very characteristic way)" (Malmberg 1951: 46; our translation). Fant's x-ray data on these vowels, which have been reproduced in small size in many publications (e.g. Fant 1973: 11), are reproduced here in figure 9.12 in a larger size. The evidence they provide is not entirely in agreement with Malmberg's 1951 account. At least for this speaker, ʉ is much higher than the mid vowel eː. The three vowels i, yː, ʉ have similar (although not identical) tongue positions; yː has a more open and more protruded lip position; ʉ has a fairly close approximation of the upper and lower lip, but without protrusion. In measurements of labial gestures of eight speakers of Swedish, Linker (1982) found that the same distinctions applied to her subjects. McAllister, Lubker and Carlson (1974), who came to a similar conclusion, also note that these high vowels have a consonantal offglide in Swedish; the offglide for y is the protruded semivowel ɥ, whereas ʉ has an offglide that they symbolize β. Vanvik (1972) also noted that u and ʉ in Standard Norwegian share the same lip position, whereas the third vowel y has protrusion.

All these observations, together with our own investigations of these languages, lead us to conclude that there are two lip position parameters for vowels, vertical lip compression and protrusion. In most languages these parameters are implemented jointly (and, also, linked to the front-back dimension), and it is sufficient to distinguish rounded (either compressed or protruded) vowels from unrounded vowels. In a small number of languages the two parameters are independently controlled. Some languages may choose to use lip compression rather than the form of rounding that has lip protrusion. Edwin Pulleyblank (personal communication) notes that Japanese u can be regarded as having compressed lips rather than being simply unrounded. This vowel shows its labiality by the fact that it alternates with w in verbal inflections. Pulleyblank also notes that the Japanese allophone of h that occurs before u is bilabial ɸ, with what we here call compressed, rather than protruded, lips. We have not investigated the acoustic characteristics of lip compression. They are presumably similar to those of lip rounding and protrusion insofar as any decrease in lip aperture tends to lower all formant frequencies, but compression and protrusion differ with respect to their distinct effects on the length of the vocal tract.

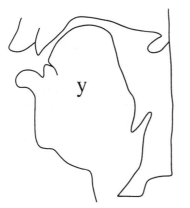 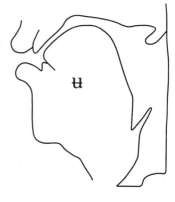

Figure 9.12 X-ray tracings of Swedish high front vowels differing in lip position. y has (horizontal) lip rounding and protrusion; ʉ has (vertical) lip compression (based on data in Fant 1973).

Table 9.7 The major features of vowel quality

HEIGHT	BACKNESS	ROUNDING	
		COMPRESSION	PROTRUSION
[high]	[front]	[compressed]	[protruded]
[mid-high]	[central]	[separated]	[retracted]
[mid]	[back]		
[mid-low]			
[low]			

Table 9.7 summarizes the major vowel features and the major phonetic categories possible within each of these features. It should be noted that Height and Backness are multi-valued, and cannot be adequately represented in binary terms.

The features and categories listed in table 9.7 might be taken to imply that there are 5 x 3 x 2 x 2 = 60 possible vowels differing only in the values of the major features of vowel quality. However, a number of combinations are so unlikely to occur that they might well be considered to be impossible. For example, there is no known language, and almost certainly could not be a language, which contrasts four lip positions among front low vowels; and it seems equally unlikely that there could be a language that contrasts five degrees of height among back unrounded vowels. It follows that the values shown in table 9.7 substantially over-represent the phonological possibilities.

They do not, however, allow for all the phonetic possibilities. In order to describe phonetic differences among vowel qualities that occur in different languages, a far greater number of distinctions must be considered. Disner

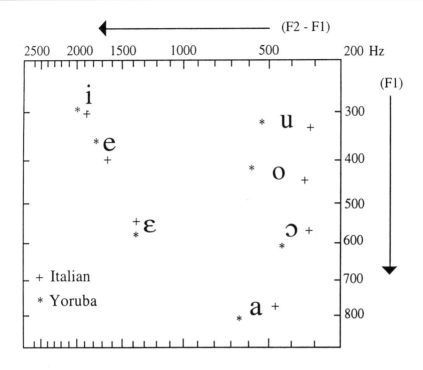

Figure 9.13 Mean formant frequencies of the vowels of Yoruba and Italian (based on data in Disner 1983).

(1983), for example, has shown that there are many small phonetic differences among the vowels that occur in different languages. Using her work, Ladefoged (1984) discussed systematic phonetic differences between two 7-vowel languages, Italian and Yoruba, both of which have vowels that may be represented as i, e, ɛ, a, ɔ, o, u. The mean formant frequencies of 25 speakers of Italian and 10 speakers of Yoruba are shown in figure 9.13. In this figure Italian vowels are marked by + and Yoruba vowels by *. The vowels of Italian are relatively evenly distributed; but in Yoruba e and o are much closer to i and u than to ɛ and ɔ respectively. The uneven distribution of the Yoruba vowels may be attributed to historical facts concerning the way in which the vowels of the original 9- or 10-vowel system (Fresco 1970) have merged to produce the current 7-vowel Yoruba system. The earlier system may have involved an additional vowel parameter, the position of the tongue root (± ATR), which we will discuss later. Synchronically, however, Yoruba vowels can be described using only the major features of vowel quality which we have been discussing in the preceding sections. The set of terms given in table 9.7 is adequate for specifying the phonological contrasts within each of these languages, but not for discussing the phonetic differences between them.

Table 9.8 The minor features of vowel quality

(1)	Nasalization	(3)	Voiceless
			Breathy
(2)	Advanced Tongue Root		Slack
	Pharyngealization		Stiff
	Stridency		Creaky
	Rhotacization	(4)	Long
	Fricative		Diphthongal

9.2 Additional Vowel Features

The Yoruba and Italian differences, and many similar variations in vowel quality such as those among Germanic languages discussed by Disner (1983), are all examples of variations in the phonetic values of what we have called major vowel features. We will now turn to other ways in which vowels differ, considering mainly how these additional vowel properties may be used to form phonological contrasts within a language. We will refer to these additional properties of vowels as the minor vowel features. Table 9.8 lists a number of additional properties that have been observed. As may be seen, they fall into four groups. The first, and by far the most commonly found of the minor vowel features is nasalization. The remaining additional vowel features fall into three main groups: those that involve special gestures of the tongue and associated structures; those that involve different phonation types; and those that involve differences in the time domain, producing variations in length and diphthongization.

Nasalized vowels

The most common minor vowel feature is nasalization, with more than one language in five using this possibility (Maddieson 1984a). The most frequent nasalized vowels are ĩ, ã, ũ, the counterparts of the most frequent oral vowels **i, a, u**. Nasalization appears to be a binary feature from a phonological point of view. But there are surface phonetic contrasts between oral, lightly nasalized, and heavily nasalized vowels in some languages. This usually occurs when a language with a phonological contrast between oral and nasalized vowels in addition has oral vowels that are contextually nasalized when adjacent to a nasal consonant. An example is shown in figure 9.14, (after Cohn 1990) comparing the nasal flow patterns of the French words *bonnet, nonnette,* and *non-être* ('cap', 'young nun', 'non-entity'). The volume of air flowing through the nose can be taken as a measure of the degree of nasality when there are comparable oral articulations. Vowel (1) is an oral vowel before a nasal consonant,

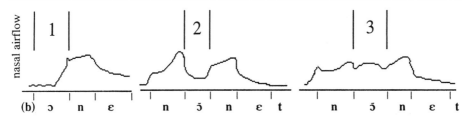

Figure 9.14 Records of nasal flow in three French words *bonnet, nonnette,* and *non-être* ('cap', 'young nun', 'non-entity'), showing the difference between oral, contextually nasalized and phonologically nasalized vowels (based on data in Cohn 1990).

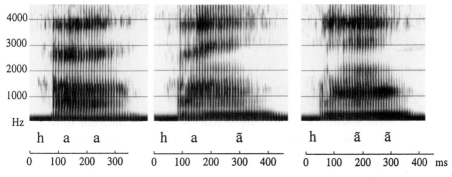

Figure 9.15 Spectrograms of the three Chinantec words in table 9.9.

resulting in the last part of the vowel being contextually nasalized; vowel (2) is considerably more nasalized, as it is between two nasal consonants; but it is not as nasalized as vowel (3), a phonologically nasalized vowel, in the same context.

Using surface phonetic contrasts such as those shown in table 9.9, Merrifield (1963) and Ladefoged (1971) noted three degrees of contrastive nasality in Palantla Chinantec, which were described as oral, lightly nasalized and heavily nasalized. This claim was supported by airflow data (recorded by W. S-Y. Wang and Peter Ladefoged; unfortunately this data is no longer available) showing that there was a higher maximum rate of nasal airflow in the fully nasalized vowels than in the lightly nasalized vowels. Auditory and acoustic analysis of such items show clear differences between the two types of nasalized vowels in the relative timing of the onset and offset of nasality. The vowels that were described as lightly nasalized are in fact audibly nasalized through only the latter part of their duration. Figure 9.15 shows spectrograms of the words in table 9.9. In the first word, with a fully oral vowel, the first two formants are very close together with the center between them being at about 1000 Hz. Both these formants are of approximately equal intensity. At the beginning of the second word the first two formants are in the same position, but the first is weaker than the second due to the incidence of a nasal zero. The

Table 9.9 Words illustrating contrasts among oral, partly nasalized, and nasalized vowels in Palantla Chinantec

háa	'so, such'	**háã**	'(he) spreads open'	**hã́ã**	'foam, froth'

third formant in this word moves up as the nasalization increases. In the third word the third formant is high from the beginning, and the first formant is even weaker, indicating that this word is fully nasalized throughout. The second of these three words can thus be seen to consist of a movement from a vowel like that in the first word followed by a vowel that is more like the third. A better description of the three Chinantec contrasts might be as being between oral vowels, oral-nasal diphthongs and nasalized vowels.

Advanced tongue root

There are fashions in the descriptions of vowels, resulting in some of the terms in table 9.8 being more discussed at certain times than others. For the last decade or so, the most discussed of the minor vowel features has been ATR (Advanced Tongue Root). For many years before that it was the Tense/Lax opposition; and earlier still, at the end of the last century, dichotomies such as Narrow/Wide and Primary/Wide were used. There is some overlap in the usage of each of these terms. We will begin by considering sets of vowels that can be said to differ in ATR; later we will compare these vowels with those that are said to be Tense as opposed to Lax.

Many West African languages have vowels that differ in the position of the tongue root (Ladefoged 1964). This difference is often most obvious in the case of high vowels. Tracings of the vocal tract shape in Igbo high vowels as shown by x-ray cinematography are given in figure 9.16. In each of these pairs the height of the tongue is very much the same. This is true irrespective of which of the two classic measures of tongue height is used, the location of the highest point of the tongue, or the height of the tongue body as a whole. Clearly, the most striking difference is that the root of the tongue is more retracted in the one case than in the other.

Another language in which there are two sets of vowels differing in ATR is Akan. Diagrams of the vocal tract shape (redrawn from data in Lindau 1975) are shown in figure 9.17. As Lindau has pointed out, in this language (and probably in most languages in which ATR distinguishes two sets of vowels), the difference is not simply in the tongue root gesture, but in the enlargement of the whole pharyngeal cavity, partly by the movement of the tongue root, but also by the lowering of the larynx. Lindau suggests that the term Expanded is the most appropriate name for this feature. The lowering of the larynx sometimes results in these vowels having a slightly breathy quality.

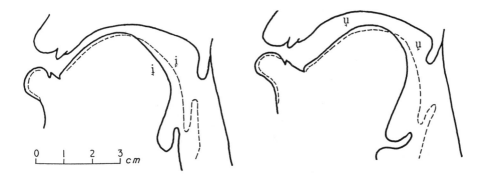

Figure 9.16 Tracings from x-ray cinematography films of Igbo vowels ị as in ọ́bị̀ (óbì in the standard Igbo orthography) 'heart'; ị as in ụ̀bị̀ (ùbì)poverty of ability'; ụ as in ịbụ́ (íbú) 'weight'; and ụ as in ọbụ̀ (obu) 'it is'. In accordance with current IPA usage ˌ and ˌ are used to indicate Advanced and Retracted Tongue Root, respectively.

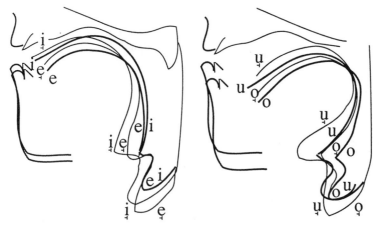

Figure 9.17 The articulatory positions in non-low vowels of the Akyem dialect of Akan, based on Lindau (1975). Front vowels are in the left panel, back vowels in the right panel. Advanced Tongue Root vowels are shown by the lighter lines. The positions for the lips are estimated.

Acoustic analysis also shows why retracted tongue root vowels have sometimes been described as having a difference in voice quality (e.g by Berry 1955).
Figure 9.18 shows the spectra of a pair of Degema vowels with similar formant
frequencies, the retracted tongue root front vowel ị, and the advanced tongue
root front vowel ị. The auditory qualities of these two vowels are similar; but
the advanced tongue root vowel sounds 'brighter' because of the greater
amount of energy in the higher part of the spectrum. There is a noticeable difference in the bandwidths of the formants; those of the advanced tongue root
vowel are narrower, probably because there is greater tension of the vocal tract

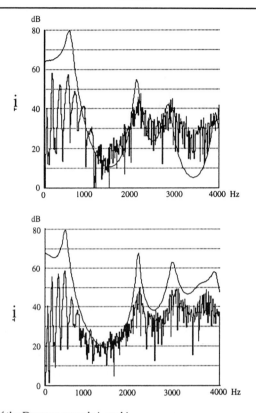

Figure 9.18 Spectra of the Degema vowels i̩ and i̩.

walls and fewer acoustic losses in the region of the resonances. This would also add to the 'brighter' tone of this vowel. Similar differences in bandwidth have been found with ATR contrasts in Akan (Hess 1992). However we should point out that in most cases that we have heard, the West African languages using ATR do not have markedly different voice qualities.

Tense/Lax and ATR

The Akan vowels in figure 9.17 also differ in the height of the tongue in the front part of the oral cavity. This leads us to consider whether the differences between [+ATR] and [-ATR] vowels are the same as the differences between so-called Tense and Lax vowels, which may also differ in both the height of the tongue and the position of the root of the tongue. There are differences of this kind in Germanic languages, as exemplified by pairs of English words such as *heed–hid* and *bait–bet*. Following Jones (1956) and a long British tradition, we regard the members of these pairs of vowels as being

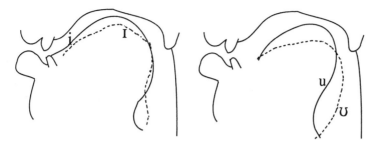

Figure 9.19 X-ray tracings of the articulatory positions in some so-called Tense/Lax pairs of vowels in English (redrawn from data in Perkell 1969).

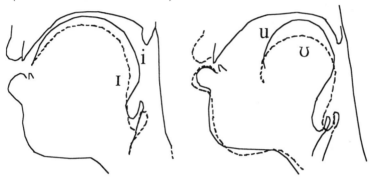

Figure 9.20 X-ray tracings of the articulatory positions in some so-called Tense/Lax pairs of vowels in German (after Bolla and Valaczkai 1986).

distinguished by variations of the major vowel qualities, Height and Backness (and perhaps Rounding). We note, of course, that the differences may involve diphthongization implemented through variation in Height and the members of each pair also differ in length. But we do not find it necessary to consider any additional parameters such as tenseness.

We recognize, however, that there is also a long tradition in which these vowels are considered as being distinguished by the feature Tense (e.g. by Bloch and Trager 1942, and by Chomsky and Halle 1968). This leads us to consider two related questions that might be asked at this point. Firstly, are we correct in our phonetic characterization of these vowels as differing only in the regular vowel dimensions of Height and Backness (and Rounding), plus Length? Secondly, are ATR variations the same as Tense/Lax variations? We can get a partial answer to these questions by comparing the vocal tract shapes shown for the Igbo vowels in figure 9.16 and the Akan vowels in figure 9.17, with the pairs of English vowels shown in figure 9.19 or the pairs of German vowels in figure 9.20. In Igbo and Akan the tongue height is not correlated with the tongue root position. In English the position of the tongue root is correlated with the tongue height (more so for the back vowels than for the front). In

German the same is true of the back vowels, but in the front vowels what difference there is in root position would favor the so-called lax vowel having a more advanced tongue root. There is no common setting of the tongue root for the so-called lax vowels that distinguishes them from the so-called tense vowels. This conclusion is supported by statistical analyses of tongue shapes, in which it has been shown that the saggital position of the tongue in sets of English vowels containing the Tense/Lax pairs can be specified very completely by reference to only two variables (Harshman, Ladefoged and Goldstein 1977, Ladefoged and Harshman 1979). Using similar techniques, Jackson (1988) has also substantiated the finding that in English there does not appear to be a separate control of the root of the tongue; but he did find that there were three independent parameters of tongue shape in Akan. Tiede's (1993) three-dimensional study of pharynx volume using MRI shows further differences between Akan and English. In the pharyngeal region below the epiglottis, Akan shows a positive correlation between the transverse width of the space and tongue root advancement, whereas in English transverse width is negatively correlated with advancement. Accordingly it seems that the situation in English (and other Germanic languages) is not the same as that in West African languages. Although there may be some increase in the height of the tongue accompanying the advancement of the tongue root in Akan, the changes in tongue height are small in comparison with the expansion that occurs in the pharyngeal region. Furthermore, on some occasions there may be virtually no increase in tongue height for [+ATR] vowels, as is shown in the case of the Igbo vowels in figure 9.16. We conclude that the advancement of the tongue root is a separable tongue gesture in languages such as Igbo and Akan. In Germanic languages, however, it is simply one of the concomitants of vowel Height.

If the advancement of the tongue root is an independent gesture that can be learned as part of the sound pattern of a language, then it must have observable acoustic consequences that distinguish it from all other possible ways of achieving similar acoustic effects.

Lindau (1979) has also pointed out that there are differences between ATR and Tense/Lax characterizations of vowels in the acoustic domain. Figure 9.21 shows the acoustic characteristics of ATR differences in a number of languages. The Akan data is from Lindau (1979), the DhoLuo from Jacobson (1978), and the remaining languages are from our own files. It may be seen that in virtually all cases the [+ATR] vowel appears to be raised and advanced in the acoustic space. The only exception is the Ebira lower mid back vowel which is raised, but only very slightly advanced. Among front vowels, pairs of vowels differing in ATR have formant frequency characteristics that are reminiscent of so-called tense-lax pairs of vowels in Germanic languages, such as English *bead–bid; bade–bed*; both retracted tongue root vowels and the lax vowels are lowered and more central in the acoustic space. Among front vowels there is this parallel between [+ ATR] and [-ATR] tongue root vowels on the one hand, and Tense and Lax vowels on the other, but among back vowel pairs

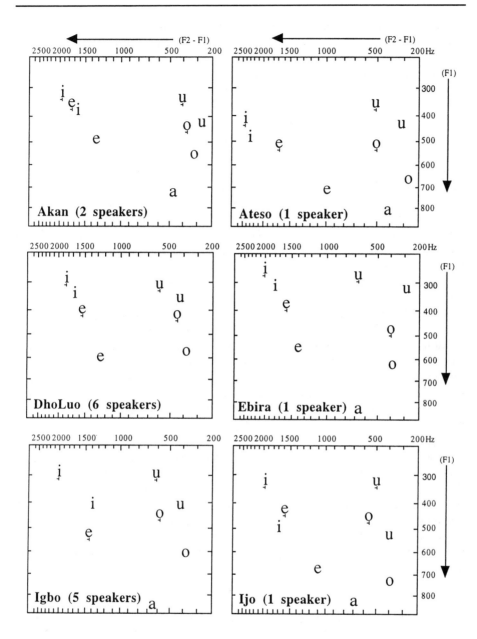

Figure 9.21 The acoustic effects of ATR in a number of languages. Vowels that are [+ ATR] are indicated by the subscript ₌.

there is no such parallel. The high back retracted tongue root vowel is always further back than its counterpart, rather than further forward, as is the case for the traditional lax back vowels. Lax vowels of all kinds are normally taken to be more centralized. Retracted tongue root vowels do not always have this characteristic.

Pharyngealized vowels

Another gesture of the tongue root involves its active retraction rather than advancement. This gesture takes several different forms, resulting in vowels that are variously called pharyngealized, epiglottalized, sphincteric or strident. Among the languages which have been described as having pharyngealized vowels is Even, a Tungus language of North-Central Siberia (Novikova 1960). This language has two sets of vowels as exemplified by the words in table 9.10. The vowels in the set labeled pharyngealized all have a narrower pharyngeal passage and a raised larynx. Tracings of x-rays of the vocal tract shape in these vowels are shown in figure 9.22. (As drawn in the originals these tracings imply that all these vowels are nasalized. That seems unlikely, and we do not know what to make of it. Obviously, we should be cautious in fully accepting the validity of the rest of the indicated vocal tract shape.) There is considerable similarity between these pairs of vowels and those we have been discussing in Akan. Furthermore, it is interesting to note that the two sets of vowels in Even also constitute vowel harmony sets in much the same way as the two sets in Akan: roots must contain vowels that are all of one set or the other.

Despite these similarities, both the examination of the x-ray tracings and Novikova's comments on the acoustic characteristics of these vowels suggest that there is a greater degree of pharyngeal narrowing in Even than in Akan. We will therefore consider these vowels to be characterized by pharyngealization rather than by ATR. Vowels with even more retraction of the tongue root occur primarily in two language families: Caucasian and Khoisan. In Caucasian languages such as Tsakhur and Udi each of the five vowels **i, e, a, o, u** has a pharyngealized counterpart (Catford, ms in preparation). Tsakhur also has a sixth vowel, which Catford symbolizes ɤ, that has a

Table 9.10 Words illustrating plain and pharyngealized vowels in Even (Novikova 1960)

PLAIN		PHARYNGEALIZED	
is li	'plucked'	iˤsliˤ	'reached'
us	'weapons'	uˤs	'guilt'
oj	'summit'	ɔˤj	'clothing'
əkən	'older sister'	akan	'older brother'

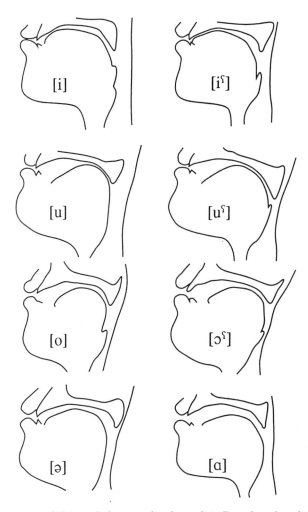

Figure 9.22 X-ray tracings of plain and pharyngealized vowels in Even (based on data in Novikova 1960).

pharyngealized counterpart (and Udi has three other vowels that do not have such counterparts). Catford reports formant frequencies for all these vowels. The most noticeable point in the acoustic structure is that the frequency of the third formant is markedly lower in the pharyngealized vowels. The frequency of the first formant is also somewhat higher.

X-rays of Tsakhur and Udi pharyngealized vowels are shown in figure 9.23. In addition Gaprindashvili (1966) has published some x-rays of pharyngealized vowels in two different dialects of Dargi. These all show that there is considerable narrowing in the pharynx near the tip of the epiglottis.

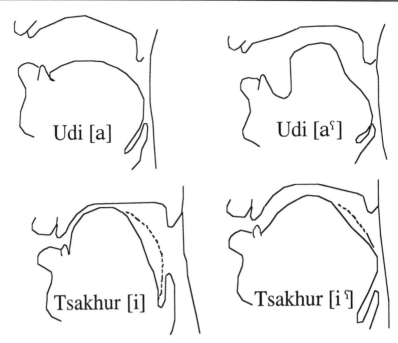

Figure 9.23 X-ray tracings of plain and pharyngealized vowels in Tsakhur and Udi (based on data in Catford ms in preparation, and Dzhejranishvili 1959). The original sources are not completely explicit, but the dashed lines presumably represent raised portions of the sides of the tongue.

Table 9.11 Additional vowel properties in !Xóõ. (See text for an explanation of the phonetic notation)

PLAIN	k‖áã	'camelthorn tree'
PHARYNGEALIZED	qâˤa	'long ago'
STRIDENT	ʔŋ!ào	'base'
BREATHY VOICED	k!ao	'slope'

What is equally interesting is that the whole front part of the tongue is bunched up, with a pronounced hollowing of the part of the tongue below the uvula. This results in the vocal tract having three cavities rather than just the usual front and back cavities produced by a single constriction. As Catford (1988a) has noted, a similar vocal tract configuration also occurs in some American English rhotic vowels, which like the Caucasian vowels, have a low F3.

There are also pharyngealized vowels in some of the Khoisan languages. In these languages only the back vowels **a, o, u** have pharyngealized counterparts; but there are additional contrasts among vowels (which we will discuss later), as shown for the vowel **a** in table 9.11. Traill (1985) has given good descriptions of all these sounds. Figure 9.24 is based on tracings from his

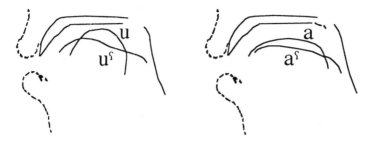

Figure 9.24 X-ray tracings of plain and pharyngealized vowels in !Xóõ (based on data in Traill 1985).

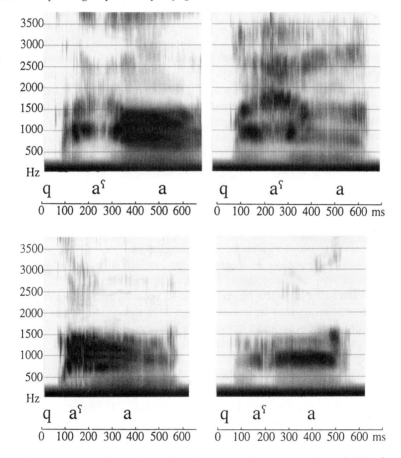

Figure 9.25 Spectrograms of the word **qaˤa** as pronounced by four speakers of !Xóõ, showing a pharyngealized vowel, followed by a non-pharyngealized vowel.

cine-radiology film of a speaker of !Xóõ, showing aˤ and uˤ (a̰ and ṵ in his transcription; we follow IPA practice in using ˤ for pharyngealization, keeping the
subscript tilde for indicating creaky voice). The tongue positions for the plain
back vowels **a, u** are also shown. It may be seen that there are considerable
overall differences between the tongue shapes of the pharyngealized and non-
pharyngealized members of each pair, very noticeably so in the case of the high
vowel **u**. In fact, as Traill notes, on the basis of the tongue shape alone it would
be difficult to regard uˤ as being in any sense a high back vowel; the reasons for
symbolizing it in this way are largely auditory and phonological.

The auditory and acoustic effects of pharyngealization in !Xóõ do not seem
to be the same as in the two Caucasian languages. We have heard recordings of
all these languages, and have ourselves worked with speakers of !Xóõ and
other Khoisan languages. Figure 9.25 shows spectrograms of the word **qaˤa** as
pronounced by four speakers of !Xóõ. This word is especially interesting because it contains two vowels that are the same except for the pharyngealization
that occurs on the first. The acoustic effects of pharyngealization are observable in only the first part of the word. The lowering of the third formant is
similar to that reported in the Caucasian languages; but in the Khoisan examples, there is also a considerable *raising* of the lower formants, accompanied by
a diminution of the energy around 400–700 Hz. This is comparable to the
acoustic effects seen in pharyngeal consonants and discussed in chapter 2.

Strident vowels

The Khoisan pharyngealized vowels that we have been discussing so far are
not the so-called strident vowels of these languages. Traill (1985) suggests that
the strident vowels may be regarded phonologically as pharyngealized
breathy voiced vowels. He goes on, however, to emphasize that the vocal tract
shape is not the same as in the pharyngealized vowels, and the laryngeal action
is very different from that in breathy voiced vowels. It is clear that from a
phonetic point of view strident vowels are best considered as involving a distinct articulatory mechanism of their own, which he has labelled 'sphincteric'
(Traill 1986).

Traill (1985, 1986) has provided a great deal of valuable data on these vowels. Figure 9.26 shows, in addition to the plain and pharyngealized vowels discussed above, the strident vowels which, for want of better symbols, we will
represent by a̰ and ṵ. Traill, in accordance with his phonological analysis, transcribes them as a̰h and ṵh. It is clear that the whole body of the tongue is much
lower for the strident vowels. In addition the back wall of the pharynx, which
is shown by the dashed line, is drawn forward, and, "the epiglottis vibrates
rapidly during these sounds" (Trail 1985).

More details are apparent from the enhanced x-ray of Traill's own pronunciation of a strident vowel shown in figure 9.27. Only the pharyngeal and

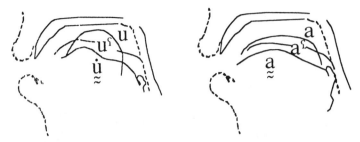

Figure 9.26 X-ray tracings of plain, pharyngealized and strident vowels in !Xóõ, based on data in Traill (1985).

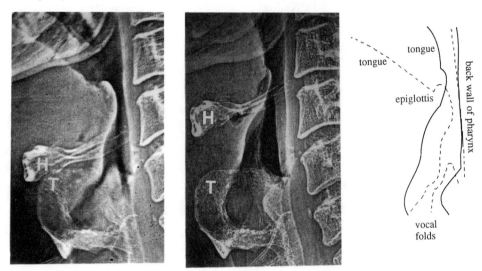

Figure 9.27 Photographs (courtesy of A. Traill) of his pronunciation of a strident vowel in !Xóõ (compare Traill 1985). The left-hand picture shows the larynx and the pharyngeal area when at rest and the right-hand picture shows the phonation of a strident vowel. The diagram on the right shows the two tongue positions superimposed, with the dashed lines indicating the strident vowel. An H in both photographs marks the hyoid bone, and a T marks the thyroid cartilage.

laryngeal areas of the vocal tract are shown. The right-hand part of this figure shows our tracings (from the original photographs) of the shape of the vocal tract. In addition to the constriction at the root of the glottis, shown in figure 9.26, there is also a major constriction between the part of the tongue below the epiglottis and the tips of the arytenoid cartilages in the upper part of the larynx. As may be seen by comparison of the two photographs, this constriction is achieved by pulling the hyoid bone (marked by H) and the thyroid cartilage (marked by T) closer together. A constriction of this kind does not occur in the pharyngealized vowels of !Xóõ or other Khoisan languages, and is also not apparent in any of the data that we have seen showing the pharyngealized

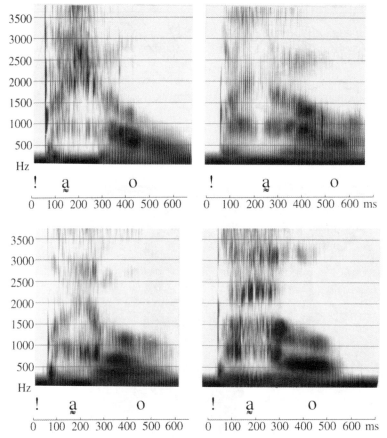

Figure 9.28 Spectrograms of the pronunciation of the word !ao containing the low back strident vowel, spoken by four speakers of !Xóõ.

vowels in Caucasian languages. Consequently in table 9.8 we listed strident among those vowel properties that depend on variations in vocal tract shape, although, in fact, it is not simply the vocal tract shape that characterizes these vowels.

As we have seen, strident vowels have a constriction between the part of the tongue below the epiglottis and the tips of the arytenoid cartilages in the upper part of the larynx. This constriction results in these vowels having a specific phonation type. Traill (1985) notes that "the arytenoid cartilages vibrate vigorously." He also notes, however, that the vocal cords themselves do not vibrate during this tight constriction in the upper part of the larynx. This whole shape, in which the vocal cords are stiff and comparatively close together, is certainly not at all like that normally associated with what is called murmur or breathy voice. Figure 9.28 provides acoustic data from our own field recordings of strident vowels produced by four speakers. The first of these speakers is the subject who provided the data in figure 9.24 and figure 9.26.

These data support Traill's description. They show that there are irregular, noisy vibrations that might well have been produced by the approximated arytenoid cartilages and/or the epiglottis, rather than by the vocal cords themselves. The spectrograms show even more upward displacement of the first and second formants than in the pharyngealized vowels we discussed in the previous section. Again the third formant generally shifts downward.

We have discussed ATR, pharyngealized and strident vowels as if they were characterized by separate properties. However, as we noted, [– ATR] vowels are very much akin to pharyngealized vowels, and strident vowels might be regarded as a more extreme form of pharyngealized vowels. All these vowels are characterized by some degree of pharyngeal narrowing and larynx raising. Languages seldom use more than one of the three possibilities. We cannot reduce these three possibilities to a single binary contrast because of the contrastive use of plain, pharyngealized and strident vowels in !Xóõ. But the most suitable phonological parameters to use in describing these vowels are not clear to us at this moment.

Rhotic vowels

As we mentioned above there is yet another class of vowels in which the root of the tongue is often retracted, namely the rhotic (r-colored) vowels. These sounds are very unusual, and occur in less than one percent of the world's languages (Maddieson 1984a). They are, however, comparatively well known, in that they occur both in some forms of English, and in some forms of Chinese. The common attribute of all rhotic vowels is in their acoustic structure, rather than in their articulation. Rhotic vowels always have a lowered frequency of the third formant. Sometimes these sounds are produced with the tip of the tongue up, and sometimes with it down; often the tongue is bunched up in the anterior-posterior direction; and there is usually a narrowing of the vocal tract in the region of the epiglottis. As discussed in chapter 7, the syllabic peak in words such as *herd* in many varieties of American English is regarded as a syllabic version of the consonant ɹ, but other vowels often take on a rhotic coloring before ɹ.

What may be a different kind of rhotacization has been reported by Emeneau (1939) in Badaga, a Dravidian language. He suggests that in this language there are five vowel qualities, **i, e, a, o, u**, each of which can be "normal, half-retroflexed, (or) fully retroflexed." The half-retroflex vowels are described as being "produced with the edges and tip of the tongue retroflexed or curved upward to approach the alveolar ridge, but without touching or causing friction at any point; the front of the blade of the tongue seems to be raised also in this manner of vowel production." His description of the fully retroflexed

Table 9.12 Words illustrating two degrees of rhotacization in Badaga vowels as pronounced by conservative speakers

PLAIN		SLIGHTLY RHOTACIZED		FULLY RHOTACIZED	
be	'mouth'	**be˞**	'bangle'	**be˞˞**	crop
kaːsu	'coin'	**ha˞ːsu**	'spread out'	**ka˞˞ːsu**	'remove'

vowels is as follows: "In the vowels with fully-retroflexed resonance the whole tongue is strongly retracted, the edges are curved upwards towards the hard palate well behind the alveolar ridge but without touching or causing friction at any point, and a channel is left in the center of the tongue well visible at the tip in a V-formation." Emeneau offers good evidence for all these 15 vowels being phonologically contrastive. Emeneau's fieldwork was conducted in the 1930s, and it seems that the form of Badaga he investigated is no longer spoken. We have made recordings of a large number of Badaga speakers, going from one end of their dialect region to another. Our speakers included the son of Emeneau's informant and others from the same district. We found only a few speakers from very conservative groups who maintained a three-way contrast, and then it was in only one or at the most two vowels. However, two speakers did reliably distinguish the words shown in table 9.12.

Fricative vowels

The next added vowel feature to be discussed is frication. Fricative vowels can usually be thought of as syllabic fricatives that are allophones of vowels. The best known examples are the allophones of **i** that occur after retroflex (flat post-alveolar) and palatal fricatives and affricates respectively in Standard Chinese. These vowels are made with the tongue in essentially the same position as in the corresponding fricatives. Because of the articulation used in the retroflex case, these vowels have sometimes been referred to as 'apical' vowels. This term is not appropriate for the palatal cases. In addition, in Liangshang Yi there are fricative vowels which are syllabic variants of a labial fricative (Maddieson and Hess 1986) and in Czech a laminal **r** can occur as a fricative vowel (Ladefoged 1971, and see chapter 7). These non-Chinese cases indicate that the more general term fricative vowel is preferable. Fricative vowels are reconstructable for Proto-Bantu (they are usually referred to by Bantuists as 'superclose' vowels, written ụ, ị). The fricative vowel pronunciation is retained in some languages in the northwestern part of the Bantu area, but has often resulted in frication of a preceding consonant elsewhere. In both Yi and Czech the fricative vowels may be not only fricated but also trilled. In the case of the Yi labial vowel, it is the lips that are trilled.

Phonation types

The phonation types listed in table 9.8 were defined in chapter 3, when we discussed the different states of the glottis that can occur in conjunction with stops (and other consonants). Most languages use only the two different phonation types, voiced and voiceless; and these two types usually contrast only among consonants. For vowels, the status of phonological contrasts between voiced and voiceless possibilities is not always clear. They have been reported to have some phonological role in Ik (Heine 1975) and Dafla (Ray 1967). As a surface phonetic phenomenon they are an important areal feature of the Amerindian languages of the Plains and the Rockies. In some of these languages they appear to be phonologically contrastive. For example, Miller and Davis (1963) reconstruct voiceless vowels for Proto-Keresan. In other languages, such as Acoma (Miller 1966), they are not underlying phonemes; in yet others, such as Comanche, their status is problematic (Armagost 1986). Voiceless vowels also occur in the Bantu languages of the Congo basin and the Indo-Iranian languages in the Indic/Iranian border region; but here they are simply surface phonetic phenomena. Voiceless vowels occur as allophones of regularly voiced vowels in many languages, including English (e.g. in the first syllables of 'peculiar' and 'particular'). In Japanese there is a contrast between the voiceless allophones of i and u between voiceless obstruents, as in kiʃi 'shore' and kuʃi 'comb'.

Many languages have phonemic contrasts involving other kinds of phonation. Some languages exploit a breathy voice quality which some linguists call 'murmur' (Ladefoged 1971, Pandit 1957), but which in this book we are calling breathy voice. As shown in table 9.13, Gujarati has developed surface phonetic contrasts between plain and breathy voiced vowels, in addition to the more common Indo-Aryan contrasts between plain and breathy voiced stops, discussed in chapter 3. !Xóõ contrasts involving breathy voice have already been illustrated in table 9.11.

Another type of vowel is produced with the body of the vocal folds, the vocalis muscle, stiffened, forming what we are here calling stiff voice. A good example occurs in Mpi, a language with six tones, each of which may occur with a plain or a laryngealized vowel, so that the same articulatory sequence,

Table 9.13 Words illustrating contrasts between voiced and breathy voiced vowels in Gujarati. (For further comparison, contrasts between voiceless aspirated, voiced aspirated, voiceless, and voiced consonants are also shown)

	Voiced initial		Voiceless initial	
Plain vowel	baɾ	'twelve'	pɔɾ	'last year'
Breathy vowel	ba̤ɾ	'outside'	pɔ̤ɾ	'early morning'
Aspirated consonant	bʱaɾ	'burden'	pʰɔdz	'army'

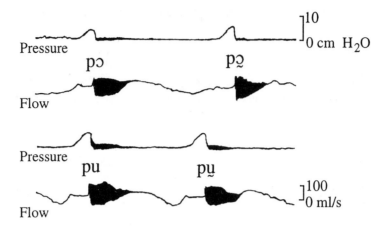

Figure 9.29 Airflow and intra-oral pressure records of two pairs of words with stiff and slack voicing in Parauk (retraced from the original recordings).

Table 9.14 Contrasting phonation types and tones occurring on the segments si in Mpi. The 12 glosses are appropriate for the segments si with the tones and phonation types as shown

	TONE	MODAL VOICE	STIFF VOICE
1	low rising	'to be putrid'	'to be dried up'
2	low	'blood'	'seven'
3	mid rising	'to roll'	'to smoke'
4	mid	(a color)	(classifier)
5	high rising	'to die'	(man's name)
6	high	'four'	(man's name)

si, has 12 different meanings depending on accompanying tone and phonation type, as shown in table 9.14.

Often the contrast is not so much between regular voicing and stiff voicing, but instead is between a slightly breathy and slightly stiff type of phonation. Parauk (Wa), a Mon-Khmer language, uses two such contrasting phonation types, neither of which is as breathy or as creaky as the contrasting phonation types in the other languages we have been considering in this chapter; both are much closer to modal voice. The small differences in Parauk vowels are illustrated in the aerodynamic records of two pairs of words shown in figure 9.29 (from Maddieson and Ladefoged 1985). There are insignificant variations in the pressure, due to various factors such as the sequence in which the words were read. However, for a given pressure, there is always a higher mean flow for the slack vowels, which, accordingly, must have been produced with a less constricted glottis.

Table 9.15 Words illustrating creaky (laryngealized), breathy (murmured) and modal (plain) vowels in Jalapa Mazatec

MODAL VOICE	BREATHY	CREAKY
já	ja̤	ja̰
'tree'	'he carries'	'he wears'
ntʰǽ	nda̤ǽ	nda̰ǽ
'seed'	'arse'	'horse'

A more extreme type of laryngealization, creaky voice, occurs in some languages, such as Jalapa Mazatec, an Otomanguean language spoken in Mexico (Kirk, Ladefoged and Ladefoged 1993). As we noted in the case of stop consonants, the distinction drawn between creaky voice and stiff voice is somewhat arbitrary. We have, ourselves, referred to the voice quality in Mpi as creaky (Ladefoged 1982), although, in comparison with the Jalapa Mazatec vowels, Mpi vowels definitely have a less constricted glottis. Jalapa Mazatec is exceptional in that it has a three way contrast between creaky (laryngealized), breathy (murmured) and modal (plain) vowels, as illustrated in table 9.15, and the vowel contrasts are therefore worth examining in some detail.

The acoustic cues distinguishing vowels with different phonation types have been described at length by Ladefoged, Maddieson and Jackson (1988). As a general rule, vowels with stiff voice or creaky voice have more energy in the harmonics in the region of the first and second formants than those with modal voice. Conversely, vowels with slack or breathy voice have comparatively more energy in the fundamental frequency. There is also a tendency (though not in all languages) for vowels with creaky voice to have a more irregular vocal cord pulse rate (more jitter), and for breathy voice vowels to have more random energy (a larger noise component) in the higher frequencies. These points can be seen in the narrow band power spectra of the creaky, modal and breathy vowels of five speakers of Jalapa Mazatec, shown in figure 9.30.

Figure 9.31 shows the difference between the amplitude of the fundamental and that of the first formant in each of these spectra. It thus illustrates the way in which some of these differences can be expressed quantitatively. Data for each of the five speakers is shown separately, followed by the mean for all five. The lowest set of three bars shows that the mean difference in amplitude between the fundamental and the first formant for creaky voice (black bar) is −17 dB, i.e. the fundamental has 17 dB less amplitude than the first formant, which is thus considerably stronger. The mean for modal voice (shaded bar) is −7 dB, and that for breathy voice (white bar) is +5 dB (i.e. for breathy voice there is a comparatively large amount of energy in the fundamental rather than in the first formant). There is considerable variation from speaker to speaker in the value for each of the three phonation types, but for all speakers the value for breathy voice is higher than that for modal voice for any speaker. Creaky

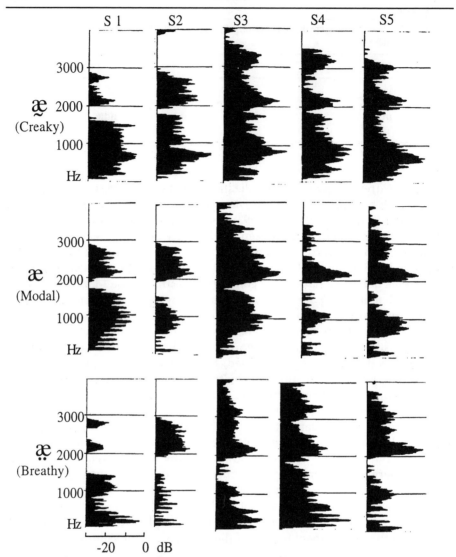

Figure 9.30 Narrow band power spectra of the creaky, modal and breathy vowels of five speakers of Jalapa Mazatec, taken during the middle of the vowels in the last row of table 9.15.

voice and modal voice show some overlap of values, but it is still true that for every speaker creaky voice it has a relatively lower value than modal voice.

Some of the differences between the three phonation types can also be seen in records of the waveforms of these vowels. Figure 9.32 shows the three vowels as produced by one speaker. The creaky vowel has more irregular pulses and a comparatively undamped waveform corresponding to the narrow

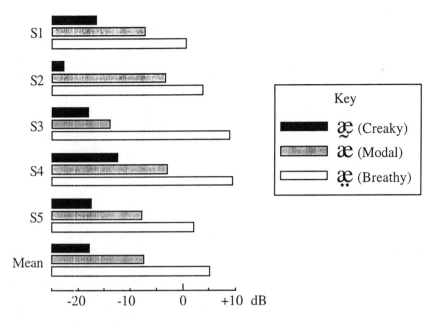

Figure 9.31 Relative amplitude of the fundamental and the first formant in Jalapa Mazatec vowels for five speakers and the mean of all five.

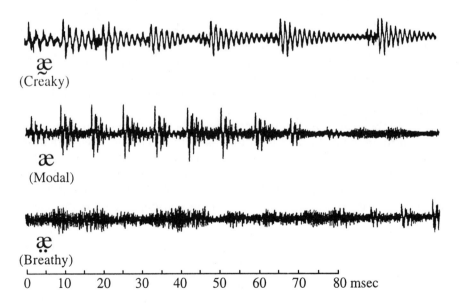

Figure 9.32 Waveforms of the three vowels in the first row of table 9.15 as spoken by one speaker.

bandwidth of the formants in this vowel. In the breathy vowel it is hard to see the individual pulses because of the high frequency noise components.

In summarizing the use of variations in phonation type to differentiate among vowels, we should emphasize (as we did in the discussion of stops) that there is a continuum going from a glottal state in which the vocal cords are in the voiceless position with the arytenoid cartilages far apart, to one involving a creaky voice with the arytenoid cartilages pressed firmly together. Most languages do not use any differences between these glottal states to distinguish among vowels. A number of languages use two, selecting various possibilities within the continuum. A few rare languages, such as Jalapa Mazatec, have three contrasts of this kind.

Length

Numerous languages distinguish long and short vowels. Occasionally, as in Estonian, there are three contrasting vowel lengths. In this language, however, as has been pointed out by Lehiste (1970), the significant differences in quantity are not simply lexical, but are related to the structure of the word. The only language that we know of that has persuasively been shown to use three degrees of length to contrast lexical items is Mixe (Hoogshagen 1959). Lehiste (1970), commenting on Hoogshagen's description of this language, concludes that "vowel quantity in Mixe is segmental, i.e., does not depend on syllable structure or on word patterns as was the case in Estonian." Our reading of Hoogshagen's data leads to the same conclusions; Hoogshagen provides numerous examples, mainly monosyllabic words, showing that there are three degrees of contrastive vowel length, independent of the syllable pattern, the vowel quality, the preceding or following consonants, the stress, the pitch and the intonation. Examples are given in table 9.16. Yavapai also has distinctions between vowels of three different lengths which seem to be lexical (Thomas and Shaterian 1990).

Larger numbers of length differences have been observed in some languages, but these are associated with the distinction between vowels that are contained in one syllable versus those which form more than one syllable. Whiteley and Muli (1962) suggested that KiKamba has four degrees of length. Although they pointed out that the very long vowels have cognate forms in neighboring languages with an intervening consonant within the vowel

Table 9.16 Words illustrating the three contrastive vowel lengths in Mixe (data from Hoogshagen 1959)

poʃ	'guava'	pet	'climb (n)'	piʃ	'flea'
po·ʃ	'spider'	pe·t	'broom'	pi·ʃ	'marigold'
po:ʃ	'knot'	pe:t	'Peter'	tʃi:t	'cat'

Table 9.17 Words illustrating long and short vowels, and vowel hiatus in KiKamba (from Roberts-
Kohno 1994)

SHORT VOWEL	**kokona**	'to hit'
LONG VOWEL	**kóómã**	'to dry'
SHORT + SHORT	**ko.ómã**	'to bite'
SHORT + LONG	**nétóṇubáné.éetê**	'we have chosen for everyone and are still choosing'

sequence, they saw no obvious reason to consider these very long vowels as consisting of more than one syllable. Roberts-Kohno (1994) has clarified the situation: there is a four-way distinction between vowel lengths because there are two independent factors. There are long and short vowels, and identical vowels may have a syllable boundary (or 'hiatus') between them. This yields the difference **V**, **V:**, **V.V**, and **V.V:** (neither **V:.V** nor **V:.V:** occurs). Examples of each type are given in table 9.17. In the case of hiatus, non-identical vowel sequences also occur, as in **ko.úmã** 'to curse'. Two identical short vowels in hiatus are much longer than a long vowel; Roberts-Kohno measured the mean duration of the bisyllabic vowel sequence in **kotó.ómeðja** 'to cause to bite us' as 232 ms, but the long vowel in **kotóómeðja** 'to dry us' as only 127 ms.

Diphthongs

If we consider phonetic descriptions of vowels to be equivalent to statements about the targets of vocalic gestures, then we can consider diphthongs to be vowels that have two separate targets. There is a problem with this definition, in that it does not distinguish between diphthongs and long vowels, which may well be considered to be vowels that have two identical targets. Accordingly we must stipulate that diphthongs must have two different targets. Lindau, Norlin and Svantesson (1985) have calculated that diphthongs occur in about a third of the world's languages. They also note that diphthongs of the **ai**-type occur in 75 percent of these languages, and of the **au**-type in 65 percent of these languages.

As with all sounds with two targets, the time-course of the movement from one target to the next has to be specified. Lindau, Norlin and Svantesson (1985) examined diphthongs in Arabic, Hausa, Standard Chinese, and English, and showed that there are differences in the way that the diphthong targets are joined. For some of the diphthongs in these languages certain general principles seemed to apply. For example, for the **ai** diphthong in English, and for the upward moving diphthongs in Chinese it was true that "the further to go, the longer it takes." But for other Chinese diphthongs, and for English **au** diphthongs, this was not true. In addition Hausa and Arabic had significantly shorter diphthongal transitions than English and Chinese. Peeters and Barry (1989) have also shown that there are language specific differences in the movements within diphthongs.

The kinds of vowels that occur as targets in diphthongs are no different from those that occur as single vowels. Consequently, in this book, in which our aim is to describe the set of phonologically contrastive sounds that occur in the languages of the world, there is little extra to be said about diphthongs. No new features are needed. Of course from a phonological point of view, diphthongs pose many interesting problems, such as why some sequences are preferred to others. But these are outside our present purview.

9.3 Vowel-like Consonants

Traditional phonetic classification has often set up a category of sounds known as semi-vowels. These are vowel-like segments that function as consonants, such as **w** and **j**. These sounds have also been termed 'glides', based on the idea that they involve a quick movement from a high vowel position to a lower vowel. This term, and this characterization of the nature of these sounds is inappropriate; as with other consonants they can occur geminated, for example in Marshallese, Sierra Miwok and Tashlhiyt.

Vowel-like segments that function as consonants are common in the world's languages. Of the world's languages 85 percent have the palatal approximant **j** and 76 percent the labial-velar approximant **w** (Maddieson 1984a). Other semi-vowels are far less common, occurring in less than 2 percent of languages. Table 9.18 illustrates the contrasts between the labial-palatal approximant **ɥ** and the two more familiar semivowels **j**, **w** in French. The (unrounded) velar approximant **ɰ** is even less common. It occurs in Axininca where it contrasts with "a bilabial approximant [IPA β] which has no simultaneous velar … articulation as **w** would," (Payne 1981) as well as with the palatal approximant **j**.

There has been a great deal of discussion about the relationship between vowels and semivowels. It is clear that there is a contrast between English words such as *east* and *yeast* and between words such as *woos* and *ooze*. But Jakobson, Fant and Halle (1952) suggested that this does not necessitate setting up a category of semivowels. In their view, there is only an allophonic difference between semivowels and vowels. Thus Jakobson, Fant and Halle transcribed the words *woo* and *ye* as **uuu** and **iii**, instead of **wuw** and **yiy** as was the

Table 9.18 Words illustrating contrasting semivowels in French

mjet	'guava'	mɥet	'mute'	mwet	'sea gull'
lje	'spider'	lɥi	'him'	lwi	'Louis'
jø	'eyes'	ɥit	'eight'	wi	'yes'

contemporary practice for American English. But, irrespective of phonological arguments, Maddieson and Emmorey (1985) have shown that there is a clear articulatory difference between vowels and semivowels such as these in three very different languages, Amharic, Yoruba and Zuni. There are cross-language differences between the semivowels in these languages, and these differences are correlated with cross-language differences between the vowels. But within each language the semivowels differ from the corresponding vowels in that they are produced with narrower constrictions of the vocal tract.

In addition to j, w, ɥ, ɰ, there are a number of other non-syllabic vowel-like sounds that might also be considered as semivowels. Two of these are forms of 'r' and are more appropriately considered in chapter 7, which is concerned with all forms of rhotics. But we should note here that, for many speakers of American English, the approximant ɹ at the beginning of the word 'red' bears the same relationship to the vowel ɚ in 'bird' as the approximant j in 'yes' does to the vowel i in 'heed'. Similarly, the Danish 'r' sound in words such as 'raad' (council) is not a uvular approximant as some textbooks (Bredsdorf 1958) describe it, but a pharyngeal approximant with an articulatory position similar to that in a low back vowel.

We should also consider whether there are semivowels corresponding to mid-vowels in a language. A possibility of this sort can be seen by considering the resyllabifications of vowel elisions that occur in Nepali, shown in table 9.19. In this language there are several possible sequences of vowels that occur in a slow, formal style of speech. In normal, colloquial speech one or other of two adjacent vowels becomes non-syllabic. The examples cited in the tables sound like two syllables in slow speech, but like single syllables in normal speech, both to us and to the Nepali linguist B.M. Dahal, who suggested them to us. Sometimes it is the first of the two vowels that is affected, and sometimes the second. The six vowels of the language may be described in terms of three vowel heights: i, u; e, o; ə, a. Kelkar (personal communication.) has pointed out that when a sequence includes a high or mid-vowel, and a vowel of a lower height, the higher vowel in the sequence becomes non-syllabic, irrespective of whether it is the first or second vowel in the sequence. The high vowels become the semivowels j, w; and, when a mid-vowel occurs with a low vowel, the mid-vowels become the non-high semivowels, ĕ, ŏ. When high or mid-vowels of equal height occur in sequence, either of them may become non-syllabic, so that either of the possible semivowels is produced. Only when two low vowels alone occur in sequence (i.e. in a sequence without a mid- or high vowel), is the first of the two elided. Facts such as these not only indicate the possibility of non-high semivowels, but also support the notion of vowel heights forming a multi-valued ordered set that cannot be expressed in binary terms.

While not actually semivowels, we will also consider here the bilabial approximant β and the labiodental approximant ʋ. Hindi is a good example of a language in which there is no v or w, but instead the most common allophone

Table 9.19 Vowel elisions in Nepali

	Slow, formal		Normal, colloquial	
	die	→	dje	'they gave'
	tei	→	tej	'same'
	pia	→	pja	'cause to drink'
	gai	→	gaj	'cow'
	ao	→	aŏ	'come (pl.)'
	dʱoa	→	dʱŏa	'cause to wash'

Table 9.20 Words illustrating contrasting labial fricatives and approximants in Urhobo

	Labialized or Labial-velar		Labiodental	
Fricative	òɣʷó	'soup'	èṽà	'monitor lizards'
Approximant	éwé	'ponds'	eʋá	'divination'

of the sound that might be symbolized using one of those symbols is actually β, in, for example, nɔβ̃ ninth'. A labiodental approximant ʋ contrasts with a labiodental fricative v in Urhobo; this language also has a labialized velar fricative ɣʷ as well as a labial-velar approximant w (Ladefoged 1968, Kelly 1969), as illustrated in table 9.20. Ladefoged (1968) had w̰ in place of ɣʷ, but we now consider Kelly (1969) to be correct. As Elugbe (1989) has pointed out, the friction is the result of the velar articulation alone.

The neighboring language, Isoko, has a similar set of contrasts. Photographs of the lip positions in three of the four possibilities are shown in figure 9.33. It may be seen that the labialized velar fricative ɣʷ in the word éɣʷé 'hoe' has a very small aperture, with the lips being tightly pressed together. The spectrogram accompanying the photograph shows that this tight constriction produced formant transitions like those in a labial-velar approximant w, but with a great decrease in the intensity of the sound, so that there is a stop-like gap without a following release burst. Unfortunately we do not have a comparable data for the labial-velar approximant, which occurs in the word ɔwa 'age-grade'. But we do have photographs of both the fricative in évé 'how' and the approximant labiodental in éʋé 'breath'. The spectrogram of the fricative shows that there is also a considerable decrease in intensity, but without the large formant transitions that occur in ɣʷ. In this particular token there is very little fricative energy apparent. The approximant has a much wider lip aperture; but, as may be seen from additional photographs in Ladefoged (1968), the aperture is not as great as that in the surrounding vowels. As the lower lip is so far from the upper teeth and the upper lip, it is not possible to say whether this sound is better classified as a bilabial approximant β̞, or a labiodental

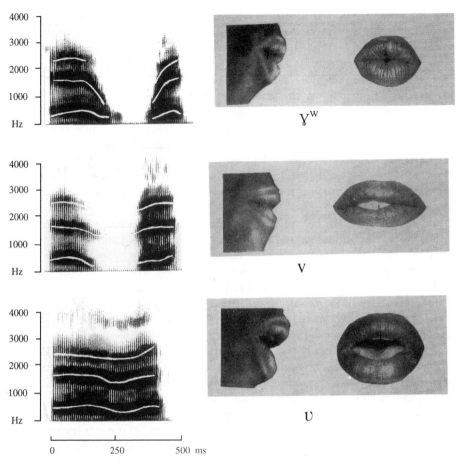

Figure 9.33 Photographs of the lips in the Isoko words ɛɣʷɛ́ 'hoe', ɛ́vɛ́ 'how' and ɛ́ʋɛ́ 'breath'. The photographs were determined to be in the middle of the consonants by observing the click of the camera shutter on a simultaneous recording. The spectrograms on the left are of repetitions of these words recorded immediately after the photographic session. Center formant frequencies have been outlined in white.

approximant ʋ. The spectrogram shows that there are smaller formant movements associated with this sound and very little diminution of amplitude.

Many of the semivowels and central approximants that we have been considering in this section also have voiceless counterparts. In addition, two sounds mentioned in the chapter on fricatives, **h** and **ɦ**, should also be discussed here. These sounds have been described as voiceless or breathy voiced counterparts of the vowels that follow them (Ladefoged 1971). But, as Keating (1988) has shown, the shape of the vocal tract during **h** or **ɦ** is often simply that of the surrounding sounds. In saying the word *ahead*, for example, there is usually a breathy voiced ɦ during which the formants are moving from those associated with ə to those associated with ɛ. Accordingly, in such cases it is more appropriate to regard **h** and **ɦ** as segments that have only a laryngeal specification, and are unmarked for all other features. There are other languages which show a more definite displacement of the formant frequencies for **h**, suggesting it has a constriction associated with its production. Laufer (1991) argues that a glottal constriction is observable in Hebrew and Arabic. A few languages contrast **h** and **ɦ**. One group of languages which does is the Masa group of Chadic languages. Sachnine (1982) gives examples of contrasts in Lame, such as **hàs** 'to cut' vs. **ɦàs** 'warmth'. A detailed study of the related language Musey is being conducted by Shryock (in progress). In this language the contrast between **h** and **ɦ** is not primarily encoded as a voicing difference. Both segments are more often than not produced with vocal fold vibration, but **ɦ** tends to have a laxer laryngeal setting and a lower fundamental frequency.

The voiceless counterparts of the central approximants **j** and **w** occur as contrastive segments in a number of languages, such as Yao (Purnell 1965), Klamath (Barker 1964) and Aleut (Bergsland 1956). They also occur in some dialects of English. Most speakers of English differentiate between words such as **ju** 'you' and what is usually transcribed as **hju** *hue*. The onset in the second word is normally a voiceless palatal approximant, j̊, for which the IPA has no unitary symbol. In some dialects (e.g. most of those spoken in Scotland), the words *weather* and *whether* contrast, the latter beginning with a non-fricative ʍ. No language that we know of contrasts a voiceless labial-velar fricative and a non-fricative ʍ, just as no language contrasts the voiceless lateral approximant l̥ and the voiceless lateral fricative ɬ as discussed in chapter 6. In addition, the voiceless counterpart of **w** cannot have friction at both the labial and velar places of articulation, as we will discuss in chapter 10, so if it is a fricative, it is better described as a voiceless labialized velar fricative. Other voiceless approximants, such as voiceless laterals are discussed in chapter 6, and voiceless rhotics in chapter 7

Summary

Finally, we will compare our findings in this chapter with those of the most comprehensive previous survey, that of Lindau (1978). We are largely in accord with respect to the major features Height and Backness, noting only that recent evidence has suggested that there may be as many as five distinctive vowel heights. Our differences on the third major feature, Rounding, are more in form than in substance. We regard Rounding as a feature that dominates both Compression and Protrusion, a possibility that was not open to Lindau before the advent of hierarchical phonological structures, although she recognized the distinction between these two types of lip action. Among the additional vowel properties, nasalization is now slightly better understood, but remains as a binary feature. We have proposed a slightly larger set of tongue body features, re-arranging Lindau's feature Expanded to allow for distinctions in ATR, Pharyngealization and Stridency, in addition to Rhotacization, which both classificatory systems include; we have not, however, found it necessary to distinguish between peripheral and non-peripheral vowels as she did. In addition we have noted further distinctions among vowels involving phonation types and variations in dynamic properties.

10

Multiple Articulatory Gestures

Most consonantal segments can be described by specifying a single oral articulatory gesture, together with its accompanying laryngeal and velic gestures. But there are a considerable number of types of sounds in which more than one articulatory gesture is employed. These sounds will be the topic of this chapter. In the traditional phonetic literature (e.g. Abercrombie 1967), a distinction is made between segments with double articulations and segments with secondary articulations. The basis of this distinction rests on the establishment of a scale of stricture, consisting of three degrees: closure, narrow approximation (such as to produce friction), and open approximation (as in an approximant or vowel). Doubly-articulated segments are those which have two simultaneous articulations of the same degree of stricture, such as two oral closures or two open approximations. When two co-occurring articulations have different degrees of stricture, the one with the greater stricture is labeled primary and the lesser one is labeled secondary. This traditional terminology allows for doubly-articulated fricatives, and for a fricative to be the secondary articulation accompanying a stop. We will argue below that the world's languages do not use segments that combine two fricative elements, and that secondary articulations are actually always approximant-like. Moreover, we will suggest that doubly-articulated approximants, such as [w], are not really parallel to segments with two closures, which is why they were discussed in the chapter on vowels and approximants. This leaves two major classes of segments with multiple gestures: stops and nasals with two closures, and stops, nasals, liquids and fricatives with an approximant secondary articulation. The basic framework of this chapter is to deal with these in turn, together with the issues that arise.

10.1 Preliminary Considerations

Before proceeding, however, it should be stressed that this chapter is only concerned with categorizing segments in which there are multiple articulations that are effectively simultaneous from the phonetic point of view. By this, we mean that the onsets and the offsets of the articulatory gestures are timed to occur very closely together, and that they may only be produced with this close timing pattern. There are many additional types of complex phonetic events that have been considered at one time or another to be single segments because of phonological considerations, but which are articulatory sequences from the phonetic point of view. That is, one of the articulations leads or lags behind the other by a substantial part of the total time required for their production. These phonetic events are not distinguishable from events which would be accepted as segment sequences in another language that lacked the phonological pattern to motivate their interpretation as single segments. Some of these sequences will be referred to in the course of the chapter in order to clarify what kinds of segments we consider to have phonetic simultaneity.

This chapter is also not concerned with the many situations in which different gestures show degrees of coarticulation and coproduction as part of the regular concatenation of speech sounds. The velar and alveolar articulations in an English word such as *cactus* overlap in time so that the release of the velar closure produces no audible sound; the lip rounding of a rounded vowel in Swedish is anticipated throughout a preceding consonant cluster, producing phonetically labialized clusters (McAllister 1978). However, alveolar-velar doubly-articulated plosives are not part of the phonological inventory of English; rather they are part of a characteristic production strategy by which abutting plosives with different places of articulation both word-internally and across word-boundaries are overlapped in this fashion (Byrd 1994). The degree of this overlap is highly variable, unlike the relatively invariable timing observed between the articulations in multiply-articulated single segments. Similarly, the anticipation of rounding in Swedish is part of a production strategy, rather than a feature that enlarges the contrastive possibilities in the language.

The other preliminary matter to be considered concerns the possibility of multiply-articulated fricatives. It is clear that generation of audible friction at two different locations in the oral cavity at the same time is very difficult. As noted in chapter 3, a fricative requires a more precise adjustment of the articulators than a stop or an approximant. The size of the inter-articulator aperture and the velocity of the airflow must be within critical limits for friction to be generated. To achieve two of these critical adjustments at the same time, especially when the flow requirements might be different for different places, is obviously problematical. From the auditory point of view, even if two sources of friction exist, the one further forward in the mouth is very likely to mask the acoustic effect of the more rearward one. Doubly-articulated fricatives would therefore seem to be linguistically undesirable segments; they are hard to produce and poorly distinctive. Nonetheless, in a small number of languages it has been claimed that such segments do occur. We have examined some of these cases and found them to be instances of either fricative segments with a secondary articulation, or instances of a sequence of two fricatives that has been interpreted as a single segment for phonological reasons.

The most well-known case is the Swedish segment that has been described as a doubly-articulated voiceless palato-alveolar-velar fricative, i.e.ʃ͡x. The IPA even goes so far as to provide a separate symbol for this sound on its chart, namely ɧ. The sound in question is one variant of the pronunciation of the phonological element ʃ, which is highly variable in Swedish dialects, receiving pronunciations ranging from a palatalized bilabial sound to a velarized palato-alveolar one to a fully velar one. As we showed in chapter 5 it is not clear that any of the variants is actually a doubly-articulated fricative.

Another similar example is mentioned by Catford (1977a). He reports that the bilabial-palatal fricatives ɸ͡ç, β͡ʝ occur in Abkhaz. He notes, of doubly-articulated fricatives in general, that "it is often somewhat difficult to discern whether there actually is turbulent (fricative) air-flow at each of the two stricture locations" (p. 190). Concerning the Abkhaz sounds specifically, he notes that although one may choose to regard them as coordinate fricative articulations, the "impression from hearing two or three speakers of each dialect, is that in the Abzhui (literary) dialect of Abkhaz the labial articulation dominates somewhat – generating stronger turbulence – whereas in the Bzyb dialect the palatal articulation is somewhat dominant." (p. 191).

We have heard recordings of a speaker of each of these dialects and to our ears the sounds in question sound like labialized palato-alveolars, with frication only from the palatal stricture. The two dialects do differ. In Literary Abkhaz there are extended slow rising F1 and F2 transitions from the fricative to the following vowel of the sort that are typical of a w-like secondary articulation accompanying a consonant release. On the other hand, in the Bzyb dialect, the formant transitions are less extensive in duration and in frequency range, and more symmetrical between consonant onset and release, as illustrated in figure 10.1. We believe this is the result of just rounding the lips without any accompanying raising of the back of the tongue. A major effect is to reduce the frequency range of the fricative energy generated at the post-alveolar constriction as it passes through the narrowed labial aperture in front. In neither case do there seem to be two sources of frication; rather, there is one post-alveolar fricative source accompanied by one of two different types of accompanying secondary articulation. The distinction between these two types of labialization is discussed further in section 10.3.

A case where there are clearly two separate sources of friction is found in SePedi (Northern Sotho). Lombard (1985) transcribes the segments f͡s, f͡ʃ, β͡ʒ in words such as βofsa 'youth', lefʃeːra 'coward' and β͡ʒalwa 'beer' and describes

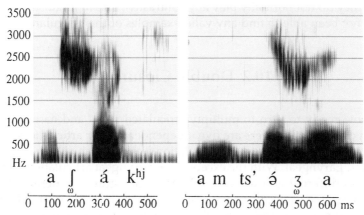

Figure 10.1 Abkhaz "bilabial-palatal" fricatives in the words **aʃakʰʲ** and **amts'əʒa** spoken by a male speaker of the Bzyb dialect.

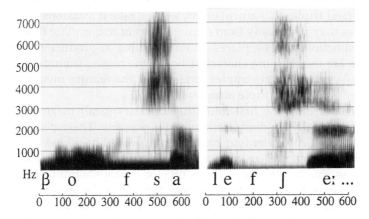

Figure 10.2 Spectrograms of the SePedi words **βofsa** 'youth' and **lefʃeːra** 'coward' spoken by a male speaker.

them as labiodental-alveolar, labiodental-prepalatal and bilabial-prepalatal fricatives respectively. Because of the lack of other sequences in SePedi and the restrictions on their distribution, this description may be appropriate in phonological terms. However, as the spectrograms in figure 10.2 demonstrate, these are phonetic sequences. One articulation follows the other, so that for example, SePedi **fs** is not very different from the **fs** in an English word like *offset*. The phonetic description given, namely, that they have two simultaneous fricative articulations, is incorrect. Another similar case is discussed in connection with 'labiodentalization' as a secondary articulation below. Although doubly-articulated fricatives are not impossible to produce, we suspect that they do not normally play any contrastive role in linguistic phonetics. We have not been able to find any valid examples of their regular occurrence.

10.2 Double Closures

We are now ready to turn to multiply-articulated stops and nasals. We have argued in chapter 2 that there are five independent major articulators and, correspondingly, five major place of articulation features, Labial, Coronal, Dorsal, Radical and Laryngeal. With the exception of Laryngeal articulations, there are a number of different gestural possibilities in each grouping defined by these major features. For example, Labial gestures may be bilabial or labiodental and Coronal gestures may be linguo-labial, dental, alveolar or post-alveolar, as well as being apical, laminal or sub-apical. The features that control these variations are subordinate to the major place features, as indicated in table 2.11. For double (and triple, etc.) articulations, we will take it as axiomatic that multiple gestures may result only from combinations of major place features. Subordinate distinctions among places do not combine to produce multiple gestures. These are the defining characteristics of the major/subordinate distinction and apparent counterexamples require that the feature inventory be adjusted rather than the principle abandoned.

If we consider only the first four (the supralaryngeal) major articulators, there are theoretically six double articulations possible. These possibilities are listed in table 10.1. A further four combinations would be added to the total if pairings of a supraglottal articulator with a Laryngeal articulation were included. These involve the production of glottal stops simultaneously with other articulations. In these cases, however, the role of the larynx as a place of articulation needs to be considered in relation to its role as the initiator of an airstream or as a modification of the phonation, as discussed in other chapters. We will not consider supraglottal-glottal combinations any further here. We will exemplify all those combinations in table 10.1 which we know to occur in languages, and consider if the patterns of occurrence and non-occurrence provide a basis for proposing that the number of such combinations is restricted.

Table 10.1 Possible pairings of major supraglottal articulators

LABIAL-CORONAL		
LABIAL-DORSAL	CORONAL-DORSAL	
LABIAL-RADICAL	CORONAL-RADICAL	DORSAL-RADICAL

Labial-Dorsals

We will deal first with Labial-Dorsal combinations, since by far the most common double stop articulation is a bilabial and velar one. Languages with bilabial-velar stops are especially common in West Africa and northern Central Africa, where they occur in several different families. Idoma, Yoruba, Gwandara, Logbara and many other African languages exemplify the Labial-Dorsal category of table 10.1. Sounds of this type are also found in several New Guinea languages, such as Kate, Ono, Mape, Dedua and Yeletnye. Examples from Idoma are given in table 10.2.

Doubly-articulated stops and nasals have durations comparable to those of stops and nasals with single articulations. This is an important factor in their recognition as single sounds. Measurements of the acoustically determined closure duration of g͡b, k͡p and b in Yoruba are given in table 10.3. In another smaller data set, duration of simple k was measured as 134 ms. In these data there is no significant difference between the duration of g͡b and b; k͡p is significantly longer than both g͡b and b ($p < 0.01$) but by little more than is often found for voiceless stops compared to voiced ones.

The closure durations of bilabial, velar and labial-velar stops in Ewe, measured from the acoustic waveform displays of ten tokens each, are shown in table 10.4. Here velar stops are shorter than bilabial ones, and labial-velars are 25–30 ms longer than bilabials.

Table 10.2 Bilabial-velar sounds in Idoma

VOICELESS STOP	àk͡pà	'bridge'
VOICED STOP	àg͡bà	'jaw'
VOICED NASAL	aŋmàa	'body painting'

Table 10.3 Durations of g͡b, k͡p and b in Yoruba (two repetitions of nine words each, matched for vowels and tones)

	g͡b	b	k͡p
MEAN DURATION	132	128	148
STANDARD DEVIATION	12.5	17.6	16.5

Table 10.4 Mean closure durations of Ewe bilabial, velar and labial-velar stops in aCa context (ten repetitions from one speaker)

	VOICELESS		VOICED	
VELAR	k	142	g	133
BILABIAL	p	158	b	150
LABIAL-VELAR	k͡p	174	g͡b	179

Table 10.5 Labial, velar and labial-velar stops and clusters in Eggon (tones omitted)

SINGLE SEGMENTS

pom	abu	aku	gom	k͡pu	g͡bu
'pound (v.)'	'dog'	'room'	'break'	'die'	'arrive'

SEQUENCES

kba	g͡bga	ak͡pki	bga	kpu	gba
'dig'	'grind'	'stomach'	'beat, kill'	'kneel'	'divide'

Clusters typically have from one and a half to two times the duration of single segments of comparable type (Haggard 1973, Hardcastle and Roach 1977, Catford 1977a), even when their articulations partially overlap in time, as would usually be the case for stop sequences in English in words such as *actor* or *aptly*. Thus, doubly-articulated stops are shorter than segment sequences. Very few languages include both complex labial-velar stops and sequences of juxtaposed labial and velar stops, but one which does is Eggon (Maddieson 1981, Sibomana 1985). This language even includes sequences combining a labial-velar with a labial or velar stop, as the examples in table 10.5 show.

Unlike in English, in Eggon the first member of a stop cluster is clearly released; hence the clusters are easily distinguished from simple stops. In cases where labials, velars and labial-velars are involved the second member of the cluster is frequently lenited in more relaxed speech. Note that lenition does not occur in clusters containing alveolars (e.g. in the words **atku** 'calabash', **odga** 'leg'), suggesting that this may be a further strategy for marking the potentially ambiguous clusters. These features may be seen in the words illustrated in the spectrograms in figure 10.3 which include examples of both doubly-articulated consonants and clusters. Whereas only a single stop release is seen in the words **ok͡pu** and **ag͡bu**, the separate release of the stops in a sequence can be clearly seen in the remaining words. When the sequence is voiced, the release between them has the character of a short vowel-like segment, but there is no contrast of quality in this segment.

Their briefer duration disambiguates labial-velars from sequences but, of course, does not distinguish them from single articulations. However, in a great majority of cases the complex nature of labial-velar articulation is clearly detectable by auditory/acoustic means. In the majority of intervocalic labial-velar stops we have heard, the dominant auditory impression of the transition from preceding vowel to stop is of a velar closure, while the dominant auditory impression of the transition from stop to following vowel is of a labial release. (We do not think that it is an accident that these sounds are normally transcribed as k͡p, g͡b rather than p͡k, b͡g.) The impression is that the velar articulation leads the labial one by a brief time, and is released shortly before the labial one too, so that labial characteristics dominate the release. Note that if the duration of one articulation was contained within the duration of the other,

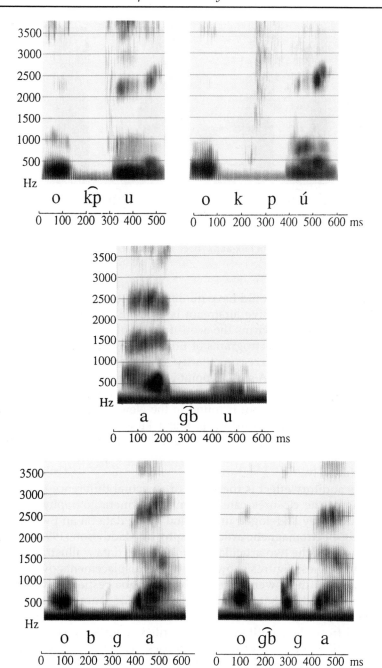

Figure 10.3 Spectrograms of words containing k͡p, g͡b, kp, bg and g͡bg in Eggon.

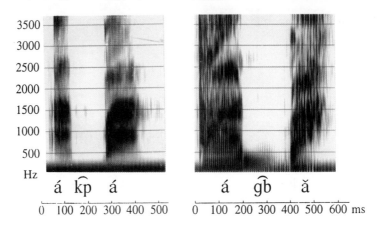

Figure 10.4 Spectrograms of k͡p in Efik **ák͡pá** 'river' and g͡b in Logbara **à g͡bǎ** 'I hit'.

the shorter articulation would have minimal acoustic consequences (assuming a simple pulmonic egressive airstream is used). Examination of data from a number of languages confirms the acoustic basis of our auditory impressions. As can be seen in the spectrograms of Efik and Logbara in figure 10.4, the labial-velar closure does have a similarity to a velar one while its release has similarity to a labial one. A similar point is made concerning Ibibio by Connell (1987). This feature is typical not just of the well-known West African languages with labial-velars, but is found in the New Guinea languages as well. Examples from Dedua contrasting **p**, **k** and k͡p are given in figure 10.5. This figure also includes spectra of a window centered on the release burst, enabling the acoustic similarity of the k͡p release to the **p** release to be seen even more persuasively.

That this auditory effect is the result of an actual difference in the articulatory timing of the closures can be seen from cineradiography of an Idoma speaker studied by Ladefoged in 1962 and in the data on an Ewe speaker obtained using electromagnetic articulography by Maddieson (1993). The temporal asymmetry of the two articulations in the Ewe data is illustrated in figures 10.6 and 10.7. These figures show the vertical displacements over time of the tongue back and the lower lip for **akp͡a** and **ag͡ba** respectively. The vertical scale is normalized so that comparisons can be made more easily between the two movements. The time scale is relative to the release of the labial closure, as determined from the simultaneously recorded acoustic waveforms. For both **akp͡a** and **ag͡ba** the raising of the tongue back occurs faster and peaks earlier than the raising of the lower lip. As the first movement upward of both articulators coincides closely, asymmetry of the closures appears to be achieved by making the upward movement of the lip slower than its downward movement.

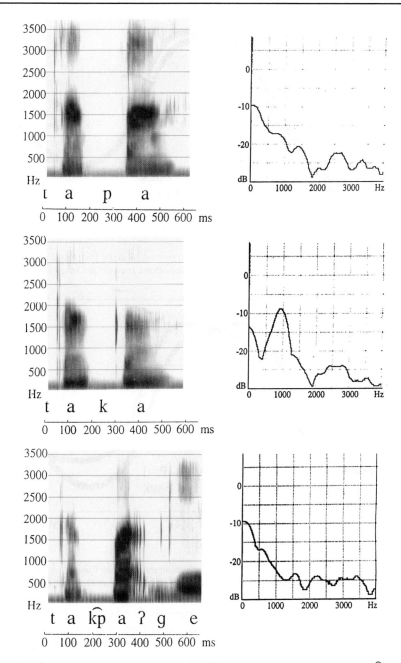

Figure 10.5 Spectrograms and stop burst spectra of Dedua words contrasting **p**, **k** and **k͡p**.

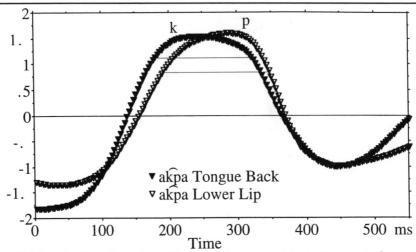

Figure 10.6 Coordination of lower lip and tongue back movements in the Ewe word **ak͡pa** (vertical displacement, normalized scale expressed in standard deviations, mean of ten tokens aligned at release).

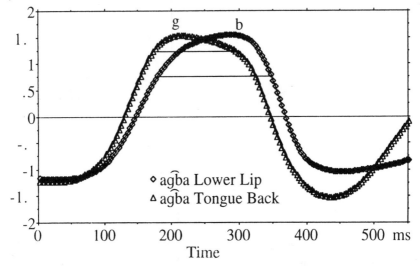

Figure 10.7 Coordination of lower lip and tongue back movements in the Ewe word **ag͡ba** (vertical displacement, normalized scale expressed in standard deviations, mean of ten tokens aligned at release).

In both figures 10.6 and 10.7, the consonant release is at 350 ms. Two horizontal lines have been drawn on these figures. One connects the lower lip height at the time of release on the labial movement trajectory to the preceding point at the same height on the closing phase of the lip movement. A similar line connects the tongue back height at the mean time of onset of closure (from table 10.4) to the following point with the same height on the downward trajectory of the tongue back. These lines visualize the likely durations of contact.

Table 10.6 Estimates of closure duration and timing offsets in labial-velars (in ms)

	ak͡pa	ag͡ba
ESTIMATED DURATION OF VELAR CLOSURE	148	130
ESTIMATED DURATION OF LABIAL CLOSURE	164	174
OFFSET BETWEEN CLOSURES	10	5
OFFSET BETWEEN RELEASES	26	49
NET OFFSET	16	44

More precise estimates of the closure durations of the velar and labial components of the labial-velar stops are given in table 10.6. These were obtained in
the following way. For the labial closure durations, the time point with the
nearest articulator height to the height at labial release on the upward lower lip
movement was subtracted from the release time. For the velar closure the
mean time at closure was subtracted from the time point with the nearest
height to the height at closure on the downward movement of the tongue back.

  These estimates have a number of sources of error, including the basic assumption that closure and release occur at similar heights of the articulators.
The plausibility of this assumption is supported by comparison between the
height at closure onset and at release of simple bilabial and velar stops, where
the time of both onset and release of closure are known from the acoustic
records. For each of the four comparisons between onset and release height in
the set **apaa, abaa, aka** and **aga** there is less than 1 mm difference; the difference
between one sample point and the next in these phases of the movement tracks
is typically over 0.5 mm. (The movement data is sampled about every 3 ms.)
Comparison of the data in tables 10.5 and 10.6 shows that three of the four
estimated closure durations for the component articulations in labial-velars
are very similar to the durations of Ewe simple bilabial and velar stops of the
same voicing category. The differences are 6 ms or less. The exception is the
considerably longer duration of the estimated labial closure in g͡b compared
with the measured duration of **b** (174 vs 150 ms). This extends the offset between the velar and labial releases in g͡b.

  Connell's multi-speaker study of Ibibio suggests that the mean total duration for k͡p of about 160 ms can be interpreted as a standard closure duration
plus the slight asynchrony of the velar and labial articulations. That is, k͡p duration is the sum of the duration of **p**, measured as about 138 ms, plus the
amount of time by which the velar articulation leads the labial one, which he
estimates at 20 ms.

  These timing features would seem to be sufficient to distinguish labial-velars
from labial + velar sequences on the one hand and from simple labial or velar
stops on the other. However, as Ladefoged (1968) showed, there are frequently

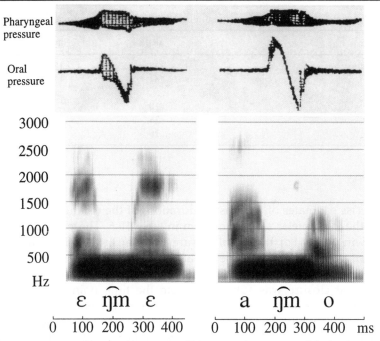

Figure 10.8 Pressure records and spectrograms of Idoma words containing labial-velar nasals with oral pressure reduction.

also aerodynamic features which distinguish labial-velars from singly-articulated stops or nasals. Ladefoged, using a system which measured air pressure in the oral and pharyngeal cavities, observed types of labial-velar stops during whose production the air pressure in the oral cavity is reduced. He concluded that a velaric ingressive airstream was involved. He also observed labial-velar nasals in which there is rarefaction of the air in the oral cavity while pulmonic air continues to pass through the velo-pharyngeal port behind the velar closure. Figure 10.8. shows pressure records and spectrograms of tokens from Idoma in which pressure reduction occurred. These too were described as having a velaric ingressive airstream.

We now feel that some of these descriptions might be rephrased in order to avoid the possibly misleading implication that these sounds are made in the same way as clicks. Let us first consider labial-velar nasals of the Idoma type. These have a bilabial closure and voiced pulmonic air flowing out through the nose. If they are also straightforwardly described as being produced with the velaric airstream mechanism, then they are effectively equated with nasalized bilabial clicks such as occur in !Xóõ. Yet they are clearly a different sound altogether, principally because they lack the salient burst of a click and are acoustically predominantly resonant in character. The spectrograms of Idoma ŋ͡m in

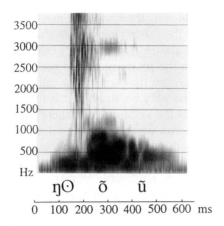

3500
3000
2500
2000
1500
1000
500
Hz

ŋʘ   õ   ũ

0 100 200 300 400 500 600 ms

Figure 10.9 Spectrogram illustrating a nasalized bilabial click in ǂHóã̃.

figure 10.8 can be compared with ǂHóã̃ ŋ͡ʘ in figure 10.9. In addition to the acoustic differences observed between these two types of sounds, differences in the aerodynamic patterns can also be noted. In Idoma ŋ͡m the air pressure in the oral cavity often rises initially. Since this is a nasal, we can be fairly certain that this is because the air volume between the velar and labial closures is being compressed as the jaw and the tongue dorsum continues to rise, reducing the size of the cavity between the closures. An oral pressure rise *could* occur as a result of pulmonic air pressure if the labial closure was formed before the velar closure, but only if the nasal passage remained closed until after the labial closure had been formed. Otherwise the pulmonic air would escape through the nose and there would be no pressure build-up in the oral cavity. Thus if the oral pressure increase was due to pulmonic air we would observe two additional features; first, there would be a simultaneous rise in pharyngeal pressure (since pulmonic air would only reach the oral cavity if the oral and pharyngeal cavities are not divided into two separate chambers by a closure at the velum); second, when the nasal escape was initiated there would be burst-like release of pressure through the nose. Neither the aerodynamic nor the acoustic records of Idoma support the view that the oral pressure increase can be due to pulmonic pressure, since these phenomena are absent.

In the nasals we are examining, following the oral pressure increase, the air pressure is then reduced as the cavity expands with the lowering of the tongue, sometimes reaching a level below atmospheric pressure, as in the two tokens in figure 10.8, but sometimes only reaching equality with atmospheric pressure, as in other tokens in the same data set. On the other hand, in ŋ͡ʘ there is always substantial oral cavity expansion (see the discussion relating to figures 10.15 and 10.16 below, and compare chapter 8), creating greater negative pressure. The difference in timing between the two closure releases in ŋ͡m and ŋ͡ʘ also contributes to their acoustic dissimilarity. In ŋ͡m the velar release typically precedes the labial one and so the oral air pressure, which is reduced as the tongue initiates its lowering gesture, is equalized or is on its way to equalization with the pharyngeal and nasal air pressure before the labial release occurs. Consequently there is typically no ingressive oral airflow. Although the velar release may be audible, it is not acoustically strong. In ŋ͡ʘ the labial release precedes the velar one and there is oral inflow with a definite acoustic effect. In the Idoma doubly-articulated nasals, it may be that the reduction in oral air pressure should be viewed as a by-product of the double articulation, whereas in production of ŋ͡ʘ (or any other click) rarefaction of the oral air is essential. It seems preferable to reserve the term 'velaric airstream mechanism' for the latter kind of situation, and to merely note the presence of an 'oral pressure reduction' in the other.

Since the articulatory gesture appears the same in the stops and nasals, the same rephrasing should apply to Idoma labial-velar stops, as well as many of those from Yoruba, Edo and other languages, described in Ladefoged (1968) as being produced with both the pulmonic egressive and velaric ingressive airstream mechanisms. Oral and pharyngeal pressure records of three repetitions of the words ɔk͡pa and ik͡pa extracted from an Edo sentence are shown in figure 10.10. A striking fact is the difference between the two words in the oral pressure records. Following work by Silverman and Jun (1994) on coarticulated **k** + **p** sequences in Korean, we now have an explanation for differences of this type. They are due to interactions between the differing movements required for the vowel sequences in these words and the overlapping consonantal gestures. In ɔk͡pa there is initially an increase in oral pressure, which then declines to a slightly or strongly negative value before the release. In the third repetition the increase in pharyngeal pressure substantially leads the increase in the oral pressure, confirming that the velar closure leads the labial one here and leading to the inference that the oral pressure rise is due to jaw and tongue movement. In ik͡pa on the other hand there is miminal or no oral pressure increase initially, suggesting that upward movement of the jaw and tongue is completed before labial closure occurs, and, at a later point, consistently strong negative oral pressure. The retraction of the tongue involved in passing from the **i** to **a** may account for a substantial part of this rarefaction. The timing of release is harder to read from these records. In ik͡pa the return to positive oral pressure before release probably indicates that the velar closure has been released before labial release, allowing the positive pharyngeal pressure to spread into the oral cavity. In this case there will of course be a burst, but one that is not click-like in nature. In other tokens the fall in pharyngeal air pressure and the rise from negative oral air pressure seem to be coextensive in time. This may be because the closures are released more or less simultaneously.

The situation is different when a labial-velar stop articulation is accompanied by downward movement of the larynx. Larynx lowering was inferred from the rarefaction of air in the pharyngeal cavity, observed consistently in

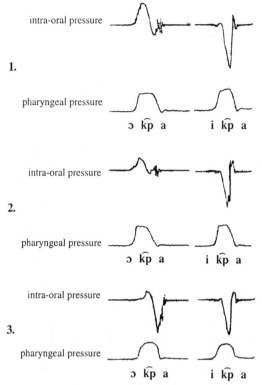

Figure 10.10 Aerodynamic records of the words ɔk͡pa and ik͡pa extracted from three repetitions of an Edo sentence.

both k͡p and g͡b in Idoma by Ladefoged (1968). Larynx lowering might also be contributing to the decay of pharyngeal pressure build-up in some of the Edo stops shown in figure 10.10. Connell (1987) observed substantial inward air-flow, accompanied by pre-voicing, in Ibibio k͡p. Both these features are consist-ent with use of a glottalic airstream. Hence, in some languages at least it seems appropriate to 'talk of labial-velar implosives, although these do not contrast with labial-velar plosives. (Recall that the Central Igbo labial implosives dis-cussed in chapter 3 are derived from labial-velar plosive segments.) Other languages in which an inward airflow occurs with the labial release seem likely also to be using a glottalic ingressive airstream mechanism if the velar closure leads the labial one in the usual fashion.

Other Doubly-articulated Closures

Although Labial-Dorsal sounds are relatively common, it is much rarer to find languages combining a bilabial closure with anything other than a velar one.

Some languages have been reported with Labial-Coronal sounds; t͡p occurs as an allophone of k͡p in Dagbani (Wilson and Bendor-Samuel 1969, Ladefoged 1968) and in Nzema (Chinebuah 1963), and as a variant of **tʷ** for at least some speakers of Abkhaz (Catford 1972) and Lak (Khaidakov 1966). Here Catford describes the labial contact as 'light'; moreover, in these Caucasian cases the labial component involves considerable forward protrusion of the lips and the contact is between the inner surfaces. Photographs taken by Catford show this is quite different from the normal contact for **p**, and it might be more justifiable to consider this gesture as phonetically a secondary articulation, since it seems related to lip rounding. Two Chadic languages frequently cited as having labial-alveolars, Margi and Bura (Hoffman 1963, Ladefoged 1968, Halle 1983), on closer examination prove to have labial + alveolar sequences rather than double articulations (Maddieson 1983, 1987). For example, **bd** is considerably longer than **b** or **d**. Moreover, a labial release can be detected well before the alveolar one.

In view of these findings, Maddieson (1983) expressed doubts about whether contrastive labial-alveolar segments occurred in any language and proposed that the only true double articulations are labial-velar ones. However, phonemic segments with simultaneous bilabial and alveolar closures do occur in Yeletnye, spoken on Rossel Island, Papua New Guinea. This language has plosives and nasals at bilabial, front alveolar, slightly post-alveolar and velar positions. Bilabial articulation can co-occur with the three other places, producing bilabial-alveolar, bilabial-post-alveolar and bilabial-velar stops and nasals. Examples are given in table 10.7 based on our own fieldwork, with

Table 10.7 Single and double articulations in Yeletnye

	BILABIAL	ALVEOLAR	POST-ALVEOLAR	VELAR
VOICELESS STOP	**paa** 'side'	**taa** 'knife'	**ʈoo** 'tongue'	**kaa** 'spear'
PRENASALIZED VOICED STOP	**mbee** 'carry'	**nde** 'food'	**ɳɖe** 'firewood'	**ŋkaa** '(tree)'
VOICED NASAL	**maa** 'road'	**nii** 'juice'	**ɳaa** 'feast'	**ŋa** 'lease'

	LABIAL-ALVEOLAR	LABIAL-POST-ALVEOLAR	LABIAL-VELAR
VOICELESS STOP	t͡pənə 'lung'	ʈ͡pənə 'horn'	k͡pene 'coconut bag'
PRENASALIZED VOICED STOP	n͡md͡boo 'pulp'	ɳ͡md͡boo 'many'	ŋ͡mg͡bo 'fog'
VOICED NASAL	n͡mo 'bird'	ɳ͡mo 'we'	ŋ͡mo 'breast'

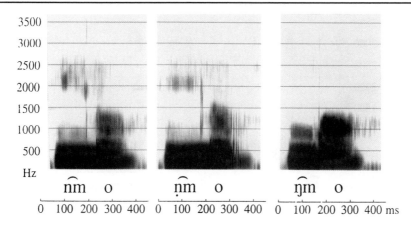

Figure 10.11 Spectrograms of the three Yeletnye doubly-articulated nasals in the words on the last row of table 10.7 as spoken by a female speaker.

some additional words taken from Henderson and Henderson (1987). Prenasalized examples are included in this table. The language also has a full series of nasally released stops including at least two of these double places of articulation (see chapter 4).

Spectrograms illustrating the three doubly-articulated nasals are given in figure 10.11. In these spectrograms, which represent careful citation forms of these words, the effects of separate releases of the two closures can be seen in each case. This is because these are nasals. As the more rearward closure is released, a transient is produced and the resonance characteristics of the cavity in front of the nasal escape are altered. Note that this result would not occur if the labial closure was the first to be released, since this would leave the shape of the cavity which gives the nasal its characteristic quality unchanged. Spectrograms of the three doubly-articulated stops are given in figure 10.12.

We are not aware of any language which has plosive or nasal sounds involving simultaneous Coronal and Dorsal articulation, such as alveolar-velars. Some accounts of Kinyarwanda and of certain dialects of Shona have been interpreted as indicating the occurrence of segments such as t͡k, d͡g. Although phonological arguments can be marshalled in favor of treating these events as single segments (Sagey 1986, 1990), they are phonetically quite unambiguous. They are sequences of two stops. This point is made by Jouannet (1983) for Kinyarwanda and can be shown in our own data from the Zezuru dialect of Shona (Maddieson 1990b). Figure 10.13 shows audio waveforms and records of the pressure of the air in the mouth behind an alveolar closure but in front of a velar closure during the phrase **tkwana tkwangu** 'my little child'. The release of **t** preceding **k** can be clearly seen, both in the acoustic record and in the fact that the intra-oral pressure, sensed in a location between the alveolar and the

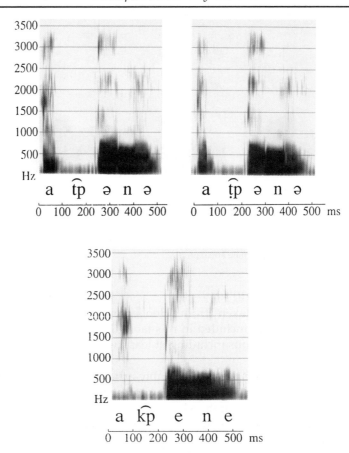

Figure 10.12 Spectrograms illustrating the three Yeletnye doubly-articulated plosives in stem-initial position of nouns preceded by the first person singular possessive prefix **a-**.

velar closures, falls well before the burst for the velar release. The alveolar and velar closures do not overlap at all.

Dental-palatal articulations occur in some dialects of Isoko (Elugbe 1989) and have also been reported in some Australian languages, such as Maung (Capell and Hinch 1970). Most dialects of Isoko have laminal dental plosives and nasals contrasting with apical alveolar plosives and nasals as exemplified in chapter 2. But Elugbe notes that in some dialects the laminal dentals are realized with two simultaneous articulatory contacts, one in the dental and one in the palatal region. We regard these sounds, which do not contrast with either dental or palatal sounds, as having accidental contacts in two articulatory regions, rather than as having double articulations. The dental-palatal segments reported in Australian languages are variants of the laminal post-

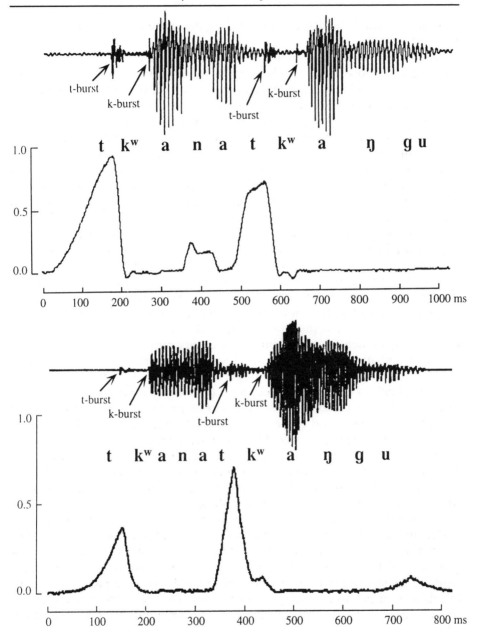

Figure 10.13 Waveforms and intra-oral pressure records of **tk** cluster in Shona from two male speakers. The pressure records are calibrated in terms of the speaker's maximum (= 1).

alveolars with an extended closure covering the entire region from the teeth to the hard palate.

Thus, if we restrict our attention to sounds made with the pulmonic airstream and to those which involve only the most commonly used articulatory regions – Labial, Coronal and Dorsal – the pattern of permitted combinations of articulatory closures is that only a Labial articulation occurs with one at another place; and we know of only one language, Yeletnye, in which the combination is anything other than labial-velar at the phonological level.

This limitation is significant, but it should not be taken as evidence that other combinations are absent from human languages. As Halle (1983) suggests, the Coronal-Dorsal combination that might be expected from the articulatory independence of the tongue tip/blade and tongue body is to be found in click articulations. Clicks, of course, require a double closure for their production. However, the place of articulation given for a click has traditionally referred only to the location of the front closure, and the back closure has not been considered as a place of articulation. The velar closure involved in producing a click is usually regarded by phoneticians solely as the basis of the airstream mechanism employed, hence the name velaric airstream mechanism (Pike 1943). We believe that this view is mistaken in that it allocates only one role to the back closure. The distinction drawn in chapter 8 between click type and click accompaniment is convenient for expository purposes, but the expository device of conflating several properties together as an 'accompaniment' should not be taken as indicating that the properties cannot be separated. We take the view that Halle is correct and clicks have (at least) two places of articulation, one of which is provided by the back closure. A precursor of this point of view is found in Chomsky and Halle (1968: 319), who argued that clicks are stops produced with 'extreme velarization' and assigned the features [+high, +back] to them. These features are shared by velar and velarized sounds in the SPE scheme, and so clicks are described as velar in place. The one argument cited by Chomsky and Halle for their view is that in Nama the back closure can vary in its manner of release, and that the resulting abrupt versus affricated contrast is an articulatory difference. There are at least two other points that can be added. In Bantu languages with clicks, such as Zulu and Xhosa, nasal + stop clusters must be homorganic. Prefixes which contain a final nasal undergo a place assimilation rule when the nasal abuts a stop (or almost any other consonant). When such a prefix abuts a click, the nasal is not assimilated to the dental, alveolar or palato-alveolar place of the front closure of the click but rather to the velar place (Doke 1926: 78). Illustrative examples from Zulu are given in table 10.8.

Doke argues that before a click "with the back of the tongue touching the velum . . . the nasal homorganic to the clicks must be the pure velar nasal ŋ." While it is true that when a nasal is *simultaneously* articulated with a click the effective closure for that nasal must be the back closure for the click, it is important to note that a nasal *preceding* a click need not necessarily be produced

Table 10.8 Nasal assimilation in Zulu noun class prefix izin-

	SINGULAR	PLURAL	
PLOSIVES	u-pʰapʰɛ	izim-papʰɛ	'feather(s)'
	u-tʰi	izin-ti	'stick(s)'
	u-gu	iziŋ-gu	'river-bank(s)'
CLICKS	u-k|ʰuʃela	iziŋ-k|uʃela	'sharp instrument(s)'
	u-k!ʰududu	iziŋ-k!ududu	'tall careless person(s)'
	u-k‖ʰuʃela	iziŋ-k‖uʃela	'sharp instrument(s)'

with a velar articulation. The velar closure could be formed later than the front closure, i.e. not until the click itself is being produced. Given what actually happens, it is clear that the velar closure is not acting solely as the initiator of the airstream for the click but is also functioning as a place of articulation whose influence spreads to the adjacent pulmonic nasal segment.

The second additional argument is based on the contrast that occurs in some of the Khoisan languages, such as !Xóõ, ǂHóã and ‖Ani, where the back closure itself may differ in place, being either velar or uvular. Contrasts from !Xóõ have been illustrated in table 8.4 above. Not only does !Xóõ have contrasting velar and uvular accompaniments to the clicks, but the language also contrasts abrupt with affricated release of the back closure in the velar place. Hence, the back closure in clicks is an articulatory gesture, with contrasts in both place and manner dimensions, even though it also forms the basis of the airstream mechanism. Since the back closure of a click must be viewed as parallel to place of articulation features in other segments, we may confirm that Coronal-Dorsal double articulations occur, since they are commonly found in clicks. We will mention clicks again when we turn to discussion of sounds with three simultaneous articulations.

Our treatment in chapter 2 of the tongue root and epiglottis as another major articulatory region suggest the possibility of double articulations combining a Radical articulation with one at the Labial, Coronal or Dorsal positions. However, within the terms of our present discussion – limited to closure articulations – very few cases would be expected. Recall that nasals with Radical articulations are not possible and stops are rare. Given that double articulations are themselves uncommon, the chances of a Radical articulation co-occurring with another closure would therefore seem to be very slight. Though there are a number of well-known languages, such as Arabic and Ubykh, with stops that are produced with an accompanying secondary constriction of the pharynx, we know of no language which has a doubly-articulated stop including a Radical closure. It does not seem improbable that, through an intensification of the pharyngeal articulation accompanying an alveolar stop (as in Arabic) or a bilabial or uvular one (as in Ubykh), a language could develop

Labial-Radical, Coronal-Radical or Dorsal-Radical stops. The fact that we do not know of a language which has done so does not provide a basis for ruling out the possibility.

Triple Stop and Nasal Articulations

Although he did not know of an example, Halle (1983) anticipated that triply-articulated Labial-Coronal-Dorsal segments would be found. With the addition of Radical (not to mention Glottal) to the list of major articulators, the list of conceivable triple combinations increases. However, we do not know of any linguistically contrastive segment which is regularly produced with a triple closure, and we would argue that none should be expected. This expectation has to do with how the presence of multiple articulations can be perceived. Recall that in the case of a double articulation on the pulmonic airstream, onsets and releases of the two closures are usually not exactly coterminous but slightly staggered, as indicated schematically in figure 10.14 (a). For example, in a labial-velar stop, formation of the velar closure fractionally precedes the labial one and the labial one is released fractionally after the velar one. This enables different transitional cues to be heard at the onset and offset of such segments and these reveal that the segment has a complex articulation. If, say, the velar closure was both formed earlier than and released later than the labial one, only velar transitions would be apparent. On the other hand, in a click the back closure is usually formed before and is always released after the front closure, as shown in figure 10.14 (b). In this case the front closure *must* be released first in order for the velaric suction mechanism to produce an audible burst. This release produces the place cues relating to the front closure of the click. The place of the back closure is perceived because of cues that are carried in the pulmonic (or glottalic) airflow that surrounds the click articulation. The two places involved are perceived because their cues are carried in two separate airstreams. Hence in both these types of doubly-articulated segments the two contributing closures can be readily perceived from separate cues.

Now, consider what would happen if three closures were involved. The onsets of the three closures can be staggered, but this strategy does not produce a clear indication of the complex articulation involved. When only pulmonic air is used, a closure whose duration is entirely contained within the duration of a longer closure will have no acoustic transitions in adjoining segments and under most circumstances its presence will be imperceptible. This includes the case in figure 10.14 (c) where closure 2 is included within the longer duration formed by the overlap of closure 1 and closure 3. Rescheduling the timing, say, as in figure 10.14 (d) does not help. Under no possible arrangement can more than two transitions occur; one at the beginning of the first closure and a second at the release of the last closure.

Of course, transitions are not the only acoustic cues to the presence of a

Two closures

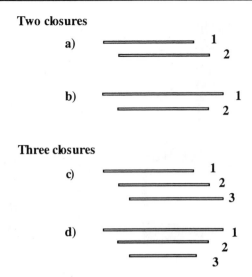

Three closures

Figure 10.14 Some relative timing possibilities among multiple closures.

particular type of articulatory closure. We must also consider the burst phenomena heard when a closure is released and the resonance characteristics of
the sound produced while the closure is maintained. In the case of stops, the
burst characteristics are more important, whereas in nasals the resonance characteristics (of the nasal murmur) are more important. When a plosive with
multiple closures is produced, only the last closure to be released can have the
full character of a burst, since only that one can have both a build-up of
pulmonic air pressure behind the closure and the opportunity for the sound to
be radiated into the air outside the speaker's mouth. A closure released while
another is maintained further forward in the mouth will not radiate the burst
energy. One that is released while another is maintained further back in the
mouth will not have a pressure build-up behind it and hence will have little or
no acoustic energy. No arrangement of three overlapping closures can avoid
one or other of these situations, so place cues inherent in bursts will be ineffec-
tive supplements to the transitional cues.

In nasals, the particular quality of the nasal murmur depends principally on
the size of the oral cavity in front of the velo-pharyngeal port. When there are
multiple oral closures, the size of this cavity is determined by the closure clos-
est to the velar region. It is therefore theoretically possible for changes in the
quality of the nasal murmur to provide cues to complex articulations as closures are added or released. For example, if figure 10.14 (c) represents a nasal
in which closure 1 is labial, closure 2 is alveolar and closure 3 is velar, then at
the onset of the nasal a rapid shifting of the nasal murmur from a quality characteristic of labial place to a quality characteristic of alveolar place and finally

Figure 10.15 Palatograms of !Xóõ bilabial clicks from five speakers, based on data in Traill (1985).
The three in the upper row show the only lingual contact to be in the velar region. The lower two
have a tongue front contact as well as the labial and velar contacts and are those described as having
"three points of articulation" by Traill.

to a quality characteristic of velar place might be observed. The brief alveolar
portion would provide the cue to the presence of an articulation which would
not be cued by transitions to and from surrounding segments. We do not
know how long this portion would need to be in order for its presence to be
noticeable, but, given the relative difficulty of discriminating between nasal
murmurs, we suspect that it may need to be quite long or its presence will be
missed. And if it is long enough to be perceived, then conflict may arise with
the principle that single complex segments have duration comparable to that
of simple segments of the same phonetic class in the same environment. Instead of a single multiply-articulated nasal, a sequence of several nasal segments may be perceived (and production adjusted to that program). In either
case, it is easy to see that circumstances do not favor the development and
stability of triply-articulated nasals any more than plosives.

As for clicks, there are two ways in which they could be produced with triple closures. One way is to have two closures, one Labial and the other
Coronal, in front of the velar or uvular closure required for the click mechanism. It is possible to imagine that these closures could be timed so that the
first is formed just before the back closure is made, thus providing a transitional cue on the pulmonic airstream. If this closure is released first, the second
forward closure would then be the place of articulation of the velaric airstream, and the back closure would be released into pulmonic airflow. All
three closures would then have audible cues to their presence. However, we
know of no clicks that are produced without the back closure overlapping the

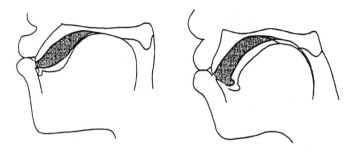

Figure 10.16 Tracings from x-ray films of !Xóõ bilabial clicks (based on Traill 1985). The shaded area shows the cavity between the two closures before the tongue is lowered. The position before release is shown by the lower tongue outline.

forward oral closure. With this overlap, if two forward closures are formed only the second to be released is likely to produce an audible burst. The presence of the other closure contributes little or nothing. In fact, palatograms of !Xóõ bilabial clicks show that two of five speakers also formed a closure in the dental-alveolar region during the click (Traill 1985: 103). The palatograms are shown in figure 10.15. Although Traill says that these 'bilabial-dental' clicks have "three points of articulation" there is no indication that these variants sound any different from the bilabial clicks of other speakers. From his discussion, it is clear that the dental contact is released well before the labial one is, since cavity expansion for labial clicks is achieved "by a lowering and retraction of the front part of the tongue" (Traill, 1985: 106). Tracings from x-ray films of the same two subjects who show dental closure on the palatograms indicate that the labial closure is maintained after the tongue tip is well away from the upper teeth. A figure based on these tracings is shown as figure 10.16. The third closure for these clicks is consequently of no significance, as we would predict.

The second way that a click can be formed with three closures is for a Radical or Glottal closure to be added behind the back closure for the click. We know of no cases with a Radical closure, but clicks produced with an accompanying glottal closure are relatively common in Khoisan languages. The relative timing of the gestures involved is discussed in chapter 8, where we interpret the glottal closure as either contributing an accompanying glottalic airstream, modifying the release of the back closure, or as forming a separate glottal stop that is released about 150–200 ms after the click. In neither case is it a place of articulation of the click segment.

In summary, we would argue that for pragmatic reasons a contrastive function for segments with three oral closures is not to be expected. Our arguments will apply *a fortiori* to segments with four simultaneous closures. We now turn to discussion of cases with articulations of differing degrees of stricture.

10.3 Secondary Articulations

We will begin our discussion of secondary articulations by considering two points of a general nature; what combinations of stricture form possible sounds with secondary articulations, and what are the timing relations involved. As noted at the beginning of this chapter, the standard phonetic definition of a secondary articulation is that it is an articulation of a lesser degree of stricture accompanying a primary articulation of a higher degree. This definition allows for the possibility of a secondary fricative articulation combined with a primary stop articulation. We suggest that, from a phonetic point of view, secondary articulations are always approximant-like in nature and do not include fricatives superimposed on stops.

When stop-fricative combinations have been treated as single segments for phonological reasons the phonetic descriptions provided often assert or imply simultaneity. An example is Lombard's analysis of SePedi, where **ps^h**, **pʃ** are described as simultaneous plosive and fricative in words like **ps^hio** 'kidney' and **yopʃa** 'to dry up'. These words are illustrated by the spectrograms in figure 10.17. In these examples we do not know how early the tongue is positioned for the alveolar or post-alveolar fricative during the closure phase of the bilabial stop. There is certainly some articulatory overlap, since the stop is released directly into the fricative, indicating that the tongue is already positioned for the fricative before the stop is released, but there is no frication before the stop in the SePedi examples whereas there is a relatively steady-state fricative portion after the stop release, indicating that the temporal centre of the fricative gesture is later than that of the stop. The timing seems similar to that found in English words such as *topsheet* or *caption*. Here, despite the syllable break between the two consonants, considerable articulatory overlap

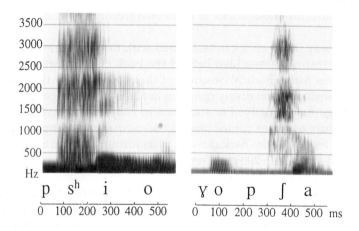

Figure 10.17 Spectrograms of the SePedi words **ps^hio** 'kidney' and **yopʃa** 'to dry up'.

of stop and fricative articulations also occurs, but acoustically the two sounds form a sequence, as in SePedi.

From the aerodynamic and acoustic points of view no frication can be generated or be audible during an actual stop closure. Therefore it seems likely that the phonetic intent in items such as the SePedi words above is to create the sequence of acoustic events, rather than to simultaneously produce the articulatory events – only if the less constricted articulation is prolonged or delayed relative to the other is audible friction produced. Naturally, when the articulatory requirements for a stop-fricative sequence do not entail conflicting positions for the same articulator, coarticulatory overlap is to be expected. But there seems to be no occurrence of secondary fricative articulations as a phonetic possibility distinct from such sequences. It therefore follows, given a three-way partition of degree of stricture, that only the combinations of closure + open approximation, and close approximation (frication) + open approximation remain as ways of combining a primary and a secondary articulation. In other words, secondary articulations will always be approximant or vowel-like in their degree of stricture.

The timing of secondary articulations in relation to the primary ones they accompany is the second general issue that requires more discussion. In the case of double articulations, the scope of the discussion was limited to those phonetic events in which two gestures occur virtually simultaneously. Even though it was argued that small timing offsets between the articulations may have great phonetic importance, the total duration of the gestures does not equal that of a (carefully spoken) sequence of two articulations in a cluster. The same considerations apply to secondary articulations, but the difficulties of demarcating comparable boundaries between a primary and a secondary articulation are greater than for doubly-articulated stops. Formation and release of a closure provide definite landmarks, but approximant articulations lack comparable boundaries. Nonetheless we feel that a useful distinction can be drawn between a consonant with a secondary articulation and a sequence of a consonant and an approximant. In practice, this distinction can be difficult to make, and many published descriptions of languages are written without such a distinction in mind. We will return to this question at several points in the discussion that follows.

There are several different types of secondary articulations which we will describe below. Articulatory gestures involving closure or close approximation can be accompanied by less extreme gestures involving raising the tongue body towards the front or back of the palate or by retracting the root of the tongue, whenever these articulators are not pre-empted for the primary articulation. Such added articulations are customarily referred to as palatalization, velarization and pharyngealization respectively. None of these is as common as labialization, a secondary articulation involving the lips. Since it is most common, labialization will be discussed first.

Labialization

The addition of a lip rounding gesture is referred to as labialization. It may occur even when the primary articulation is made at the lips. In the great majority of cases where lip rounding is employed as a secondary articulation, there is also an accompanying raising of the back of the tongue, i.e. a velarization gesture. This is parallel to, and functionally related to, the familiar prevalence of lip rounding paired with backness in vowels (see chapter 5 for further discussion of this point). This double secondary articulation type is sometimes called labiovelarization, but we will use the term labialization to refer to this complex and propose the term 'simple labialization' to describe instances where lip rounding alone needs to be distinguished. However, the combination of lip rounding and raising of the front of the tongue will be referred to as labiopalatalization. As far as we are aware, labiopalatalization only occurs as an allophonic variant of labialization in front vowel contexts in certain languages. In Akan, for example, labiopalatalized alveolar plosives are the allophonic variants of labialized velars that occur before front vowels (Dolphyne 1987).

Labialization is the most widely found secondary consonantal articulation, both with respect to the number of different types of segments with which it co-occurs, and the number of languages in which it is found. It is especially common with velar obstruents and, relative to their frequency, with uvulars. Many languages, including such varied ones as Amharic, Wantoat and Guarani, permit labialization only of such back consonants. Examples from Kwakw'ala, another language with such a restriction are given in table 10.9. (Note that the velar sounds in this language are more fronted than in many others, and have sometimes been described as palatalized.)

Other languages, including certain Australian and Caucasian languages, permit labialization of a much wider range of consonants, including those whose primary place of articulation is labial. Examples from Arrernte are given in table 10.10.

Table 10.9 Words illustrating the labialized consonants and contrasting plain velar and uvular consonants in Kwakw'ala (from Grubb 1977)

	VELAR	LABIALIZED VELAR	UVULAR	LABIALIZED UVULAR
VOICELESS PLOSIVE	'kasa 'beat soft'	kʷe'sa 'splashing'	qe'sa 'coiling'	qʷe'sa 'peeling'
VOICED PLOSIVE	'gisgas 'incest'	gʷe'su 'pig'	'ɢaɢas 'grandparent'	'ɢʷalas 'lizard'
VOICELESS FRICATIVE	xe'sa 'lost'	'xʷasa (a dance)	'χasa 'rotten'	'χʷat'a 'sparrow'
EJECTIVE STOP	'k'ata 'writing'	kʷ'e'sa 'light (weight)'	'q'asa 'sea otter'	'qʷ'asa 'crying'

Table 10.10 Labialized consonants in Arrernte. The two blank cells in this table may be accidental gaps in the data available; the cells marked with dashes indicate systematic gaps.

	BILABIAL	LAMINAL DENTAL	APICAL ALVEOLAR	LAMINAL POSTALVEOLAR	APICAL RETROFLEX	VELAR
PLOSIVES	pʷapə 'whirlwind'	jit̪ʷəŋə 'maybe'	at̪ʷatə 'gap'	aṯʷə 'calf'	aʈʷə 'man'	akʷəkə 'small'
NASALS	mʷaɻə 'good'		anʷənə '(1 pl) marrying'	ṉʷəɻpə 'wrong for'	aɳʷəɾə 'hum'	aŋʷənə 'who'
PRESTOPPED NASALS	pmʷanə 'coolamon'	t̪n̪ʷəɻət̪ə 'rock pigeon'	atnʷarə 'heel'		aʈɳʷəɾə 'wild'	kŋʷəḻə 'dog'
PRENASALIZED STOPS	mpʷəɾə 'maggot'	n̪t̪ʷəɻkə 'guts'	jəṉt̪ʷarə 'over there'	aṉt̪ʷə 'nest'	mpaɳʈʷə 'Alice Springs'	ŋkʷənə 'bone'
LATERALS	——	al̪ʷə 'blood'	al̪ʷaɾə 'swollen'	aḻʷəkə 'stone knife'	aɭʷə 'boulder'	——
RHOTICS AND APPROXIMANTS	——	——	arʷə 'handle of shield'	ajʷə 'old man'	aɻʷə 'rock wallaby'	——

It is interesting to note that in several languages, including Arrernte, linguistic analyses have shifted between interpretation of the rounding feature as a property of the consonant system or of the vowel system. Better data and analysis suggest that, at least for the Arandic languages, rounding plays no role in the underlying system of vowels (Wilkins 1986); instead there are the large number of labialized consonants indicated above. As indicated in chapter 9, we assume an analysis of Arrernte with two underlying vowels, **a** and **ə**.

In most languages with which we are familiar a stronger acoustic effect of the lip action is seen at the release the primary stricture of a labialized consonant than is seen at the onset of this stricture. We believe this arises because of an asymmetry in the timing between the primary and secondary articulations that is not unlike that seen in most labial-velar stops. Thus we can say that labialization is typically concentrated on the release phase of the primary articulation that it accompanies. This observation has both phonetic and phonological significance. Many more languages have a restriction between the presence of labialization and the choice of following vowel, than between its presence and the choice of preceding vowel, and in many languages with labialized consonants the set of syllable-final consonants, if any, does not include labialized ones.

Although it is rare, final labialization does occur. Pohnpeian, for example, has a contrast between plain and labialized bilabial stops and nasals in both initial and final position. Examples are given in the spectrograms in figure 10.18. The final labialized consonants have releases which are audibly quite distinct from the plain counterparts. Labial consonants are accompanied by a low second formant transition in adjoining vowels. When they are labialized the second formant is even lower. In accord with our observation that the stronger effect of labialization is seen at the release of the consonant, the lowest formant values in the examples in figure 10.18 are seen after the release of a labialized consonant; before a syllable-final labialized consonant the value is not as low.

In these words, it can also be seen that the formants of the **a** vowel are less affected by a preceding labialized consonant than they are by a following one. These effects on the vowel show a further interesting asymmetry. When formants are measured in the center of the vowels, both F1 and F2 are significantly lower after an initial labialized consonant than after a plain bilabial. Before a final labialized consonant, F1 is significantly lower, but F2 is not. Our interpretation of this observation is that the two component gestures involved in the secondary articulation of labialization, lip rounding and tongue back raising, have somewhat different timing in relation to the primary articulation, with the tongue backing starting earlier. Tongue raising can be expected primarily to affect F1 (compare the raising of vowels before velars that occurs in some dialects of English), whereas rounding of the lips can be expected to lower all formants in most vowels.

Simple labialization, not accompanied by any raising of the back of the tongue, is most often found as an "enhancing" feature (Stevens, Keyser and Kawasaki 1986) which supplements a primary contrast of another kind. The example of liprounding in the ʃ segments of English and French (Abry, Boë, Gentil, Descout and Graillot 1979) is well known; a degree of rounding of the lips seems to serve to distinguish the sibilant pair s–ʃ by further lowering the center of gravity of the spectrum of ʃ. However, in Shona there is a pair of rounded fricatives that we will symbolize ş , z̧ which are distinguished from unrounded s, z by the presence of simple labialization. In some dialects these are further distinguished from the sequences sw, zw and şw, z̧w (other dialects pronounce these sequences as **skw, zgw** etc., see Doke 1931a,b, Maddieson 1990b). The lip positions for s and ş as produced by a Karanga speaker, are shown in figure 10.19 (after Doke 1931b). As mentioned in the discussion of purported doubly-articulated fricatives at the beginning of this chapter, the Abkhaz labialized palato-alveolars may occur with a similar type of simple labialization, but in that language there is no contrast between different types of labialization.

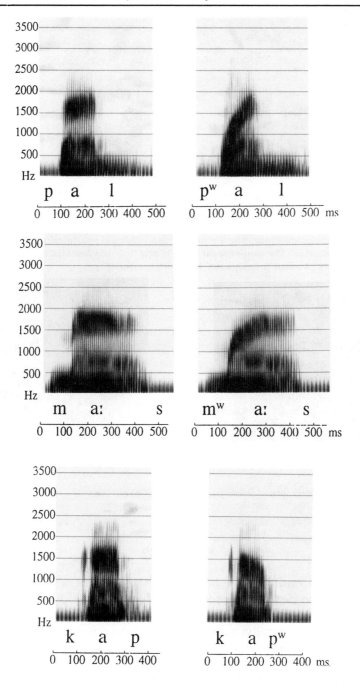

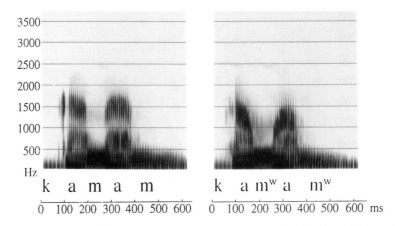

Figure 10.18 Spectrograms illustrating contrast of word-initial and final labialized bilabial plosives and nasals in Pohnpeian. The words are **pal** 'to hack', **pʷal** 'to be slit', **maːs** 'face', **mʷaːs** 'worm', **kap** 'bundle', **kapʷ** 'new', **kamam** 'to enjoy kava', **kamʷamʷ** 'to exhaust'.

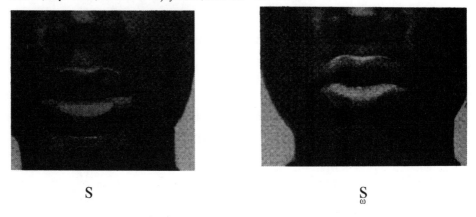

Figure 10.19 Lip photographs of Shona [s] and [s̰] (after Doke 1931b).

Velarization

Velarization, the raising of the back of the tongue, differs from labialization in that it is not so clearly anchored to the release. This leads us to expect patterns of a different type when we have velarization by itself as a secondary articulation: phonologically, more restrictions between consonant and preceding vowel, and, phonetically, more anticipation than is the case with labialization. This anticipation is observed in English l. This segment is often described as having plain allophones in syllable-initial position and velarized allophones in syllable- final position. While this is true for many speakers, a considerable number of speakers of American English varieties use a velarized

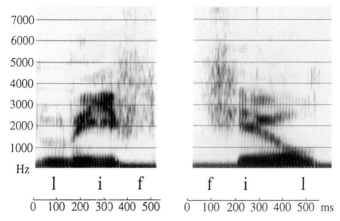

Figure 10.20 Spectrograms of an American English speaker's pronunciation of *leaf, feel* using velarized laterals in both words.

pronunciation in all positions. Representative spectrograms from such a speaker pronouncing the words *leaf* and *feel* are given in figure 10.20. The velarization is in this case shown in the acoustic pattern by a low F2 during the lateral. This is somewhat lower in the final lateral, indicating that it is more strongly velarized than the initial lateral. There is also a timing difference in the transitions; in *leaf* the F2 transition at the onset of the vowel is comparatively short, in *feel* the F2 transition before the final lateral is longer and the low F2 value is fully achieved before the consonantal occlusion begins. This pattern is consistent with velarization being anchored nearer the beginning of the consonantal articulation than the end. A different view has been expressed by Sproat and Fujimura (1993) who suggest that a secondary articulation will always be implemented closer to the syllable nucleus than the primary articulation. In their view a secondary articulation is realized closer to the end of an initial consonant, but closer to the beginning of a final consonant. This would predict that, for speakers of the type of English who have velarized laterals in all positions, *leaf* and *feel* should appear more like mirror images of each other than they do. It would also predict that we would not see the asymmetrical results that labialization produces.

The number of languages which clearly involve contrastive velarization is quite small. The set of Russian palatalized ('soft') sounds is often said to be opposed to a set of velarized consonants, but a study of the available x-rays of the articulations in question suggests that the term velarized may be appropriate only for the laterals. A clearer instance of contrast is provided by Marshallese, which has plain and velarized nasals and liquids. Among stops, the contrast is restricted to bilabials. Some examples of the bilabial nasals, spoken by a male speaker, are provided in the spectrograms and spectra in figure

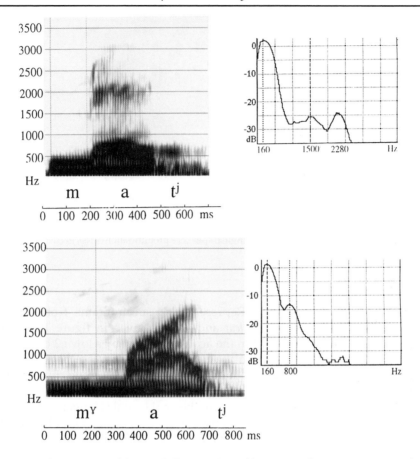

Figure 10.21 Spectrograms of the Marshallese words **matʲ** 'eye' vs **mˠatʲ** 'eel, worm', illustrating the contrast of plain and velarized nasals. Panels on the right show spectra of the nasal steady state. Frequencies of spectral peaks are indicated.

10.21. The second peak in the nasal spectrum is low throughout the velarized nasal in 'snake'; whereas the equivalent resonance in the plain bilabial is at about 1500 Hz. In Marshallese, the main properties of short vowels, apart from height, are largely determined by the surrounding consonants, especially by their secondary articulations (Bender 1968, Maddieson 1991, Choi 1992). In the minimal pair illustrated in the figure, F2 has essentially a straight-line interpolation from the initial consonant to the final in both words.

The velarization contrast in Marshallese laterals is illustrated by the spectrograms of a female speaker in figure 10.22. Each of the first three words contains two laterals, but in the first they are both plain, in the second both velarized, and in the third the first is plain but the second is velarized. The fourth word is a form incorporating a reduplication of the third word, result-

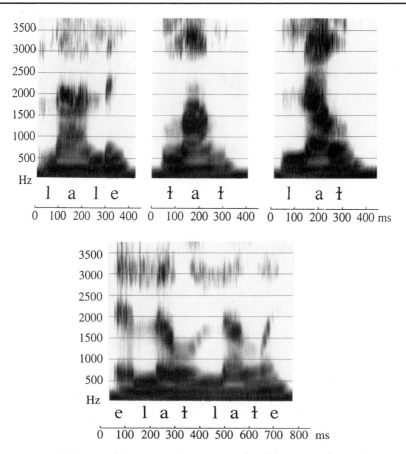

Figure 10.22 Marshallese **lale** 'check' vs **ɫaɫ** 'knock' vs **laɫ** 'earth' vs **elaɫlate** 'he's a down-to-earth person'.

ing in a medial cluster of a velarized followed by a plain lateral. In this form, anticipation of the velarization in the first **a** can be very clearly seen, although it is not so clear that there is more anticipation than perseveration of the velarization of the final lateral. Note also that in the second word there is just about as much perseveration as anticipation. This would indicate that in Marshallese velarization might be realized in the middle of the consonant.

Palatalization

Palatalization is the superimposition of a raising of the front of the tongue toward a position similar to that for **i** on a primary gesture. Like labialization it is often more apparent at the release than at the formation of a primary

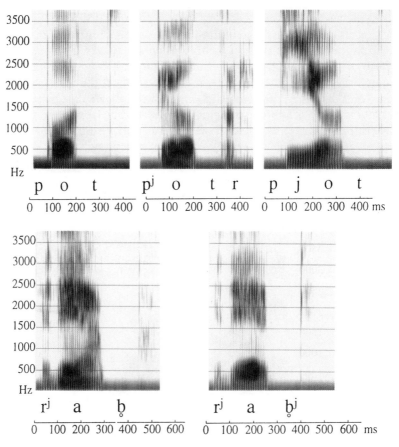

Figure 10.23 Spectrograms contrasting Russian plain and palatalized bilabial stops in the words **pot** 'sweat', **pʲotr** 'Peter', **rʲab̥** 'pock-marked', and **rʲab̥ʲ** 'ripples' spoken by a male speaker from St Petersburg. The top line also shows the sequence **pj** in **pjot** 'drink' (3 sg.).

constriction. Since bilabial sounds do not require any specific position of the tongue for their articulation, the tongue body can assume an **i**-like position during their production without any conflict with the demands of the primary articulation. Plain and palatalized bilabials in initial and final position in Russian are illustrated in the spectrograms in figure 10.23. It can be seen that the high F2 position associated with palatalization is more extreme at the release of the initial labial stop than it is at the onset of the final one (even, as in these examples, when the initial consonant is also palatalized and contributes to raising F2). This figure also illustrates the distinction between palatalization and a sequence with **j**. In **pʲotr** 'Peter' the transition away from the palatal position, indicated by a falling F2, begins immediately on consonant release. In contrast, in **pjot** 'drinks' there is a short steady state before the transition begins.

The situation is more complex with Coronal primary articulations in which specific aspects of the tongue configuration are essential for the primary consonant articulation. In this situation palatalization consists of a displacement of the surface of the tongue front from the position that it would assume in the non-palatalized counterpart, when its role is to support the movement of the tongue tip or blade. A palatalized articulation can be viewed as the summation of two movements, with the displacement of the tongue front often producing a slightly different primary constriction location. Some examples of this process have been discussed in chapter 2 on place of articulation.

In the case of Dorsal articulations, an attempt to combine a tongue-body position like that for a front vowel with a position for a consonant that is not also front will result in a modification of the primary place of articulation. Velars in all languages show variability in primary constriction location due to vowel context (though the range of variation is greater in some than in others). Palatalization of velars can be thought of therefore as producing the variant of a velar that would normally appear in a high front vowel context when the vowel context is in fact something other than a high front vowel.

Pharyngealization

The remaining type of secondary articulation involving the tongue body is pharyngealization. As with other secondary articulations, this is a feature of vowels, as discussed in chapter 9. It is most familiar from those dialects of Arabic in which the distinction between the traditional classes of plain and "emphatic" coronals is made by forming a secondary constriction in the pharynx (not all Arabic varieties make the distinction in this way; some have velarization rather than pharyngealization). Tracings of the contrast between [s] and [sˤ], based on x-ray photographs in Bukshaisha (1985) of a Qatari Arabic speaker, are shown in figure 10.24. Comparison across languages suggests that there are distinguishable higher and lower secondary pharyngeal gestures, just as there are higher and lower primary gestures in the pharyngeal area, as

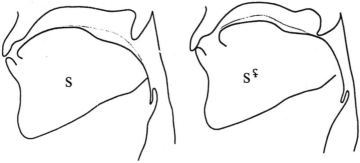

Figure 10.24 X-ray tracings of s and sˤ spoken by a Qatari Arabic speaker in the words **sad** 'to prevail' and **sˤad** (name of the letter).

described in chapter 2. Hess (1992) suggests that the lower pharyngeal gesture can be found in the pharyngealized consonants of Tsakhur. (The pharyngealized vowels in this language were illustrated in figure 9.23.) For most Arabic speakers for whom articulatory data in the form of x-ray photographs has been published (over a dozen) the narrowest constriction in the pharyngeal region is formed approximately midway between the uvula and the level of the epiglottis. The secondary gesture thus has a higher location than the constriction usually observed for the primary pharyngeal consonants of Arabic.

Other secondary articulations

A further secondary articulation type, labiodentalization, is noted by Ladefoged (1968) as occurring in Kom and Kuteb. The phenomenon in question involves the narrowing of the passage between the lower lip and the upper teeth, as in simple labiodental segments, while another articulatory position is being held. In the phonology of Kom (Hyman 1980), this phenomenon is regarded as an aspect of the vowel system of the language, to be compared with other instances of fricative vowels described in chapter 5. The nucleus of a syllable can consist of a syllabic sound which ranges from a high back rounded vowel to a lax **v**. In the phonetic domain, the labiodental articulation characteristic of this vowel can be anticipated in a range of preceding consonants, including velar stops and coronal affricate and fricative segments. In **iku** 'death' the stop is released into a quite strong voiceless bilabial fricative which is followed by a voiced more vowel-like articulation, as can be seen in the spectrogram on the left of figure 10.25. The fact that the labial constriction is coarticulated with the velar closure can be seen from the sharp drop of the second formant before the closure. In **iʒu** 'sky' the coronal fricative has a voiced labiodental fricative offglide. The ʒ segment is probably also produced with some labial constriction The consequences of this coarticulation include the presence of a lower range of frequencies in the frication from those that would be expected from the coronal articulation alone. It is unlikely that there is a second source of frication during the coronal segment; if so, this coarticulated variant would exemplify the rare possibility of a doubly-articulated fricative. More likely, the different acoustic effect is a result of modification of the outlet channel in front of the frication source.

The Kuteb 'labiodentalization' is a positional variant of the labial-velar approximant **w** in clusters that begin with a fricative or affricate. Ladefoged (1968) shows that this articulation can also be anticipated in a preceding segment, as in the laminagram reproduced as figure 10.26. A similar phenomenon has been more recently observed in Angami, a Tibeto-Burman language of Northwest India. In Kom, Kuteb and Angami labiodentalization is not a contrastive feature, but it does constitute a striking characteristic of the phonetic structure of these languages.

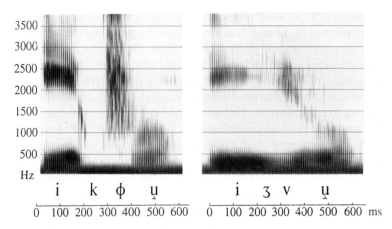

Figure 10.25 Spectrograms illustrating the effect of Kom fricative vowel ʮ, inducing labiodental offglide of preceding consonants in the words **iku** 'death', and **iʒu** 'sky'.

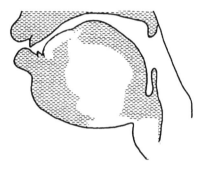

Figure 10.26 Laminagram of Kuteb laminal post-alveolar fricative z̰ as pronounced before v allophone of **w** (after Ladefoged 1968).

A final candidate for the status of a secondary articulation is sulcalization. This is a term that describes a deep grooving of the back of the tongue (Catford 1977a). A deep groove is typical of productions of s in English, as can be seen from the data on English **s** in chapter 3. It seems likely that the grooved shape helps to focus the airflow toward the obstacle at the teeth so that high-amplitude noise is produced for this sibilant. We do not know whether such grooving is typical of all sibilants. Catford (1977a) suggests that it is not. His observations indicate that different degrees of sulcalization may characterize sounds with differing places of articulation within a language, and may also contribute to the differences between languages, but they do not by themselves distinguish segments within any language.

Finally, it is perhaps worth stressing that the terms labialization and palatalization have phonological and historical linguistic uses that differ from the phonetic sense in which we use these terms. Labialization may be used to describe a sequence of a consonant and **w**, and palatalization has been used to describe a situation, especially in languages of the Slavic group, where a class of consonants possesses shared distributional characteristics resulting from historical assimilations to front vowels. Not all members of such classes necessarily will share the phonetic trait of palatalization. Several examples of the place contrasts discussed in chapter 2 and elsewhere in this book are the result of processes of palatalization in this historical sense, and are not what we would now call palatalized consonants. In fact, an important source of differences of place among consonants in the history of individual languages is the process by which simple coarticulation in particular contexts becomes fixed as secondary articulations on consonants, and in turn these complex consonants evolve into new blended articulations that can no longer be separated into primary and secondary components. Today's secondary articulations may be the primary articulations of the future.

11

Coda

One of our hopes for this book is that it might provide a basis for future work on phonological feature theories. The great variety of data that we have presented shows that the construction of an adequate theory of universal features is much more complex than hitherto thought. In this brief coda we will summarize just the main oppositions that such a theory will have to take into account. We should emphasize that we are not presenting this summary as a feature theory in the usual sense. It is simply an account of the major phonetic categories that languages employ. Furthermore, we would like to recall the introductory remarks in chapter 1, where we suggested that the description of phonetic events involves the establishment of parameters along which variation can be measured, and a set of categorial values along these parameters. These categorial values can be regarded as labels for classifying similar distinctions in different languages. But one of the main themes of this book is that many phonetic phenomena need to be described as variants of these categories. We have shown that there is a continuous range of values within the parameters. Thus we saw that when a wide range of data from different languages is considered, it is difficult to say that there is a certain specific number of places of articulation. It is equally hard to determine a specific number of states of the glottis. Similarly, we found that there is no sharp division between ejectives and plosives accompanied by a glottal stop. We also noted that there is a gradient between one form of voiced plosive and what is clearly a voiced implosive; there are not two clearly defined classes. The same kind of notion appears throughout the book, becoming, perhaps, most apparent towards the end in the discussion of vowels. Comparing vowels in different languages obviously involves considering values of parameters rather than fixed categories. Nonetheless, the notion of distinguishable categories is basic to understanding the way that languages

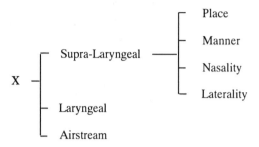

Figure 11.1 An overview of the relation between a segment (or root node) X and different types of phonetic variation.

maintain contrast between lexical items, and we also noted that there are readily apparent preferences for what we have called modal possibilities on many of the phonetic parameters. Bearing these points in mind, we can now summarize the major phonetic categories.

The basic framework that we have adopted is shown in figure 11.1. We began by discussing contrasts in Place, and went on to discuss contrasts involving other Manners of articulation and Nasality. In these discussions we considered variations in Laryngeal actions. When we discussed different Manners of articulation, we also considered different Airstream mechanisms.

The major place features and individual places of articulation were summarized in table 2.11. We can regard these possibilities as an expansion of the Place term in figure 11.1 as shown in table 11.1.

In chapter 3 and subsequent chapters we considered various manners of articulation, leading to an expansion of the MANNER term in figure 11.1 as shown in table 11.2. The most important distinction among manners is that of STRICTURE. It is not clear how TAP and TRILL relate to this parameter, but the other four terms form an ordered set. Traditional phonetic classifications would include Nasal and Lateral among the manners, but we have taken these to be independent parameters. In chapter 4 we showed that there is a wide variety of possible nasal sounds, but we did not have to consider degrees of nasality, so no further expansion of the NASAL term is needed. Similarly we noted that sounds could differ in degree of laterality, but from a phonological point of view, sounds are either CENTRAL or LATERAL.

Each of the terms in the third column of table 11.2 was considered in some detail, the first two being discussed in separate chapters (chapter 3 Stops, and chapter 5 Fricatives). The fricative chapter discusses some special considerations affecting this class of sounds that have been omitted in this summary; here we mention only the difference between Sibilant and Non-Sibilant. TAP and TRILL are major concerns of chapter 7 Rhotics. Discussions of APPROXIMANTS occur in chapter 6 Laterals, and in chapter 7 Rhotics, but the most common

Table 11.1 The relationship between the major place features and individual places of articulation

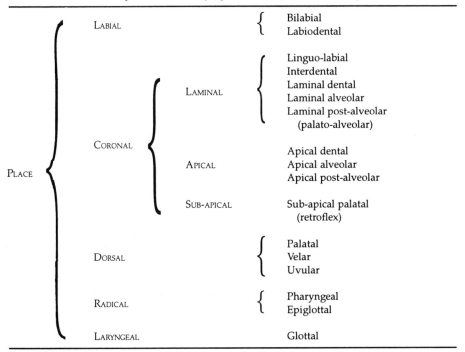

Table 11.2 Manners of articulation

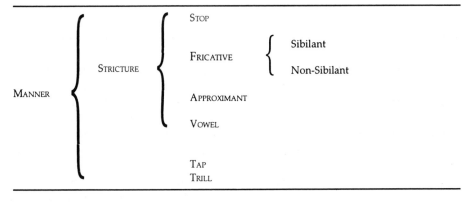

Table 11.3 Parameters and categories for approximants and vowels

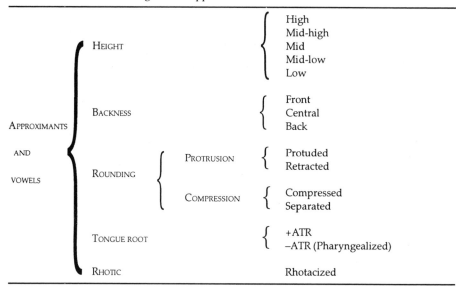

APPROXIMANTS AND VOWELS	HEIGHT		High / Mid-high / Mid / Mid-low / Low
	BACKNESS		Front / Central / Back
	ROUNDING	PROTRUSION	Protuded / Retracted
		COMPRESSION	Compressed / Separated
	TONGUE ROOT		+ATR / −ATR (Pharyngealized)
	RHOTIC		Rhotacized

Table 11.4 Types of phonation

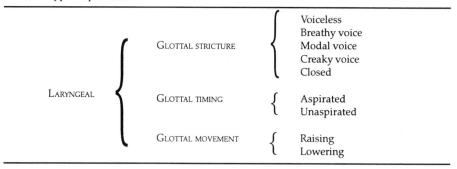

LARYNGEAL	GLOTTAL STRICTURE	Voiceless / Breathy voice / Modal voice / Creaky voice / Closed
	GLOTTAL TIMING	Aspirated / Unaspirated
	GLOTTAL MOVEMENT	Raising / Lowering

type of approximant is a semivowel. For this reason approximants receive their fullest discussion in the chapter devoted to VOWELS. The same parameters apply to both such approximants and vowels, as shown in table 11.3. These parameters are also available for describing secondary articulations.

Throughout the book we considered a variety of phonation types. We can take these into account by expanding the LARYNGEAL term in Figure 11.1 as shown in table 11.4.

Variations in airstream mechanisms were considered partly in the Chapter on clicks, but also in other chapters, notably Chapter 3 Stops, and Chapter 5 Fricatives. A possible expansion of the AIRSTREAM term in figure 11.1 is shown in table 11.5. This arrangement is different from the traditional approach

Table 11.5 Variations involving different airstream mechanisms

which includes a glottalic airstream mechanism as one of the possibilities. We have preferred to regard implosives and ejectives as characterized by a Laryngeal parameter of movement.

We will not attempt to turn this set of oppositions into a coherent set of universal features for use in phonological descriptions. Producing the present book has taken many years, and we are happy to let other linguists take this next step.

Appendix

List of Languages Cited

This index lists all the languages that are discussed in the text. The language names as we have used them are listed alphabetically. Common alternative names or spellings are provided in parentheses, as are dialects mentioned in the text. Next, a brief indication of the genetic affiliation of the language is given; this lists the largest reasonably uncontroversial family to which the language belongs. For languages of the Americas this tends to be a relatively small family, but in other parts of the world less cautious classifications are followed. In the second column there is an indication of the country or region in which the language is principally spoken.

Language (alternate names or spellings) and genetic affiliation	Principal location(s)
Abkhaz. North Caucasian.	Georgia
Abua. Niger-Kordofanian.	Nigeria
Acehnese. Austronesian.	Indonesia
Achang. Tibeto-Burman.	China
Acoma (Western Keres). Keresan.	New Mexico, USA
Adyghe (Shapsug dialect). North Caucasian.	Russia and Turkey
Afar. Afro-Asiatic.	Ethiopia
Agul (Burkikhan dialect). North Causasian.	Russia
Akan (Akyem and Akwapem Twi and Fante dialects). Niger-Kordofanian.	Ghana

Alawa. Australian.	Australia
Albanian. Indo-European.	Albania
Aleut. Eskimo-Aleut.	Alaska, USA and Russia
Alyawarra. Australian.	Australia
Amharic. Afro-Asiatic.	Ethiopia
Angami (Khonoma dialect). Tibeto-Burman.	India
Ao. Tibeto-Burman.	India
Arabana. Australian.	Australia
Arabic (Iraqi, Palestinian, Tunisian dialects). Afro-Asiatic.	Arabia and North Africa
Archi. North Causasian.	Russia
Armenian (Eastern and Western dialects). Indo-European.	Armenia
Arrente (Aranda). Australian.	Australia
Assamese. Indo-European.	India
Avokaya. Nilo-Saharan.	Sudan, Zaire.
Axluxlay (Chulupí). Mataco-Guaicuru.	Paraguay
Badaga. Dravidian.	India
Barasano. Tucanoan.	Columbia
Bardi. Australian.	Australia
Beembe (Bembe). Niger-Kordofanian.	Zaire
Bella Coola. *See* Nuxalk.	
Bondei. Niger-Kordofanian.	Tanzania
Breton. Indo-European.	France
Bulgarian. Indo-European.	Bulgaria
Bumo. Niger-Kordofanian.	Nigeria
Bura. Afro-Asiatic.	Nigeria
Burmese Tibeto-Burman.	Myanmar
Catalan. Indo-European.	Spain
Chechen-Ingush (Nakh, Nax. Chechen, Ingush dialects). North Caucasian.	Russia
Chemehuevi (?Dialect of Ute language). Uto-Aztecan.	California, USA
Chinantec. See Palantla Chinantec.	
Chinese, including the following languages or dialects: Yue (Cantonese), Jiaonan, Standard Mandarin (Pekingese, Putonghua), Quingdao, Rongcheng, Shandong, Zhongshan. Sinitic.	China
Chipewyan. Na-Dene.	Canada
Chumburung. Niger-Kordofanian.	Ghana
Cofan. Classification uncertain.	Ecuador and Colombia
Columbian Salish (Wenatchi). Salishan.	Washington, USA
Comanche. Uto-Aztecan.	Oklahoma, USA

Comox. Salishan.	Canada
Czech. Indo-European.	Czech Republic
Dafla. Tibeto-Burman.	India
Dagbani. Niger-Kordofanian.	Ghana
Dahalo. Afro-Asiatic.	Kenya
Damin (Special language of Lardil; extinct). Australian.	Australia
Danish. Indo-European.	Denmark
Dargi. North Caucasian.	Russia
Dedua. Papuan.	Papua New Guinea.
Degema. Niger-Kordofanian.	Nigeria
DhoLuo (Luo). Nilo-Saharan.	Kenya
Diegueño. Hokan.	California, USA and Mexico
Diyari (Dieri). Australian.	Australia
Djapu. Australian.	Australia
Djauan (Jawoñ, Jawony). Australian.	Australia
Djingili. Australian.	Australia
Dutch. Indo-European.	The Netherlands
Edo (Bini). Niger-Kordofanian.	Nigeria
Eggon. Niger-Kordofanian.	Nigeria
English (including Californian, Southern British, Scottish, South African dialects). Indo-European	USA, Canada, UK, South Africa, Australia, New Zealand, Jamaica, Guyana, etc.
Estonian. Uralic.	Estonia
Even. Altaic.	Russia
Ewe (Vhe, Gbe). Niger-Kordofanian.	Ghana
Faroese. Indo-European.	Faroe Islands
Farsi. Indo-European.	Iran
Fijian. Austronesian.	Fiji
Finnish. Uralic.	Finland
French. Indo-European.	France, Belgium, Canada, etc.
Fula (Fulani, Peul). Niger-Kordofanian.	West Africa
Gaelic. Indo-European.	Scotland
Garawa. Australian.	Australia
Gbeya. Niger-Kordofanian.	Central African Republic
Georgian (Kartvelian). South Caucasian.	Georgia
German. Indo-European.	Germany, Austria, Switzerland. etc.
Ghotuọ. Niger-Kordofanian.	Nigeria
Gimi. Papuan.	Papua New Guinea

Gonja. Niger-Kordofanian.	Ghana
Guajiro (Goajiro, Wayuu). Arawakan.	Colombia and Venezuela
Guarani. Tupi.	Paraguay
Gujarati (Gujerati). Indo-European.	India
Gununa-Kena (Tehuelche). Chon.	Argentina
Gwandara. Afro-Asiatic.	Nigeria
Hadza. Possibly Khoisan.	Tanzania
Haida. Na-Dene.	Canada
Hausa. Afro-Asiatic.	Nigeria
Hawaiian. Austronesian.	Hawaii, USA
Hebrew (Ashkenazic dialect). Afro-Asiatic.	Israel
Hindi. Indo-European.	India
Hmar. Tibeto-Burman.	India
Hmong (Hmong Daw, White Hmong). Hmong-Mien.	Thailand
Hungarian. Uralic.	Hungary
Hupa. Na-Dene.	California, USA
Iaai. Austronesian.	New Caledonia
Ibibio. Niger-Kordofanian.	Nigeria
Icelandic. Indo-European.	Iceland
Idoma. Niger-Kordofanian.	Nigeria
Igbo. Niger-Kordofanian.	Nigeria
Ik (Teuso). Nilo-Saharan.	Uganda
Ilwana (Elwana, Malakote). Niger-Kordofanian.	Kenya
Ingush. *See* Chechen-Ingush.	
Iraqw. Afro-Asiatic.	Tanzania
Irish (Gaelic, Erse). Indo-European.	Ireland
Isoko (Uzere dialect). Niger-Kordofanian.	Nigeria
Italian. Indo-European.	Italy
Izon (Ijo). Niger-Kordofanian	Nigeria
Jalapa Mazatec. Oto-Manguean.	Mexico
Japanese. (Classification uncertain, possibly Altaic).	Japan
Jaqaru. Aymaran.	Peru
Javanese. Austronesian.	Indonesia
Jeh. Austro-Asiatic.	Vietnam
Jingpho (Jinghpo). Tibeto-Burman.	Myanmar and China
Jino. Tibeto-Burman.	China
K'ekchi. Mayan.	Guatemala
Kabardian. North Caucasian.	Russia
Kaingang. Macro-Ge.	Brazil
Kaititj (Kayteyt). Australian.	Australia
Kalabari. Niger-Kordofanian.	Nigeria
Kanite. Papuan.	Papua New Guinea
Karok. Hokan.	California, USA

Kashaya. Hokan.	California, USA
Kâte. Papuan.	Papua New Guinea
Kelabit. Austronesian.	Malaysia
Kele. Austronesian.	Papua New Guinea
KeSukuma (Sukuma). Niger-Kordofanian.	Tanzania
Khanty (Xanty, Eastern Ostyak). Uralic.	Russia
KiChaka (Chagga). Niger-Kordofanian.	Tanzania
Kiche (Quiche). Mayan.	Guatemala
KiKamba (Kamba). Niger-Kordofanian.	Kenya
Kinyarwanda. Niger-Kordofanian.	Uganda
Klamath. Penutian.	Oregon, USA
Kom. Niger-Kordofanian.	Cameroon
Komi. Uralic.	Russia
Konda. Dravidian.	India
Korean. (Classification uncertain, possibly Altaic).	Korea
Kotoko. Afro-Asiatic.	Cameroon
Kurti. Austronesian.	Papua New Guinea
Kurtjar. Australian.	Australia
Kuteb. Niger-Kordofanian.	Nigeria
Kuvi. Dravidian.	India
Kuy. Dravidian.	India
Kwakw'ala (Kwakiutl). Wakashan.	Canada
Kwambi. Niger-Kordofanian.	Namibia
Kwangali. Niger-Kordofanian.	Namibia
Kwanyama. Niger-Kordofanian.	Namibia
Lak. North Caucasian.	Russia
Lakkia (Laka). Daic.	China
Lamé. Afro-Asiatic.	Cameroon
Lardil. Australian.	Australia
Late. Niger-Kordofanian.	Ghana
Latin (extinct except for special purposes). Indo-European.	Former Roman Empire
Lendu. Nilo-Saharan.	Zaire
Liangshang Yi. Tibeto-Burman.	China
Limba. Niger-Kordofanian.	Sierra Leone
Logba. Niger-Kordofanian.	Ghana
Lua (Niellim). Niger-Kordofanian.	Chad
LuGanda. Niger-Kordofanian.	Uganda
Lugbara. Nilo-Saharan.	Uganda
Luiseño. Uto-Aztecan.	California, USA
Lungchow (Longzhou, Nung). Daic.	Vietnam and China
Luquan Yi. Tibeto-Burman.	China
Maidu. Penutian.	California, USA
Maithili. Indo-European.	India

Malagasy. Austronesian.	Malagasy Republic
Malay (Pattani dialect). Austronesian.	Thailand
Malayalam. Dravidian.	India
Maori. Austronesian.	New Zealand
Mape. Papuan.	Papua New Guinea
Mapuche (Mapudungun). Araucanian.	Chile
Marathi. Indo-European.	India
Margi. Afro-Asiatic.	Nigeria
Marshallese. Austronesian.	Marshall Islands
Mazatec. *See* Jalapa Mazatec.	
Melpa. Papuan.	Papua New Guinea
Mid-Waghi. Papuan.	Papua New Guinea
Mien (Yao). Hmong-Mien.	China and Vietnam
Mixtec (dialect cluster). Oto-Manguean.	Mexico
Montana Salish (Flathead). Salishan.	Montana, USA
Mpi. Tibeto-Burman.	Thailand
Muinane. Witotoan.	Colombia
Mundari. Austro-Asiatic.	India
Murinhpatha. Australian.	Australia
Naʔahai. Austronesian.	Vanuatu
Nama. Central Khoisan.	Namibia and South Africa
Nambiquara. Nambiquaran.	Brazil
Naron. Central Khoisan.	Botswana
Nasioi. Papuan.	Papua New Guinea
Navajo (Navaho). Na-Dene.	New Mexico, USA
Ndonga. Niger-Kordofanian.	Namibia and Angola
Nepali. Indo-European.	Nepal
Newari. Tibeto-Burman.	Nepal
Nez Perce. Penutian.	Idaho, USA
Ngizim. Afro-Asiatic.	Nigeria
Ngwo. Niger-Kordofanian.	Cameroon
Niaboua (Nyabwa). Niger-Kordofanian.	Côte d'Ivoire
Nias. Austronesian.	Indonesia
Nimboran. Papuan.	Indonesia
Nivkh (Gilyak). Language isolate.	Russia
Nunggubuyu. Australian.	Australia
Nuxalk (Bella Coola). Salishan.	Canada
Nweh (Ngwe). Niger-Kordofanian.	Nigeria
Nzema. Niger-Kordofanian.	Ghana
Occitan (Languedoc, Provençal). Indo-European.	France
Ojibwa, Eastern. Algic.	Canada
Olgolo. Australian.	Australia
Ono. Papuan.	Papua New Guinea

'O'odham (Pima, Papago). Uto-Aztecan.	Arizona, USA
Pacoh. Austro-Asiatic.	Vietnam
Palantla Chinantec. Oto-Manguean.	Mexico
Palauan. Austronesian.	Republic of Belau
Panjabi. Indo-European.	India
Parauk (Wa). Austro-Asiatic.	China
Pare. Niger-Kordofanian.	Tanzania
Pirahã. (Classification uncertain).	Brazil
Pitjantjara. Australian.	Australia
Pitta-Pitta. Australian.	Australia
Pohnpeian (Ponapean). Austronesian.	Pohnpei, Micronesia
Pokomo. Niger-Kordofanian.	Kenya
Polish. Indo-European.	Poland
Pomo, South-Eastern. Hokan.	California, USA
Portuguese (Brazilian dialect). Indo-European.	Brazil
Quechua. Quechuan.	Bolivia and Peru
RuGciriku. Niger-Kordofanian.	Namibia and Angola
Russian. Indo-European.	Russia
Saami (Lule dialect) (Lappish). Uralic.	Sweden
Sandawe. Possibly Khoisan.	Tanzania
Sedang (Roteang). Austro-Asiatic.	Vietnam
SePedi (Northern Sotho). Niger-Kordofanian.	South Africa
Serbo-Croatian. Indo-European.	Serbia, Croatia and Bosnia
Serer. Niger-Kordofanian.	Senegal
Shambaa (Shambala). Niger-Kordofanian.	Tanzania
Shilluk. Nilo-Saharan.	Sudan
Shona (Zezuru dialect). Niger-Kordofanian.	Zimbabwe
Shubi. Niger-Kordofanian.	South Africa
SiNdebele (Ndebele). Niger-Kordofanian.	Zimbabwe and South Africa
Sindhi. Indo-European.	India
Sinhala (Sinhalese). Indo-European.	Sri Lanka
Siona. Tucanoan.	Colombia
Siya (Avatime). Niger-Kordofanian.	Ghana
Somali. Afro-Asiatic.	Somalia
Spanish (Peninsular Standard, Mexican, Peruvian, Chicano, etc. dialects). Indo-European.	Spain, USA, Caribbean, Central and South America
Sre (Koho). Austro-Asiatic.	Vietnam
Stieng. Austro-Asiatic.	Vietnam and Cambodia
Sui. Daic.	China
Sundanese. Austronesian.	Indonesia

Swedish. Indo-European.	Sweden
Tabasaran. North Caucasian.	Russia
Tamil. Dravidian.	India
Teke. Niger-Kordofanian.	Zaire
Telugu (Telegu). Dravidian.	India
Temne. Niger-Kordofanian.	Sierra Leone
Thai (Siamese). Daic.	Thailand
ThiMbukushu. Niger-Kordofanian.	Namibia
Tibetan. Tibeto-Burman.	Tibet
Tiddim Chin. Tibeto-Burman.	Myanmar
Tiwi. Australian.	Australia
Tlingit. Na-Dene.	Alaska, USA
Toda. Dravidian.	India
Tongan. Austronesian.	Tonga
Tsakhur. North Caucasian.	Russia
Tsimshian (Gitskan dialect). Penutian.	Canada
Tsonga. Niger-Kordofanian.	South Africa
Tsou. Austronesian.	Taiwan
Tucano. Tucanoan.	Brazil
Ubykh. North Caucasian.	Turkey
Udi. North Caucasian.	Azerbaijan
Uduk. Nilo-Saharan.	Sudan
UMbundu. Niger-Kordofanian.	Angola
Umotina. Macro-Ge.	Brazil
Urhobo. Niger-Kordofanian.	Nigeria
Uripiv. Austronesian.	Vanuatu
V'enen Taut (Thenen Taut, Big Nambas). Austronesian.	Vanuatu
Vao. Austronesian.	Vanuatu
Venda. Niger-Kordofanian.	South Africa
Waffa. Papuan.	Papua New Guinea
Wangganuru. Australian.	Australia
Wangurri. Australian.	Australia
Wantoat. Papuan.	Papua New Guinea
Wapishana. Arawakan.	Guyana
Warlpiri. Australian.	Australia
Welsh (Cymraeg). Indo-European	UK
Wenatchi. *See* Columbian Salish.	
Wintu. Penutian.	California, USA
Xhosa. Niger-Kordofanian.	South Africa
Yagaria. Papuan.	Papua New Guinea
Yanyuwa. Australian.	Australia
Yei. Niger-Kordofanian.	Namibia
Yeletnye (Rossel Island, Yele). Papuan.	Papua New Guinea
Yoruba. Niger-Kordofanian.	Nigeria

Zapotec. Oto-Manguean.	Mexico
Zhuǀʼhõasi (dialect of !Xū). Northern Khoisan.	Namibia
Zulu (IsiZulu). Niger-Kordofanian.	South Africa
Zuni. Classification uncertain.	New Mexico, USA
!Xóõ. Southern Khoisan.	Botswana
!Xū (!Kung). Northern Khoisan.	Angola and Namibia
ǂKhomani (extinct). Southern Khoisan.	Botswana
ǂHóã. Southern Khoisan.	Botswana
ǀXam (recently extinct). Southern Khoisan.	South Africa
ǁAni (ǁKanikhoe). Central Khoisan.	Namibia

References

Abercrombie, David. 1967. *Elements of General Phonetics.* Aldine, Chicago.

Abramson, Arthur S. 1986. "The perception of word-initial consonant length: Pattani Malay." *Journal of the International Phonetic Association* 16: 8–16.

Abramson, Arthur S. 1991. "Amplitude as a cue to word-initial consonant length: Pattani Malay." In *Proceedings of the 12th International Congress of Phonetic Sciences*, ed. by M. Rossi et al. Université de Provence, Aix-en-Provence: 98–101.

Abry, C., L. J. Boë, M. Gentil, R. Descout and P. Graillot. 1979. "La géométrie des lèvres en français – protrusion vocalique et protrusion consonantique." Paper presented at 10èmes Journées d'Étude sur la Parole, Grenoble.

Al-Ani, Salman H. 1970. *Arabic Phonology: An Acoustical and Physiological Investigation.* (Janua Linguarum, Series Practica 61.) Mouton, The Hague.

Amayo, Moses Airen. 1976. *A Generative Phonology of Edo.* Ph. D. thesis. University of Ibadan.

Anceaux, J. C. 1965. *The Nimboran Language: Phonology and Morphology.* Martinus Nijhoff, The Hague.

Anderson, Stephen R. 1978. "Syllables, segments and the Northwest Caucasian languages." In *Syllables and Segments*, ed. by A. Bell and J. B. Hooper. North-Holland, Amsterdam: 47–58.

Anderson, Victoria B. and Ian Maddieson. 1994. "Acoustic characteristics of Tiwi coronal stops." *UCLA Working Papers in Phonetics* 87: 131–62.

Armagost, James L. 1986. "Three exceptions to vowel devoicing in Comanche." *Anthropological Linguistics* 28: 255–65.

Arnott, David. 1970. *The Nominal and Verbal Systems of Fula.* Clarendon Press, Oxford.

Austin, Peter A. 1981. *A Grammar of Diyari.* Cambridge University Press, Cambridge.

Balasubramanian, T. 1972. *The Phonetics of Colloquial Tamil.* Ph.D. thesis. University of Edinburgh.

Ball, Martin J. and Nicole Müller. 1992. *Mutation in Welsh.* Routledge, London and New York.

Barker, M. A. R. 1964. *Klamath Grammar.* University of California Press, Berkeley.

Barry, Martin. 1985. "A palatographic study of connected speech processes." *Cambridge Papers in Phonetics and Experimental Linguistics* 4: 1–16.

Batibo, Herman. 1976 [1985]. *Le Kesukuma: Phonologie, Morphologie.* Thèse de troisième cycle, Paris. Available from Éditions Recherche sur les Civilisations, Paris (1985).

Baucom, Keith L. 1974. "The Wambo languages of South West Africa and Angola." *Journal of African Languages* 11: 45–73.

Bauer, Laurie, J. Dienhart, H. Hartvigson and L. Jakobsen. 1980. *American English Pronunciation: Supplement, Comparison with Danish.* Gyldendalske Boghandel, Copenhagen.

Baumbach, E. J. M. 1974. *Introduction to the Speech Sounds and Speech Sound Changes of Tsonga.* van Schaik, Pretoria.

Baumbach, E. J. M. 1987. *Analytical Tsonga Grammar.* University of South Africa, Pretoria.

Beach, Douglas M. 1938. *The Phonetics of the Hottentot Language.* W. Heffer, Cambridge.

Bell-Berti, Fredericka. 1975. "Control of pharyngeal cavity size for English voiced and voiceless stops." *Journal of the Acoustical Society of America* 57: 456–61.

Bender, Byron W. 1968. *Marshallese Dictionary.* University of Hawaii Press, Honolulu.

Benguerel, André and Tej K. Bhatia. 1980. "Hindi stop consonants: an acoustic and fiberscopic study." *Phonetica* 37: 134–48.

Benguerel, A.-P., H. Hirose, M. Sawashima and T. Ushijima. 1977. "Velar coarticulation in French: a fiberscopic study." *Journal of Phonetics* 5: 149–58.

Bentick, J. 1975. "Le niaboua, langue sans consonnes nasales." *Annales de l'Université d'Abidjan, Série H, Linguistique* 8: 5–14.

Bergsland, Knut. 1956. "Some problems of Aleut phonology." In *For Roman Jakobson*, ed. by M. Halle. Mouton, The Hague: 38–43.

Berry, Jack. 1955. "Some notes on the phonology of the Nzema and Ahanta dialects." *Bulletin of the School of Oriental and African Studies* 17: 160–5.

Bgazhba, X. S. 1964. *Bzybskij Dialekt Abkhazskogo Jazyka (The Bzyb Dialect of the Abkhaz Language).* Metsniereba, Tbilisi.

Bhaskararao, Peri and Peter Ladefoged. 1991. "Two types of voiceless nasals." *Journal of the International Phonetic Association* 21: 80–8.

Bhat, D. N. Shankara. 1974. "The phonology of liquid consonants." *Working Papers in Language Universals (Stanford University)* 16: 73–104.

Bladon, R. A. W. 1979. "The production of laterals: Some articulatory properties and their acoustic implications." In *Current Issues in the Phonetic Sciences*, ed. by H. Hollien and P. Hollien. John Benjamins, Amsterdam: 501–8.

Bladon, R. A. W. and A. Al-Bamerni. 1976. "Coarticulation resistance of English /l/." *Journal of Phonetics* 4: 135–50.

Bladon, R. A. W. and E. Carbonaro. 1978. "Lateral consonants in Italian." *Journal of Italian Linguistics* 3: 43–54.

Bladon, R. A. W. and Francis Nolan. 1977. "A videofluorographic investigation of tip and blade alveolars in English." *Journal of Phonetics* 5: 185–93.

Blake, Barry. 1979. "Pitta-Pitta." In *Handbook of Australian Languages, Volume 1*, ed. by R. M. W. Dixon and B. J. Blake. Australian National University Press, Canberra and John Benjamins, Amsterdam: 183–242.

Blankenship, Barbara, Peter Ladefoged, Peri Bhaskararao and Nichümeno Chase. 1993. "Phonetic structures of Khonoma Angami." *Linguistics of the Tibeto-Burman Area* 16: 69–88.

Bleek, Wilhelm H. I. and Lucy C. Lloyd. 1911. *Specimens of Bushman Folklore.* G. Allen and Co., London.

Bloch, Bernard and George Trager. 1942. *Outline of Linguistic Analysis.* Waverly Press, Baltimore.

Bloomfield, Leonard. 1956. *Eastern Ojibwa.* University of Michigan Press, Ann Arbor.

Blust, Robert. 1974. "A double counter-universal in Kelabit." *Papers in Linguistics* 7: 309–24.

Blust, Robert. 1993. "Kelabit-English vocabulary." *Sarawak Museum Journal, New Series* 65: 141–226.

Boff Dkhissi, Marie-Christine. 1983. "Contribution à l'étude expérimentale des consonnes d'arrière de l'Arabe Classique (locuteurs marocains)." *Travaux de l'Institut de Phonétique de Strasbourg* 15.

Bolla, Kálmán. 1980. *Magyar Hangalbum (A Phonetic Conspectus of Hungarian).* (Magyar Fonetikai Füzetek (Hungarian Papers in Phonetics) 6). Hungarian Academy of Sciences, Budapest.

Bolla, Kalmán. 1981. *A Conspectus of Russian Speech Sounds.* Böhlau Verlag, Köln.

Bolla, Kalmán. 1982. *Orosz Hangalbum (A Phonetic Conspectus of Russian).* Magyar Fonetikai Füzetek (Hungarian Papers in Phonetics) 11). Hungarian Academy of Sciences, Budapest.

Bolla, Kalmán and I. Valaczkai. 1986. *Német Beszédhangok Atlasza (A Phonetic Conspectus of German).* (Magyar Fonetikai Füzetek (Hungarian Papers in Phonetics) 16). Hungarian Academy of Sciences, Budapest.

Borden, Gloria J. and Katherine S. Harris. 1980. *Speech Science Primer: Physiology, Acoustics and Perception of Speech.* Williams and Wilkins, Baltimore.

Borman, M. B. 1962. "Cofan phonemes." In *Studies in Ecuadorian Indian Languages, Vol. 1.* Summer Institute of Linguistics, University of Oklahoma, Norman: 45–9.

Bothorel, André. 1969–70. "Contribution à l'étude descriptive des latérales de l'Albanais." *Travaux de l'Institut de Phonétique de Strasbourg* 2: 133–44.

Bothorel, André. 1982. *Etude Phonétique et Phonologique du Breton parlé à Argol (Finistere-sud).* Thèse de troisième cycle. Atelier National Reproduction des Thèses, Université Lille III, Lille.

Bouvier, Jean-Claude. 1976. *Les Parlers Provençaux de la Drome: Étude de Géographie Phonétique* (Bibliothèque Française et Romane, Série A, 33.) Klincksieck, Paris.

Boyeldieu, Pascal. 1985. *La Langue Lua ("Niellim").* Cambridge University Press for SELAF, Paris.

Bredsdorff, E. 1958. *Danish, An Elementary Grammar and Reader.* Cambridge University Press, Cambridge.

Bright, William. 1978. "Sibilants and naturalness in aboriginal California." *Journal of California Anthropology, Papers in Linguistics* 1: 39–63.

Bronstein, Arthur. 1960. *The Pronunciation of American English.* Appleton-Century-Crofts, Inc., New York.

Browman, Catherine P. and Louis M. Goldstein. 1986. "Towards an articulatory phonology." *Phonology Yearbook* 3: 219–52.

Browman, Catherine P. and Louis M. Goldstein. 1992. "Articulatory phonology: An overview." *Phonetica* 49: 155–80.

Bubrikh, D. V. 1949. *Grammatika Literaturnogo Komi Jazyka.* Leningrad State University, Leningrad.

Buckley, Eugene L. 1990. "Glottalized and aspirated sonorants in Kashaya." In *Papers from the 1990 Hokan-Penutian Workshop (= Occasional Papers in Linguistics 15),* ed. by M. Langdon. Southern Illinois University, Carbondale, IL: 75–91.

Buckley, Eugene L. 1993. *Theoretical Aspects of Kashaya Phonology and Morphology.* Ph. D. thesis. University of California, Berkeley.

Bukshaisha, Fouzia. 1985. *An Experimental Study of some Aspects of Qatari Arabic.* Ph.D. thesis. University of Edinburgh.

Butcher, Andrew. In progress. *The Phonetics of Australian Languages.*

Byrd, Dani. 1994. *Articulatory Timing in English Consonant Sequences (UCLA Working Papers in Phonetics 85).* Ph.D. thesis. University of California, Los Angeles.

Cairns, Charles E. and Mark H. Feinstein. 1982. "Markedness and the theory of syllable structure." *Linguistic Inquiry* 13: 193–226.

Camden, William. 1979. "Parallels in structure of lexicon and syntax between New Hebrides Bislama and the South Santo language as spoken at Tangoa." *Papers in Pidgin and Creole Languages 2* (Pacific Linguistics, Series A 57): 51–117.

Cao, Jianfen and Ian Maddieson. 1992. "An exploration of phonation types in Wu dialects of Chinese." *Journal of Phonetics* 20: 77–92.

Capell, Arthur and H. E. Hinch. 1970. *Maung Grammar: Texts and Vocabulary.* Mouton, The Hague.

Carnochan, Jack. 1948. "A study on the phonology of an Igbo speaker." *Bulletin of the School of Oriental and African Studies, London University* 22: 416–27.

Carnochan, Jack. 1952. "Glottalization in Hausa." *Transactions of the Philological Society* (1952): 78–109.

Catford, J. C. 1939. "On the classification of stop consonants." *Le Maître phonétique* 65: 2–5.

Catford, J. C. 1972. "Labialization in Caucasian languages, with special reference to Abkhaz." In *Proceedings of the Seventh International Congress of Phonetic Sciences,* ed. by A. Rigault and R. Charbonneau. Mouton, The Hague: 679–82.

Catford, J. C. 1977a. *Fundamental Problems in Phonetics.* Indiana University Press, Bloomington.

Catford, J. C. 1977b. "Mountain of tongues: The languages of the Caucasus." *Annual Review of Anthropology* 6: 283–314.

Catford, J. C. 1983. "Pharyngeal and laryngeal sounds in Caucasian languages." In *Vocal Fold Physiology: Contemporary Research and Clinical Issues,* ed. by D. M. Bless and J. H. Abbs. College Hill Press, San Diego: 344–50.

Catford, J. C. 1988a. *A Practical Introduction to Phonetics.* Clarendon Press, Oxford.

Catford, J. C. 1988b. "Notes on the phonetics of Nias." In *Studies in Austronesian Linguistics,* ed. by R. McGinn. Ohio University Center for International Studies, Athens, Ohio: 151–72.

Catford, J. C. ms, in preparation. *The Phonetics of Caucasian Languages.* University of Michigan, Ann Arbor.

Chadwick, Neil. 1975. *A Descriptive Study of the Djingili Language.* Australian Institute of Aboriginal Studies, Canberra.

Chan, Marjorie Kit Man. 1980. *Zhongshan Phonology: A Synchronic and Diachronic Analysis of a Yue (Cantonese) Dialect.* M. A. thesis. University of British Columbia, Vancouver.

Chao, Yuan Ren. 1948. "Zhongshan fangyan [Zhongshan dialect]." *Bulletin of the Institute of History and Philology, Academia Sinica* 21: 49–73.

Chao, Yuan Ren. 1951. "Taishan Yuliao [Taishan texts]." *Bulletin of the Institute of History and Philology, Academia Sinica* 23: 25–76.

Chao, Yuan Ren. 1968. *A Grammar of Spoken Chinese.* University of California Press, Berkeley.

Chinebuah, Isaac K. 1963. "The category of number in Nzema." *Journal of African Languages* 2: 244–59.

Cho, S. B. 1967. *A Phonological Study of Korean.* Almqvist and Wiksells, Uppsala.

Cho, Young-Mee Yu. 1990. *Parameters of Consonantal Assimilation.* Ph. D. thesis. Stanford University.

Choi, John D. 1991. "Kabardian vowels revisited." *Journal of the International Phonetic Association* 21: 4–12.

Choi, John D. 1992. *Phonetic Underspecification and Target Interpolation: an Acoustic Study of Marshallese Vowel Allophony (UCLA Working Papers in Phonetics 82).* Ph. D. thesis. University of California, Los Angeles.

Chomsky, Noam and Morris Halle. 1968. *The Sound Pattern of English.* Harper and Row, New York.

Clements, G. N. 1985. "The geometry of phonological features." *Phonology Yearbook* 2: 225–52.

Cohen, Patrick D. 1966. "Presyllables and reduplication in Jeh." *Mon-Khmer Studies* 2: 31–40.

Cohn, Abigail C. 1990. *Phonetic and Phonological Rules of Nasalization (UCLA Working Papers in Phonetics 76).* Ph. D. thesis. University of California, Los Angeles.

Cohn, Abigail C. 1993. "The status of nasalized continuants." In *Nasals, Nasalization, and the Velum,* ed. by M. K. Huffman and R. A. Krakow. Academic Press, San Diego: 329–67.

Connell, Bruce. 1987. "Temporal aspects of labiovelar stops." *Work in Progress, Department of Linguistics, University of Edinburgh* 20: 53–60.

Coustenoble, Hélène N. 1945. *La Phonétique du Provençal Moderne en Terre d'Arles.* Stephen Austin, Hertford.

Dai, Qinxia. 1985. "Achangyude qingbiyin [Voiceless nasals in the Achang language]." *Minzu Yuwen* 2: 11–15.

Dantsuji, Masatake. 1986. "Some acoustic observations on the distinction of place of articulation for voiceless nasals in Burmese." *Studia Phonologica* 20: 1–11.

Dart, Sarah N. 1987. "An aerodynamic study of Korean stop consonants: measurements and modeling." *Journal of the Acoustical Society of America* 81: 138–47.

Dart, Sarah N. 1991. *Articulatory and Acoustic Properties of Apical and Laminal Articulations (UCLA Working Papers in Phonetics 79).* Ph. D. thesis. University of California, Los Angeles.

Dart, Sarah N. 1993. "Phonetic properties of O'odham stop and fricative contrasts." *International Journal of American Linguistics* 59: 16–37.

Dave, Radhekant. 1977. "Retroflex and dental consonants in Gujerati: a palatographic and acoustical study." *Annual Report of the Institute of Phonetics, University of Copenhagen* 11: 27–156.

Davey, Anthony, Lioba Moshi and Ian Maddieson. 1982. "Liquids in Chaga." *UCLA Working Papers in Phonetics* 54: 93–108.

Delattre, Pierre. 1971. "Pharyngeal features in the consonants of Arabic, German, Spanish, French and American English." *Phonetica* 23: 129–55.

Delattre, Pierre and D. C. Freeman. 1968. "A dialect study of American r's by x-ray motion picture." *Linguistics* 44: 29–68.

Demolin, Didier. 1988. "Some problems of phonological reconstruction in Central Sudanic." In *Phonological Reconstruction: Problems and Methods (Belgian Journal of Linguistics 3)*, ed. by M. Dominicy and J. Dor. Free University of Brussels, Brussels: 53–102.

Demolin, Didier. In press. "The phonetics and phonology of glottalized consonants in Lendu." In *Phonology and Phonetic Evidence: Papers in Laboratory Phonology 4*, ed. by B. Connell and A. Arvaniti. Cambridge University Press, Cambridge.

Dent, Hilary. 1984. "Coarticulate devoicing in English laterals." *Work In Progress, Phonetics Laboratory, University of Reading* 4: 111–34.

Disner, Sandra F. 1983. *Vowel Quality: The Relation Between Universal and Language-Specific Factors (UCLA Working Papers in Phonetics 58)*. Ph. D. thesis. University of California, Los Angeles.

Dixit, R. Prakash. 1975. *Neuromuscular Aspects of Laryngeal Control, with Special Reference to Hindi*. Ph. D. thesis. University of Texas, Austin.

Dixit, R. Prakash. 1989. "Glottal gestures in Hindi plosives." *Journal of Phonetics* 17: 213–37.

Dixon, Robert M. W. 1970. "Proto-Australian laminals." *Oceanic Linguistics* 9: 79–103.

Dixon, Robert M. W. 1980. *The Languages of Australia*. Cambridge University Press, Cambridge.

Dodi, Anastas. 1970. *Fonetika e Gjuhës së sotme Shqipe (Phonetics and the Sounds of Albanian)*. University of Pristina, Pristina (Kosovo, Yugoslavia).

Doke, Clement M. 1925. "The phonetics of Ců Bushman." *Bantu Studies* 2: 129–65.

Doke, Clement M. 1926. *The Phonetics of the Zulu Language*. (Bantu Studies Special Number.) University of the Witwatersrand Press, Johannesburg.

Doke, Clement M. 1931a. *Report on the Unification of the Shona Dialects*. Stephen Austin & Sons, Hertford, for the Government of Southern Rhodesia.

Doke, Clement M. 1931b. *A Comparative Study in Shona Phonetics*. University of the Witwatersrand, Johannesburg.

Doke, C.M. 1937. "An outline of ǂKhomani Bushman phonetics." In *Bushmen of the Southern Kalahari*, ed. by J. D. Rheinallt Jones and C. M. Doke. University of the Witwatersrand Press, Johannesburg: 61–8.

Dolphyne, Florence A. 1987. *The Akan (Twi-Fante) Language, its Sound Systems and Tonal Structure*. University of Ghana Press, Accra.

Donwa, Shirley O. 1982. *The Sound System of Isoko*. Ph. D. thesis. University of Ibadan.

Duckworth, Martin, George Allen, William Hardcastle and Martin J. Ball. 1990. "Extensions to the International Phonetic Alphabet for the transcription of atypical speech." *Clinical Linguistics and Phonetics* 4: 273–80.

Dunstan, Elizabeth. 1964. "Towards a phonology of Ngwe." *Journal of West African Languages* 1.1: 39–42.

Durie, Mark. 1985. *A Grammar of Acehnese*. (Verhandelingen van het Koninklijk Instituut voor Taal-, Land- en Volkenkunde 112.) Foris, Dordrecht.

Dyen, Isadore. 1971. "Malagasy." In *Current Trends in Linguistics, Volume 8. Linguistics in Oceania*, ed. by T. Sebeok. Mouton, The Hague: 211–39.

Dzhejranishvili, E. F. 1959. "Faringalizovanye glasnye v Tsakhursko-Rutul'skom i Udinskom jazykakh." *Iberijsko-Kavkazkoe Jazykoznanie* 11: 339–59.

Eek, A. 1984–5. "Problems of quantity in Estonian word prosody." *Estonian Papers in Phonetics* 13–66.

Elert, Claes Christian. 1964. *Phonologic Studies of Quantity in Swedish*. Almqvist and

Wiksells, Stockholm.

Elugbe, Ben Ohi. 1973. *A Comparative Edo Phonology*. Ph. D. thesis. University of Ibadan.

Elugbe, Benjamin O. 1978. "On the wider application of the term 'tap'." *Journal of Phonetics* 6: 133–40.

Elugbe, Benjamin O. 1980. "Reconstructing the lenis feature in Proto-Edoid." *Journal of African Languages and Linguistics* 2: 39–67.

Elugbe, Benjamin O. 1989. *Comparative Edoid: Phonology and Lexicon* (Delta Series 6). University of Port Harcourt Press, Port Harcourt.

Emeneau, Murray B. 1939. "The vowels of the Badaga language." *Language* 15: 43–7.

Emeneau, Murray B. 1984. *Toda Grammar and Texts*. American Philosophical Society, Philadelphia.

Engstrand, Olle. 1987. "Preaspiration and the voicing contrast in Lule Sami." *Phonetica* 44: 103–16.

Engstrand, Olle. 1989. "Towards an electropalatographic specification of consonant articulation in Swedish." *PERILUS (Phonetic Experimental Research at the Institute of Linguistics, University of Stockholm)* 10: 115–56.

Everett, Daniel L. 1982. "Phonetic rarities in Pirahã." *Journal of the International Phonetic Association* 12: 94–6.

Fagan, Joel L. 1988. "Javanese intervocalic stop phonemes: the light/heavy distinction." In *Studies in Austronesian Linguistics*, ed. by R. McGinn. Ohio Center for International Studies, Center for Southeast Asia Studies, Athens, Ohio: 173–200.

Fant, Gunnar. 1960. *Acoustic Theory of Speech Production*. Mouton, The Hague.

Fant, Gunnar. 1968. "Analysis and synthesis of speech processes." In *Manual of Phonetics*, ed. by B. Malmberg. North-Holland, Amsterdam: 171–272.

Fant, Gunnar. 1973. *Speech Sounds and Features*. MIT Press, Cambridge, MA.

Feinstein, Mark H. 1979. "Prenasalization and syllable structure." *Linguistic Inquiry* 10: 243–78.

Feldman, D. 1972. "On utterance-final [l] and [u] in Portuguese." In *Papers in Linguistics and Phonetics to the Memory of Pierre Delattre*, ed. by A. Valdman. Mouton, The Hague: 129–42.

Fischer-Jørgensen, Eli. 1985. "Some basic vowel features, their articulatory correlates, and their explanatory power in phonology." In *Phonetic Linguistics: Essays in Honor of Peter Ladefoged*, ed. by V. A. Fromkin. Academic Press, Orlando, FL: 15–24.

Fischer-Jørgensen, Eli. 1987. "A phonetic study of the stød in Standard Danish." *Annual Report of the Institute of Phonetics of the University of Copenhagen* 21: 55–65.

Flege, James E. 1982. "Laryngeal timing and phonation onset in utterance-initial English stops." *Journal of Phonetics* 10: 177–92.

Flemming, Edward, Peter Ladefoged and Sarah Thomason. 1994. "Phonetic structures of Montana Salish." *UCLA Working Papers in Phonetics* 87: 1–33.

Fox, Greg J. 1979. *Big Nambas Grammar (Pacific Linguistics, Series B 60.)* Research School of Pacific Studies, Australian National University, Canberra.

Fresco, Edward. 1970. *Topics in Yoruba Dialect Phonology*. (Studies in African Linguistics Supplement 1.) University of California, Los Angeles.

Fujimura, Osamu. 1961. "Bilabial stop and nasal consonants: A motion picture study and its acoustical implications." *Journal of Speech and Hearing Research* 4: 233–47.

Fujimura, Osamu. 1962. "Analysis of nasal consonants." *Journal of the Acoustical Society of America* 34: 1865–75.

Fuller, J. M. 1990. "Pulmonic ingressive fricatives in Tsou." *Journal of the International*

Phonetic Association 20: 9–14.

Furby, C. E. 1974. "Garawa phonology." *Papers in Australian Linguistics (Pacific Linguistics, Series A 37)* 7: 1–11.

Gai, X. 1981. "Jinnuo gaikuang [A brief description of the Jino language]." *Minzu Yuwen* 1: 65–78.

Gaprindashvili, Shota G. 1966. *Fonetika Darginskogo Jazyka (The Phonetics of the Dargi Language).* Metsniereba, Tbilisi.

Garnes, Sara. 1974. *Quantity in Icelandic: Production and Perception.* Ph. D. thesis. Ohio State University. (Published in 1986 as Hamburger Phonetische Beiträge, 18. Buske Verlag, Hamburg.)

Gartenberg, Robert D. 1984. "An electropalatographic investigation of allophonic variation in English /l/ articulations." *Work in Progress, Phonetics Laboratory, University of Reading* 4: 135–57.

Gerzenstein, Ana. 1968. *Fonologia de la lengua Gununa-Kena.* (Cuadernos de Lingüística Indigena 5.) Centro de Estudios Lingüísticos, University of Buenos Aires, Buenos Aires.

Ghazeli, Salem. 1977. *Back Consonants and Backing Coarticulation in Arabic.* Ph. D. thesis. University of Texas, Austin.

Giles, S. B. and K. L. Moll. 1975. "Cinefluorographic study of selected allophones of English /l/." *Phonetica* 31: 206–27.

Gilley, Leoma G. 1992. *An Autosegmental Approach to Shilluk Phonology.* Summer Institute of Linguistics and University of Texas at Arlington, Arlington, TX.

Gimson, A. C. 1970. *An Introduction to the Pronunciation of English.* Edward Arnold, London.

Goldstein, Louis M. and Catherine P. Browman. 1986. "Representation of voicing contrasts using articulatory gestures." *Journal of Phonetics* 14: 339–42.

Golla, Victor K. 1970. *Hupa Grammar.* Ph. D. dissertation. University of California, Berkeley.

Gowda, K. S. Gurubasave. 1972. *Ao-Naga Phonetic Reader.* Central Institute of Indian Languages, Nanjangud, Mysore State.

Goyvaerts, Didier L. 1988. "Glottalized consonants: a new dimension." In *Phonological Reconstruction: Problems and Methods (Belgian Journal of Linguistics 3)*, ed. by M. Dominicy and J. Dor. Free University of Brussels, Brussels: 97–102.

Green, M. M. and G. E. Igwe. 1963. *A Descriptive Grammar of Igbo.* Akademie Verlag for Oxford University Press, Berlin.

Greenberg, Joseph H. 1970. "Some generalizations concerning glottalic consonants, especially implosives." *International Journal of American Linguistics* 36: 123–45.

Gregores, E. and Jorge A. Suarez. 1967. *A Description of Colloquial Guarani.* Mouton, The Hague.

Grubb, David M. 1977. *A Practical Writing System and Short Dictionary of Kwakw'ala.* (National Museum of Man Mercury Series 34.) National Museums of Canada, Ottawa.

Gulya, Janos. 1966. *Eastern Ostyak Chrestomathy.* (Indiana University Publications, Uralic and Altaic Series 51.) Indiana University, Bloomington.

Guthrie, Malcolm. 1948. *The Classification of the Bantu Languages.* Oxford University Press for the International African Institute, London.

Hagège, Claude. 1981. *Le Comox Lhaamen de Colombie Britannique: Présentation d'une Langue amerindienne.* (Amerindia, numéro spécial 2.) AEA, Paris.

Haggard, Mark. 1973. "Abbreviation of consonants in English pre- and post-vocalic clusters." *Journal of Phonetics* 1: 9–25.

Hagman, Roy C. 1977. *Nama Hottentot Grammar*. Indiana University, Bloomington IN.

Hála, Bohuslav. 1923. *K Popisu Prazske Vyslovnosti: Studie z Experimentalni Fonetiky*. (Rozpravy Ceske Akademie Ved a Umeni, Trida 3, 56.) Ceske Akademie Ved a Umeni, Prague.

Hale, Kenneth and David Nash. Unpublished manuscript. *Lardil and Damin Phonotactics*. Massachusetts Institute of Technology, Cambridge MA.

Halle, Morris. 1970. "Is Kabardian a vowelless language?" *Foundations of Language* 6: 95–103.

Halle, Morris. 1983. "On distinctive features and their articulatory implementation." *Natural Language and Linguistic Theory* 1: 91–105.

Halle, Morris, G. W. Hughes and J. P. A. Radley. 1957. "Acoustic properties of stop consonants." *Journal of the Acoustical Society of America* 29: 107–16.

Halle, Morris and Jean-Roger Vergnaud. 1980. "Three dimensional phonology." *Journal of Linguistic Research* 1: 83–105.

Han, Mieko S. and Raymond S. Weitzman. 1970. "Acoustic features of Korean /P, T, K/, /p, t, k/ and /ph, th, kh/." *Phonetica* 22: 112–28.

Hardcastle, William J. 1973. "Some observations on the tense-lax distinction in initial stops in Korean." *Journal of Phonetics* 1: 263–72.

Hardcastle, William J. 1974. "Instrumental investigations of lingual activity during speech: A survey." *Phonetica* 29: 129–57.

Hardcastle, William J. and Peter Roach. 1977. "An instrumental investigation of coarticulation in stop consonant sequences." *Work in Progress, Phonetics Laboratory, University of Reading* 1: 27–44.

Hardman, Michael J. 1966. *Jaqaru: Outline of Phonological and Morphological Structure*. (Janua Linguarum, Series Practica 22.) Mouton, The Hague.

Harris, Katharine S. 1958. "Cues for the discrimination of American English fricatives in spoken syllables." *Language and Speech* 1: 1–7.

Harshman, Richard, Peter Ladefoged and Louis Goldstein. 1977. "Factor analysis of tongue shapes." *Journal of the Acoustical Society of America* 62: 693–707.

Hashimoto, Oi-Kan Yue. 1972. *Phonology of Cantonese*. (Studies in Yue Dialects 1.) Princeton University Press, Princeton.

Haudricourt, André-Georges. 1950. "Les consonnes préglottalisées en Indochine." *Bulletin de la Société Linguistique de Paris* 46: 172–82.

Hayes, Bruce. 1984. "The phonetics and phonology of Russian voicing assimilation." In *Language Sound Structure: Studies in Phonology Presented to Morris Halle by his Teachers and Students*, ed. by M. Aronoff and R. T. Oehrle. MIT Press, Cambridge, MA: 318–28.

Hayes, Bruce. 1986. "Inalterability in CV phonology." *Language* 62: 321–51.

Heine, Bernd. 1975. "Ik – eine ostafrikanische Restsprache." *Afrika und Übersee* 59: 31–56.

Henderson, James and Anne Henderson. 1987. *Nt:u Kópu Dyuu U Puku Dmi (Rossel Dictionary)*. (Dictionaries of Papua New Guinea No 9). Summer Institute of Linguistics, Ukarumpa.

Herbert, Robert K. 1986. *Language Universals, Markedness Theory and Natural Phonetic Processes*. Mouton de Gruyter, Berlin.

Hercus, Louise. 1973. "The prestopped nasal and lateral consonants in Arabana-Wanganura." *Anthropological Linguistics* 14: 293–305.

Hess, Susan. 1992. "Assimilatory effects in a vowel harmony language: An acoustic analysis of Advanced Tongue Root in Akan." *Journal of Phonetics* 20: 475–92.

Hinnebusch, T. J. 1975. "A reconstructed chronology of loss: Swahili class 9/10." In *Proceedings of the Sixth Conference on African Linguistics (= Working Papers in Linguistics 20)*, ed. by R. K. Herbert. Ohio State University, Columbus, OH: 32–9.

Hoard, James E. 1978. "Obstruent voicing in Gitskan: some implications for distinctive feature theory." In *Linguistic Studies of Native Canada*, ed. by E.-D. Cook and J. Kaye. University of British Columbia Press, Vancouver: 111–19.

Hockett, Charles F. 1958. *A Course in Modern Linguistics*. Macmillan, New York.

Hoffman, Carl. 1957. *A Grammar of the Bura language*. Ph. D. thesis. Hamburg.

Hoffman, Carl. 1963. *A Grammar of Margi*. Oxford University Press, Oxford.

Holder, William. 1669. *The Elements of Speech*. Printed by T. N. for J. Martyn, London.

Holmer, Nils M. 1949. "Goajiro (Arawak) 1: Phonology." *International Journal of American Linguistics* 14: 45–56.

Homma, Yayoi. 1981. "Durational relationships between Japanese stops and vowels." *Journal of Phonetics* 9: 273–81.

Hoogshagen, S. 1959. "Three contrastive vowel lengths in Mixe." *Zeitschrift für Phonetik, Sprachwissenschaft und Kommunikationsforschung* 12: 111–15.

Hooper, Joan Bybee. 1976. *An Introduction to Natural Generative Phonology*. Academic Press, New York.

Houde, R. A. 1967. *A Study of Tongue Body Motion During Selected Speech Sounds*. Ph. D. thesis. University of Michigan.

Hubbard, Kathleen. In press. "Towards a theory of phonological and phonetic timing: Evidence from Bantu." In *Phonology and Phonetic Evidence: Papers in Laboratory Phonology 4*, ed. by B. A. Connell and A. Arvaniti. Cambridge University Press, Cambridge.

Hudgins, C. V. and R. H. Stetson. 1935. "Voicing of consonants by depression of the larynx." *Archives Néerlandaises de Phonétique Expérimentale* 11: 1–28.

Hughes, W. and Morris Halle. 1956. "Spectral properties of fricative consonants." *Journal of the Acoustical Society of America* 28: 303–10.

Hunter, G. G. and Eunice V. Pike. 1969. "The phonology and tone sandhi of Molinos Mixtec." *Linguistics* 47: 24–40.

Hurd, C. and P. Hurd. 1966. *Nasioi Language Course*. Department of Information and Extension Services, Papua New Guinea, Port Moresby.

Hyman, Larry M. 1980. "Babanki and the Ring group." In *Les Classes Nominales dans le Bantou des Grassfields*, ed. by L. M. Hyman and J. Voorhoeve. SELAF, Paris: 223–58.

Inouye, Susan B. 1991a. *Taps and Trills in Variation (manuscript)*. University of California, Los Angeles.

Inouye, Susan B. 1991b. *The Phonetics and Phonology of Palauan 'r' and 'rr'*. Paper presented at Sixth International Conference on Austronesian Linguistics, Honolulu, Hawaii.

International Phonetic Association. 1949. *The Principles of the International Phonetic Association*. Department of Phonetics, University College, London, London.

International Phonetic Association. 1989. "Report on the 1989 Kiel Convention." *Journal of the International Phonetic Association* 19: 67–80.

Jackson, Michel. 1988. *Phonetic Theory and Cross-linguistic Variation in Vowel Articulation (UCLA Working Papers in Phonetics 69)*. Ph. D. thesis. University of California, Los Angeles.

Jacobson, L. C. 1978. *Dholuo Vowel Harmony: A Phonetic Investigation (UCLA Working Papers in Phonetics 43).* Ph. D. thesis. University of California, Los Angeles.

Jacquot, André. 1981. *Etudes Beembes (Congo): I Esquisse linguistique, II Devinettes et proverbes. (Travaux et Documents de l'ORSTOM 133.)* ORSTOM, Paris.

Jaeger, Jeri J. 1983. "The fortis/lenis question: evidence from Zapotec and Jawoñ." *Journal of Phonetics* 11: 177–89.

Jakobson, Roman, Gunnar Fant and Morris Halle. 1952. *Preliminaries to Speech Analysis.* (Technical Report 13.) Acoustics Laboratory, Massachusetts Institute of Technology, Cambridge, MA (Reprinted by MIT Press, Cambridge, MA. 1963.).

Jassem, Wiktor. 1962. *Noise Spectra of Swedish, English, and Polish Fricatives.* Proceedings of the Speech Communication Seminar, Stockholm, Royal Institute of Technology Speech Transmission Laboratory.

Jassem, Wiktor. 1968. "Acoustic description of voiceless fricatives in terms of spectral parameters." In *Speech Analysis and Synthesis,* ed. by W. Jassem. Państwowe Wydawnictwo Naukowe, Warsaw: 189–206.

Javkin, Hector. 1977. "Towards a phonetic explanation for universal preferences in implosives and ejectives." In *Proceedings of the Third Annual Berkeley Linguistics Society Conference*: 559–65.

Jazić, J. H. 1977. *Osnovi Fonetike Ruskog Jezika: Ruski Glasovni Sustem u Poredenju sa Srpskohrvatskom.* Naucna Kniga, Beograd.

Jespersen, Otto. 1897–9. *Fonetik.* Det Schubotheske Forlag, Copenhagen.

Johnson, Keith, Peter Ladefoged and Mona Lindau. 1993. "Individual differences in vowel production." *Journal of the Acoustical Society of America* 94: 701–14.

Jones, Daniel. 1950. *The Phoneme: Its Nature and Use.* Heffer, Cambridge.

Jones, Daniel. 1956. *An Outline of English Phonetics.* (8th edition.) Heffer, Cambridge.

Jouannet, François. 1983. "Phonétique et phonologie. Le systeme consonantique du kinyarwanda." In *Le Kinyarwanda: Études Linguistiques,* ed. by F. Jouannet. SELAF, Paris: 55–74.

Kagaya, Ryohei. 1974. "A fiberscopic and acoustic study of the Korean stops, affricates and fricatives." *Journal of Phonetics* 2: 161–80.

Kagaya, Ryohei. 1978. "Soundspectrographic analysis of Naron clicks: A preliminary report." *Annual Bulletin of the Research Institute of Logopedics and Phoniatrics, Faculty of Medicine, University of Tokyo* 12: 113–25.

Kagaya, Ryohei. 1993. *A Classified Vocabulary of the Sandawe Language.* Institute for the Cultures and Languages of Asia and Africa, Tokyo.

Kagaya, Ryohei and Hajime Hirose. 1975. "Fiberoptic, electromyographic and acoustic analyses of Hindi stop consonants." *Annual Bulletin of the Research Institute of Logopedics and Phoniatrics* 9: 27–46.

Keating, Patricia A. 1984a. "Phonetic and phonological representation of stop consonant voicing." *Language* 60: 286–319.

Keating, Patricia A. 1984b. "Aerodynamic modeling at UCLA." *UCLA Working Papers in Phonetics* 59: 18–28.

Keating, Patricia A. 1984c. "Physiological effects on stop consonant voicing." *UCLA Working Papers in Phonetics* 59: 29–34.

Keating, Patricia A. 1988. "Underspecification in phonetics." *Phonology* 5: 275–92.

Keating, Patricia A. and Aditi Lahiri. 1993. "Fronted velars, palatalized velars, and palatals." *Phonetica* 50: 73–101.

Kelkar, Ashok R. 1968. *Studies in Hindi-Urdu 1: Introduction and Word Phonology.*

Postgraduate and Research Institute, Deccan College, Pune.

Kelly, J. 1969. "Urhobo." In *Twelve Nigerian Languages,* ed. by E. Dunstan. Longmans, London: 153–62.

Kent, Raymond D. and Kenneth L. Moll. 1969. "Vocal-tract characteristics of the stop cognates." *Journal of the Acoustical Society of America* 46: 1549–55.

Kent, Raymond D. and Kenneth L. Moll. 1972. "Cinefluorographic analyses of selected lingual consonants." *Journal of Speech and Hearing Research* 15: 453–73.

Key, Mary Ritchie. 1978. "Lingüística comparativa auracana." *Vicus Cuadernos, Lingüística* 2: 45–55.

Khaidakov, Said M. 1966. *Ocherki po Lakskoj Dialektologii.* Nauka, Moscow.

Kim, Chin-Wu. 1965. "On the autonomy of the tensity feature in stop classification (with special reference to Korean stops)." *Word* 21: 339–59.

Kirk, Paul L., Jenny Ladefoged and Peter Ladefoged. 1993. "Quantifying acoustic properties of modal, breathy and creaky vowels in Jalapa Mazatec." In *American Indian Linguistics and Ethnology in Honor of Laurence C. Thompson,* ed. by A. Mattina and T. Montler. University of Montana: 435–50.

Kirton, Jean F. and Bella Charlie. 1978. "Seven articulatory positions in Yanyuwa consonants." *Papers in Australian Linguistics 11 (Pacific Linguistics Series A 51)*: 179–97.

Kitazawa, Shigeyoshi and Shuji Doshita. 1984. "Nasal consonant discrimination by vowel independent features." *Studia Phonologica* 18: 46–58.

Kodzasov, Sandro V. 1977. "Fonetika Archinskogo Jazyka." In *Opyt Structurnogo Opisanija Archinskogo Jazyka (Sketch of a Structural Description of the Archi language),* ed. by A.E. Kibrik, S. V. Kodzasov, I. P. Olyannikova, and D. S. Samedov. Moscow University, Moscow: 184–355.

Kodzasov, Sandro V. 1990. "Fonetika." In *Sopostavitelnoe Izuchenie Dagestanskix Jazykov (Comparative Study of Dagestanian Languages),* ed. by A. E. Kibrik and S. V. Kodzasov. Moscow University, Moscow: 338–41.

Kodzasov, S. V. and I. A. Muravjeva. 1982. "Fonetika Tabasaranskogo jazyka." In *Tabasaranskie Etjudy.* Moscow University, Moscow: 6–16.

Köhler, Oswin. 1981. "Les langues khoisan." In *Les Langues dans le Monde ancien et moderne, Première Partie, les Langues de l'Afrique Subsaharienne,* ed. by G. Manessy. Centre Nationale de la Recherche Scientifique, Paris: 455–615.

Köhler, Oswin, Peter Ladefoged, Jan Snyman, Anthony Traill and Rainer Vossen. 1988. "The symbols for clicks." *Journal of the International Phonetic Association* 18: 140–2.

Koneczna, Halina and W. Zawadowski. 1956. *Obrazy Rentgenograficzne Glosek Rosyjskich.* (Prace jezykoznawcze 9.) Państwowe Wydawnictwo Naukowe, Warsaw.

Krönlein, Johann Georg. 1889 [1969]. *Nama Wörterbuch.* Deutsche Kolonialgesellschaft (revised edition, F. Rust (ed.) University of Natal Press, Pietermaritzburg, 1969), Berlin.

Kudela, Katarzyna. 1968. "Spectral features of fricative consonants." In *Speech Analysis and Synthesis,* ed. by W. Jassem. Państwowe Wydawnictwo Naukowe, Warsaw: 93–188.

Kuipers, Aert H. 1960. *Phoneme and Morpheme in Kabardian.* (Janua Linguarum, Series Minor 8.) Mouton, The Hague.

Kumari, B. Syamala. 1972. *Malayalam Phonetic Reader.* Central Institute of Indian Languages, Mysore.

Kurowski, Kathleen M. and Sheila Blumstein. 1987. "Acoustic properties for place of articulation in nasals." *Journal of the Acoustical Society of America* 81: 1917–27.

Kutch Lojenga, Constance. 1991. "Lendu: a new perspective on implosives and glottalized stops." *Afrika und Übersee* 74: 77–86.

Ladefoged, Peter. 1957. "Use of palatography." *Journal of Speech and Hearing Disorders* 22: 764–74.

Ladefoged, Peter. 1964. *A Phonetic Study of West African Languages: An Auditory-instrumental Survey.* (1st edition.) Cambridge University Press, Cambridge.

Ladefoged, Peter. 1967. *Three Areas of Experimental Phonetics.* Oxford University Press, London.

Ladefoged, Peter. 1968. *A Phonetic Study of West African Languages.* (2nd edition.) Cambridge University Press, Cambridge.

Ladefoged, Peter. 1971. *Preliminaries to Linguistic Phonetics.* (Midway reprint 1981.) University of Chicago Press, Chicago.

Ladefoged, Peter. 1975. *A Course in Phonetics.* (1st edition.) Harcourt Brace Jovanovich, New York.

Ladefoged, Peter. 1982. *A Course in Phonetics.* (2nd edition.) Harcourt Brace Jovanovich, New York.

Ladefoged, Peter. 1983. "The linguistic use of different phonation types." In *Vocal Fold Physiology: Contemporary Research and Clinical Issues,* ed. by D. Bless and J. Abbs. College Hill Press, San Diego: 351–60.

Ladefoged, Peter. 1984. "'Out of chaos comes order': Physical, biological, and structural patterns in phonetics." In *Proceedings of the Tenth International Congress of Phonetic Sciences,* ed. by M. P. R. van den Broecke and A. Cohen. Foris Publications, Dordrecht and Cinnaminson, NJ: 83–96.

Ladefoged, Peter. 1988. "Hierarchical features of the International Phonetic Alphabet." In *Berkeley Linguistics Society, Proceedings of the Fourteenth Annual Meeting,* ed. by S. Axmaker, A. Jaisser and H. Singmaster. Berkeley: 124–41.

Ladefoged, Peter. 1990a. "Some reflections on the IPA." *Journal of Phonetics* 18: 335–46.

Ladefoged, Peter. 1990b. "What do we symbolize? Thoughts prompted by bilabial and labiodental fricatives." *Journal of the International Phonetic Association* 20: 33–6.

Ladefoged, Peter. 1992. "The many interfaces between phonetics and phonology." In *Phonologica 1988,* ed. by W. U. Dressler, H. C. Luschitzky, O. E. Pfeiffer and J. R. Rennison. Cambridge University Press, Cambridge: 165–79.

Ladefoged, Peter. 1993. *A Course in Phonetics.* (3rd edition.) Harcourt Brace Jovanovich, New York.

Ladefoged, Peter. In press. "Instrumental phonetic fieldwork." In *A Handbook of Phonetic Science,* ed. by W. Hardcastle and J. Laver. Blackwell, Oxford.

Ladefoged, Peter and Peri Bhaskararao. 1983. "Non-quantal aspects of consonant production: A study of retroflex consonants." *Journal of Phonetics* 11: 291–302.

Ladefoged, Peter, Anne Cochran and Sandra F. Disner. 1977. "Laterals and trills." *Journal of the International Phonetic Association* 7: 46–54.

Ladefoged, Peter, Ruth Glick and Clive Criper. 1968. *Language in Uganda.* Oxford University Press, Nairobi.

Ladefoged, Peter and Richard Harshman. 1979. "Formant frequencies and movements of the tongue." In *Frontiers of Speech Communication,* ed. by B. Lindblom and S. Öhman. Academic Press, New York: 25–34.

Ladefoged, Peter and Mona Lindau. 1989. "Modeling articulatory-acoustic relations: A comment on Stevens' 'On the quantal nature of speech'." *Journal of Phonetics* 17: 99–106.

Ladefoged, Peter, Ian Maddieson and Michel T.T. Jackson. 1988. "Investigating phonation types in different languages." In *Vocal Physiology: Voice Production, Mechanisms and Functions*, ed. by O. Fujimura. Raven, New York: 297–317.

Ladefoged, Peter and Anthony Traill. 1984. "Linguistic phonetic description of clicks." *Language* 60: 1–20.

Ladefoged, Peter and Anthony Traill. 1994. "Clicks and their accompaniments." *Journal of Phonetics* 22: 33–64.

Ladefoged, Peter, Kay Williamson, Benjamin O. Elugbe and A. Uwulaka. 1976. "The stops of Owerri Igbo." *Studies in African Linguistics* Supplement 6: 147–63.

Ladefoged, Peter and Zhongji Wu. 1984. "Places of articulation: An investigation of Pekingese fricatives and affricates." *Journal of Phonetics* 12: 267–78.

Ladefoged, Peter and Elizabeth Zeitoun. 1993. "Pulmonic ingressive phones do not occur in Tsou." *Journal of the International Phonetic Association* 23: 13–15.

Lahiri, Aditi and Sheila E. Blumstein. 1984. "A re-evaluation of the feature coronal." *Journal of Phonetics* 12: 133–46.

Lahiri, Aditi and Jorge Hankamer. 1988. "The timing of geminate consonants." *Journal of Phonetics* 16: 327–38.

Langdon, Margaret. 1970. *A Grammar of Diegueño, Mesa Grande Dialect*. (University of California Publications in Linguistics 66). University of California Press, Berkeley and Los Angeles.

Lanham, Leonard W. 1964. "The proliferation and extension of Bantu phonemic systems influenced by Bushman and Hottentot." In *Proceedings of the Ninth International Congress of Linguists*, ed. by H. G. Lunt. Mouton, The Hague.

Laufer, Asher. 1991. "The 'glottal fricative'." *Journal of the International Phonetic Association* 21: 91–3.

Laufer, Asher and Iovanna D. Condax. 1979. "The epiglottis as an articulator." *Journal of the International Phonetic Association* 9: 50–6.

Laufer, Asher and Iovanna D. Condax. 1981. "The function of the epiglottis in speech." *Language and Speech* 24: 39–61.

Lehiste, I. 1964. *Acoustical Characteristics of Selected English Consonants*. Indiana University, Bloomington.

Lehiste, Ilse. 1966. *Consonant Quantity and Phonological Units in Estonian*. Indiana University, Bloomington.

Lehiste, Ilse. 1970. *Suprasegmentals*. MIT Press, Cambridge, MA.

Lehiste, Ilse, Katherine Morton and M. A. A. Tatham. 1973. "An instrumental study of consonant gemination." *Journal of Phonetics* 1: 131–48.

Li, Fang Kuei. 1948. "The distribution of initials and tones in the Sui language." *Language* 24: 160–7.

Lindau, Mona. 1975. *[Features] for Vowels (UCLA Working Papers in Phonetics 30)*. Ph. D. thesis. University of California, Los Angeles.

Lindau, Mona. 1978. "Vowel features." *Language* 54: 541–63.

Lindau, Mona. 1979. "The feature expanded." *Journal of Phonetics* 7: 163–76.

Lindau, Mona. 1984. "Phonetic differences in glottalic consonants." *Journal of Phonetics* 12: 147–55.

Lindau, Mona. 1985. "The story of r." In *Phonetic Linguistics*, ed. by V. A. Fromkin. Academic Press, Orlando, FL: 157–68.

Lindau, Mona, Kjell Norlin and Jan-Olof Svantesson. 1985. "Cross-linguistic differences in diphthongs." *UCLA Working Papers in Phonetics* 61: 40–4.

Lindblad, Per. 1980. *Svenskans sje- och tje-ljud i ett Allmänfonetisk Perspektiv. Travaux de l'Institut de Linguistique de Lund 16.* C. W. K. Gleerup, Lund.

Lindblom, Björn. 1990. "Models of phonetic variation and selection." *PERILUS (Phonetic Experimental Research, Institute of Linguistics, University of Stockholm)* 11: 65–100.

Lindblom, Björn and Ian Maddieson. 1988. "Phonetic universals in consonant systems." In *Language, Speech and Mind: Studies in Honor of Victoria A. Fromkin*, ed. by L. M. Hyman and C. N. Li. Routledge, London and New York: 62–80.

Linker, Wendy. 1982. *Articulatory and Acoustic Correlates of Labial Activity in Vowels: A Cross-linguistic Study (UCLA Working Papers in Phonetics 56).* Ph. D. thesis. University of California, Los Angeles.

Lisker, Leigh. 1984. "On the temporal relationship and syllable affinity of intervocalic stops." In *Papers in Phonetics and Phonology*, ed. by B. B. Rajapurohit. Central Institute of Indian Languages, Mysore: 1–16.

Lisker, Leigh and Arthur S. Abramson. 1964. "A cross language study of voicing in initial stops: Acoustical measurements." *Word* 20: 384–422.

Lisker, Leigh and Arthur S. Abramson. 1967. "Some effects of context on voice onset time in English stops." *Language and Speech* 10: 1–28.

Lombard, Daan. 1985. *An Introduction to the Grammar of Northern Sotho.* van Schaik, Pretoria.

Long, James B. and Ian Maddieson. 1993. "Consonantal evidence against the Quantal Theory." *UCLA Working Papers in Phonetics* 83: 141–7.

Louw, J. A. 1977. "Clicks as loans in Xhosa." In *Bushman and Hottentot Linguistic Studies 1975 (Papers of a Seminar held on 25 October 1975)*, ed. by J. W. Snyman. University of South Africa, Department of Bantu Languages, Pretoria: 82–100.

Lunt, Horace G. 1973. "Remarks on nasality: The case of Guarani." In *A Festschrift for Morris Halle*, ed. by S. R. Anderson. Holt, Rinehart and Winston, New York: 131–9.

Lyman, Thomas A. 1979. *Grammar of Hmong Njua (Green Miao): A Descriptive Linguistic Study.* The author. Reprinted 1985 Blue Oak Press, Sattley CA.

Lytkin, V. I. 1966. "Komi-Zyrjanskij jazyk." In *Jazyki Narodov SSSR*, ed. by V. V. Vinogradov. Nauka, Leningrad: 281–99.

Maddieson, Ian. 1981. "Unusual consonant clusters and complex segments in Eggon." *Studies in African Linguistics* Supplement 8: 89–92.

Maddieson, Ian. 1983. "The analysis of complex phonetic elements in Bura and the syllable." *Studies in African Linguistics* 14: 285–310.

Maddieson, Ian. 1984a. *Patterns of Sounds.* Cambridge University Press, Cambridge.

Maddieson, Ian. 1984b. "The effects on F_0 of a voicing distinction in sonorants and their implications for a theory of tonogenesis." *Journal of Phonetics* 12: 9–15.

Maddieson, Ian. 1985. "Phonetic cues to syllabification." In *Phonetic Linguistics*, ed. by V. A. Fromkin. Academic Press, Orlando: 203–21.

Maddieson, Ian. 1987. "The Margi vowel system and labiocoronals." *Studies in African Linguistics* 18: 327–55.

Maddieson, Ian. 1989a. "Linguo-labials." In *VICAL 1: Oceanic Languages, Part 2*, ed. by R. Harlow and R. Cooper. Linguistic Society of New Zealand, Auckland: 349–76.

Maddieson, Ian. 1989b. "Aerodynamic constraints on sound change: The case of bilabial trills." *UCLA Working Papers in Phonetics* 72: 91–115.

Maddieson, Ian. 1990a. "Prenasalized stops and speech timing." *Journal of the International Phonetic Association* 19: 57–66.

Maddieson, Ian. 1990b. "Shona velarization: Complex consonants or complex onsets?" *UCLA Working Papers in Phonetics* 74: 16–34.

Maddieson, Ian. 1991. "Articulatory phonology and Sukuma 'aspirated nasals'". In *Proceedings of the 17th Annual Meeting of the Berkeley Linguistic Society, Special Session on African Language Structures*, ed. by K. Hubbard. Berkeley Linguistics Society, Berkeley: 145–54.

Maddieson, Ian. 1993. "Investigating Ewe articulations with electromagnetic articulography." *Forschungsberichte des Instituts für Phonetik und Sprachliche Kommunikation der Universität München* 31: 181–214.

Maddieson, Ian. 1995. "Gestural economy." Proceedings of the 13th International Congress of Phonetic Sciences, Stockholm.

Maddieson, Ian and Victoria B. Anderson. 1994. "Phonetic structures of Iaai." *UCLA Working Papers in Phonetics* 87: 163–82.

Maddieson, Ian and Karen Emmorey. 1984. "Is there a valid distinction between voiceless lateral approximants and fricatives?" *Journal of Phonetics* 41: 181–90.

Maddieson, Ian and Karen Emmorey. 1985. "Relationship between semivowels and vowels: Cross-linguistic investigations of acoustic difference and coarticulation." *Phonetica* 42: 163–74.

Maddieson, Ian and Jack Gandour. 1977. "Vowel length before aspirated consonants." *Indian Linguistics* 38: 6–11.

Maddieson, Ian and Susan Hess. 1986. "'Tense' and 'lax' revisited: more on phonation type and pitch in minority languages in China." *UCLA Working Papers in Phonetics* 63: 103–9.

Maddieson, Ian and Peter Ladefoged. 1985. "'Tense' and 'lax' in four minority languages of China." *Journal of Phonetics* 13: 433–54.

Maddieson, Ian and Peter Ladefoged. 1993. "Phonetics of partially nasal consonants." In *Nasals, Nasalization and the Velum*, ed. by M. K. Huffman and R. A. Krakow. Academic Press, San Diego: 251–301.

Maddieson, Ian, Siniša Spajić, Bonny Sands, and Peter Ladefoged. 1993. "The phonetic structures of Dahalo." *Afrikanistische Arbeitspapiere* 36: 5–53.

Magometov, A. A. 1967. "Agul'skij jazyk [Agul language]." In *Jazyki Narodov SSSR*, ed. by V. V. Vinogradov. Nauka, Moscow: 562–79.

Malécot, André. 1956. "Acoustic cues for nasal consonants: an experimental study involving tape-splicing techniques." *Language* 32: 274–84.

Malécot, André. 1968. "The force of articulation of American stops and fricatives as a function of position." *Phonetica* 18: 95–102.

Malmberg, Bertil. 1951. *Svensk Fonetik*. C. W. K. Gleerup, Lund.

Malmberg, Bertil. 1956. "Distinctive features of Swedish vowels, some instrumental and structural data." In *For Roman Jakobson*, ed. by M. Halle. Mouton, The Hague: 316–21.

Manley, Timothy M. 1972. *Outline of Sre Structure*. (Oceanic Linguistics Special Publication 12.) University of Hawaii Press, Honolulu.

Maran, La Raw. 1971. *Burmese and Jingpho: A Study of Tonal Linguistic Processes*. (Occasional Papers of the Wolfenden Society on Tibeto-Burman Linguistics 4.) University of Illinois, Urbana.

Martinet, André. 1964. *Économie des Changements Phonétiques; Traité de Phonologie Diachronique*. (2nd edition.) A. Francke, Berne.

McAllister, Robert. 1978. "Temporal asymmetry in labial coarticulation." *Papers from the Institute of Linguistics, University of Stockholm* 35: 1–16.

McAllister, Robert, James Lubker and Johann Carlson. 1974. "An EMG study of some characteristics of the Swedish rounded vowels." *Journal of Phonetics* 2: 267–78.

McCarthy, John J. 1988. "Feature geometry and dependency: a review." *Phonetica* 45: 84–108.

McCawley, James D. 1968. *The Phonological Component of a Grammar of Japanese.* Mouton, The Hague.

McCutcheon, Martin J., Akira Hasegawa and Samuel G. Fletcher. 1980. "Effects of palatal morphology on /s, z/ articulation." (Abstract) *Journal of the Acoustical Society of America* 67, Supplement 1: S94.

McDonough, Joyce and Peter Ladefoged. 1993. "Navajo stops." *UCLA Working Papers in Phonetics* 84: 151–64.

McGowan, Richard S. 1992. "Tongue-tip trills and vocal tract wall compliance." *Journal of the Acoustical Society of America* 91: 2903–10.

McIntosh, Mary. 1984. *Fulfulde Syntax and Verbal Morphology.* KPI in association with the University of Port Harcourt Press, Boston.

McKay, G. R. 1980. "Medial stop gemination in Rembarrnga: a spectrographic study." *Journal of Phonetics* 8: 343–52.

Merrifield, William R. 1963. "Palantla Chinantec syllable types." *Anthropological Linguistics* 5: 1–16.

Miller, Wick R. 1966. *Acoma Grammar and Texts.* (U. C. Publications in Linguistics 40.) University of California Press, Berkeley and Los Angeles.

Miller, W. R. and I. Davis. 1963. "Proto-Keresan Phonology." *International Journal of American Linguistics* 29: 310–30.

Milner, George B. 1956. *Fijian Grammar.* Fiji Government Printer, Suva.

Mohanan, K. P. and Tara Mohanan. 1984. "Lexical phonology of the consonant system of Malayalam." *Linguistic Inquiry* 15: 575–602.

Moll, Kenneth L. and T. H. Shriner. 1967. "Preliminary investigation of a new concept of velar activity during speech." *Cleft Palate Journal* 4: 58–69.

Monnot, Michel and Michael Freeman. 1972. "A comparison of Spanish single-tap /r/ with American /t/ and /d/ in post-stress intervocalic position." In *Papers in Linguistics to the Memory of Pierre Delattre*, ed. by A. Valdman. Mouton, The Hague: 409–16.

Mooshammer, Christine. 1992. *Artikulatorische Untersuchung mit EMA – die Zungenbewegung bei der Produktion von VCV-Sequenzen mit velarer Konsonanz und langem und kurzem Erstvokal.* Hausarbeit zur Erlangung des Magistergrades (M.A. thesis). University of Munich.

Morphy, Frances. 1983. "Djapu, a Yolngu dialect." In *Handbook of Australian Languages* 3, ed. by R. M. W. Dixon and B. J. Blake. John Benjamins, Amsterdam: 1–188.

Nater, H. F. 1984. *The Bella Coola Language.* (Canadian Ethnology Service Paper 92.) National Museum of Man, Ottawa.

Navarro Tomás, Tomás. 1968. *Manual de Pronunciación Española.* (14th edition.) Consejo Superior de Investigaciones Científicas, Madrid.

Newman, Paul. 1980. "The two R's in Hausa." *African Language Studies* 17: 77–87.

ní Chasaide, Ailbhe. 1985. *Preaspiration in Phonological Stop Contrasts.* Ph. D. thesis. University College of North Wales, Bangor.

Nihalani, Paroo. 1974. "An aerodynamic study of stops in Sindhi." *Phonetica* 29: 193–224.

Nihalani, Paroo. 1991. "A re-evaluation of implosives in Sindhi." *UCLA Working Papers in Phonetics* 80: 1–5.

Nord, Lennart. 1976. "Perceptual experiments with nasals." *Quarterly Progress and Status Report, Speech Transmission Laboratory (KTH, Stockholm)* 1976: 5–8.

Novikova, K. A. 1960. *Ocherki Dialektov Evenskogo Jazyka.* Izdatjelstvo Akademii Nauk SSSR, Moscow.

Ohala, John J. 1975. "Phonetic explanations for nasal sound patterns." In *Nasálfest: Papers from a Symposium on Nasals and Nasalization (1975),* ed. by C. A. Ferguson, L. M. Hyman and J. J. Ohala. Language Universals Project, Stanford: 289–316.

Ohala, John J. and Carol Riordan. 1979. "Passive vocal tract enlargement during voiced stops." In *Speech Communication Papers presented at the 97th Meeting of the Acoustical Society of America,* ed. by J. Wolf and D. Klatt. Acoustical Society of America, New York: 89–92.

Ohala, Manjari. 1983. *Aspects of Hindi Phonology.* (MLBD series in Linguistics.) Motilal Barnarsidass, Delhi.

Ohlsson, S. Ö., J. P. Nielsen and K. Schaltz. 1977. "Om r-gränsen pa öland: på östfronten intet nytt?" *Arkiv for Nordisk Filologi* 92: 177–99.

Ohnesorg, K. and O. Svarný. 1955. *Études Expérimentales des Articulations Chinoises.* (Rozpravy Ceskoslovenské Akademie Ved 65.) Prague.

Ozanne-Rivierre, Françoise. 1976. *Le Iaai, Langue Mélanésienne d'Ouvéa (Nouvelle-Calédonie): Phonologie, Morphologie, Esquisse Syntaxique.* (Langues et Civilisations à Tradition Orale 20.) SELAF, Paris.

Painter, Colin. 1970. *Gonja: A Phonological and Grammatical Study.* Mouton, The Hague.

Pandit, P. B. 1957. "Nasalization, aspiration and murmur in Gujarati." *Indian Linguistics* 17: 165–72.

Parker, E. M. and Richard J. Hayward. 1985. *An Afar-English-French Dictionary (with Grammatical Notes in English).* School of Oriental and African Studies, University of London, London.

Passy, Paul. 1899. *Les Sons du Français.* (5th edition.) Association Phonétique Internationale, Paris.

Paulian, Christiane. 1975. *Le Kukuya – Langue Teke du Congo (Phonologie; Classes Nominales).* (Bibliothèque de la SELAF 49–50.) SELAF, Paris.

Payne, David L. 1981. *The Phonology and Morphology of Axininca Campa.* Summer Institute of Linguistics, Dallas.

Peeters, W. J. and William J. Barry. 1989. *Diphthong dynamics: production and perception in Southern British English.* European Conference on Speech Communication and Technology, ed. by J. P. Tubach and J. J. Mariani. CEP Consultants, Paris: 55–8.

Perkell, Joseph S. 1969. *Physiology of Speech Production: Results and Implications of a Quantitative Cineradiographic Study.* (Research Monograph 53.) MIT Press, Cambridge, MA.

Perkell, Joseph S., Suzanne Boyce and Kenneth N. Stevens. 1979. "Articulatory and acoustic correlates of the [s-š] distinction." In *Speech Communication Papers presented at the 97th Meeting of the Acoustical Society of America,* ed. by J. J. Wolf and D. K. Klatt. Acoustical Society of America, New York: 109–13.

Pétursson, Magnus. 1971. "Étude de la réalisation des consonnes islandaises þ, ð, s, dans la prononciation d'un sujet islandais à partir de la radiocinématographie." *Phonetica* 23: 203–16.

Pétursson, Magnus. 1976. "Aspiration et activité glottale: examen expérimental à partir de consonnes islandaises." *Phonetica* 33: 78–198.

Pike, Kenneth L. 1943. *Phonetics: A Critical Analysis of Phonetic Theory and a Technique for the Practical Description of Sounds.* University of Michigan Press, Ann Arbor.

Pike, Kenneth L. and Eunice V. Pike. 1947. "Immediate constituents of Mazatec syllables." *International Journal of American Linguistics* 13: 78–91.

Pinkerton, Sandra. 1986. "Quichean (Mayan) glottalized and nonglottalized stops: A phonetic study with implications for phonological universals." In *Experimental Phonology*, ed. by J. J. Ohala and J. J. Jaeger. Academic Press, Orlando: 125–39.

Prator, Clifford H. and Betty W. Robinett. 1985. *Manual of American English Pronunciation.* Holt, Rinehart and Winston, New York.

Price, P. David. 1976. "Southern Nambikwara phonology." *International Journal of American Linguistics* 42:

Puppel, Stanisław, Jadwiga Nawrocka-Fisiak and Halina Krassowska. 1977. *A Handbook of Polish Pronunciation for English Learners.* Państwowe Wydawnictwo Naukowe, Warsaw.

Purnell, Herbert C. 1965. *Phonology of a Yao dialect.* Hartford Seminary Foundation, Hartford.

Qi, Yingyong and Robert A. Fox. 1992. "Analysis of nasal consonants using perceptual linear prediction." *Journal of the Acoustical Society of America* 91: 1718–26.

Quilis, Antonio. 1963. *Fonética y Fonología del Español.* Consejo Superior de Investigaciones Científicas, Madrid.

Quilis, Antonio. 1981. *Fonética Acústica de la Lengua Española.* Biblioteca Románica Hispánica, Madrid.

Quilis, Antonio and J. A. Fernández. 1964. *Curso de Fonética y Fonología Españolas.* Instituto Miguel Cervantes, Madrid.

Ray, Punya Sloka. 1967. "Dafla phonology and morphology." *Anthropological Linguistics* 9: 9–14.

Recasens, Daniel. 1983. "Place cues for nasal consonants with special reference to Catalan." *Journal of the Acoustical Society of America* 73: 1346–53.

Recasens, Daniel. 1984a. "Timing constraints and coarticulation: alveo-palatals and sequences of alveolar + [j] in Catalan." *Phonetica* 41: 125–39.

Recasens, Daniel. 1984b. "Vowel-to-vowel coarticulation in Catalan VCV Sequences." *Journal of the Acoustical Society of America* 76: 1624–35.

Recasens, Daniel. 1991. "On the production characteristics of apicoalveolar taps and trills." *Journal of Phonetics* 19: 267–80.

Reddy, B. Ramakrishna, Susheela P. Upadhyaya and Joy Reddy. 1974. *Kuvi Phonetic Reader.* (CIIL Phonetic Reader Series 11.) Central Institute of Indian Languages, Mysore.

Renck, G. L. 1975. *A Grammar of Yagaria.* (Pacific Linguistics, Series B 40.) Research School of Pacific Studies, Australian National University, Canberra.

Roach, Peter J. 1983. *English Phonetics and Phonology: A Practical Course (Tutor's Book).* Cambridge University Press, Cambridge.

Roberts-Kohno, R. Ruth. 1994. "Vowel coalescence and hiatus in Kikamba: Evidence for empty consonants." Paper presented at Twenty-fifth Annual Conference on African Linguistics. Rutgers University, New Brunswick, NJ.

Robins, R. H. 1957. "Vowel nasality in Sundanese: a phonological and grammatical study." In *Studies in Linguistics (Special Volume of the Philological Society)*. Basil Blackwell, Oxford: 87–103.

Rochette, Claude E. 1973. *Les Groupes de Consonnes en Français: Étude de l'enchaînement articulatoire á l'aide de la radiocinématographie et de l'oscillographie.* (Bibliothèque Française et Romane, Série A 23/1–2.) Klincksieck, Paris.

Sachnine, Michka. 1982. *Le Lamé (Nord-Cameroun).* SELAF, Paris.

Sagey, Elizabeth. 1986. *The Representation of Features and Relations in Nonlinear Phonology.* Ph. D. thesis. MIT, Cambridge, MA.

Sagey, Elizabeth. 1990. *The Representation of Features in Nonlinear Phonology: The Articulator Node Hierarchy.* (Outstanding Dissertations in Linguistics.) Garland Publishing, New York.

Samarin, William J. 1966. *The Gbeya Language.* University of California Press, Berkeley and Los Angeles.

Sands, Bonny. 1991. "Evidence for click features: Acoustic characteristics of Xhosa clicks." *UCLA Working Papers in Phonetics* 80: 6–37.

Sands, Bonny, Ian Maddieson and Peter Ladefoged. 1993. "The phonetic structures of Hadza." *UCLA Working Papers in Phonetics* 84: 67–88.

Sapir, Edward and Harry Hoijer. 1967. *The Phonology and Morphology of the Navaho Language.* University of California Press, Berkeley and Los Angeles.

Scatton, Ernest. 1984. *A Reference Grammar of Bulgarian.* Slavica, Cambridge, MA.

Schadeberg, Thilo C. 1982. "Nasalization in UMbundu." *Journal of African Languages and Linguistics* 4: 109–32.

Schroeder, Manfred R., Bishnu S. Atal and J. L. Hall. 1979. "Objective measure of certain speech signal degradations based on masking properties of human auditory perception." In *Frontiers of Speech Communication Research,* ed. by B. Lindblom and S. Öhman. Academic Press, San Francisco: 217–29.

Shadle, Christine H. 1985. *The Acoustics of Fricative Consonants.* Ph. D. thesis. MIT, Cambridge, MA.

Shadle, Christine H., Pierre Badin and André Moulinier. 1991. "Towards the spectral characteristics of fricative consonants." In *Proceedings of the Twelfth International Congress of Phonetic Sciences,* ed. by M. Rossi et al., Université de Provence, Aix-en-Provence: 42–5.

Shadle, Christine H., André Moulinier, C. Dobelke and Celia Scully. 1992. "Ensemble averaging applied to the analysis of fricative consonants." In *Proceedings of the International Conference on Spoken Language Processing,* ed. by J. J. Ohala, T. Nearey, B. Derwing, N. Hodge and G. Wiebe. University of Alberta, Banff: 53–6.

Shafeev, D. A., translated and edited by Herbert H. Paper. 1964. *A Short Grammatical Outline of Pashto.* (Publications in Anthropology 33.) Research Center in Anthropology, Folklore and Linguistics, Indiana University, Bloomington.

Shalev, Michael, Peter Ladefoged and Peri Bhaskararao. 1994. "Phonetics of Toda." *PILC Journal of Dravidian Studies* 4: 19–56.

Shibatani, Masayoshi. 1990. *The Languages of Japan.* Cambridge University Press, Cambridge.

Shimizu, Katsumasa and Masatake Dantsuji. 1987. "A cross-language study on the perception of [r – l] – a preliminary report." *Studia Phonologica* 21: 10–19.

Short, David. 1987. "Czech and Slovak." In *The World's Major Languages,* ed. by B. Comrie. Oxford University Press, New York: 367–90.

Shryock, Aaron. In progress. *Investigating Laryngeal Contrasts: An Acoustic Study of Consonants in Musey.* Ph. D. thesis. University of California, Los Angeles.

Sibomana, Leo. 1985. "A phonological and grammatical outline of Eggon." *Afrika und Übersee* 68: 43–68.

Sievers, Eduard. 1876. *Grundzüge der Lautphysiologie.* Breitkopf und Härtel, Leipzig.

Silverman, Daniel and Jungho Jun. 1994. "Aerodynamic evidence for articulatory overlap in Korean." *Phonetica* 51: 210–20.

Simon, Péla. 1967. *Les Consonnes Françaises.* (Bibliothèque Française et Romane, Série A 14.) Klincksieck, Paris.

Skalozub, Larisa G. 1963. *Palatogrammy i Rentgenogrammy Soglasnyx Fonem Russkogo Literaturnogo Jazyka.* Izdatelstvo Kievskogo Universiteta, Kiev.

Slis, I. H. 1971. "Articulatory effort and its durational and electromyographic correlates." *Phonetica* 23: 171–88.

Smalley, William A. 1976. "The problems of consonants and tone: Hmong (Meo, Mio)." In *Phonemes and Orthography: Language Planning in Ten Minority Languages of Thailand (Pacific Linguistics, Series C 43),* ed. by W. A. Smalley. Research School of Pacific Studies, Australian National University, Canberra.

Smith, Bruce L. and Ann McLean-Muse. 1987. "Kinematic characteristics of postvocalic labial stop consonants produced by children and adults." *Phonetica* 227–37.

Smith, Caroline L. 1992. *The Timing of Vowel and Consonant Gestures.* Ph. D. thesis. Yale University.

Smith, Caroline L. In press. "Prosodic patterns in the coordination of vowel and consonant gestures." In *Phonology and Phonetic Evidence: Papers in Laboratory Phonology 4,* ed. by B. A. Connell and A. Arvaniti. Cambridge University Press, Cambridge.

Smith, Kenneth D. 1968. "Laryngealization and delaryngealization in Sedang phonemics." *Linguistics* 38: 52–69.

Snider, Keith L. 1984. "Vowel harmony and the consonant l in Chumburung." *Studies in African Linguistics* 15: 47–58.

Snyman, Jan W. 1970. *An Introduction to the !Xũ Language.* Balkema, Cape Town.

Snyman, Jan W. 1975. *Žuǀʼhoasi Fonologie en Woordeboek.* Balkema, Cape Town.

Snyman, Jan W. 1978. "The clicks of Zhuǀʼhõasi." In *Second Africa Languages Congress of UNISA,* ed. by E. J. M. Baumbach. University of South Africa, Pretoria.

Snyman, Jan W. 1980. "The relationship between Angolan !Xũ and Žuǀʼhõasi." In *Bushman and Hottentot Linguistic Studies 1979,* ed. by J. W. Snyman. University of South Africa, Pretoria: 1–58.

Spajić, Siniša, Peter Ladefoged and Peri Bhaskararao. 1994. "The rhotics of Toda." *UCLA Working Papers in Phonetics* 87: 35–66.

Sproat, Richard and Osamu Fujimura. 1993. "Allophonic variation in English /l/ and its implications for phonetic implementation." *Journal of Phonetics* 21: 291–312.

Stell, Nelida N. 1972. "Fonologia de la lenga aˣluˣlaj." *Cuadernos de Lingüística Indigena (Universidad de Buenos Aires)* 8: 21–55.

Steriade, Donca. 1982. *Greek Prosodies and the Nature of Syllabification.* Ph. D. thesis. MIT, Cambridge, MA.

Steriade, Donca. 1993a. "Segments, contours and clusters." In *Actes du 15ème Congrès International des Linguistes,* ed. by A. Crochetière, J.-C. Boulanger and C. Ouellen. Presses Universitaires Laval, Sainte Foy, Québec: 71–82.

Steriade, Donca. 1993b. "Closure, release and nasal contours". In *Nasals, Nasalization and the Velum,* ed. by M. K. Huffman and R. A. Krakow. Academic Press, San Diego: 401–70.

Stetson, R. H. 1951. *Motor Phonetics: A Study of Speech Movement in Action.* (2nd edition.) North-Holland Publishing Co., Amsterdam.

Stevens, Kenneth N. 1972. "The quantal nature of speech: Evidence from articulatory-acoustic data." In *Human Communication, A Unified View*, ed. by P. B. Denes and E. E. David Jr. McGraw-Hill, New York: 51–66.

Stevens, Kenneth N. 1988. "Modes of vocal fold vibration based on a two-section model." In *Vocal Physiology: Voice Production, Mechanisms and Functions*, ed. by O. Fujimura. Raven Press, New York: 357–67.

Stevens, Kenneth N. 1989. "On the quantal nature of speech." *Journal of Phonetics* 17: 3–46.

Stevens, Kenneth N. and Sheila E. Blumstein. 1975. "Quantal aspects of consonant production and perception: A study of retroflex consonants." *Journal of Phonetics* 3: 215–33.

Stevens, Kenneth N. and Arthur S. House. 1955. "Development of a quantitative model of vowel articulation." *Journal of the Acoustical Society of America* 27: 484–93.

Stevens, Kenneth N., S. Jay Keyser and Haruko Kawasaki. 1986. "Toward a phonetic and phonological theory of redundant features." In *Invariance and Variability in Speech Process*, ed. by J. S. Perkell and D. Klatt. Lawrence Erlbaum Associates, Hillsdale, NJ: 426–49.

Stevens, Kenneth N. and S. Jay Keyser. 1989. "Primary features and their enhancement in consonants." *Language* 65: 81–106.

Stojkov, Stojko. 1942. *Bulgarski Knizhoven Izgovor: Opitno Izsledovanie (Bulgarian literary pronunciation: preliminary investigations).* (Sbornik na Bulgarskata Akademija na Naukite u Izkustvata 37.3.) Durzhavna Pechatnitsa, Sofia.

Stojkov, Stojko. 1961. *Uvod v Bulgarskata Fonetika.* (2nd revised edition.) Nauka i Izkustvo, Sofia.

Stolte, J. and N. Stolte. 1971. "A description of Northern Barasano phonology." *Linguistics* 75: 86–92.

Stone, Maureen. 1991. "Towards a model of three-dimensional tongue movement." *Journal of Phonetics* 19: 309–20.

Story, Gillian and Constance Naish. 1973. *Tlingit Verb Dictionary.* University of Alaska, College, AK.

Straka, Georges. 1965. *Album Phonétique.* Université Laval, Québec.

Strevens, Peter D. 1960. "Spectra of fricative noise in human speech." *Language and Speech* 3: 32–49.

Stringer, M. and J. Hotz. 1973. "Waffa phonemes." In *The Languages of the Eastern Family of the East New Guinea Highland Stock*, ed. by H. McKaughan. University of Washington Press, Seattle: 523–29.

Subtelny, J. D. and J. C. Mestre. 1964. "Comparative study of normal and defective articulation of /s/ related to malocclusion and deglutition." *Journal of Speech Disorders* 29: 269–85.

Subtelny, J. D. and N. Oya. 1972. "Cineradiographic study of sibilants." *Folia Phoniatrica* 24: 30–50.

Sung, Margaret M. Y. 1986. *Phonology of Eight Shandong Dialects.* Paper presented at 19th International Conference on Sino-Tibetan Languages and Linguistics, Columbus, OH.

Svarný, O. and Kamil Zvelebil. 1955. "Some remarks on the articulation of the 'cerebral' consonants in Indian languages, especially in Tamil." *Archiv Orientalni* 23: 374–407.

Sweet, Henry. 1877. *A Handbook of Phonetics, Including a Popular Exposition of the Principles of Spelling Reform.* Clarendon Press, Oxford.

Sweet, Henry. 1879. "Sounds and forms of spoken Swedish." *Transactions of the Philo-*

logical Society 187: 457–543.

Taljaard, P. O. and Jan W. Snyman. 1990. *An Introduction to Zulu Phonetics.* M. Lubbe, Hout Bay.

Thomas, Alan R. 1992. "The Welsh language." In *The Celtic Languages*, ed. by D. MacAulay. Cambridge University Press, Cambridge: 251–345.

Thomas, Kimberly D. and Alan Shaterian. 1990. "Vowel length and pitch in Yavapai." In *Papers from the 1990 Hokan-Penutian Languages Workshop*, ed. by M. D. Langdon. Department of Linguistics, University of Southern Illinois, Carbondale, IL: 144–53.

Thráinsson, H. 1978. "On the phonology of Icelandic preaspiration." *Nordic Journal of Linguistics* 1: 3–54.

Tiede, Mark K. 1993. "An MRI-based study of pharyngeal volume contrasts in Akan." *Haskins Laboratories Status Reports on Speech Research* 113: 107–30.

Tilkov, Dimitur. 1979. "Akustichen sustav u distributsija na palatalnite suglacnu v knizhovnija Bulgarsku ezik." In *Vuprosi na Suvremennija Bulgarski Knizhoven Ezik*, Instituta za Bulgarski Ezik, Bulgarska Akademija na Naukite, Sofia: 32–79.

Tracy, Frances V. 1972. "Wapishana phonology." In *Languages of the Guianas*, ed. by J. E. Grimes. Summer Institute of Linguistics, University of Oklahoma, Norman, OK: 78–84.

Trager, George L. and Henry L. Smith. 1956. *An Outline of English Structure.* (Studies in Linguistics, Occasional Papers, 3.) Battenburg Press, Norman, Oklahoma.

Traill, Anthony. 1985. *Phonetic and Phonological Studies of !Xóõ Bushman.* (Quellen zur Khoisan-Forschung 5.) Helmut Buske, Hamburg.

Traill, Anthony. 1986. "The laryngeal sphincter as a phonatory mechanism in !Xóõ." In *Variation, Culture and Evolution*, ed. by R. Singer and J. K. Lundy. Witwatersrand University Press, Johannesburg: 123–31.

Traill, Anthony. 1991. "Pulmonic control, nasal venting and aspiration in Khoisan languages." *Journal of the International Phonetic Association* 21: 13–18.

Traill, Anthony. 1992. "The feature geometry of clicks." In *Festschrift for E. B. van Wyk*, ed. by P. von Staden. Via Afrika, Pretoria: 134–40.

Traill, Anthony. 1994. *A !Xóõ Dictionary.* (Quellen zur Khoisan-Forschung 9.) Rüdiger Köppe, Köln.

Traill, Anthony and Michel Jackson. 1988. "Speaker variation and phonation type in Tsonga nasals." *Journal of Phonetics* 16: 385–400.

Traill, Anthony, J. S. M. Khumalo and P. Fridjhon. 1987. "Depressing facts about Zulu." *African Studies* 46: 255–74.

Traunmüller, Hartmut. 1982. "Vokalismus in der westniederösterreichischen Mundart." *Zeitschrift für Dialektologie und Linguistik* 2: 289–333.

Tryon, Darrell T. 1976. *New Hebrides Languages: An Internal Classification.* (Pacific Linguistics, Series C 50.) Research School of Pacific Studies, Australian National University, Canberra.

Tsuji, Nobuhisa. 1980. *Comparative Phonology of Guangxi Yue Dialects.* Kazama Shobo, Tokyo.

Tucker, A., M. Bryan and J. Woodburn. 1977. "The East African click languages: a phonetic comparison." In *Zur Sprachgeschichte und Ethnohistorie in Afrika: Neue Beiträge Afrikanistischer Forschungen*, ed. by W. J. G. Möhlig. Dietrich Reimer, Berlin: 300–22.

Uldall, Elizabeth. 1958. "American 'molar' R and 'flapped' T." *Revista do Laboratorio de Fonetica Experimental, Universidad de Coimbra* 4: 103–6.

Uldall, H. J. 1933. *A Danish Phonetic Reader.* University of London Press, London.

Vages, K., E. Ferrero, Emmanuela Magno-Caldognetto and C. Lavagnoli. 1978. "Some acoustic characteristics of Italian consonants." *Journal of Italian Linguistics* 3: 69–85.

Vaissière, Jacqueline. 1983. "Prediction of articulatory movement of the velum from phonetic input." Unpublished paper, circulated by AT&T Bell Laboratories, Murray Hill, NJ.

Vanvik, Arne. 1972. "A phonetic-phonemic analysis of Standard Eastern Norwegian." *Norwegian Journal of Linguistics* 27: 130–9.

Vatikiotis-Bateson, Eric. 1984. "The temporal effects of homorganic medial nasal clusters." *Research in Phonetics (Indiana University, Bloomington)* 4: 197–233.

Velayudhan, S. 1971. *Vowel Duration in Malayalam: An Acoustic Phonetic Study.* The Dravidian Linguistic Society of India, Trivandrum.

Vossen, Rainer. 1986. "Zur Phonologie der ‖Ani-Sprache." In *Contemporary Studies on Khoisan 2* (Quellen zur Khoisan-Forschung, 5.2), ed. by R. Vossen and K. Keuthmann. Helmut Buske, Hamburg: 321–45.

Walton, James and Janice Walton. 1967. "Phonemes of Muinane." In *Phonemic Systems of Colombian Languages*, ed. by V. Waterhouse. Studies in Linguistics, University of Oklahoma, Norman OK: 37–47.

Wängler, Hans-Heinrich. 1961. *Atlas deutscher Sprachlaute.* Akademie-Verlag, Berlin.

West, Betty and Birdie Welch. 1967. "Phonemic system of Tucano." In *Phonemic Systems of Colombian Languages*, ed. by V. Waterhouse. Summer Institute of Linguistics, University of Oklahoma, Norman, OK: 11–24.

Westbury, John R. 1983. "Enlargement of the supraglottal cavity and its relation to stop consonant voicing." *Journal of the Acoustical Society of America* 73: 1322–36.

Westbury, John R. and Patricia A. Keating. 1986. "On the naturalness of stop consonant voicing." *Journal of Linguistics* 22: 145–66.

Wheeler, Alva and Margaret Wheeler. 1962. "Siona phonemics (Western Tucanoan)." In *Studies in Ecuadorian Indian Languages.* Summer Institute of Linguistics, University of Oklahoma, Norman, OK: 96–111.

Whiteley, W. H. and M. G. Muli. 1962. *Practical Introduction to Kamba.* Oxford University Press, London.

Wiesemann, Ursula. 1972. *Die Phonologische und Grammatische Struktur der Kaingang-Sprache.* Mouton, The Hague.

Wilkins, David L. 1986. *The Mparntwe Dialect of Arrernte.* Ph. D. dissertation. Australian National University, Canberra.

Williamson, Kay. 1969. "Igbo." In *Twelve Nigerian Languages*, ed. by E. Dunstan. Longmans Green, London: 85–96.

Wilson, W.A.A. and John T. Bendor-Samuel. 1969. "The phonology of the nominal in Dagbani." *Linguistics* 52: 56–82.

Wright, Richard and Peter Ladefoged. Forthcoming. "A phonetic study of Tsou." *Bulletin of the Institute of History and Philology, Academia Sinica.*

Yadav, Ramawater. 1984. "Voicing and aspiration in Maithili: a fiberoptic and acoustic study." *Indian Linguistics* 45: 27–35.

Yamuna, R. 1986. "A spectrographic study of /r/ and /R/ in Malayalam." In *Acoustic Studies in Indian Languages*, ed. by B. B. Rajapurohit. Central Institute of Indian Languages, Mysore: 61–4.

Young, Rosemary. 1962. "The phonemes of Kanite, Kamano, Benabena and Gahuku." *Oceania Linguistic Monographs* 6: 35–48.

Zee, Eric. 1981. "Effect of vowel quality on perception of post-vocalic nasal consonants in noise." *Journal of Phonetics* 9: 35–48.

Zee, Eric. 1985. "Sound change in syllable final nasal consonants in Chinese." *Journal of Chinese Linguistics* 13: 291–330.

Zhou, Dianfu and Zhongji Wu. 1963. *Articulation Album of Putonghua.* Shangwu Yingshuguan, Beijing.

Zinder, Lev R., Lija V. Bondarko and L. A. Berbitskaja. 1964. "Akustičeskaja xarakteristika različija tverdyx i mjagkix soglasnyx v russkom jazyke [Acoustic nature of the distinction between hard and soft consonants in Russian]." In *Voprosy Fonetiki (Učenye Zapiski LGU, No. 325)*, ed. by M. I. Matusevič. Leningrad State University, Leningrad: 28–36.

Zvelebil, Kamil V. 1970. *Comparative Dravidian Phonology.* Mouton, The Hague.

Index

THE INTERNATIONAL PHONETIC ALPHABET (revised to 1993)

CONSONANTS (PULMONIC)

	Bilabial	Labiodental	Dental	Alveolar	Postalveolar	Retroflex	Palatal	Velar	Uvular	Pharyngeal	Glottal
Plosive	p b			t d		ʈ ɖ	c ɟ	k g	q ɢ		ʔ
Nasal	m	ɱ		n		ɳ	ɲ	ŋ	N		
Trill	B			r					R		
Tap or Flap				ɾ		ɽ					
Fricative	ɸ β	f v	θ ð	s z	ʃ ʒ	ʂ ʐ	ç ʝ	x ɣ	χ ʁ	ħ ʕ	h ɦ
Lateral fricative				ɬ ɮ							
Approximant		ʋ		ɹ		ɻ	j	ɰ			
Lateral approximant				l		ɭ	ʎ	L			

Where symbols appear in pairs, the one to the right represents a voiced consonant. Shaded areas denote articulations judged impossible.

CONSONANTS (NON-PULMONIC)

Clicks		Voiced implosives		Ejectives	
ʘ	Bilabial	ɓ	Bilabial	'	as in:
ǀ	Dental	ɗ	Dental/alveolar	p'	Bilabial
ǃ	(Post)alveolar	ʄ	Palatal	t'	Dental/alveolar
ǂ	Palatoalveolar	ɠ	Velar	k'	Velar
ǁ	Alveolar lateral	ʛ	Uvular	s'	Alveolar fricative

VOWELS

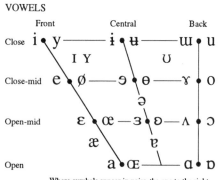

Where symbols appear in pairs, the one to the right represents a rounded vowel.

OTHER SYMBOLS

- ʍ Voiceless labial-velar fricative
- w Voiced labial-velar approximant
- ɥ Voiced labial-palatal approximant
- ʜ Voiceless epiglottal fricative
- ʢ Voiced epiglottal fricative
- ʡ Epiglottal plosive
- ɕ ʑ Alveolo-palatal fricatives
- ɺ Alveolar lateral flap
- ɧ Simultaneous ʃ and x

Affricates and double articulations can be represented by two symbols joined by a tie bar if necessary.

k͡p t͡s

SUPRASEGMENTALS

- ˈ Primary stress
- ˌ Secondary stress
  - ˌfoʊnəˈtɪʃən
- ː Long eː
- ˑ Half-long eˑ
- ̆ Extra-short ĕ
- . Syllable break ɹi.ækt
- | Minor (foot) group
- ‖ Major (intonation) group
- ‿ Linking (absence of a break)

TONES & WORD ACCENTS

LEVEL		CONTOUR	
e̋ or ˥	Extra high	ě or ˄	Rising
é ˦	High	ê ˅	Falling
ē ˧	Mid	e᷄ ˧	High rising
è ˨	Low	e᷅ ˧	Low rising
ȅ ˩	Extra low	e᷈ ˧	Rising-falling
↓ Downstep		↗ Global rise	etc.
↑ Upstep		↘ Global fall	

DIACRITICS

Diacritics may be placed above a symbol with a descender, e.g. ŋ̊

̥ Voiceless	n̥ d̥	̤ Breathy voiced	b̤ a̤	̪ Dental	t̪ d̪
̬ Voiced	s̬ t̬	̰ Creaky voiced	b̰ a̰	̺ Apical	t̺ d̺
ʰ Aspirated	tʰ dʰ	̼ Linguolabial	t̼ d̼	̻ Laminal	t̻ d̻
̹ More rounded	ɔ̹	ʷ Labialized	tʷ dʷ	̃ Nasalized	ẽ
̜ Less rounded	ɔ̜	ʲ Palatalized	tʲ dʲ	ⁿ Nasal release	dⁿ
̟ Advanced	u̟	ˠ Velarized	tˠ dˠ	ˡ Lateral release	dˡ
̠ Retracted	i̠	ˤ Pharyngealized	tˤ dˤ	̚ No audible release	d̚
̈ Centralized	ë	̴ Velarized or pharyngealized	ɫ		
̽ Mid-centralized	e̽	̝ Raised	e̝ (ɹ̝ = voiced alveolar fricative)		
̩ Syllabic	ɹ̩	̞ Lowered	e̞ (β̞ = voiced bilabial approximant)		
̯ Non-syllabic	e̯	̘ Advanced Tongue Root	e̘		
˞ Rhoticity	ɚ	̙ Retracted Tongue Root	e̙		